COLLECTED POEMS
OF WILLIAM ELLERY CHANNING
THE YOUNGER, 1817-1901

WILLIAM ELLERY CHANNING

THE YOUNGER, 1817-1901

THE COLLECTED POEMS

of

WILLIAM ELLERY CHANNING

THE YOUNGER, 1817-1901

FACSIMILE REPRODUCTIONS

EDITED WITH AN INTRODUCTION

BY

WALTER HARDING

GAINESVILLE, FLORIDA

SCHOLARS' FACSIMILES & REPRINTS

1967

SCHOLARS' FACSIMILES & REPRINTS
1605 N.W. 14TH AVENUE
GAINESVILLE, FLORIDA, 32601, U.S.A.
HARRY R. WARFEL, GENERAL EDITOR

L.C. CATALOG CARD NUMBER: 67-21749

MANUFACTURED IN THE U.S.A.

FOR

TED BAILEY

THOREAUVIAN STOCKBROKER

TABLE OF CONTENTS

INTRODUCTION

I

William Ellery Channing was born in Boston, Massachusetts, the son of Walter Channing, a physician and professor of obstetrics at Harvard Medical School, on November 29, 1817. (The date 1818 usually given is incorrect, I am informed by Professor Frederick McGill, Jr., who has examined Walter Channing's obstetrical records.) He was named for his paternal uncle, the great Unitarian divine, with whom he is now unfortunately frequently confused in literary histories and bibliographical records. To distinguish the two it is the common practice to refer to the poet as "Ellery," "W. Ellery," or "William Ellery Channing the Younger." Edward T. Channing, the famed Boylston Professor of Rhetoric at Harvard, was another uncle.

Channing's mother died when he was but a boy and he spent an unhappy childhood with relatives. He attended the famous Round Hill School in Northampton, Massachusetts, and later the Boston Latin School. In 1834 he entered Harvard College, but dropped out after only a few months, pronouncing compulsory chapel "a bore" and the whole curriculum "tiresome."

Since his father provided him with a small, regular income, he felt no need to do anything as prosaic as earning a living and instead devoted himself to writing poetry. In 1839 he tried farming a quarter-section in pioneer McHenry County in Illinois, but soon abandoned the experiment. Returning to the East, he began to associate with Transcendentalists such as Emerson and to contribute poetry to various periodicals, the *Dial* in particular.

In 1842 he married Margaret Fuller's sister Ellen and in 1843 settled down in Concord, Massachusetts, to be near Emerson. Never making a serious effort to support his growing family, he drove his wife's relatives—and his own—to distraction. On a few occasions he worked briefly for newspapers in New York City and New Bedford, Massachusetts, but for the most part, he was content to go his carefree way, leaving the more practical problem of the care of his family to others. Meanwhile he continued to write poetry and, as they became better acquainted, to devote more and more of his time to companionship with Henry David Thoreau, one of the few people willing to overlook his eccentricities, though even Thoreau at times found him impossible.

In the mid-1850's he became so entirely negligent of his family that his wife, on the advice of relatives, left him; when she died shortly thereafter, his children were assigned to the care of others. Channing continued to live on alone in Concord, spending the greater part of his time in accompanying Thoreau on his walks. After Thoreau's death in 1862, Channing retreated more and more into himself and lived alone in a house on Academy Lane. In his old age he was generously taken into the home of Franklin Benjamin Sanborn, the self-styled "last of the Transcendentalists," and died there on December 23, 1901, at the age of eighty-four.

II

Despite his irresponsibility in other directions, Channing did devote himself to the muse of poetry. His first published poem, "The Spider," appeared in the *New England Magazine* for October, 1835, when he was only seventeen. It had been submitted without his knowledge by a friend to the editor of the magazine, Park Benjamin, and accepted immediately. From then until his death sixty-six years later he produced a steady stream of poetry, publishing it in periodicals, gift books, biographies, church Christmas annuals, or any other publication that would accept it. He published seven volumes of verse during his lifetime—*Poems* in 1843, *Poems: Second Series* in 1847, *The Woodman and Other Poems* in 1849, *Near Home* in 1858, *The Wanderer* in 1871, *Eliot* in 1885, and

John Brown and the Heroes of Harper's Ferry in 1886. A collection, *Poems of Sixty-Five Years,* was in preparation at the time of his death and appeared the next year, 1902. No book was a financial success. Some were underwritten by his friends. Samuel G. Ward, for example, paid for the publication of the 1843 *Poems* and James H. Bentley and Henry S. Borneman for the publication of *Poems of Sixty-Five Years.* Thoreau was so astonished to hear someone actually asking for a copy of the 1843 volume in a bookstore that he wrote Emerson of the event. *The Wanderer,* the only volume that seemed to arouse any great interest in the reading public, had its sales cut short by a fire at the publishers which destroyed all the unsold stock.

Nor did his books fare well at the hands of reviewers. The then all-powerful *North American Review,* discussing his first book, declared him unable to write verse and sense at the same instant. James Russell Lowell, in *Fable for Critics* (1848), derided him for too closely imitating Emerson. But the most devastating criticism was that made by Edgar Allan Poe in a review in *Graham's Magazine* of Channing's 1843 volume. Poe, as is well known, could be a vitriolic reviewer and his commentary on Channing was perhaps the most vitriolic of all he wrote. He said, in part: "His book contains about sixty-three things, which he calls poems, and which he no doubt seriously supposes so to be. They are full of all kinds of mistakes, of which the most important is that of their having been printed at all. They are not precisely English—nor will we insult a great nation by calling them Kickapoo; perhaps they are Channingese." And then he went on to cite example after example of what he considered bad lines, bad rhymes, and preposterous grammar.

Even Channing's cousin, William Henry Channing, in a review of the same 1843 volume in *The Present*, chided him, though on the basis of the content of the poems rather than of their literary merit. W. H. Channing was an activist in many reform movements—anti-slavery, Fourierism, and so on—and he could not understand why Ellery seemed to concern himself more with Nature than with Mankind: "Your daily thoughts are better poems than you can write. . . . Never shall you know the full music of your shell, and thread the strings of your lyre with the grateful tears of your brothers, your countrymen, till you own yourself to be one beating pulse of this wonderful mankind, struggling as it is towards symmetry and perfectness."

Unquestionably Channing deserved some of the harsh criticism he received. A great deal of the poetry he wrote was third-rate. His devotion to the muse of poetry was quantitative rather than qualitative. If he had published fewer poems and had spent more time polishing those he did publish, he could have achieved a higher rank as a poet. But he was at heart a dilettante, always ready to toss off a new line of poetry, but rarely willing to settle down and work over a line already committed to paper. He worked by inspiration rather than by perspiration. The result was that on occasion he could toss off some really outstanding lines, but he could rarely sustain a high level throughout a poem. It is significant that his best known poem, "A Poet's Hope," was written on the spur of the moment. Mrs. Samuel G. Ward challenged him to write a poem. He withdrew to an adjacent room and in a very short time improvised this seventy-eight line poem. It is equally significant that the poem became well-known not for the unity, structure, or significance of the poem as a whole, but for one brief line—

"If my bark sinks, 'tis to another sea."

It has been well said that Channing has been and in all likelihood will remain a poet known chiefly within the limits of quotation marks.

His poems have a significance beyond the purely belletristic. He was at the very heart of the Transcendentalist movement. On intimate terms with all of the leading Transcendentalists, he portrays them frequently in his poems. Emerson is the subject of the lengthy "Ode" of the *Poems: Second Series* and the "large and generous man" of *The Wanderer*. His son Edward is the "little boy" of "Too ——, Three Years Old," and Waldo is the "Sleeping Child" of the poem of that name. Elizabeth Hoar is the "Lady" of "Believe, that thus a humble worshipper." Marston and Mary Russell Watson are the host and hostess of "Hillside" in *The Wanderer.* But most extensive and most important are the portraits in poetry of Henry David Thoreau as the "Rudolpho" of *Near Home,* the "Hermit" of *The Wanderer* and, of course, as the central subject of the "Memorial Verses" Channing appended to *Thoreau, the Poet-Naturalist.* Here we get an intimate close-up of Thoreau that we can find nowhere else.

Channing is also important as an example of the Transcendentalist mind at work. He was the very epitome of the Transcendentalist in his individualism. He shared most of the diverse interests and enthusiasms of his fellow Transcendentalists. He was an inveterate reader and in his poems we can find expression of his enthusiasm for the typical and varied favorites of the Transcendentalists from the Greek classics to Shelley, from Francis Quarles to Wordsworth. He felt drawn towards reform movements from anti-slavery to Fourierism; John Brown became one of his major heroes. Above all, he shared with the others a deep and abiding love for Nature and natural history, and while he never acquired Thoreau's knowledge of the flora and fauna of New England, he did share Thoreau's fondness for rambles in the countryside.

To be sure, in his personal life Channing often carried his individualism—and his Transcendentalism—to absurd extremes. But he thus enables us to study the philosophy in an exaggerated form and see to what extremes both its strengths and its weaknesses can carry one.

It is true that Channing fared badly at the hands of most of his reviewers. There is one notable exception. His friend Ralph Waldo Emerson examined a number of his poems at length in the first volume of the *Dial.* His words there are perhaps a fitting summary of Channing's poetry at its best: "Our first feeling on reading them was a lively joy. . . . Here is poetry more purely intellectual than any American verses we have yet seen, distinguished from all competition by two merits; the fineness of perception; and the poet's trust in his own genius to that degree, that there is an absence of all conventional imagery, and a bold use of that which the moment's mood had made sacred to him."

III

I have tried to include in this volume every poem of Channing's that has reached print. My basic texts are of course the seven volumes published during his lifetime, and they are reproduced in exact facsimile and in chronological order. These are followed by the texts of his uncollected poems presented in their chronological order of publication, and again, where possible, reproduced in facsimile. It is possible that a few of the poems that I have taken from the *Dial* are not by Channing. Many poems printed there were unsigned, and I have simply followed George Willis Cooke's identifications. It is only fair to point out that Cooke himself indicated that he was not certain that "Song," "Sweet Love, I cannot show thee in this guise," "Let not my love implore of thee in vain," "Spring," and "The Song of Birds in Spring" were by Channing, but since to my knowledge they have not been proved otherwise, I have included them.

I have included pieces from *Poems of Sixty-five Years* only as a last resort. F. B. Sanborn was its editor, and anyone acquainted with Transcendentalist scholarship should be fully aware of his idiosyncracies as an editor. Here, as with his other editorial work, he did not hesitate to change, add or subtract words, lines, stanzas and titles as he saw fit. The result is, of course, more Sanborn than Channing. So, if I could find any other version of a poem, I used it. An exception has been made for the poems from Channing's biography of Thoreau and for "Flight of Geese," where in both cases Sanborn's 1902 edition of Channing's biography of Thoreau was used because the type was more suited to reproduction and the editorial changes were minor.

To the best of my knowledge I have included every poem of Channing's that has hitherto appeared in print. A few of his poems appeared in variant versions here and there—sometimes the variants having different titles and even different first lines—but if they were obviously variants of poems I had already included, I omitted them.

I cannot close this brief introduction without expressing my gratitude to the staff of the Houghton Library of Harvard University for providing me with facsimiles of the texts of six of Channing's seven published books of verse; to the staffs of the State University College at Geneseo Library, Princeton University Library, Rutgers University Library, the New York Public Library, the New York State Library, and the Newberry Library for providing me with facsimiles of some of the uncollected poems; to Professor Harry Warfel for the cooperation, guidance, and kindness I have come to expect from him as we have worked together on this and my two previous volumes published under his aegis; and to my secretary, Miss Freda Hark, for making indexes, collating some of the texts, and doing many of the other mundane tasks involved in the preparation of such an edition. To Professor Frederick T. McGill, Jr., I am indebted for all sorts of help and encouragement. As the foremost Channing scholar he has been unstinting in sharing his knowledge. This volume could hardly have come into being without his help.

WALTER HARDING

State University College
Geneseo, New York
June 9, 1966

POEMS

BY

WILLIAM ELLERY CHANNING.

BOSTON:
CHARLES C. LITTLE AND JAMES BROWN.
MDCCCXLIII.

BOSTON:
PRINTED BY FREEMAN AND BOLLES,
WASHINGTON STREET.

CONTENTS.

POEMS.

EDWARD AND MARGARET.

Not rudely built that ancient hall, whose doors
Held widely open by the unsparing hand
Of active charity, gave amplest welcome;
Nor unadorned around with graceful trees,
Whose music all the seasons through was heard
Within the cheerful mansion. This abode,
Framed for the occupation of content,
Looked down upon a valley, where one lake
Received into its depths some circling hills,
Green in the summer, with majestic growth
Of lofty cedars, and time-hallowed oaks,
And the gay foliage of the birch and ash.

The sudden storms, nursed in the mountain's arms,
Visited that tranquil landscape in brief kind,
Coming with mighty speed, scarce touching there,
As if that valley were too fair for violence.

In this calm spot dwelt the sweet Margaret,
A maid of ruddy cheek and meaning eye,
Gentle, and good, and eloquently fair.
From earliest childhood, she had trod the paths
Leading among those wild precipitous hills,
Delight to trace the mountain-brook's descent,
Through shelving rocks, and deep, embowered linns,
Where, when the first warm beams of spring had come,
The fearless birds sang with the dashing spray.
Nor less in winter, mid the glittering banks
Heaped of unspotted snow, the maiden roved,
Charmed by the neat severity of frost.

And Margaret dwelt within the ancient hall,
The sunlight of her home, her parents' joy;
So framed for social converse, that the hut,
Or poorest shed of sorry cottager,

Had laughed with pleasure in her gladsome smile.
Her mind had harbored only virtuous thoughts,
Good wisdom that the Book of Life had taught,
Unceasing love for man, respect for worth,
And such calm judgment as a happy life,
Spent with industrious aims and filial pride,
Confers upon an innocent maiden's heart.
Sixteen fair summers bloomed upon her cheek,
That cheek unchannelled by an angry tear,
And dimpled with the modesty of youth.
But, from that clear, free air in which she lived,
The breath of mountain independence, she
Had caught a purpose firm and resolute,
Exacting honesty of speech, and something
Masculine almost, though softly carved in grace.

A stranger to the hamlet, Edward came,
From cities built afar, a nervous voyager,
To whom the streets crowded with anxious toil
Were weariness of life. But twenty years
Had marked his thoughtful brow, and this small space
Filled with irregular days, and nights as sad,

Sufficed to bruise a sympathetic heart,
Asking for love, — receiving careless words.
A narrow bridge across life's arrowy foam,
Is all that shrinking poverty controls,
And yields this straitened path to forward wealth.

To Edward's mind, the outward world supplied
The decorative gauds of pomp and show ;
The liberal sky blazed freely forth for him,
The countless worlds of space, the landscape smiled,
And days among the hills were days of gold.
To him, this calm, secluded hamlet seemed
A tranquil island in the ocean's storm.
He did forget what he had lately shared, —
To follow mutely after empty state,
Supply by thought the indolence of wealth,
And frame for others that they could not shape.
The influences of this serene isle
Composed his turbulent fancies into dream.
Couched on the grass, beneath the monarch trees,
He drew fine pictures on the swimming air.
No longer careworn with his daily needs,

He revelled in a future, shining gay.
Thus might his life have passed in gentle thoughts,
If only silent trees, and purling brooks
Had varied that small hamlet's seeming calm.

But he had seen upon those lonely hills
A maiden's form, one mellow evening, stand,
Gazing in mute surprise upon the clouds
That piled their snowy summits in the west.
Lost as in trance, he dwelt upon the lines
Rounding her vermeil cheek, her stately brow,
Until her image, stamped upon his heart,
Defied the golden sunset, the bright clouds,
And broke that soft tranquillity in twain,
In one swift instant, never more to form.

On the next Sabbath, to the village church
Edward and Margaret came, how different!
She cast a modest glance upon the youth,
His stranger mien demanding some respect,
Then studious bent her soul on pious quest,
The youth forgotten, as he had not been.

How should she mark that wild and eager eye,
How should she read the secrets of his heart!
The week went by, and still another came,
And Edward sought the prints of Margaret's foot,
Along the streamlet's bank, and up the dell,
Even to the midst of that deep solitude
Where she was seated, braiding a green wreath,
Of the broad ferns that seek the utmost shade.
Yet even here a sunbeam wandered down,
And touched a golden curl of Margaret's hair,
And as she turned at Edward's soft approach,
That thread of light caught in her sparkling eye,
As if to pierce the rash intruder through.

Then first, she listened to dread passion's voice,
Toned with rich melody, but echoing
A dark and awful fate, if unreturned.
In gentle accents, with unheeded pace,
The youth thus poured his inmost thoughts for her:
  Nay! look not on me with surprised air.
Have I not marked thy wanderings even here,
Where but the wind has entrance? Am I not,

One of thy lineage, though less beautiful?
Do not these shapely trees associate near,
To listen with glad ears to those sweet songs,
Which the wild birds pour in united notes,
And speeding on the way, the headlong brook
Conceals not its clear charms from any eye.
O! if these forms thus picture forth my heart,
How much more thou, twin image of my soul,
Myself, concealed in a diviner shape.
I do remember thee, as first I saw
Thy sweet, proud figure, where the setting sun
Vainly contrived to render thee more bright,
And dressed with splendor mosses at thy feet,
And built sublimest palaces within
The sky; yet only thee I saw, and now
And ever thou art in my eyes the same.
I wander through where never man hath trod,
I seek most desolate regions, and dim caves,
Where only reptiles crawl and hiss at me,
I stand below the precipice, and ask
The mighty rocks to fall and bury me,
So that I may shut out thy speechless beauty,

That compels me on, through wood, and fell, and moor,
Alone, yet in the breath of thy own being.
This gale, beneath which all my powers have bent,
Has borne me to thy feet, and now I seek
The shelter of thy love, my only hope. —

Its own wild music, by this wilder tale
Was hushed, the brook no longer foamed, the wind
Among the trees was stilled asleep, at least
To Margaret and Edward in their trance.
By different ways they left that lonely spot,
And Margaret mused upon her blessed home.

Next morn some peasants passing by the lake,
Saw the fresh morning gild a floating corpse,
Outstretched in placid slumber. On the face
A tender smile was lingering, as to say, —
This place of sepulture is girded round
With an enchanting beauty, once like thine. —

When Margaret heard the tale of Edward's death,
More solemn seemed the duties of her home,

And to her mother, who had heard the tale
Of helpless love, and Edward's frenzied looks,
She said: — How sad a fate was this, so young,
So fragrant was this flower, so soon cut off
By this strange mystery. — Then she replied: —
O Margaret, let us still more learn from this,
How the small bounds of home embrace the whole,
And never leave these sweet and sheltered spots.
As I have taught you, cheerful industry,
And regular tasks pursued with patient thought,
And the loved fireside of domestic peace,
With reverence for man, and charity,
Will strengthen, and preserve us from the dark,
Impenetrable agonies of life.

MEMORY.

I.

I saw the pine trees on the shore
  Stand solemn in their dark green shroud,
I heard the winds thy loss deplore,
  Whose beauty worlds had fleetly bowed.

Thy beauty! God's own hand did press
  Thy rich curls round thy Grecian brow,
And wound thee in lithe loveliness;—
  I see thee standing by me now.

I hear thy solemn anthem fall
  Of richest song upon my ear,
That clothes thee in thy golden pall,
  As this wide sun flows on the mere.

Away — 't is Autumn in the land,
  Though Summer decks the green pine's bough,
Its spires are plucked by thy white hand, —
  I see thee standing by me now.

II.

I dress thee in the withered leaves,
  Like forests when their day is done,
I bear thee as the wain its sheaves,
  Which crisply rustle in the sun.

Thou trackest me, as bloodhounds scent
  The wanderer's feet, all down the glen;
Thy memory is the monument
  That dies not out my heart again.

So swift the circling years run round
Their dizzy course, I hope to hide;
But till they lay me 'neath the ground,
My resting-day shall be denied.

Thou, summer sun, wilt pity me,
Thy beams once gladly sought my brow,
My love, I wandered then with thee,—
I see thee standing by me now.

III.

A thousand flowers enchant the gale
With perfume sweet as love's first kiss,
And odors in the landscape sail,
And charm the sense with sudden bliss.

But fate, who metes a different way
To me, since I was falsely sold,
Hath gray-haired turned the sunny day,
Bent its high form, and made it old.

Age freezes me on every side,
  Since thy sweet beauty died to me,
And I had better youthful died,
  Than broke such loving troth to thee.

I see the hills where heaven stoops
  To seize the shadows off their brow,
But there my nature downward droops,—
  I see thee standing by me now.

IV.

Come Time — come Death, and blot my doom
  With feller woes, if they be thine,
Clang back thy gates, sepulchral tomb,
  And match thy barrenness with mine.

O moaning wind along the shore,
  How faint thy sobbing accents come!
Strike on my heart with maddest roar,
  Thou meet'st no discord in this home.

Sear, blistering sun, these temple veins;
Blind, icy moon, these coldest eyes;
And drench me through, ye winter rains,—
Swell, if ye can, my miseries.

Those dark, deep orbs are meeting mine,
That white hand presses on my brow,
That soft, sweet smile I know, 't is thine,—
I see thee standing by me now.

DREAMING.

TO ——.

Now may I thee describe a Paradise,
That in the olden day I chanced to see,
And plainly in my inward mirror lies
The shape of that divine festivity;
So, brief may I interpret it to thee,
Return for graceful prose of such a measure
As in no rhyme will e'er pertain to me;
For I have not of life abounding leisure,
I live not in gay rhyme, though that would be my pleasure.

—

There was a plain beneath a summer sky,
Stretching away to mountains like blue air,
Whose points, though surely not to heaven nigh,
Did ever a most azure vestment wear,

On whose pure heights man's life became more rare;
So when we meet a soul of great design,
Its noble presence is a weight to bear,
Capped with pure snows, on which the few rays shine
Of this world's gratitude, now in a swift decline.

Scattered upon the plain were holy trees,
Those moving, yet immovable ideas;
They trembled for the little western breeze,
So full of thought, so subdued to bright fears,
While they o'erlast the number of our years.
Birds reared their young in them, fearing no harm,
For then upon the plain were shed no tears,
But all were swelling in the sunlight calm,
There was most perfect peace, that never felt alarm.

On a clear stream, o'er pebbles tinkling shrill, —
In the embraces of a varied mass
Of very sumptuous trees, whose mouths could fill
Its roof with music from the winds that pass,
Mixed with some whispers from the bright green
grass,

A temple stood, — its roof enchased all
With artists' history. What tale it was
I cannot think; a solemn funeral
It may perchance have been, teaching from that gray wall.

This temple was a font of the best art,
A juvenescent shape of pleasant thought,
Such as would steal within thy inmost heart;
Oh, with what precious hands, its figures wrought,
By learning from a life of love, 't was brought:
The pillars rose with fine proportioned air,
To them the entire world was plainly nought,
They such complete self grace did always wear,
And in the radiant light their pious roof upbear.

And underneath this solemn, stately roof,
Two dwelt, save when they wandered near the plain,
Who from each other never kept aloof,
But sometimes from the beach would hear the main,

Or see the early stars, a mild, sweet train,
Come out to bury the diurnal sun.
There was such steadfast union in the twain
They both each day of life at once begun,
With them each day of life at the same time was done.

One's hair was brown and soft, and liked to play
Around a neck whose meaning was quite clear,
It fell about her face, — an early day,
So she did in a kind of mist appear;
Her eye was liquid with a gentle fear,
She felt a joy in her timidity:
The other did her imitate most near,
But not so mild nor eloquent was he,
And both at morn and eve he bent the willing knee.

I leave thee — the maid spoke to the true youth —
This is the day I promised to return;
But soon I come to you again, in truth
To tend the fire perpetual of our urn,
Of our delightful plain again to learn

Rich lessons. — The sun lay upon the line
Of the last height; the stars were soon to burn,
The youth his front in silence could decline,
In a most pure belief his every thought resign.

Long time had passed; the maid was drest in state,
Wild flared the odorous lamps, church music rung,
The hour was of the darkest midnight late,
As tolled the heavy bell with iron tongue;
Meantime in dewy woods brisk crickets sung,
And shrieked from nodding towers the sharp-toned owl,
Sitting upon his throne with ivy hung:
And miserable priest drew tight his cowl,
And in the city's depths the murderous deeds broke foul.

With the fair maid a youth of beauty stood,
Whose countenance was touched with withering scorn;
Of no content and reverential mood,
But a poor wanderer of the world forlorn,
In whom the bad array was ever born

Of discord, hate, and forms I will not name,
  A sun uprising in a cloudy dawn,—
The maid was loving this enamored same,
For burned within her breast a most disastrous flame.

* * * * *

Lying on fragrant leaves the youth was seen,
  In the sweet temple on the plain so wide.
What perfect picture had his short life been!
  His ways had joyous nature ne'er belied,—
  But then, how was it he so soon had died?
For a few bones were in the temple fair,
  The graceful pillars round it did abide;
Fanned them the softly entering, singing air,
The same mild aspect rose, was all devoid of care.

A meek old man was reading from a page,
  Reclined not far from the sweet temple's door;
He must have been a man of longest age,
  And promised now to last of years a store.
  The sunlight painted him all freshly o'er;

With quiet face and soft entrancing eye
He sate, as silent as a rocky shore,
That listens to the ocean's lullaby,
Nor moves its placid front though waves roar frightfully.

Presently came along the unworn road
A troop of people, and their mules, whose bells
Merrily jingled o'er oppressive load.
They stopped to breathe at one of the clear wells
Of that old country, which forever swells
From a most curious, ancient, carved stone ;
And musical a tale it always tells,
Ever a thinking song it sings alone,
Coming from middest earth, and of the blessed Unknown.

They quickly passed away ; the sage sate still,
And twilight melted down on stream and vale ;
Nor did he move from his repose until
The moon was gleaming like torn silver mail,
And through ethereal deeps went gently pale ;

Then closing up his book, he silently
 Removed, saying in thought,—Shall not avail
This summer rest, O lovely one! To thee,
Who ere thy real time put on that sanctity.

—

To thee should these few simple lines convey
 A pleasurable sense of my own mind,
Which from my earliest youth, the frailest lay
 Has to me shadowed out in no great kind,—
 In that I shall a perfect pleasure find;
And in a future day may thee present
 With thoughts as permanent as shifting wind.
Yet now believe that these are kindly meant,
Though with no real life is this small story blent.

AUTUMN ODE.

By the waterfall, and the lone road side
Flowers of an hundred hues have died ;
For the lonely gale is sighing deep,
Over the valley and over the steep,
And the soul of Autumn is haunting the day,
And nothing but sorrow, for nothing is gay.

The leaves of the forest are changing their hue,
They are yellow and red like a carpeted pew,
They moan in the wind like an orphan child
Whose mother lies dead on the moorland wild.
Not so in the Spring
When the green leaves cling
To the truthful trees, like a lover's heart
To her whom he loves, and who cannot part.

Then sang the Spring like a hymn of joy,
  In the sunny sheen of the glossy bough,
Whilst her breath with the wavy grass did toy, —
  The grass which is withered so yellow now, —
Notes of the breeze, of the sweet breeze warm,
A thousand leagues off from a thought of storm.

Then, on the banks of the rushing stream,
  The tall polished stalks of the flowers rose up,
Then must one lie and sweetly dream,
  While happiness glowed in his full life's cup, —
    It is over now.

Chill and cold comes the autumn wind,
Snow and ice it is hiding behind,
And its hands are full of unnumbered blights,
To stand in the room of the sunny lights,
Which wove the gold fruits on the orchard's breast,
And lined the soft wall of the wood-bird's nest.

The song of the Summer has faded away,
Her life she gave up in the last warm day.

No more are her steps on the flowery hills,
No more the soul of the wood she fills
With those snatches of joy, and that rustling light
That sparkled like gems in the sun so bright.

THE EARTH SPIRIT.

* * * * * *

Then spoke the Spirit of the Earth,
  Her gentle voice like a soft water's song; —
None from my loins have ever birth,
  But what to joy and love belong;
I faithful am, and give to thee
Blessings great, and give them free.
  I have woven shrouds of air
    In a loom of hurrying light,
  For the trees which blossoms bear,
    And gilded them with sheets of bright;

I fall upon the grass like love's first kiss,
I make the golden flies and their fine bliss.
I paint the hedge-rows in the lane,
And clover white and red the pathways bear,
I laugh aloud in sudden gusts of rain,
To see the ocean lash himself in air;
I throw smooth shells and weeds along the beach,
And pour the curling waves far o'er the glassy reach;
Swing birds' nests in the elms, and shake cool moss
Along the aged beams and hide their loss.
The very broad rough stones I gladden too;
Some willing seeds I drop along their sides,
Nourish the generous plant with freshening dew,
Till there, where all was waste, true joy abides.
The peaks of aged mountains, with my care
Smile in the red of glowing morn elate;
I bind the caverns of the sea with hair,
Glossy, and long, and rich as king's estate;
I polish the green ice, and gleam the wall
With the white frost, and leaf the brown trees tall.

* * * * * *

'T was so, — t' was thine. Earth! thou wast true:
I kneel, thy grateful child, I kneel,
Thy full forgiveness for my sins I sue,
My mother! learn thy child can think and feel.
Mother dear! wilt pardon me,
Who loved not the generous sun,
Nor thy seasons loved to hear
Singing to the busy year; —
Thee neglected, — shut his heart,
In thy being had no part?
Mother dear! I list thy song
In the autumn eve along;
Now thy chill airs round the day
And leave me my time to pray.
Mother dear! the day must come,
When I, thy child, shall make my home,
My long, last home amid the grass,
Over which thy warm hands pass.
Ah me! do let me lie
Gently on thy breast to die;
I know my prayers will reach thy ear,

Thou art with me while I ask,
Nor a child refuse to hear,
Who would learn his little task.
Let me take my part with thee
In the gray clouds, or thy light,
Laugh with thee upon the sea,
Or idle on the land by night.
In the trees I will with thee,
In the flowers, like any bee.

I feel it shall be so. We were not born
To sink our finer feelings in the dust;
And better to the grave with feelings torn,
So in our step strides truth and honest trust
In the great love of things, than to be slaves
To forms, whose ringing sides each stroke we give
Stamps with a hollower want. Yes, to our graves
Hurry, before we in the heavens' look live,
Strangers to our best thoughts, and fearing men,
And fearing death, and to be born again.

TO A FRIEND ON HIS MARRIAGE.

A LIGHT is in thine eyes,—an endless day
Has risen, and an eterne sun now paints
The dim and drear cold regions of this world.
She whom thy love did honor, now hath pledged
Obedience, faithful care, and life to thee.
Now the stern winter, with his snowy hair,
Droops thy fine fantasy with no vile frost,
And disappointment with a keen-edged knife
Cuts never more the cable of thy joys.
Down to the inlet's shores, wherein thy bark
Rides at its anchor, the sweet flowers are edged;
Violets and roses bloom, and the green grass.
Whatever scents the air, like hidden notes

Of some rare instrument, or charms the gaze,
This lives for thee. — I also honor thee.
Though outward cold, and wanting show of love,
My memory haunts the gladness of old days;
And in the sunny nooks of those warm thoughts
Which are the pictures of *our* former years,
I, like a tired child, still love to lie.

By the dark river; — in the magic tents
Of the rich trees, with sunlight creeping through,
I wander yet, and see thee stand amazed
At all the prodigal beauty. And beyond,
Where level fields, their distance marked by elms,
Stretch to the azure river, I yet roam;
Or on the mountains stand, as in those days;
So fair, so glad are those past years to me.
Those are my jewels; for these later times
Are drawn in other figures. Not friendless,
While thou yet hauntest here, the truest friend,
Whom idlesse, distance, form and show of love
Cannot dissever. Thanks for all to thee.

A shade is on my life. No more to me
The green trees and blue skies yield up their joy;
A fatal, fatal shade is on my days,
And though I smile, and seem to be as light,
As merry, and as humorsome as most,
The past, dear friend, casts darkness upon me.
No more, — no more of this. Joy to thee, friend,
Long life, and always glad; like a green tree,
Whose branches sing a summer melody.
And now farewell! The moon is riding up
The serene azure. The keen stars are now
Dressed in their whitest garments. Thro' the mask
Of that consuming beauty which burns out
In song, in picture, most of all in love,
I see how Heaven hath blessed thee. Now farewell.
It is a word, — sometime a thought of joy,
Sometime of sorrow. Joy to thy future.

THE HARBOR.

No more I seek, the prize is found,
  I furl my sails, my voyage is o'er;
The treacherous waves no longer sound
  But sing thy praise along the shore.

I steal from all I hoped of old,
  To throw more beauty round thy way;
The dross I part, and melt the gold,
  And stamp it with thy every-day.

I did not dream to welcome thee;
  Like all I have thou camest unknown,
An island in a misty sea,
  With stars, and flowers, and harvests strown.

A well is in the desert sand
  With purest water cold and clear,
Where overjoyed at rest I stand,
  And drink the sound I hoped to hear.

THE NIAGARA FALL.

'T is the boom of the fall with a heavy pour,
Solemn and slow as a thunder cloud,
Majestic as the vast ocean's roar,
Though the green trees round its singing crowd ;
And the light is as green as the emerald grass,
Or the wide leaved plants in the wet morass.

It sounds over all, and the rushing storm
Cannot wrinkle its temples, or wave its hair.
It dwells alone in the pride of its form,
A lonely thing in the populous air.
From the hanging cliffs it whirls away,
All seasons through, all the livelong day.

THOUGHTS.

I.

The Bible is a book worthy to read,
The life of those great Prophets is the life we need,
From all delusive seeming ever freed.

Be not afraid to utter what thou art,
'Tis no disgrace to keep an open heart;
A soul free, frank, and loving friends to aid,
Not even does this harm a gentle maid.

Strive as thou canst, thou wilt not value o'er
Thy life; — thou standest on a lighted shore,
And from the depths of an unfathom'd sea
The noblest impulses flow tenderly to thee;
Feel them as they arise, and take them free.

Better live unknown,
No heart but thy own
Beating ever near,
To no mortal dear
In thy hemisphere,
Poor and wanting bread
Steeped in poverty,
Than to be in dread,
Than to be afraid
From thyself to flee.
For it is not living,
To a soul believing,
To change each noble joy
Which our strength employs,
For a state half rotten,
And a life of toys;
Better be forgotten
Than lose equipoise.

How shall I live? In earnestness.
What shall I do? Work earnestly.

What shall I give ? A willingness.
What shall I gain ? Tranquillity.
But do you mean a quietness
In which I act, and no man bless ?
Flash out in action, infinite and free,
Action conjoined with deep tranquillity,
Resting upon the soul's true utterance,
And life shall flow as merry as a dance.

Being, — not seeming,
Thinking, — not dreaming,
Heavenward tending,
To all nature bending,
In transport unending;
Then shalt thou follow
The flight of the swallow ; —
In a green flowery spring
Thy life 's on the wing.

II.

Life is too good to waste, enough to prize ;
Keep looking round with clear unhooded eyes ;

Love all thy brothers, and for them endure
Many privations, the reward is sure.

A little thing! There is no little thing;
Through all a joyful song is murmuring,
Each leaf, each stem, each sound in winter drear
Hath deepest meanings for an anxious ear.

Thou seest life is sad; the father mourns his wife and
child;
Keep in the midst of sorrows a fair aspect mild.

A howling fox, a shrieking owl,
A violent distracting Ghoul,
Forms of the most infuriate madness,—
These may not move thy soul to gladness,
But look within the dark outside,
Nought shalt thou hate, and nought deride.

Thou meetest a common man,
With a delusive show of *can*;

His acts are petty forgeries of natural greatness,
That show a dreadful lateness
Of this world's mighty impulses; a want of truthful
earnestness:
He seems, not does, and in that shows
No true nobility,
A poor ductility
That no proper office knows,
Not even estimation small of human woes.

Be not afraid;
His understanding aid
With thy own pure content,
On highest purpose bent.

Leave him not lonely,
For that his admiration
Fastens on self and seeming only.
Make a right dedication
Of all thy strength to keep
From swelling, that so ample heap

Of lives abused and virtue given for nought.
And thus it shall appear for all in nature hast thou
wrought.
If thou unconsciously perform what 's good
Like nature's self thy proper mood.

A life well spent is like a flower
That had bright sunshine its brief hour;
It flourished in pure willingness,
Discovered strongest earnestness,
Was fragrant for each lightest wind,
Was of its own particular kind,
Nor knew a tone of discord sharp;
Breathed alway like a silver harp,
And went to immortality,
A very proper thing to die.

A POET'S LOVE.

I CAN remember well
  My very early youth,
My sumptuous Isabel,
  Who was a girl of truth;
Of golden truth; — we do not often see
Those whose whole lives have only known to be.

So sunlight, very warm,
  On harvest fields and trees,
Could not more sweetly form
  Rejoicing melodies
For these deep things, than Isabel for me;
I lay beneath her soul as a lit tree.

That cottage where she dwelt
  Was all o'er mosses green;
I still forever felt
  How nothing stands between
The soul and truth; why starving poverty
Was nothing — nothing, Isabel, to thee.

Grass beneath her faint tread
  Bent pleasantly away;
From her ne'er small birds fled,
  But kept at their bright play,
Not fearing her; it was her endless motion,
Just a true swell upon a summer ocean.

They who conveyed her home, —
  I mean who led her where
The spirit does not roam, —
  Had such small weight to bear,
They scarcely felt. How softly was thy knell
Rung for thee that soft day, girl Isabel!

I am no more below,
My life is raised on high;
My fantasy was slow
Ere Isabel could die,
It pressed me down; but now I sail away
Into the regions of exceeding day.

And Isabel and I
Float on the red-brown clouds,
That amply multiply
The very constant crowds
Of serene shapes. Play on mortality!
Thy happiest hour is that when thou may'st die.

—

The running winds are not more fleet
That pace along the blue sea's floor,
Than are thy tender childhood's feet,
O girl, the best that nature bore.

GIFTS.

A DROPPING shower of spray,
  Filled with a beam of light, —
The breath of some soft day, —
  The groves by wan moonlight, —
    Some rivers flow,
    Some falling snow,
  Some bird's swift flight; —

A summer field o'erstrown
  With gay and laughing flowers,
And shepherd's clocks half blown,
  That tell the merry hours, —
    The waving grain,
    The spring soft rain, —
  Are these things *ours*?

THE STARS.

SILENT companions of the blinded earth,
Day's recollection, enemies of time, —
How like an angel troop with folded hopes
Ye stand, each separate in the azure.
Hear! 'T is the rushing of the midnight wind,
Falling with his resistless scimitar
Upon the mournful memories of the wood:
Whirling before it to the South they flee,
In sad confusion, to the sheltering South.
The yellow grass moans in the chilling air,
Each living thing runs to its in-door home;
But ye, clear stars, look with untrembling eyes
On the fierce blast, far in your upper sphere.

Where the wild battle rages, and the streams
Run crimson to the sea, and frightened death
Falls shuddering at the slaughter, pressing hard
His icy palms upon his saddened eyes,
Your soft and dewy light floats gently o'er
Sweet as a mother's thoughts by sleeping babe.

In your deep light I look and see the abode
Of greater spirits than our life sends forth
To wander in the paths of the green earth.
I see a wisdom which this noisy day,
That jars our phantom forms with rude uproar,
Shall never emulate. Unsleeping Stars!
Who can distrust the love that reigns the world,
Or think, though unheard, that your sphere is dumb.

THE LOVER'S SONG.

BEE in the deep flower bells,
Brook in the cavern dim,
Fawn in the woodland dells
Hideth him.

I hide in thy deep flower eyes,
In the well of thy dark cold eye;
In thy heart my feelings rise,
There they lie.

Sing love, sing, for thy song
Filleth the life of my mind;
Thou bendest my woes along
Like a wind.

Green of the spring and flower,
Fruit of the summer day,
Midnight and moon-lit hour —
What say they?

Centre of them thou art,
Building that points on high;
Sun, — for it is in thy heart,
Will not die.

SEA SONG.

Our boat to the waves go free,
By the bending tide, where the curled wave breaks,
Like the track of the wind on the white snow flakes;
Away! — away! 'T is a path o'er the sea.

Blasts may rave, — spread the sail,
For our spirits can wrest the power from the wind,
And the gray clouds yield to the sunny mind,
Fear not we the whirl of the gale.

Waves on the beach, and the wild sea-foam,
With a leap, and a dash, and a sudden cheer,
Where the sea-weed makes its bending home,
And the sea birds swim on the crests so clear,
Wave after wave, they are curling o'er
While the white sand dazzles along the shore.

BOAT SONG.

THE River calmly flows
Through shining banks, through lonely glen,
Where the owl shrieks, though ne'er the cheer of men
Has stirred its mute repose;
Still if you should walk there, you would go there again.

The stream is well alive;
Another passive world you see,
Where downward grows the form of every tree,
Like soft light clouds they thrive;
Like them let us in our pure loves reflected be.

A yellow gleam is thrown
Into the secrets of that maze
Of tangled trees, that late shut out our gaze,
Refusing to be known;
It must its privacy unclose,—its glories blaze.

Sweet falls the summer air
Over her form who sails with me,
Her way like it is beautifully free,
Her nature far more rare,
And is her constant heart of virgin purity.

A quivering star is seen
Keeping its watch above the hill;
Though from the sun's retreat small light is still
Poured on earth's saddening mien:
We all are tranquilly obeying Evening's will.

Thus ever love the Power;
To simplest thoughts dispose the mind;
In each obscure event a worship find
Like that of this dim hour,—
In lights, and airs, and trees, and in all human kind.

We smoothly glide below
The faintly glimmering worlds of light:
Day has a charm, and this deceptive night
Brings a mysterious show;
He shadows our dear earth, but his cool stars are white.

REVERENCE.

—— As an ancestral heritage revere
All learning, and all thought. The painter's fame
Is thine, whate'er thy lot, who honorest grace.
And need enough in this low time, when they,
Who seek to captivate the fleeting notes
Of heaven's sweet beauty, must despair almost,
So heavy and obdurate show the hearts
Of their companions. Honor kindly then
Those who bear up in their so generous arms
The beautiful ideas of matchless forms;
For were these not portrayed, our human fate,—
Which is to be all high, majestical,
To grow to goodness with each coming age,
Till virtue leap and sing for joy to see

So noble, virtuous men, — would brief decay;
And the green, festering slime, oblivious, haunt
About our common fate. Oh honor them!

But what to all true eyes has chiefest charm,
And what to every breast where beats a heart
Framed to one beautiful emotion, — to
One sweet and natural feeling, lends a grace
To all the tedious walks of common life,
This is fair woman, — woman, whose applause
Each poet sings, — woman the beautiful.
Not that her fairest brow, or gentlest form
Charm us to tears; not that the smoothest cheek,
Where ever rosy tints have made their home,
So rivet us on her; but that she is
The subtle, delicate grace, — the inward grace,
For words too excellent; the noble, true,
The majesty of earth; the summer queen:
In whose conceptions nothing but what's great
Has any right. And, O! her love for him,
Who does but his small part in honoring her;
Discharging a sweet office, sweeter none,

Mother and child, friend, counsel and repose; —
Nought matches with her, nought has leave with her
To highest human praise. Farewell to him
Who reverences not with an excess
Of faith the beauteous sex; all barren he
Shall live a living death of mockery.

Ah! had but words the power, what could we say
Of woman! We, rude men, of violent phrase,
Harsh action, even in repose inwardly harsh;
Whose lives walk blustering on high stilts, removed
From all the purely gracious influence
Of mother earth. To single from the host
Of angel forms one only, and to her
Devote our deepest heart and deepest mind
Seems almost contradiction. Unto her
We owe our greatest blessings, hours of cheer,
Gay smiles, and sudden tears, and more than these
A sure perpetual love. Regard her as
She walks along the vast still earth; and see!
Before her flies a laughing troop of joys,
And by her side treads old experience,

With never-failing voice admonitory;
The gentle, though infallible, kind advice,
The watchful care, the fine regardfulness,
Whatever mates with what we hope to find,
All consummate in her — the summer queen.

To call past ages better than what now
Man is enacting on life's crowded stage,
Cannot improve our worth; and for the world
Blue is the sky as ever, and the stars
Kindle their crystal flames at soft-fallen eve
With the same purest lustre that the east
Worshipped. The river gently flows through fields
Where the broad-leaved corn spreads out, and loads
Its ear as when the Indian tilled the soil.
The dark green pine, — green in the winter's cold,
Still whispers meaning emblems, as of old;
The cricket chirps, and the sweet, eager birds
In the sad woods crowd their thick melodies;
But yet, to common eyes, life's poetry
Something has faded, and the cause of this
May be that man, no longer at the shrine

Of woman, kneeling with true reverence,
In spite of field, wood, river, stars and sea
Goes most disconsolate. A babble now,
A huge and wind-swelled babble, fills the place
Of that great adoration which of old
Man had for woman. In these days no more
Is love the pith and marrow of man's fate.

Thou who in early years feelest awake
To finest impulses from nature's breath,
And in thy walk hearest such sounds of truth
As on the common ear strike without heed,
Beware of men around thee. Men are foul,
With avarice, ambition and deceit;
The worst of all, ambition. This is life
Spent in a feverish chase for selfish ends,
Which has no virtue to redeem its toil
But one long, stagnant hope to raise the self.
The miser's life to this seems sweet and fair;
Better to pile the glittering coin, than seek
To overtop our brothers and our loves.
Merit in this? Where lies it, though thy name

Ring over distant lands, meeting the wind
Even on the extremest verge of the wide world.
Merit in this? Better be hurled abroad
On the vast whirling tide, than in thyself
Concentred, feed upon thy own applause.
Thee shall the good man yield no reverence;
But, while the idle, dissolute crowd are loud
In voice to send thee flattery, shall rejoice
That he has scaped thy fatal doom, and known
How humble faith in the good soul of things
Provides amplest enjoyment. O my brother,
If the Past's counsel any honour claim
From thee, go read the history of those
Who a like path have trod, and see a fate
Wretched with fears, changing like leaves at noon,
When the new wind sings in the white birch wood.
Learn from the simple child the rule of life,
And from the movements of the unconscious tribes
Of animal nature, those that bend the wing
Or cleave the azure tide, content to be,
What the great frame provides, — freedom and grace.
Thee, simple child, do the swift winds obey,

And the white waterfalls with their bold leaps
Follow thy movements. Tenderly the light
Thee watches, girding with a zone of radiance,
And all the swinging herbs love thy soft steps.

THE SPIDER.

Habitant of castle gray,
Creeping thing in sober way,
Visible sage mechanician,
Skilfullest arithmetician,
Aged animal at birth,
Wanting joy and idle mirth;
Clothed in famous tunic old,
Vestments black, of many a fold,
Spotted mightily with gold;
Weaving, spinning in the sun
Since the world its course has run;
Creation beautiful in art,
Of God's providence a part,—
What if none will look at thee,
Sighing for the humming bee,

Or great moth with heavenly wings,
Or the nightingale who sings ? —
Curious spider, thou 'rt to me
Of a mighty family.

Tender of a mystic loom,
Weaving in my silent room
Canopy, that haply vies
With the mortal fabric wise ;
Everlasting procreator,
Ne'er was such a generator.
Adam wondered at thy skill,
And thy persevering will,
That continueth to spin,
Caring not a yellow pin
For the mortals' dire confusion ;
Sager in profound conclusion
Than astronomer at night,
When he brings new worlds to light.
Heaven has furnished thee with tools,
Such as ne'er a heap of fools

Have by dint of sweat and pain
Made for use, and made in vain.

When mild breeze is hither straying,
Sweetest music kindly playing,
Raising high the whispering leaves
And the covering of the sheaves,
Thou art rocking, airy thing,
Like a proud exalted king;
Conqueror thou surely art,
And majestical of heart.
There are times of loneliness
When a living thing we bless;
Times of miserable sin,
Cold without, and dark within;
Then, old spider, haply I
Seek thy busy factory;
Always finding thee at home,
Too forecasting e'er to roam;
So we sit and spin together
In the gayest, gloomiest weather.

THE PICTURE.

My mind obeys the power
  That through all persons breathes,
And woods are murmuring,
And fields begin to sing,
  And in me nature wreathes.

Thou too art with me here,—
  The best of all design;
Of that strong purity
Which makes it joy to be
  A distant thought of thine.

A SONG OF SPRING.

Leaves on the trees,
And buds in the breeze,
And tall grass waving on the meadows' side,
And a showerlet sweet,
While the soft clouds meet
Again in their golden robes when day has died.

The scholar his pen
Hath mended again,
For the new life runs in his wearied veins;
While the wild child flies
Mid the flowers' fresh dyes,
And the happy bird gushes with sudden strains.

WINTER SONG.

Cold blows the blast,
And the snow falls fast
On meadow and moor, and the deep blue lake;
And the wind it is keen
In the snow-white sheen,
As the glances which the Envies make.

Merrily by the hearthstone we
Sit with a song of social glee,
While the blaze of the red fire glows,
Painting the sides of the rafters old,
Till they shine in the roof like melted gold,
Right under the piled up, chilling snows.

Now the brooks are bound,
And make no sound,
Still as a corpse in its coffin drear;
While the icicles shine
As stately and fine
As the lamps of the church o'er the death-cold bier.

But it troubleth not us,
There are joys for us,
And thine eye is as warm as in summer time;
Thy kiss is as sweet,
And thy loving arms meet
As were ringing abroad the soft winds' chime.

HOME.

'Tis far away, dear friend, 't is far away
Where we were born and nurtured, and grew up.
Thither to-day, as this new gate of time
Swings on its noiseless hinges slowly back,
Through the far vista of our boyish years,
Look with a saddened eye, ay! once more look,
Ere through these portals we pass idly on,
To see the coming painted on the wall.

I see a grand procession of fine hopes,
Each with his face wrapped in a sable stole,
And turned away from me their once bright eyes,
All mutely gazing on the snowy ground.

Then one, — still farther down, — this mournful troop
They carry on a bier hung round with frost.
The light is like a dying person's eye ;
For O ! our passèd years shall make us weep,
Nor shall our boyish years live but in dreams.

They say our home is in a better land ;
That we are pilgrims here, and on this march
We shall stop never, but with soilèd feet
Track the hard pavement with our dusty prints.
But yet to journey homeward were most fair,
And, no one knowing, burst upon their sight ; —
Thou art come ! — Indeed is 't thou, from the far land ? —
That joy was in their hearts. And as the lake's
Calm surface is at once waked into life
By one slight move, so should my sudden sight
Arouse their peaceful feelings. So will 't be
When some pure man makes of this world a home,
All home, — both on new-years and birth-days home,
And all the people laugh within their hearts,
That this is city of God, both then and now.

ON RECEIVING SOME DRAWINGS.

SWEET are these drawings, and though wanting that
Great finish and pretence, which modern art
Dresses its being in, to me they are
A finer exposition of the mind
From which they issued, than more labored skill,
These first faint streaks of that consuming light
Which thou shalt shed on art, and all fair things.
For thou wert made for beauty, dwell'st in it.
No other home is thine, than where the world
Winds her green tresses o'er the golden bank,
Under whose edge the wild brook leaps along,
Like a mad courser running to the sea.

Thee shall the azure fill with countless hopes,
And the soft wind of Summer in thy ear
Speak with a voice of pleasure. But thy way
Not thus for ever. There shall be a day
When perchance sorrow, with her icy smile
Shall visit thee. Then shall thy wondrous art,
With most consoling influence, beckon thee
To sweet thoughts ; — then thy pencil guide the way
Into a region of keen memories ;
And many a form spring into graceful life,
Airy and light, dispellers of thy gloom.
Ah glorious fancy, who with shaping skill
Hast visited us here, else how obscure,
And with thy splendid charms and graceful mien
Re-clothed the sere and tearful, drooping world,
So that now going onward to the tomb,
Alone and halt, beggars in love and joy,
We from thy presence catch a glance of heaven,
And on the face of nature read the life
Which we did wish to live, as though 't were so.

OUR BIRTH DAYS.

THESE are the solemnest days of our bright lives,
When memory and hope within exert
Delightful reign; when sympathy revives,
And that which late was in the soul inert
Grows warm and living; and to us, alone
Are these a knowledge, nowise may they hurt,
Or cry aloud, or frighten out the tone
Which we will strive to wear, and as calm nature own.

Whatever scenes our eyes once gratified,
Those landscapes couched around our early homes,
To which our tender, peaceful hearts replied,
To those our present happy feeling roams;

And takes a mightier joy than from the tomes
Of the pure scholar; those ten thousand sights
Of constant nature flow in us, as foams
The bubbling spring; these are the true delights
Wherewith this solemn world the sorrowful requites.

WRITTEN IN THE EVENING OF A NOVEMBER DAY.

THEE, mild autumnal day,
I felt, not for myself; the winds may steal
From any point, and seem to me alike
Reviving, soothing powers.

Like thee the contrast is
Of a new mood in a decaying man,
Whose idle mind is suddenly revived
With many pleasant thoughts.

Our earth was gratified;
Fresh grass, a stranger in this frosty clime,
Peeped from the crumbling mould, as welcome as
An unexpected friend.

How glowed the evening star,
As it delights to glow in summer's midst,
When out of ruddy boughs the twilight birds
Sing flowing harmony.

Peace was the will to-day;
Love in bewildering growth our joyous minds
Swelled to their widest bounds; the worldly left
All hearts to sympathize.

I felt for thee, — for thee,
Whose inward, outward life completely moves,
Surrendered to the beauty of the soul
Of this creative day.

INSCRIPTION FOR A GARDEN.

The spirit builds his house in the least flowers,—
A beautiful mansion; how the colors live,
Intricately delicate. Every night
An angel, for this purpose, from the heavens
With his small urn of ivory-like hue drops
A globular world of the purest element
In the flower's midst, feeding its tender soul
With lively inspiration. Wonder 't is
That man will still want knowledge; is not here,
Spread in amazing wealth, a form too rare,
A soul so inward, that with open heart
Tremulous and tender, we must ever fear
Not to see near enough, of these deep things?

THE LOVER'S FEAR.

There is a grace upon the waving trees,
A beauty in the wide and heaving sea,
A glory is there in the rushing breeze,
Yet what are all these fairy things to me?
What by the side of such an one as thee?
They weigh as dust against the purest gold;
And all the words of fine society
And all the famous thoughts great men have told,
By side of thee seem dull, — dull, heavy and most cold.

If thou art lost to me, farewell my heart!
There is one jewel for thy prizing here,
But how companionless and chilled thou art,
If this great lustre, unto thee so dear
Fall, like an autumn leaf, withered and sere,
And leave thee on the shore of time, alone;
So shall this living earth be thy true bier,
Its every sound a wretched, mournful tone,
And all thy passions' tears turned into hardest stone.

TO CLIO.

PLANETS bear thee in their hands,
  Azure skies have folded o'er thee,
Thou art sung by angel bands,
  And the deep, cold, throbbing sea;
Whispered in each sighing tree,
In each meadow's melody.

Where the sprites outwatch the moon,
  And the ghostly night breeze swells,
And the brook prolongs a tune
  Through the shimmering, shadowed dells;
There thou weavest unknown spells
To the ringing fairy bells.

In thy folded trance there hide
  Ceaseless measures of content,
And thou art of form the bride,
  Shapely picture's element.

THE BENIGHTED TRAVELLER.

He journeys on, slow moving o'er the moor.
The treacherous dark has razed his homeward path,
And like a spirit from the heavens sent,
Dances before him his old kitchen hearth,
His children round, and antique serving maid.
The pale stars glimmer through a flickering mist,
While chill the night-breeze creeps about his heart.
His unfamiliar step crushes the herb
That withered long ago, untouched before.
He stumbles o'er rude stones, and climbs the hill,
To see the waning moon with pity look
On marshes spread beneath, and endless glades
Where never fell his eye until this hour.

THE RIVER.

THERE is an inward voice, that in the stream
Sends forth its spirit to the listening ear,
And in a calm content it floweth on,
Like wisdom, welcome with its own respect.
Clear in its breast lie all these beauteous thoughts.
It doth receive the green and graceful trees,
And the gray rocks smile in its peaceful arms,
And over all floats a serenest blue,
Which the mild heaven sheds down on it like rain.
O fair, sweet stream, thy undisturbed repose
Me beckons to thy front, and thou vexed world,
Thou other turbulent sphere where I have dwelt,
Diminished into distance touch'st no more

My feelings here, than does the swaying soft,
(Made by the delicate wave parted in front,
As through the gentle element we move
Like shadows gliding through untroubled realms,)
Disturb these lily circles, these white bells.
And yet on thee shall wind come fiercely down,
Hail pelt thee with dull words, ice bind thee up;
And yet again when the fierce rage is o'er,
O smiling river, shalt thou smile once more,
And, as it were, even in thy depths revere
The sage security thy nature wears.

THE POOR MAN.

Like a lion at bay,
Like a cold still day,
Stands the poor man here,
Few friends has he,
And fewer they be
With the turn of each year;

Who can buy him no house,
Who cannot carouse,
Nor his neighbors delight;
Whose cabin is cold,
Whose vestment is old,
Whose heart only shineth bright.

They eye him askance
With a feeble glance,
Half shake him by the hand, —
'T is the poor man, he
Hath no gold to give to me;
There are richer in the land. —

But the sun shineth fair
Through the blue-woven air,
To the poor man's mind;
His ears are all ready,
And his hearing is steady,
As rushes the wind.

The seed he puts in earth,
Of its fruit hath the birth;
Tall waves the fragrant flower;
He hath carved a broad stone
That the time may be known;
The dial telleth him the hour.

The birds over his head
Their broad wings spread,
Their songs to him they sing ;
The brook runs him to meet,
And washeth gently his feet,
While the meadows their joys bring.

STILLWATER.

Thou lazy river flowing neither way
Me figurest, and yet thy banks seem gay.
I flow between the shores of this large life,
My banks are fair as thine, with joy as rife;
Thy tides will swell when the next moon comes round,
But mine far higher in their rise be found.

FAREWELL.

THE time is told when we must part
For this present, and for long;
Yet I hear thee in my heart
Sing sweet strains of childhood's song.

What I might have proved to thee,
Must the azure future say;
And my brightest memory
Paint with gold thy distant way.

MOONLIGHT.

He came and waved a little silver wand,
He dropped the veil that hid a statue fair,
He drew a circle with that pearly hand,
His grace confined that beauty in the air;—
Those limbs so gentle, now at rest from flight,
Those quiet eyes now musing on the night.

TO ANNA.

Thou golden figure of the shaded sun,
Thou stately streamlet singing on thy way,
Thou harp, that beauty plays its notes upon,
Thou silver image of departing day!

Thou summer charm, how shall the winter glow,
That thou serenely shinest through the air,
Clothing with rosy tints the once pale snow,
Until the frosts rich crimson flowers upbear!

THE SIBYL TO HER LOVER.

Roam, — the wide world before thee,
O'er mount, o'er vale, o'er stream, o'er sea,
Roam, — outspread before the gale,
Even if it rend thy swelling sail.
Beware of the sunny isles!
Trust not their rosy smiles.

I, — what am I to thee?
A speck on thy life's morning sea, —
Soon shalt thou forget me,
Thou honey-gathering bee;
With thy laden freight shalt pass
Over all the earth to day,
Sweeping, as the bending grass
Lives beneath the wild air's play.

Set thy canvass to the wind,
Thy rudder man for ocean war,
And cleaving, leave the land behind,
Thy rushing course pursuing far.
Beware of the sunny isles!
Trust not their rosy smiles.

Look not on beauty for thy mate,
Nor sparkling wine, nor fantasy;
But drink the perfect desolate
Of some wild, lofty misery.
Beware of the sunny isles!
Trust not their rosy smiles.

Thy goblet will not hold a draught.
What lips can drain from half a rim?
Nor canst thou mould it whole by craft,
Though fused its ore in starlight dim.
Away! Thou sail'st the misty sea,
A nervèd hand, and sparkling free.

Away! away! delay no more,
I see thy cavern's thunder cloud;
Put off! put off! and hate the shore,
Before thy life with storm is bowed.
Beware the sounds of single-hearted time,
For they will chill thee like the hoar frost's rime.

Weave but one circlet for thy hair,
Twine but one chaplet for thy brow;
A wreath of floating, azure air,
And into it the sunlight throw,
Let gold hide 'neath the twisted braid
Heart's blood, as it is sometimes said.

Thy robe shall stream like crimson bars,
That fleck the sunset banner wide,
And float above thy ruby wars,
As it in gore were richly dyed.
And warm and sweet thy life shall be
Across the fathoms of the sea.

Wait but the hour, — thy course is run;
Life's carpentry will build no more;
Thou shalt sit silenced in the dun,
Perpetual tempests' sluggish roar;
Those velvet tresses soft and free,
Slimed and disfigured then shall be.

Bide not thy time, heed not thy fate,
Believe no truth, respect no law,
Fling to the winds foul custom's state,
And play with every antique saw;
For in thee hides a matchless light,
That splendors all the dreaming night.

Thy bark shall be a precious stone,
In whose red veins deep magic hides;
Thy ecstasies be known to none,
Except those vast perpetual tides
Which circulate the world's wide round,
But whisper not the lightest sound.

Away! away! thou starlit breath,
On bended knees I pray thee, go!
O bind thy temples not with death,
Nor let thy shadow fall on snow.
Beware of the sunny isles!
Trust not their rosy smiles.

See how the morning gilds the main,
See how the sun sets splendidly,
And mark thy graceful vessel's gain
When thou art flashing through the sea,
While crested cliffs hiss madly near,
Or the long reach sheds seaweeds' tear.

No sunken rock shall shatter thee,
No blasting wind thy bark pursue,
But thou shalt sail as comes to me
The forest's anthem, just and true;
Spread thy green canvass to the breeze,
Thy bows surrender to the seas.

Thy music shall the sunset star
Tune spherally in liquid light,
Thy jewelled couch the south inbar
Within the curtains of the night,
And fold thee in those clustering arms,
To sing thee deep in dreamiest charms.

A POET'S HOPE.

FLYING, — flying beyond all lower regions,
Beyond the light called day, and night's repose,
Where the untrammelled soul, on her wind-pinions
Fearlessly sweeping, defies my earthly woes; —
There, — there, upon that infinitest sea,
Lady, thy hope, — so fair a hope, summons me.

Fall off, ye garments of my misty weather,
Drop from my eyes, ye scales of time's applying;
Am I not godlike? meet not here together
A past and future infinite, defying,
The cold, still, callous moment of to-day?
Am I not master of the calm alway?

Would I could summon from the deep, deep mine,
Glutted with shapely jewels, glittering bright,
One echo of that splendor, call it thine,
And weave it in the strands of living light;
For it is in me, and the sea smiles fair,
And thitherward I rage, on whirling air.

Unloose me, demons of dull care and want,
I will not stand your slave, I am your king;
Think not within your meshes vile I pant
For the wild liberty of an unclipt wing;
My empire is myself, and I defy
The external; yes! I rule the whole, or die.

All music that the fullest breeze can play
In its melodious whisperings in the wood,
All modulations which entrance the day
And deify a sunlight solitude;
All anthems that the waves sing to the ocean
Are mine for song, and yield to my devotion.

And mine the soft glaze of a loving eye,
And mine the pure shapes of the human form,
And mine the bitterest sorrow's witchery,
And spells enough to make a snow-king warm;
For an undying hope thou breathest me, —
Hope which can ride the tossing, foaming sea.

Lady, there is a hope that all men have,
Some mercy for their faults, a grassy place
To rest in, and a flower-strown, gentle grave;
Another hope which purifies our race,
That when that fearful bourne forever past,
They may find rest, — and rest *so* long to last.

I seek it not, I ask no rest for ever,
My path is onward to the farthest shores, —
Upbear me in your arms, unceasing river,
That from the soul's clear fountain swiftly pours,
Motionless not, until the end is won,
Which now I feel hath scarcely felt the sun.

To feel, to know, to soar unlimited,
Mid throngs of light-winged angels sweeping far,
And pore upon the realms unvisited,
That tesselate the unseen unthought star,
To be the thing that now I feebly dream
Flashing within my faintest, deepest gleam.

Ah! caverns of my soul! how thick your shade,
Where flows that life by which I faintly see, —
Wave your bright torches, for I need your aid,
Golden-eyed demons of my ancestry!
Your son though blinded hath a light within,
A heavenly fire which ye from suns did win.

And, lady, in thy hope my life will rise
Like the air-voyager, till I upbear
These heavy curtains of my filmy eyes,
Into a lighter, more celestial air;
A mortal's hope shall bear me safely on,
Till I the higher region shall have won.

O Time! O death! I clasp you in my arms,
For I can soothe an infinite cold sorrow,
And gaze contented on your icy charms,
And that wild snow-pile, which we call to-morrow;
Sweep on, O soft, and azure-lidded sky,
Earth's waters to your gentle gaze reply.

I am not earth-born, though I here delay;
Hope's child, I summon infiniter powers,
And laugh to see the mild and sunny day
Smile on the shrunk and thin autumnal hours;
I laugh, for hope hath happy place with me,
If my bark sinks, 't is to another sea.

THE TEMPLE.

" SEEST thou yon azure dome
Where the thoughtful stars have home,
This floor of earth, those pillars tall,
The green wreathed mountain's steadfast wall?"

A moody man, he stands apart,
Nor listens to the pleasing charm,
And yet he has a human heart,
A heart with human feelings warm.

OCTOBER.

DRY leaves with yellow ferns, they are
Fit wreath of Autumn, while a star
Still, bright, and pure, our frosty air
Shivers in twinkling points
Of thin, celestial hair,
And thus one side of heaven anoints.

I am beneath the moon's calm look,
Most quiet in this sheltered nook,
From trouble of the frosty wind
That curls the yellow blade;
Though in my covered mind
A grateful sense of change is made.

To wandering men how dear this sight,
Of a cold, tranquil autumn night,
    In its majestic, deep repose.
    Thus shall their genius be,
    Not buried in high snows,
Though of as mute tranquillity.

An anxious life they will not pass,
Nor, as the shadow on the grass,
Leave no impression there to stay;
    To them all things are thought;
    The blushing morn's decay,
Our death, our life, by this is taught.

O find in every haze that shines
A brief appearance without lines,
A single word, — no finite joy;
    For present is a Power
    Which we may not annoy,
Yet love him stronger every hour.

I would not put this sense from me,
If I could some great sovereign be;
Yet will not task a fellow man
    To feel the same glad sense;
    For no one living can
Feel, save his given influence.

THE POOR.

I do not mourn my friends are false,
I dare not grieve for sins of mine,
I weep for those who pine to death,
Great God! in this rich world of thine.

So many trees there are to see,
And fields go waving broad with grain,
And yet, — what utter misery! —
Our very brothers lie in pain.

These by their darkened hearth-stones sit,
  Their children shivering idly round,
As true as liveth God, 't were fit
  For these poor men to curse the ground.

And those who daily bread have none,
  Half starved the long, long winter's day,
Fond parents gazing on their young,
  Too wholly sad one word to say.

To them it seems, their God has cursed
  This race of ours since they were born;
Willing to toil, and yet deprived
  Of common wood, or store of corn.

I do not weep for my own woes,
  They are as nothing in my eye;
I weep for them who, starved and froze,
  Do curse their God, and long to die.

FADING AWAY.

Sunny day!
Sunny day!
Why are shorn thy golden beams?
Mortal, tell me, are thy dreams
Fading away?

Summer flowers!
Summer flowers!
Fall your leaves forever lost?
Mortal, has no sudden frost
Crisped thine hours?

Shrine of clay!
Shrine of clay!
Shall thy fine pulsations cease?
Mortal, 't is a blest release,
Fading away.

FOR A WOOD SCENE IN WINTER.

Around this spot the trees have fallen, — the path
Leads its rude way o'er the decaying trunks
Of prostrate pines. Above, against the sky,
A massy wall of splintered rock soars up,
Once gay with those green plants that smile in shade,
The broad-leaved ferns. How still it is, — how lone.
You seem to hear the silence whispering — hush!
But in the spring I heard, as here I stood,
A loud and hissing stream, and in the fall
The wind plies its wild fingers, and plucks off
The sere and crimson foliage of the ash.

Life's winter, like the silent season, mute,
Crowned by a wreath of snow as white as this,
That hangs so loosely on the leafless trees,
Like this calm place still brightens in the sun;
And winter should be dear to man, as he
In his most venerable aspect, this
Does imitate.

UNA.

We are centred deeper far
Than the eye of any star,
Nor can rays of long sunlight
Thread a pace of our delight.
In thy form I see the day
Burning, of a kingdom higher,
In thy silver net-work play
Thoughts that to the Gods aspire;
In thy cheek I see the flame
Of the studious taper burn,
And thy Grecian eye might tame
Nature's ashed in antique urn;

Yet with this lofty element
Flows a pure stream of gentle kindness,
And thou to life thy strength hast lent,
And borne profoundest tenderness
In thy Promethean fearless arm,
With mercy's love that would all angels charm.

So trembling meek, so proudly strong,
Thou dost to higher worlds belong,
Than where I sing this empty song:
Yet I, a thing of mortal kind,
Can kneel before thy pathless mind,
And see in thee what my mates say
Sank o'er Judea's hills one crimson day.
Yet flames on high the keen Greek fire,
And later ages rarefies,
And even on my tuneless lyre
A faint, wan beam of radiance dies.

And might I say what I have thought
Of thee, and those I love to-day,
Then had the world an echo caught
Of that intense, impassioned lay,
Which sung in those thy being sings,
And from the deepest ages rings.

PAST.

I WOULD I were at home again,
  My days are running fast away,
And bring me nothing true but pain,
  Though I may look so glad and gay.

My friend, this world is more to thee,
  Than to thy old companion here,
For I must always turn and flee,
  While thou advancest without fear.

The blue skies greet me without joy,
  The earth is fearful, cold and dull,
I wish I were once more a boy,
  It then all seemed so beautiful.

I cling to what I loved before,
  I joy in what I used to do, —
I cannot learn to love you more,
  But O! I long to fly to you.

Yes! I shall come and be a child
  Where I was childish, and grow glad
To hear your gentle voice so mild,
  And play again where I was sad.

For I was sad in days past by,
  But now am sad that they are past,
And all my joys in memory,
  Are perfectly and finely glassed.

THE FRIENDS.

Our village churchyard, — would I could relate
To you all that I think of it, its trees,
Its trailing grass, the hanging stones, that say,
This watch o'er human bones fatigues not us;
My boyhood's fear unsatisfied, for then
I thought a wandering wind some ghostly father,
While the sweet rustle of the locust leaves
Shot a thin crystal web of icy dread
O'er the swift current of my wild heart's blood.
One night the pastor's form among the tombs
Chased the big drops across my unseamed brow.
You smile, — believe me, lesser things than these
Can win a boy's emotions.

These graves, — you mean;
Their history who knows better than I?
For in the busy street strikes on my ear
Each sound, even inaudible voices
Lengthen the long tale my memory tells.
Now mark how reads the epitaph, — "Here lie
Two, who in life were parted, now together."
I should remember this brief record well.
And yet these two, their lives were much the same
With all who crowd the narrow bridge of life;
I see but little difference, truly;
The greatest yet, is he who still lives on.
Alas! the day seemed big with mighty pains
That laid the first of these within this tomb.
There was within the air a murmuring sound,
For all the summer's life was fluttering o'er,
While the clear autumn conquered, and was glad.
I bore a part of the coffin, and my feet
Scattered the shrouds of the green foliage;
Yellow the flowers nature spread o'er the bier.
You read no names upon this monument;
I could not have them graved; why should we name

So patiently our friends; enough we know them.
Esther her name, and who so gay as she.
Twelve years had gently smoothed the sunny hair
That showered its golden mists adown her neck,
Twelve years, — twelve little years laughed in those eyes
Where, when her mother spoke, the bright drops stood;
So glistened in the spring depths of her love
That parent's image. Joyous was her face,
But yet, below its joy, a larger import;
Even now I see her smile, deep within deep,
And never thoughtless. What a spirited grace
Danced in each bold emotion of her heart
Unshadowed by a fear.

And who the next? —
She came to this still tomb one summer's day;
New flowers were bursting from their unsunned bells
Spring's choristers now fully grown sang loud,
Sweet was the wind, the sky above as blue
As that pure woman's eye we buried then.
Some thirty years had she the footway trod,

Yet frail and delicate she wandered on,
A violet amid the rude world's briars,
Till dropped an icicle within the flower,
That tenderness could not essay to melt.
Her name, and it was Esther ; —
This likeness you will trace between the two,
The mother of the young yet sleeping fawn
Was gathered to her side.

My hairs are gray,
Yet those we buried then stood near to me.
Their forms enchant these lonelier, elder years,
And add due sacredness to human life.
That I was father to so fair a child,
And that her mother smiled on me so long,
I think of now as passing gods' estate ;
I am enraptured that such lot was mine,
That mine is others. Sleep on, unspotted ones,
Ye are immortal now ; your mirthsome hours
Beat in my shrunken pulse, and in mine ears
Sounds the rich music of your heavenly songs.

CONTENT.

Within the unpainted cottage dwell
  The spirits of serene content,
As clear as from its moss-grown well
  Rises the crystal element.

Above, the elm, whose trunk is scarred
  With many a dint of stormy weather,
Rises, a sumptuous screen, debarred
  Of nothing that links life together.

Our common life may gratify
  More feelings than the rarest art,
For nothing can aspire so high
  As beatings of the human heart.

O! value then thy daily cheer,
  Poor pensioner on nature's store,
And clasp the least, and hold most dear
  What seemeth small, and add the more.

WRITTEN AMONG THE LENOX HILLS.

Dear friend, in this fair atmosphere again,
Far from the noisy echoes of the main,
Amid the world-old mountains, and the hills
From whose strange grouping a fine power distils
The soothing and the calm, I seek repose,
The city's noise forgot, and hard, stern woes.
As thou once said'st, the rarest sons of earth
Have in the dust of cities shown their worth,
Where long collision with the human curse
Has of great glory been the frequent nurse,
And only those who in sad cities dwell,
Are of the green trees fully sensible.
To them the silver bells of tinkling streams
Seem brighter than an angel's laugh in dreams,

A clear and airy vision of the sky,
The future's seed, companions when we die.
The dawn, full noon, evening, and solemn night
Weave all around their robes of changing light,
And in the mighty forests, day's whole time
Is shadowed with a portraiture sublime;
In the dark caves dwells midnight in her stole,
While shady Even haunts a tranquil knoll.

SONG.

My sweet girl is lying still
   In her lovely atmosphere,
The gentle hopes her blue veins fill
   With pure silver, warm and clear.

O, see her hair, O, mark her breast,
   Would it not, O! comfort thee,
If thou could'st nightly go to rest
   By that virgin chastity.

TO BESSIE.

Be the blue skies thy fitting garniture,
 And the green woods be organs to thine ear,
And all that is most sweet and fine and pure
 Attend upon thee while thou dwellest here;

The stars upon thee shine their bright rays, clear
 As are the fancies of thy generous brain,
All things be gentle to thee, and no fear
 Clothed in a darkened guise, in thy sweet heart
 appear!

THE SEA.

Sound on, thou anthem of the breathless soul,
Unneeding heat, unfathomed and alone,
Thy waves in measured phalanx firmly roll,
And toss the furious wind in steadfast tone.

Sweet smiles the day-god on thy green expanse,
And purples thee with his sad, fading eve,
Yet all the livelong night thy waters dance,
While mariners the favoring harbors leave.

Thy sunken rocks are nigh th' inconstant shore,
There thou hast tribute from the fisher's boat,
Afar, thou art the play of him no more,
But mighty ships on thy high mountains float.

AUTUMN'S APPROACH.

SUMMER is going,
Cold wind is blowing,
Tale of the autumn — the autumn so drear,
No sower is sowing,
No mower is mowing,
Seed is sown, harvest mown, time almost sere.

Flowers are fading,
Autumn's wreath braiding,
To deck the sad burial — sad burial lone,
The bees have done lading
And finished their trading,
Honey made, cellars laid, hive almost grown.

Gray clouds are flying,
Gray shades replying,
Soon shall come mourning — mourning so pale,
And the babe shall be crying,
And the mother be sighing,
Coldly lie, coldly die, in the arms of the gale.

THE ISLAND.

I.

THE POINT.

THE gray wind flies with speed along,
Yet stand the clouds nor hurry by, —
Alas ! 't is but a voice of song,
To which they send no quick reply.

The sea sleeps on, — its waves' repose
Defies the pathos of the gale,
So in our hearts, the long years' woes
Ride silent with a furled sail.

Life's wind speeds on, but we are bound
  By memory to our quiet state,
And sleep in solitude profound,
  Within the caverns of our fate.

With patient arms enfolded, mute,
  We watch the clouds' unmoving day,
And mourn above our stringless lute,
  Which still refuses us to play.

Yet many a bark drives gaily by,
  And cuts the white crest's curling foam,
While over it, the azure sky
  Shines like a dear, domestic home.

Our anchored boat among the flowers,
  Is tufted with their yellow crests,
In which a merry troop of hours
  Build with sweet song their circling nests.

Yet not our song, nor home, nor mate ;—
  We smile upon them half resigned,
And view them not made desolate,
  By our dim days and sad gray wind.

II.

THE LITTLE BAY.

Thy waves are still this gentle day,
  They sweep no more with angry voice,
The wind lies sleeping far away,
  And bids thee in repose, rejoice.

I love to skim thy peaceful breast,
  My little skiff so gently tossed,
For here I feel perpetual rest,
  Where never wind my path has crossed.

I sweetly feel within thy arms,
  Such peaceful life will dwell with me,

Day shed a rain of shining charms,
  And night glow golden passed with thee.

O little bay !—O little bay !
  Why need I shun thy tranquil tide ?
Why need I weep the gusty day,
  When I at sea shall fiercely ride ?

Alas ! my little skiff drifts down
  Thy peaceful current, but to be
The victim of the ocean's frown,
  The plaything of the misty sea.

III.

THE LITTLE ISLANDS.

With what a dauntless, unconfined air
  They eye askant this other island scene,
Now when the whole expanse is smiling fair,
  And with what bold and satisfied demean

They gaze for ever at the rolling sea,—
Their glance interpreteth my destiny.

So I, an island in the cold world's tide,
Boldly stand looking at to-morrow's rise,
To-day I feel no fear what comes beside,
Nor shade with trembling hand my weakened eyes,
Yet yonder ocean rolls with fearful might,
And has its clouds and unexpected night.

My good right hand is all I have for aid,
My soul's own armor makes my whole defence,
Yet not a power I supplicate, afraid;
They shine content, but very far from hence;
Nor any man can be my constant law,
With all mankind I wage a secret war.

—

IV.

THE BRIDGES.

Lo! how hastes the coming tide,
Plying with main strength its task,
Tossing weeds and shells aside,
No assistance does it ask.

So may we our lives control,
Cast aside what we desire,
Feeling that the sweeping soul
Has than earthly path, a higher.

Life has bridged our destiny,
Walled our woes within its breast,
Runs through us a troubled sea,
Which perceiveth here no rest.

Death shall sweep the works away,
  Set our current flowing free,
Leave us no more yesterday,
  And be the thing we feebly see.

Then by the bridge I dauntless swear
  I will rise higher than before,
My head shall breathe a freer air
  Than any scattered on this shore.

DEATH.

Beneath the endless surges of the deep,
Whose green content o'erlaps them ever-more,
A host of mariners perpetual sleep,
Too hushed to heed the wild commotion's roar;
The emerald weeds glide softly o'er their bones,
And wash them gently 'mid the rounded stones.
No epitaph have they to tell their tale,
Their birth-place, age, and story all are lost,
Yet rest they deeply, as within the vale
Those sheltered bodies by the smooth slates crost;
And countless tribes of men lie on the hills,
And human blood runs in the crystal rills.

The air is full of men, who once enjoyed
The healthy element, nor looked beyond;
Many, who all their mortal strength employed
In human kindness, of their brothers fond,
And many more who counteracted fate
And battled in the strife of common hate.
Profoundest sleep enwraps them all around,
Sages and sire, the child, and manhood strong;
Shed not one tear; expend no sorrowing sound,
Tune thy clear voice to no funereal song;
For O death stands to welcome thee sure,
And life hath in its breath a steeper mystery.

I hear a bell that tolls an empty note,
The mourning anthem, and the sobbing prayer;
A grave fresh-opened, where the friends devote
To mouldering darkness a still corpse, once fair
And beautiful as morning's silver light,
And stars which throw their clear fire on the night;

She is not here who smiled within these eyes
Warmer than spring's first sunbeam through the pale
And tearful air, — resist these flatteries; —
O lay her silently alone, and in this vale
Shall the sweet winds sing better dirge for her,
And the fine early flowers her death-clothes minister.

O Death! thou art the palace of our hopes,
The storehouse of our joys, great labor's end,
Thou art the bronzed key which swiftly opes
The coffers of the past; and thou shalt send
Such trophies to our hearts, as sunny days
When life upon its golden harpstring plays.
And when a nation mourns a silent voice,
That long entranced its ear with melody,
How must thou in thy inmost soul rejoice,
To wrap such treasure in thy boundless sea;
And thou wert dignified if but one soul
Had been enfolded in thy twilight stole.

Triumphal arches circle o'er thy deep,
Dazzling with jewels, radiant with content;
In thy vast arms the sons of genius sleep,
The carvings of thy spheral monument,
Bearing no recollection of dim time,
Within thy green, and most perennial prime.
And might I sound a thought of thy decree,
How lapsed the dreary earth in fragrant pleasure,
And hummed along o'er life's contracted sea
Like the swift petrel, mimicking the wave's measure;
But though I long, the sounds will never come,
For in thy majesty my lesser voice is dumb.

Thou art not anxious of thy precious fame,
But comest like the clouds soft stealing on;
Thou soundest in a careless key the name
Of him, who to thy boundless treasury is won;
And yet he quickly cometh; for to die
Is ever gentlest to both low and high.

Thou therefore hast humanity's respect;
They build thee tombs upon the green hill side,
And will not suffer thee the least neglect,
And tend thee with a desolate sad pride;
For thou art strong O death! though sweetly so,
And in thy lovely gentleness sleeps woe.

O what are we, who swim upon this tide
Which we call life, yet to thy kingdom come?
Look not upon us till we chasten pride,
And preparation make for thy high home;
And, might we ask, make measurely approach,
And not upon these few smooth hours encroach;—
I come, I come, think not I turn away!
Fold round me thy gray robe! I stand to feel
The setting of my last frail earthly day;
I will not pluck it off, but calmly kneel;
For I am great as thou art, though not thou,
And thought as with thee dwells upon my brow.

Ah! might I ask thee, spirit, first to tend
Upon those dear ones whom my heart has found,
And supplicate thee, that I might them lend
A light in their last hours, and to the ground
Consign them still,—yet think me not too weak,—
Come to me now, and thou shalt find me meek,
Then let us live in fellowship with thee,
And turn our ruddy cheeks thy kisses pale,
And listen to thy song as minstrelsy,
And still revere thee, till our hearts' throbs fail,
Sinking within thy arms as sinks the sun
Below the farthest hills, when his day's work is done.

SONNETS.

I.

TO AN IDEAL OBJECT.

Though far away, I still shall see thee here,
Shall see thy eyes so deep, thy modest mien,
And hear that fairy laughter, which yestreen
Fell like sweet music on my spell-bound ear.

Though far away, in truth thou dwell'st as near
As wert thou daily, hourly to be seen,
Nor of thy truthfulness have I a fear,
What is with thee stands fast and shows serene.

Would thou wert real, creature of my brain!
Thy voice and laughter, and those deep, still eyes,
And I of loneliness might not complain;

Then I should be inestimably wise,
Nor end my days in this so bitter pain,
Which far within my inmost being lies.

II.

Thou art like that which is most sweet and fair,
A gentle morning in the youth of spring,
When the few early birds begin to sing
Within the delicate depths of the fine air.

Yet shouldst thou these dear beauties much impair,
Since thou art better than is every thing
Which or the woods, or skies, or green fields bring,
And finer thoughts hast thou than they can wear.

In the proud sweetness of thy grace I see,
What lies within, a pure and steadfast mind,
Which its own mistress is of sanctity,

And to all gentleness hath been refined;
So that thy least breath falleth upon me
As the soft breathing of midsummer wind.

III.

MEN change, that heaven above not more,
Which now with white clouds is all beautiful,
Soon is with gray mists a poor creature dull;
Thus, in this human theatre, actions pour

Like slight waves on a melancholy shore;
Nothing is fixed, the human heart is null,
'T is taught by scholars, ' tis rehearsed in lore;
Methinks this human heart might well be o'er.

O precious pomp of eterne vanity!
O false fool world! whose actions are a race
Of monstrous puppets; I can't form one plea

Why any man should wear a smiling face.
World! thou art one green sepulchre to me,
Through which, mid clouds of dust, slowly I pace.

IV.

HEARTS of Eternity, — hearts of the deep !
Proclaim from land to sea your mighty fate ;
How that for you no living comes too late ;
How ye cannot in Theban labyrinth creep ;

How ye great harvests from small surface reap ;
Shout, excellent band, in grand primeval strain,
Like midnight winds that foam along the main,
And do all things rather than pause to weep.

A human heart knows nought of littleness,
Suspects no man, compares with no one's ways,
Hath in one hour most glorious length of days,

A recompense, a joy, a loveliness ;
Like eaglet keen, shoots into azure far,
And always dwelling nigh is the remotest star.

V.

The brook is eddying in the forest dell
All full of untaught merriment, — the joy
Of breathing life is this green wood's employ.
The wind is feeling through his gentle bell,

I and my flowers receive this music well.
Why will not man his natural life enjoy?
Can he then with his ample spirit toy?
Are human thoughts, like wares, now baked to sell?

All up, all round, all down, a thrilling deep,
A holy infinite salutes the sense,
And incommunicable praises leap,

Shooting the entire soul with love intense
Throughout the all. Can man live on to weep,
Submitting to such heavenly influence?

VI.

THERE never lived a man, who with a heart
Resolved, bound up, concentered in the good,
However low or high in rank he stood,
But when from him yourself had chanced to start,

You felt how goodness alway maketh art;
And that an ever venerable mood
Of sanctity, like the deep worship of a wood,
Of its unconsciousness makes you a part.

Let us live amply in the joyous all;
We surely were not meant to ride the sea
Skimming the wave in that so prisoned small,

Reposing our infinite faculties utterly.
Boom like a roaring sunlit waterfall
Humming to infinite abysms; speak loud, speak free.

VII.

THE ETERNAL LANDSCAPE.

There weeps a landscape that some mortals see,
Whose time slips on to noble purpose fair,
And of an hour escaped from carking care
That sight is star of their nativity.

Falls the warm, mellow light on field and tree,
Almost it will their breathing overbear
To find this world such holy robe does wear,
And sinketh through them, privilege to be.

That time is dead, — so the swift crowd will say
Of human beings creeping down in woe,
Yet to the true, in that long-passed day

Is parent of the chief they really know;
And casting off external busy clay,
A world of memory lies like glass below.

VIII.

I MARK beneath thy life the virtue shine
That deep within the star's eye opes its day;
I clutch those gorgeous thoughts thou throw'st away,
From the profound unfathomable mine,

And with them this mean, common hour do twine,
As glassy waters o'er the dry beach play,
And I were rich as night, them to combine
With my poor store, and warm me with thy ray.

From the fixed answer of those dateless eyes
I meet bold hints of spirit's mystery
As to what 's past, and hungry prophecies

Of deeds to-day, and things which are to be;
Of lofty life that with the eagle flies,
And lowly love, that clasps humanity.

IX.

In those bright, laughing days that pierce the fall,
With sunny spears forged from the summer's glow,
The crimson leaves sail slowly on the pall
Of the warm fitful air; but there will blow

At sunset a cool breeze; then the leaves flow
In heaped-up multitudes beneath the wall;
Thus drifts of bodies to the graveyard go,
And the pinched foliage in their times recall.

That fall's warm wind is first affection's tear,
And near remembrance, with its fiery thought;
That frosty breeze is memory, all grown sere,

And consolation, curiously wrought;
That pile of sapless sheaths the hosts who died,
And those we lately added to their side.

X.

EARTH hath her meadows green, her brooklets bright;
She hath a million flowers which bloom aloft,
O'ershade her peerless glances the clouds soft,
And dances on her sward the capering light.

She hath a full glad day, a solemn night,
And showers, and trees, and waterfallings oft.
Meekly I love her, and in her delight;
I am as one who ministers in rite.

But so much soul hast thou within thy form,
Than luscious summer days thou art the more,
And far within thee there is that more warm

Than ever sunlight to the wild flowers bore,
Thou great glad gentleness, and sweetly clear,
Thou who art mine to love and to revere.

XI.

I LOVE the universe, — I love the joy
Of every living thing. Be mine the sure
Felicity, which ever shall endure;
While passion whirls the madmen, as they toy,

To hate, I would my simple being warm
In the calm pouring sun; and in that pure
And motionless silence, ever would employ
My best true powers, without a thought's annoy.

See and be glad! O high imperial race,
Dwarfing the common altitude of strength,
Learn that ye stand on an unshaken base;

Your powers will carry you to any length.
Up! earnestly feel the gentle sunset beams;
Be glad in woods, o'er sands, — by marsh, or streams.

POEMS

BY

WILLIAM ELLERY CHANNING.

SECOND SERIES.

BOSTON:
JAMES MUNROE AND COMPANY.

M DCCC XLVII.

BOSTON:
PRINTED BY THURSTON, TORRY AND CO.
31 Devonshire Street.

CONTENTS.

POEMS.

NEW ENGLAND.

I WILL not sing for gain, nor yet for fame,
Though praise I shall enjoy if come it may,
I will not sing to make my nature tame,
And thus it is if I seck Fortune's way.
But I will chant a rude heroic lay,
On rough New England's coast, whose sterile soil
Gives happiness and dignity to toil.

If I may be a Son of those stern men,
Who took this Indian land to make them free,
And grasping in my hand a Poet's pen,
Thus as a Poet their great thoughts decree,
I then shall think I strike for liberty ;
My hand, my heart, my pen all draining up,
The imperial vintage in rich Freedom's cup.

In a New England hand the lyre must beat
With brave emotions ; such the winter wind
Sweeps on chill pinions, when the cutting sleet
Doth the bare traveller in the fields half blind,
Yet freezing to the trees congeals a rind,
Next day more brilliant than the Arab skies,
Or plumes from gorgeous birds of Paradise.

A bold and nervous hand must strike the strings,
Our varying climate forms its children so,
And what we lack in Oriental things,
We render good by that perpetual blow,
Which wears away the strongest rocks we know,
Sure in supply, and constant in demand,
Active and patient, fit to serve or stand.

They do malign us who contract our hope
To prudent gain or blind religious zeal,
More signs than these shine in our horoscope,
Nobly to live, to do, and dare, and feel,
Knit to each other by firm bands of steel,
Our eyes to God we turn, our hearts to home,
Standing content beneath the azure dome.

My country, 'tis for thee I strike the lyre,
My country, wide as is the free wind's flight,
I sing New England as she lights her fire
In every Prairie's midst; and where the bright
Enchanting stars shine pure through Southern night,
She still is there the guardian on the tower,
To open for the world a purer hour.

Could they but know the wild enchanting thrill
That in our homely houses fills the heart,
To feel how faithfully New England's will
Beats in each artery, and each small part
Of this great Continent, their blood would start
In Georgia, or where Spain once sat in state,
Or Texas with her lone star desolate.

Because they shall be free, — we wish it thus;
In vain against our purpose may they turn,
They are our Brothers, and belong to us,
And on our altars Slavery shall burn,
Its ashes buried in a silent urn.
Then think not 'tis a vain New England boast, —
We love the distant West, the Atlantic coast.

'Tis a New England thought, to make this land
The very home of Freedom, and the nurse
Of each sublime emotion; she does stand
Between the sunny South, and the dread curse
Of God, who else should make her hearse
Of condemnation to this Union's life,—
She stands to heal this plague, and banish strife.

I do not sing of this, but hymn the day
That gilds our cheerful villages and plains,
Our hamlets strewn at distance on the way,
Our forests and the ancient streams' domains,
We are a band of Brothers, and our pains
Are freely shared, no beggar in our roads,
Content and peace within our fair abodes.

In my small Cottage on the lonely hill,
Where like a Hermit I must bide my time,
Surrounded by a landscape lying still
All seasons through as in the winter's prime,
Rude and as homely as these verses chime,
I have a satisfaction which no king
Has often felt, if Fortune's happiest thing.

'T is not my Fortune, which is mainly low,
'T is not my merit, that is nothing worth,
'T is not that I have stores of Thought below
Which everywhere should build up Heaven on earth,
Nor was I highly favored in my birth,
Few friends have I, and they are much to me,
Yet fly above my poor Society.

But all about me live New England men,
Their humble houses meet my daily gaze, —
The children of this land where Life again
Flows like a great stream in sunshiny ways,
This is a joy to know them, and my days
Are filled with love to meditate on them,
These native gentlemen on Nature's hem.

That I could take one feature of their life,
Then on my page a mellow light should shine ;
Their days are Holydays with labor rife,
Labor the song of praise, that sounds divine,
And better than all sacred hymns of mine ;
The patient Earth sets platters for their food,
Corn, milk, and apples, and the best of good.

See here no shining scenes for artist's eye,
This woollen frock shall make no painter's fame,
These homely tools all burnishing deny,
The beasts are slow and heavy, still or tame,
The sensual eye may think this labor lame,
'T is in the Man where lies the sweetest art,
His true endeavor in his earnest part.

The wind may blow a hurricane, but he
Goes fairly onward with the thing in hand,
He sails undaunted on the crashing sea,
Beneath the keenest winter frost does stand,
And by his Will, he makes his way command,
Till all the seasons smile delight to feel
The grasp of his hard hand encased in steel.

He meets the year confiding, no great throws,
That suddenly bring riches does he use,
But like Thor's hammer vast, his patient blows,
Vanquish his difficult tasks, he does refuse
To tread the path, nor know the way he views,
No sad complaining words he uttereth,
But draws in peace a free and easy breath.

I love to meet him on the frozen road,
How manly is his eye, as clear as air; —
He cheers his beasts without the brutal goad,
His face is ruddy, and his features fair,
His brave, good-day, sounds like an honest prayer,
This man is in his place and feels his trust,
'T is not dull plodding through the heavy crust.

And when I have him at his homely hearth,
Within his homestead, where no ornament
Glows on the mantle but his own true worth,
I feel as if within an Arab's tent,
His hospitality is more than meant;
I there am welcome, as the sunlight is,
I must feel warm to be a Friend of his.

This man takes pleasure o'er the crackling fire,
His glittering axe subdued the monarch oak,
He earned the cheerful blaze by something higher
Than pensioned blows, he owned the tree he stroke,
And knows the value of the distant smoke,
When he returns at night his labor done,
Matched in his action with the long day's sun.

I love these homely mansions, and to me
A Farmer's house seems better than a King's,
The palace boasts its art, but liberty
And honest pride and toil are splendid things;
They carved this clumsy lintel, and it brings
The man upon its front; Greece hath her art,
But this rude homestead shows the farmer's heart.

How many brave adventures with the cold,
Built up the cumbrous cellar of plain stone,
How many summer heats the bricks did mould,
That make the ample fireplace, and the tone
Of twice a thousand winds sings through the zone,
Of rustic paling round the modest yard,—
These are the verses of this simple bard.

Who sings the praise of Woman in our clime,—
I do not boast her beauty or her grace,
Some humble Duties render her sublime,
She the sweet nurse of this New England race,
The flower upon the country's sterile face,
The mother of New England's sons, the pride
Of every house where those good sons abide.

There is a Roman splendor in her smile,
A tenderness that owes its depth to toil,
Well may she leave the soft voluptuous wile,
That forms the woman of a softer soil;
She does pour forth herself a fragrant oil,
Upon the dark asperities of Fate,
And make a garden else all desolate.

From early morn to fading eve she stands,
Labor's best offering on the shrine of worth,
And labor's jewels glitter on her hands,
To make a plenty out of partial dearth,
To animate the heaviness of earth,
To stand and serve serenely through the pain,
To nurse a vigorous race and ne'er complain.

New England women are New England's pride;
'T is fitting they should be so, they are free, —
Intelligence doth all their acts decide,
Such deeds more charming than old ancestry.
I could not dwell beside them, and not be
Enamored of them greatly; they are meant
To charm the Poet, by their pure intent.

A natural honest bearing of their lot,
Cheerful at work, and happy when 't is done,
They shine like stars within the humblest cot,
And speak for freedom centred all in one.
From every river's side I hear the son
Of some New England woman answer me,
"Joy to our Mothers, who did make us free."

And when those wanderers turn to home again,
See the familiar village, and the street
Where they once frolick'd, they are less than men
If in their eyes the tear-drops do not meet,
To feel how soon their mothers they shall greet,
Sons of New England have no dearer day,
Than once again within those arms to lay.

These are her men and women, this the sight
That greets me daily when I pass their homes,
It is enough to love, it throws some light
Over the gloomiest hours, the fancy roams
No more to Italy or Greece, the loams
Whereon we tread are sacred by the lives
Of those who till them, and our comfort thrives.

Here might one pass his days, content to be
The witness of these spectacles alway,
Bring if you may your treasure from the sea,
My pride is in my Townsmen, where the day
Rises so fairly on a race who lay
Their hopes on Heaven, after their toil is o'er,
Upon this rude and bold New England shore.

Vainly ye pine-woods rising on the height,
Should lift your verdant boughs and cones aloft,
Vainly ye winds should surge around in might,
Or murmur o'er the meadow stanzas soft,
To me should nothing yield or lake or croft,
Had not the figures of the pleasant scene,
Like trees and fields an innocent demean.

I feel when I am here some pride elate,
Proud in your presence who do duty here,
For I am some partaker of your fate;
Your manly anthem vibrates in my ear,
Your hearts are heaving unconsumed by fear,
Your modest deeds are constantly supplied,
Your simple truths by which you must abide.

Therefore I love a cold and flinty realm,
I love the sky that hangs New England o'er,
And if I were embarked, and at the helm,
I ran my vessel on New England's shore,
And dashed upon her crags, would live no more,
Rather than go to seek those lands of graves,
Where men who tread the fields are cowering slaves.

I love the mossy rocks so strangely rude,
The little forests, underwood and all, —
I love the damp paths of the Solitude,
Where in the tiny brook some waterfall
Gives its small shower of diamonds to the thrall
Of light's pursuing reflex, and the trill
Of the bright cascade, making silence still.

I love the cold, sad Winter's lengthened time,
When man half aches with cold, and Nature seems
To leer and grimace with an icy smile,
And all the little life is clad in dreams,
I love it even if the far Sun-beams
Look through the clouds like faces filled with woe,
Like mourners who to funerals do go.

Search me ye wintry winds for I am proof;
New England's kindness circles round my heart.
I see afar that old declining roof
Where underneath dwells something which is part
Of Nature's sweetest music;—through me dart
Your coldest spasms, there burns manhood's fire,
I sit by that as warm as I desire.

And if the torrid August sun scalds down,
And big drops stand upon my brow like rain,
I can enjoy this fire, and call it crown
To my content; it ripens golden grain,
New England corn,—I prize the fervid pain,
An honest hand has planted comfort there,
And fragrant coolness steals throughout the air.

It seems a happy thing that I was born
In rough New England, here that I may be,
Among a race whom all mankind adorn;
A plain strong race deep-rooted as a tree,
And I am most content my ancestry
Dates back no further than New England's date,—
What worth is King or Lord, where man is State.

14

ITALIAN SONG.

THE old Tower gray
Bids purple day
Paint the grave mosses with its Tyrian hue,
And fine-toned Night
Rounds with dim light
Each crumbling stone into proportion due.

My tinkling lute
Converts the mute
And humble silence into golden singing;
The laden air
Rich scents doth bear,
Around the ruin, vase-like odors flinging.

The Tower's round song
Dances along,
Like a brown gondola through the still sea,
Its shadow sings,
My love-note brings,
How sweet is night, in my own Italy.

16

THE WANDERER.

Who is that wight, who wanders there
So often o'er those lonely fields,—
Can solitude his thought repair,
Or filch the honey that he yields?

I see him often by the brook,
He pauses on some little rock,
Or, sheltered in a sunny nook,
He sits, nor feels the sharp wind's shock.

I meet him in the lonely lane,
Where merrily I drive my team,
And seek his downcast eye in vain,
To break the silence of his dream.

And sometimes when I fell the trees,
He muses with a saddened eye,
While leaps the forest like the Seas,
When tide and wind are running high.

Yet never questions he a word,
Of what I do or where I go,
His gentle voice I never heard,
His voice so soft and sweetly low.

And once at Sunset, on the hill
He stood and gazed at scenes afar,
While fell the twilight o'er the rill,
And glittered in the west,—a star.

I cannot see his years improve,
He leaves no tokens on the way,
'T is simply breathing, or to move
Like some dim spectre through the day.

And yet I love him, for his form
Seems graceful as a Maiden's sigh,
And something beautiful and warm
Is shadowed in his quiet eye.

Thus spoke the driver of the wain,—
While solemnly he passed along,
This man unknown to fame or gain,
The hero of no Poet's song.

And there he wanders yet, I trust,
A figure pensive as the scene,
Created from the common dust,
Yet treading o'er the grasses green.

19

THE POET

OF THE OLD AND NEW TIMES.

In olden time the Poet sang,
The ancient hall with ballads rang,
Wandering he touched the golden lyre,
By the ancestral Castle's fire,
A sacred man the Poet then,
Beloved by gods, beloved by men.

Afar the Shepherd on the hill,
Saw from his height this child of skill,
And straightway left his flock to go
And greet the bard who moved below,
The stern mechanic left his work,
His hammer fell not on the berk.

The gentle ladies sat and heard
The ditties of the tuneful bird,
With fine regard they greeted him;
He sang, — their soft eyes swam so dim
They often wept; the Poet's song
To the heart's secret did belong.

The Poets recked not for their fare,
Their comfort was the People's care;
They sang, — the doors were open wide,
They loved, — the nation dowered the Bride,
They saw the wealth around them flow
Of princes, — 't is no longer so.

The wandering Bard no city claims,
The nation loves not poet's aims,
A lonely man he bides afar,
His halls are fields, his lamp a star,
Nature 's so regal, she does wait
And minister his ancient state.

The Brook must be his mirror now,
His organ in the dark Pine-bough,

For ladies' eyes the flowerets dyes,
The southern rain his lady's sighs,
The grass the carpet of his Hall,
The trees its pillars smooth and tall.

Few doors are open if he sings,
Faint welcome with his lyre he brings,
Cold eyes avert from him their gaze,
The world suspects his idle ways,
He sits not on the hearth so wide,
For Priest and Clerk him thrust aside.

Now few can comprehend his way,
The haze has overspread his day,
Forgotten, stands he quite apart,—
The life-blood of the Nation's heart,
He sings alone, the crowds go by,
And question him with curious eye.

O world, thou hast the Poet's art
Thyself, — he counterfeits thy part,
And of his age the Poet's lyre,
Is instrument of pure desire,

Most joyful let the Poet be,
It is through him that all men see.

Not ever falls the Sunshine clear,
And heavy clouds obscure the mere,
Not ever is the fruit-tree proud,
For worms weave oft its yellow shroud,
Yet smiles the sky, the tree comes green,
The Poet shall be heard and seen.

My country, in thy early hour,
I feel the magic of thy power,
Thy hands are strong, thy aims are long,
To thee the Poets shall belong,
I mark thy pride in them, and they
Shall sing thee in heroic lay.

For in thy stature there is strength,
And in thy aims an endless length,
And Bards shall praise thy features fair,
And Poesy fill all the air,
Clear as thy dazzling sunshines are,
Deep as thy forests waving far.

23

THE JOURNEY.

A breezy softness fills the air,
That clasps the tender hand of Spring,
And yet no brooklet's voice does sing,
For all is purest stillness there,
Unless the light, soft foliage waves;
The boughs are clothed in shining green,
Through which ne'er angry Tempest raves,
And sunlight shines between.

II.

Beneath the oak a Palmer lay,
Upon the green-sward was his bed,
And its luxuriance bound the gray
And silver Laurel o'er his head.

A picture framed by calm repose,
A Grecian monument of life,
Too placid for the storm of woes,
Too grateful to be worn by strife.
I should have passed, — he bade me stay,
And tranquilly these words did say.—

Thou curtain of the tender spring,
Thy graces to my old eyes bring
The recollections of those years,
When sweet are shed our early tears,
Those days of sunny April weather,
Changeful and glad with every thing,
When Youth and Age go linked together,
Like sisters twain, and sauntering
Down mazy paths in ancient woods,
The garlands of such solitudes. —

III.

I passed along,
The Palmer's song,
Still sounding with its clear content,
At length I reached my promised tent.

Around, were crags of ruin piled,
The temples of a Nation's pride,
Within their clefts the bright stars smiled,
And moonlight swept the court-yard wide.
Some Ivy-boughs o'erhung the wall,
Or bound the pillars' sculptured fall,
Whilst deepening Shade lay o'er the place,
That still the grandeur would efface.

IV.

Not long I slept,—the wind awoke,
A river from the mountains came,
All through the Temple's courts it broke,
While they were lit by lightning's flame.
The skies hurled down their bolts of dread,
But still my little Tent was good,
No drop of rain fell on my head,
Unarmed amid the war I stood.

V.

A mightier blast,—more lurid light,
The wind dispersed my sheltering fold,
I paused an instant in the night,
Then sought that mighty Temple old.

The channel of the stream I sought,
And bravely with the waters fought.
I saw the glancing fires design,
To smite the stone's colossal form
That jutted from the topmost line,—
Too cold that steady heart to warm;—
I gained beyond the Court a bank,
And fainting in the darkness sank.

THE SEXTON'S STORY.

These quiet meadows, and the sloping bank
With its green hem of hardy pines, whose leaves
The sudden frosts, and sudden Autumn rains
Cannot displace, have been the scenes of conflict.
Housed in the yielding Sand that shapes the bank,
The early Settlers lodged their sturdy frames,
And on these Meadows where the brook o'erflows,
They saw the Indians glide, their dusky hue,
Agreeing with the brown and withered grass.
Their Memory yet endures to paint this scene,
And oft as I sit musing, they become
Scarcely less living than in Days of old.
Noble adventurers, godlike Puritans!
Poets in deed, who came, and saw, and braved
The accumulated wilderness, and read

The fatal policy of Indian guile,
May we, your Sons, thus conquer the wild foes
Who aim their shafts at your sublime Design.

It was a Winter's day. The air came keen
Across the Meadows, sheeted with pure snow,
New fallen, that now as day wheeled downward
Had ceased to fall, and the clouds parting off,
Mild showers of light spread o'er the groves and fields.
And as the light grew brighter, the wind failed,
And with the calm came a most perfect frost,
That sealed the very glances of the sun,
No longer warm to Man, or beast, or field.

The Sexton of our village was an old
And weather-beaten artizan, whose life
Led him to battle with the depths of cold.
Amid the Woods he plied a vigorous arm,
The tall trees crashed in thunder 'neath his stroke,
And a hale cheer was spread about his form.
Death does not stand and falter at the cold,
And our brave Sexton plied his pickaxe bright,
Whether the soft Snow fell, or 'mid the Rains.

This day, this Winter's day, he made a grave
For a young Blossom which the frost had nipped,
And towards the sunset hour he took his way,
Across the Meadows wide, and o'er the Brook,
Beyond the bridge and through the leafless arch
Of Willows that supports the sunken road
To the sad house of Death, bearing with him
The frail, light tenement that bounds the corpse.
The Sexton's heart beat cheerly in his breast,
For constant commerce with the grave had lined
The Coffin's smooth inside with frugal wit.
He saw no Terror in the mouldering form
Of that, where late the ruddy current ran
In social sympathy, and generous mirth.
The ghastly bones, the pale, remorseless hand
That strikes those shuddering notes on Human lyres,
E'en Death himself kept company with him.
This was no stolid want of sympathy,
Or cold forgetfulness of mortal woe,
Or curious hankering thought to purchase ease,
The Sexton had forgotten what Death was,
And graves he dealt in, as some deal in Farms.

He turned when near the Bridge, for such a flush
Of crimson wandered o'er the snow, the fields
So glowed as if with Summer's fire, his heart
Bounded to meet that last gold glance of Day.
But it felt wondrous cold, and was so still,
As if the Frost had fastened on itself.
He reached the house of death, — a friendly house,
And sat in peace to see the Wood-fire flash,
His numb and stiffened fingers spread to meet
The cheerful warmth, and then he spoke as one
Who came from living worlds, for in that house,
There was a pensive figure in one seat.
The Sexton did not see that figure sad,
But the pale Mother with her tear-stained eyes,
Look'd on and drooped her head, the Father, too,
He looked and saw that youth, the cold, cold form
Of wintry Death who sits by some sad hearths.

When he stept forth upon his homeward path,
('T was a short saunter to the Village church,)
A change was in the sky, a wild wind blew,
The Frost had tired of silence, and now played

A merry Battle-march with the light snow,
That whirled across the road in dizzy sport,
White wreaths for banners, and gay sparkling sheets.
The last ray faded in the sleeping West,
Day had abandoned earth, and the weird Night
That asks from human eye no sympathy,
Called up a host of Actors for its play.
From the soft hills that hem the Meadows in,
The Sexton heard the music of the Pines,
A sudden gush of sounds, as when a flock
Of startled Birds are beating through the air,
And tossing off the light from their quick wings;
Then pauses of deep silence, that his ear
Accustomed to the sounds of cheerful day
Could not contain, and first his Inward voice.—

—It is a bitter night, but I have felt
More cold without anxiety. The snow
Beats heavily o'er the unsheltered road,
Huge drifts to-morrow, and hard sledding here.—
Then came a heavier blast than all before,
And beat upon the cheerful Sexton's front,

As the broad, tossing billows breast the Ship.
He ploughed along the way, nor fence, nor shrub,
And a dark curtain in the air. The stars
Were flickering, as the distant Light-boat moored,
Shifts to the Pilot's eye each breaking wave.
His eye not eager sought the Willow arch,
A little onward to the Bridge, he thought,
And pausing beat his stout arms on his breast,
Then turned and faced the wintry surge again. —
One step,—and then his feet sank through,—the edge
It was of the deep Brook that wandered down
The dreary Meadows, sinuous in its course.
The Sexton's feet slipped o'er the glassy plate,
He was across,—across the meadow Brook.
He sank upon the Snow, and breathed a prayer,
His heart thrilled strangely with an icy fear,
His thoughts ran in dim shapes across his brain,
A tumult of wild Images of woe,
And one dark warning figure, wintry Death,
Stood on the bank, and said with gentle voice: —
Yes, now across the Brook thy feet have come,
The deep, black Brook, 't was never known to freeze;

It has upborne thee on its icy scale
Where but a feather's weight had turned the beam.
Thou, not in battle, nor in sharp disease,
But here within the peaceful village Fields,
Hast by the veriest chance, as may'st thou think,
Been guided well through such a sudden fear,
As no dark dream had conjured in thy mind.
Yet by no chance, since this a lesson is,
To teach thee if the burial and the tomb
Consign to rest the palsied Shapes of Life,
How grand that Hour must be, when the bright soul
Led by my hand, draws nigh to the deep Stream,
Across whose icy flow no Mortal walks,
In whose still unvexed Depths, the hosts of Men,
Still ever following, sink without return.—

There stood a Laborer's cottage not afar,
Where the Day's toil was over, and they sat,
The family about the crackling fire,
In merry mood, and heard the Spinning-wheels
Hum like a swarm of bees in Summer time,
For all the wind's loud bluster, and the cold

That like a cunning Thief crept round the hut.
They sudden hear a lamentable sound,
A voice of deep despair imploring aid.
The Laborer listens and the sounds renew,
The voice comes from the Meadow, and his dog
The Laborer calls, and muffling in his frock,
He finds the Sexton by the Brook sunk down,
And stiffening like the cold and icy Night.

Next day, they traced the hardy Sexton's steps,
And found that but one narrow arch across
The meadow Brook, the spanning frost had thrown
As if in sport, to try its secret powers.
And there the Sexton crossed, — that little arch
Left him alive to guide the funeral train
That from the friendly house came forth in woe.
It taught this lesson, that in common hours
There hides deep meaning, and a sudden fear,
Nor need we track the deserts of the Pole,
To 'scape from sight of Death and life's dark Night.

35

FIELD-BIRDS' NESTS.

Beyond the Brook so swift I went,
Beyond the fields my course I bent,
Where on the height the oak grove stands,
And Hemlocks thick like iron bands.

And by the marsh, and by the pond,
Though I had wandered oft beyond,
Never before I saw those eight,
Those eight Birds' nests now desolate.

Each nest was filled with snow and leaves,
Each nest that some small songster weaves,
Yet pleasantly they seemed to me,
These little homes of yesterday.

So frail these buildings that the wind
To airy journeys them consigned,
Had not the architect displayed
The quiet cunning of his trade.

On some small twig the house was laid,
That every breath from Heaven swayed,
The nests swing easy as the bush,
The wind in vain on these may push.

Some grass and sticks together piled,
Secure as stately Palace tiled;
A twig the rock on which they stand,
As firm as acres of deep land.

Another summer comes the Bird,
Her sweetly swelling song is heard,
She hops into her little home,
Her mate then merrily does come.

Ye men who pass a wretched life,
Consumed with care, consumed with strife,
Whose gloom grows deeper day by day,
The audience at a tiresome play;

Who build the stately palaces,
Where only endless Gilding is,
Who riot in perpetual show,
In dress, and wine, and costly woe;

Who haunt the narrow City's street,
Surrounded by a thousand feet,
With weary wrinkles in your brows,
And faltering penance in your vows;

Think of the little Field-bird's nest;
Can you not purchase such a rest,
A twig, some straws, a dreamy moor,
The same some Summers going o'er.

38

THE SNOW-STORM.

THAT is the best Poem out there,
To see the snow drift by.
See how it goes,
Hear how it blows,
One continual long-drawn sigh.

Casements rattle in its blatter,
And the solid Housetop shakes,
It paints the wall,
The road and all,
With its pigment of pure flakes.

When I walk within its growling,
Soft it calleth unto me,
How cold it is,
And wet it is,
Chill the Snow-storm utterly.

Yet it seemeth warm directly,
As the Summer's middle heat,
Or some soft day
In month of May,
When the rustling leaves do beat.

How you vex me stupid Snow-storm,
With your variations bold,
Thou art so warm,
So sweet in form,
Thou art so ugly, art so cold.

A truce to thy continual sighing,
Thy hypocritic face so white,
Come dear brown earth,
Come Spring's soft birth,
Go, go, thou hoary eremite.

40

TO ANNA DE ROSE.

WAS it a dream, — I saw the lances glance,
And gaily leapt on polished helms the sun,
Was it a dream, — I saw the festal dance,
For happily the Tournament begun,
Was it a dream, — or in that softest eye,
Anna de Rose, whose name is chivalry.

Was it a dream, — I saw the ancient hall,
The warder old, and watch-dog at his feet,
Was it a dream, — I heard the Baron call,
The draw-bridge fall, the horseman in his seat,
Was it a dream, — or was thy sunny mouth,
Anna de Rose, this picture of the south.

Was it a dream, — I saw the castle fire
That lighted up the oaken Hall so wide,
Was it a dream, — when drank the wine the Sire,
And with his earnest gaze the Baron eyed,
Was it a dream, — or was that pleasing thought
Anna de Rose, thy figure richly wrought.

These dreams were Anna what thou wert to me,
A token of the Thought which in my youth
About the busy world hung Courtesy,
And colored every day with golden truth,
Then, Knights and Ladies danced along the plain,
Fair days had come, the world felt young again.

I have had dreams which were Realities,
I thought to dream no more, but thou didst come,
And I have dreamed in sooth of those sweet eyes,
That smiling mouth, and Beauty's priceless sum,
I waked yet thou wert bright, and so despair
Shall something softer, some mild aspect wear.

I have had visions which have turned to pain,
I mourn some altered friends, some misty days,
Thou bringest to me many hours again
When Sunlight fell, and oft the Star's clear rays,
Bright hours were those, I am in debt to thee,
Anna de Rose, and would thou wert to me.

No more, I said, shall any Beauty go
Before my eyes, to warm me with its fire,
No more the fairy Rivers softly flow
That bear upon them, what I may desire,
Some little beauty in the world I seek,
In vain, the place is empty, wind is bleak.

But ever as I lose my hold on Earth,
She clasps me closer with a new-found treasure,
And when I sigh she beckons infant Mirth,
And when I weep she summons gentle Pleasure,
Thus by the course of history I know,
That still in Spring the violets shall blow.

Before thee lies the world, an aimless prize,
Thou shall float onward, see the Distant near,
O youth, why forward turn thy seeking eyes,
Why not upon the Future look with fear,
Yet not in utter fear, but with some dread,
It must not be, with visions thou art fed.

And were it in my power, my Dream should be,
That Castle old, with its ancestral fire,
That Baron and the warder, bold to see,
And thou the Lady, while I touched the lyre,
What matter if those forms we see no more,
From Fancy's urn the brilliant waters pour.

Thou listenest for thy Lord as eve draws nigh,
Afar the courser fiery-footed springs,
Then nearer draws the sound, thy gladdened eye
Beams ere the Figure in the mailed rings
Passes the castle-gate, — then falls the sun,
Night is without, with thee Day has begun.

44

THE RESTLESS MIND.

By the bleak wild hill,
Or the deep lake still,
In the silent grain
On the upland plain,
I would that the unsparing Storm might rage,
And blot with gloom the fair day's sunny page.

The lightning's gleam
Should gentle seem,
The thunder's blow
Both soft and low,
For now the world hath fill of summer weather,
Ye shining days why throng you thus together.

I am possest
With strange Unrest,
My feelings jar,
My heart is war,
A spirit dances in my dreams to-day,
I am too cold, for its strange, sunny play.

Then hurry down
With angry frown,
Thou sudden storm
Come fierce and warm,
And splinter trees and whistle o'er the moor,
For in thy Bravery I can life endure.

46

TO ELIZABETH.

Thou last sweet Beam of sunny day,
    Thou latest friend,
    Before thy light I bend,
Too heavy earth to form thy shining way;
Thou last link of the golden chain,
Thou Star amid these nights of misty rain;
    Bright weather for us all,
    How joyful we are thrall.
  How wert thou sent so late,
    How was thy voice so mute,
  How many days did fate,
    Silence thy liquid lute?

Thou beacon Fire
That o'er the unsounded deep,
By thy warm heart's desire,
Lightest the harbor's steep,
Shed from thy eye the warning flame,
Ere silence writes in tears the unheeded name.
So many come and go
Like a swift Fountain's flow,
Glancing reflections of the passing scene,
The mimicries of spheres, whose Fates are all;
The woods, the clouds, blue sky, and lawny green,
One instant fixed, then nothing we can call,
And o'er the unspeaking Fall.

Weep not,—I see thine eyes
Are filled with tears,
Weep not,—for those revolving Memories
Like autumn leaves, the years
Whirl in the unvexed skies,
And dim thy fears.
For in the illimitable hand of Time,
Who sweeps forever in vast silence, the sublime

Slow-moving history of Man,
Sure winnoweth that broad fan.

Thou angel form,
Thou calm and sunny day,
Why in this storm
Pursuest thou thy way,
While we, pale Phantoms crowd around thy car,
And catch a faint complexion from thy star.
We do remember thee,
For in the radiant Past had we some light,
Thy voice reveals the key
That made the music bright,
Yet linger not so long amid our graves,
And fear the rocks that tear the angry waves.

Thou vase of Beauty,
Carved in high relief
With shapes of Gods, and forms
That best Belief
Gave to some Races towering o'er,
All the low dwellers on this misty shore,

Shall we not live, while Thou resolv'st to bear,
Thy cold, dull crown of Grief, and proudly wear
Garments of autumn foliage for an hour,
Having immortal Beauty for thy dower.

50

ARAB SONG.

MOOR yon pillars of the sand
  To my Life, this burning day,
Seize me in your sultry hand,
  Whirl me in your heat away:—
So Alek said, a youth of flame,
Whose pathway ran too smooth and tame.

II.

The Desert stretched for miles along,
  Its perilous way so drear and wide,
Where only sang the Stars their song,
  Which in the heavens did abide,

A hymn of splendid glow and state,
Though only with the Hermit mate.

III.

Beneath the Palm tree's emerald shade,
That over-roofed a sainted glade,
A spot of coolness in the heat,
Alek one day his Maid did meet.
Within her eye's unmelting ice,
He saw her Soul's deep purity,
And prized it more than softest beams,
That spoke a warm futurity.

IV.

They wandered to the glazèd Well,
Whose colors sank to deeps unknown,
And heard afar the Camel's bell,
Pitched in its sandy sultry tone;
The Nightingale sang sweet and free,
As sweet as any sound could be,
A pretty breeze toyed with the Palm,
Not wind enough to stir the calm,

And roses bled for Alek's eyes,
What melted in his rich replies.
A single glance, the Maiden sent,
One look, — that in his firmament,
Made planetary music far
Beyond the hymn of any star.

V.

'T was in the Caliph's royal room,
The hall of gilded pomp and state,
That Alek saw the Maid, once more,
And felt the presage of his fate;
For Alek's blood though highly wrought,
No Palace with its greatness bought;
He met her eye amid the crowd,
With but a slow salute she bowed,
For the Maid's rank was gently high,—
And Alek felt the cold reply.

VI.

Now mounted he his sable Steed,
Who snuffed the moonlight all elate,

Now pressed upon the tightening bit,
Then passed the City's western gate,
Where the tall Warrior saw the night,
Sparkling with gems, and told its flight.

VII.

Away, he flies o'er parchèd Sands,
The reins loose hanging from his hands;
His speed outrushing simoon's blast,
His Courser whirling gladly past.
By scattered palm, and fountain small,
By sacred tomb, by city's wall,
By river running merrily,
By Mosque enlighted splendidly;
Like gray clouds driven by the wind,
He left no trace of him behind,
Yet in his race the Maid kept by,
And Alek felt the cold reply.

54

FIRST LOVE.

It was an old, a celebrated Church;
About the aisle ran many pillars tall,
And carved wood-work the chancel gathered in;
An old, worn Church, sad was the sight to see.
How lazy through the darkened window-panes,
The sun half-way withdrawn shone dimly down;
Across those clumsy frames the spiders wove,
A dull and heavy air of Sorrow hung
About the old worn pile; upon the Texts
Graven in gold over the chancel's steps.
But when, as comes the prelude to a storm,
The deep-toned organ waked the drowsy air,
And crept up cheerfully from underneath,
The mournful building felt a sudden warmth,
Those liberal Organ notes enlivened it.

There prayed and preached a godly, pious Clerk,
To good and pious auditors most true.
It was most sad to see the crowd throng up
The dimly-lighted aisle, as if Ghosts came,
Entranced by recollections of their Sins.
Young Henry came not as a worshipper,
To bend in worship to the blessed Lord,
For in the ancient aisle one being stood,
A young and fair-haired girl, whom Henry loved;
Her name was Hester, lovely as the Spring.
To them, this reverend building was a fane,
Whereon the God of love, fair Cupid laid
Two youthful hearts, then kindled into flame.

O what is love, young Love, what liquid fire,
What undiscovered furnace lighted up,
What mirror in our breasts that thus presents
A mistress in her bloom and glorious hour.
To Henry no such thoughts, on Hester's form
The gentle youth turned gently a faint look,
More worthy to be worshipped than the Host
Which all the congregation worshippèd.

Nor had the youth e'er told the Maid his love
In words, which are the foremost curse of love.
Hester and Henry, whither have you fled, —
The ancient Church still holds the sacred form,
And hollow ghosts stalk through the gloomy aisles,
But Hester's form has fled, and Henry 's fled.

How many Sabbaths did the heavy bell,
Which pealed from out the square Tower's little arch,
Strike through young Henry's heart a thrill of fear,
Lest Hester might not be at church that day.
Yet Hester came, and week succeeded week,
And months fled by, and sometimes Hester came not.
When she was absent, Henry felt how vain,
How utterly vain and hollow was the Creed
Taught from the Liturgy and New Testament.

Not only in the sadden'd Minster's light,
Young Henry sought the lovely Hester's shape,
But when the choral stars shone bright in Heaven,
Or when to earth fell heavily the storm,
He paced the quiet street where Hester lived.

The close-drawn curtain kept his eye without,
Still his heart beat, for there within those walls
His spirit dwelt. The framework of the house
Was hung as with a hundred starry lights,
And silvery bells made music in the way.
She dwelt so near the outward air, her life
Mingled itself with the common circumstance;
But Henry could not call those happy hours.
Deep melancholy fastened on the youth,
His cheek grew pale, his heart was sorrowful,
As day by day, the swift years circled on,
Nor brought him nearer lovely Hester's form.

Where'er he wandered through four lonely years,
He saw a spirit dancing in the path,
To whom he vainly hastened, — she did fly. —
So deep below the daily life he lived,
Consumed him this pure passion, that her name,
Sometimes repeated when the youth sat near,
Choked up his utterance, and a weight of blood
Instantly stagnant, settled at his heart. —
Thou dew of life, young Love, thou morning tear,
Thus richly rises the sweet sun of youth.

58

THE DESERT.

No shining grass, or sunny tree,
  Or smiling Villa greets my eyes,
No forms of fair society,
  Or gentle domesticities,
The scanty furze grows yellow all,
Like threadbare Tapestry on the wall.

But here I wandered most content,
  With one fair spirit by my side,
A Sister to my manhood lent
  Her beaming eyes of maiden pride,
And clothed the drear rock's loneliness
With her abiding tenderness.

So should she drape the World's wide round,
  With sunny robes, and fresh Spring weather
And consecrate the loneliest ground,
  While we went wandering linked together,
Her music voice, her beaming eyes,
Give to the Silence, glad replies.

Thy sandy hills, bleak desert Waste,
  Now murmur soft like singing streams,
Thy lonely Moors with music taste
  Like temples clad in Grecian dreams,
Thou Desert, art a living thing,
Since she and I went wandering.

60

AUTUMN WOODS.

I HAVE had tearful days,
I have been taught by melancholy hours,
My tears have dropped, like these chill Autumn showers,
Upon the rustling ways.

Yes! youth, thou sorrowest,
For these dead leaves, unlike your rising Morn,
Are the sad progeny of months forlorn,
Weary and seeking rest.

Thou wert a homeless child,
And vainly clasped the solitary air,
And the gray Ash renewed thy cold despair,—
Grief was thy mother mild.

Thy days have Sunlight now,
Those Autumn leaves thy tears do not deplore,
There flames a beacon on the forest's shore,
And thy unwrinkled brow.

O holy are the Woods,
Where nature yearly glorifies her might,
And weaves a rich and frolicsome delight.
In the deep Solitudes.

Far through the fading trees
The Pine's green plume is waving bright and free,
And in the withered age of man to me
A warm and sweet Spring breeze.

62

THE LONELY ROAD.

No track had worn the lone deserted road,
Save where the Fox had leapt from wall to wall;
There were the swelling, glittering piles of snow,
Up even with the walls, and save the Crow
Who lately had been pecking Barberries,
No other signs of life beyond ourselves.
We strayed along, beneath our feet the lane
Creaked at each pace, and soon we stood content
Where the old cellar of the house had been,
Out of which now a fruit-tree wags its top.
Some scraggy orchards hem the landscape round,
A forest of sad Apple-trees unpruned,
And then a newer orchard pet of him,
Who in his dotage kept this lonely place.

In this wild scene, and shut-in Orchard dell,
Men like ourselves, once dwelt by roaring fires,
Loved this still spot, nor had a further wish.
A little wall half falling bounds a square
Where choicer fruit-trees showed the Garden's pride,
Now crimsoned by the Sumach, whose red cones
Displace the colors of the cultured growth.
I know not how it is, that in these scenes
There is a desolation so complete,
It tarries with me after I have passed,
And the dense growth of woodland, or a sight
Of distant Cottages or landscapes wide,
Cannot obscure the dreary, cheerless thought.
But why should I remember those once there,
And think of childish voices, or that kind
Caressing hands of tender parents gone,
Have twined themselves in that soft golden hair,
All fled, and silent as an unlit Cave.
Why should I stand and muse upon their lives,
Who for me truly never had more life,
Than in the glancing mind's eye ; or in Fancy
Wear this irrespective form, thus fleeting.

I people the void scene with Fancy's eye,
Her children do not live too long for me,
They vibrate in the house whose walls I rear,
The mansion as themselves, the fugitives
Of my Intent in this soft Winter day.
Nor will I scatter these faint images,
Idle as shadows that the tall reeds cast
Over the silent ice, beneath the moon,
For in these lonely haunts where Fancy dwells,
And evermore creating weaves a veil
In which all this that we call life abides,
There must be deep retirement from the day,
And in these shadowy vistas we shall meet,
Sometime the very Phantom of ourselves.—
A long Farewell, thou dim and silent spot,
Where serious Winter sleeps, or the soft hour,
Of some half dreamy Autumn afternoon;
And may no idle feet tread thy domain,
But only men to Contemplation vowed,
Still as ourselves, creators of the Past.

65

REPENTANCE.

A CLOUD upon the day is lying,
A cloud of care, a cloud of sorrow,
That will not speed away for sighing,
That will not lift upon the Morrow.

And yet it is not gloom I carry,
To shade a world else framed in lightness,
It is not sorrow that doth tarry,
To veil the joyous sky of brightness.

Then tell me what it is, thou Nature
That of all Earth art queen supremest,
Give to my grief distinctest feature,
Thou, who art ever to me nearest.

Because my lot has no distinction,
And unregarded I am standing,
A pilgrim wan without dominion,
A ship-wrecked Mariner just landing.

Resolve for me, ye prudent Sages,
Why I am tasked without a reason,
Or penetrate the lapse of ages,
And show where is my Summer season.

For let the sky be blue above me,
Or softest breezes lift the forest,
I still uncertain, wander to thee,
Thou who the lot of Man deplorest.

Nor will I strive for Fortune's gilding,
But still the Disappointment follow,
Seek steadily the pasture's wilding,
Nor grasp a satisfaction hollow.

67

THE ARCHÈD STREAM.

It went within my inmost heart,
The overhanging Arch to see,
The liquid stream, became a part
Of my internal Harmony.

So gladly rushed the full stream through,
Pleased with the measure of its flow,
So burst the gladness on the view,
It made a song of Mirth below.

Yet gray were those o'erarching stones,
And sere and dry the fringing grass,
And mournful with remembered tones,
That out of Autumn's bosom pass.

And over it the heavy road,
  Where creaks the wain with burdened cheer,
But gaily from this low abode,
  Leapt out the merry Brook so clear.

Then Nature said: My child, to thee,
  From the gray Arch shall beauty flow,
Thou art a pleasant thing to me,
  And freely in my meadows go.

Thy Verse shall gush thus freely on,
  Some Poet yet may sit thereby,
And cheer himself within the sun,
  My Life has kindled in thine eye.

69

A DREAM OUT-OF-DOORS.

Though through the Pines a soughing wind,
There 's sun within the trembling breeze,
For continents do lie behind,
Of rarest Flowers and Strawberries ;
Each chilling blast shakes Cherries down,
And tints the knurly Pear with brown.

Your sooty cloaks bright skies resume,
And weep with all-abandoned glee,
The darkening eve shoots rose perfume,
And cowslips nod, and Apple-tree
Outshines the tapestry of the King,
With red and white, a heapèd thing.

Storm, rage, and fret, thou sullen March,
Be black, or blue, or furious red,
Springs roundly the o'erhanging arch
With violets clustering o'er its head;
Thy sullen frowns I highly cheer,
The green fields float, thy atmosphere.

And long behind the Wall I lay,
The gray stone wall with mosses laid,
And heard above my head the day
With eastern fingers twisting braid,
Swift flew the wind, but I was warm,
The sun was playing his gold charm.

There as I lay, a drowsy eye
Leered at me curious, till I sank
And into sleepy lands did fly,
While Lethe murmured down the bank,
'T was warmer then than by the fire,
More music in Apollo's lyre.

I dreamed that in the Church I stood,
Dim were mine eyes the sun did blind,
I never went to church for good,
Nor this time left my rule behind;
I went to find my love who played,
The School girl like a timid maid.

They told me in the gallery then,
That I should find my love so dear;
My eyes were blind, and I was ten,
Yes ten good times the gallery near,
When sudden blindness o'er me came,
And still I went and still the same.

And when I reached the topmost stair,
Nor could my lovely Ellen see,
I shouted, Ellen, Ellen dear,—
She came from far behind to me;
You truant, was what I could say,
As in her sweet embrace I lay.

And I awoke, and the east wind
Did clamor through the old stone wall,
And as I slept, soft clouds had lined
The spanning of the azure Hall,
There 's rain meseems within the sky,
Since I in Ellen's arms did lie.

Then blow cold March your trumpets shrill,
Send if you can a biting storm,
The nooks are sunny on the hill,
The mossy stones are smooth and warm,
For I can sleep and dream of thee,
Within whose heart is Spring for me.

73

TO THE POETS.

THEY who sing the deeds of men,
From the earth upraise their fame,
Monuments in marble pen,
Keeping ever sweet their name,
Tell me Poets, do I hear,
What you sing, with pious ear?

They who sing the Maiden's Kiss,
And the silver Sage's thought,
Loveliness of inward bliss,
Or the graver learning taught,
Tell me are your skies and streams
Real, or the shape of Dreams?

Many rainy days must go,
Many clouds the sun obscure,
But your verses clearer show,
And your lovely thoughts more pure,
  Mortals are we, but you are
  Burning keenly like a star.

75

THE MOUNTAINS.

Toys for the angry lightning in its play,
Summits, and peaks, and crests untrod and steep,
And precipices where the eyes delay,
Sheer gulfs that madly plunge in valleys deep,
Overhung valleys curtained by dark forms,
Ye, nourished by the energetic storms,
  I seek you lost in spell-bound shuddering sleep.

Within your rifts hang gem-like crystal stars,
Eyeless by day they glitter through the nights,
Full-zonèd Venus, and red visaged Mars,
And that serenest Jupiter's round lights,
Peer o'er your terrible eminences near,
But throned too high to stoop with mortal fear,
  Dreading you not, ye Ocean-stemming heights.

Your awful forms pale wandering mists surround,
Dim clouds enfold you in funereal haze,
In the white frosted Winters ye abound,
And your vast fissures with the Frost-work glaze,
Slippery and careless of ascending feet,
Holding out violent death, and thus may meet
The Olympians, — mortals with unshrinking gaze.

The fierce bald Eagle builds amid your caves,
Shrieks fearless in your lonely places where
Only his brothers of the wind make waves,
Sweeping with lazy pinions the swift air,
For far below the stealthy wolf retreats,
The fox his various victims crafty greets,
Breeze-knighted birds alone make you their lair.

Sometime in the green valley peasants stand
Shading their glance at mid-day as they pass,
And wonder at such beacons in the land,
Bending again their eyes upon the grass;
Ye heaven-high Mountains deign to stand alone,
Only the airy amphitheatre to own,
Only the shapely clouds, the snows' drear mass.

What are ye, grand, unuttered words of Power,
Why stand you thus, balancing only earth,
Shall not an echo wake, an untold hour
Stir in your cavernous breasts a giant birth,
Shall ye not answer to the roar of seas,
Send back your greeting to the running breeze;
  Mountains, I hear you, in your mighty mirth.

78

TO ONE COMPLAINING.

Go to the waving tree,
The level circle's golden round,
Or on the margin of the Sea,
List to the sound.

I bid thee from the roof,
Where underneath the dreary day,
Puts thy frail spirit to the proof,
To turn away.

Speak not beneath the wall,
God hears thee not while thou art there,
But make thy consecrated hall
The endless air.

Ride on the wild wind's mane
  When scornful Autumn hisses loud,
Sing like the heavy Summer's rain,
  So stately proud.

Have never-failing Hate,
  And be forbidden in thy deed,
And make thyself all desolate,
  Nor sate thy need.

Then when thy rage is spent,
  Thou shalt sit down to tell the tale,
And as thou see'st the way thou went,
  Be clad in mail.

Bad memories shall be,
  The storehouse of thy present worth,
The Past shall win this stake for thee,
  Another birth.

80

MID-WINTER.

O SWEETLY falls the pure white snow
Over the chill and silent earth,
And warms the patient seed below,
Waiting for Spring's voluptuous birth.

Thus fall the gentle deeds of men,
And nourish in those Hearts content,
That wait for sunshine sweet again,
And touches of that element.

Thou art not cold to me, if gray
And dimly shown the Heaven's smile,
I am the child of Northern day,
And love the Snow-drift's glittering pile.

'Tis Freedom's writing, clear and white,
Which Southern skies must long deplore,
It sparkles in the depth of night,
Conceals the Stars and paints them o'er.

82

WACHUSETT.

I LIKE this Princeton, a most silent place,
Better than Chester, that I loved to pace
So many years ago; is stiller far,
Less people, they not caring who you are,
While Chester mortals have a certain wit,
By which they know you, or can fancy it.
In Princeton live a few good farming people,
Like spectres in a church-yard, while a steeple
Is pretty nigh the village, and one inn
Which Sam. Carr keeps, lonely and cool within,
One of the country taverns built before
Our recollection, shortly after Noah.
Here Boston sportsmen stop with dog and gun,
To bag shy Woodcock, and have quiet fun,

A ruddy, cheerful race, who interfere
Never with you, in truth know not you are.
No perfumed dandies smirch the lonely roads,
No artists wander with their sketchy loads,
'T is then a proper place for us to go,
Who love old solitude and hate new show.
I think it a good spot without this hill
Wachusett, — a small mountain, cool and still
As Princeton. To the summit is easy,
With scattered outlooks picturesque and breezy,
Not as flat level as a Salem beach,
And yet within a feeble body's reach.
A pleasant ramble up a rocky steep,
'Neath shady woodlands, where some Woodgods sleep,
Where maples, shad-barks, silver birches shine,
Second-growth forest where gay trees combine.

It has no grandeur like the proud White Hills,
No cataract's thunder, steal no crystal rills
Like those which line the Catskills half the way,
And furnish comfort in a summer's day,

But the road up is dry as Minot's tongue,
Or city people chance together flung.
And off the summit one sees villages,
Church spires, white houses, and their belts of trees,
Plenty of farmers' clearings, and some woods,
But no remote Sierra solitudes.
I never counted up the list of towns,
That I can see spread on the rolling downs,
Or sought for names of mountains on the map,
As Jackson might who is a Scenery-trap,
But to my notion there is matter here,
As pleasant as if larger or severe.
'T is plain New England, neither more nor less,
Pure Massachusetts-looking, in plain dress;
From every village point at least three spires,
To satiate the good villagers' desires,
Baptist, and Methodist, and Orthodox,
And even Unitarian, creed that shocks
Established church-folk; they are one to me,
Who in the different creeds the same things see,

But I love dearly to look down at them,
In rocky landscapes like Jerusalem.
The villages gleam out painted with white,
Like paper castles are the houses light,
And every gust that o'er the valley blows,
May scatter them perchance like drifting snows.
The little streams that thread the valleys small,
Make scythes or axes, driving factories all,
The ponds are damned, and e'en the petty brooks,
Convert to sluices swell the River's crooks,
And where the land 's so poor, it will not pay
For farming, winds the Railroad's yellow way.

If in the Student's eye, this Yankee vein
Of pure utility is but pure pain,
If he shall ask for august Palace wall,
Or figured arch, or learned College hall;
If he seek Landscape gardens midst those trees,
Where hammers trip it like the hum of bees,
Instead of corn-land for the shaven Lawn,
Or one sane man who will his life adorn,

Not a dry rank of Grocers, or of shops,
Or women sometime conversant with mops,
He asks for that Wachusett does not see,
A watch-tower guarding pure utility.
Why does the Student question what there is?
Grant it not Grecian, it is surely his;
Born in New England in her useful mood,
Let him not feel as if in solitude;
The child of railroads, Factories, and farms,
Let him not stand beside them with closed arms.
Dwells not within the Locomotive's heart
One of the purest ministries of Art,
Can Poet feign more airy character,
This burdened train few drops of water stir.
Hear how it thunders down the iron road,
Invulnerable horse, who drags a load,
No matter what its shape, or weight, to him,
Gallops by noon, and speechless midnight dim,
Careless across the trembling, sunken moors,
Under the mountains, past the people's doors,

Through forest-thickets where the Partridge drums,
Along the sea-beach where the salt spray comes,
Hurled by the exercise of human thought,
The man-created beast shows matter nought.
Within his magic mind, a dreamy boy
Converts this iron to a living toy,
Shuts in a moment power of distances,
Bids granite dance, and iron axles wince.
Who cares what is the weather, good or bad,
Within the Rail-car pleasant can be had, —
Who cares where is the city, by his door,
Rolls the swift engine, circling countries o'er.

The Student grants it thus, — but selfish trade
Along the fair inventions closely laid,
Converts the country to a cunning town,
Nothing can stand save beating prices down.
Man's temple is the market, and his God
Is money, fall of dollars Jovian nod.
Society is leagued against the poor,
Monopolies close up from most the door

To fortune, Industry has come to be
Competitive, all, — aristocracy;
Work is monotonous, a war for wealth,
The universe is plainly out of health.
See from this mountain in the dusty towns,
A people sorely burdened, for smiles, — frowns,
No lovely groups of rustics dig the soil,
Alone each farmer ploughs, his greedy toil
Not shared with them about him, but his hand
Closed against those, who may the nearest stand.
A piteous sight, there is the Poor-house wall,
A frightful thing, there is the Prison's hall,
The courts of Justice fatten on the broil,
The church lamps feed on poor men's sweaty oil,
Where shall this misery end, has God forsook
The dwellers in these valleys, from the Book
Of Life their names forever razed; I see
Nothing around us but deep misery.

So spoke the Student; in his eye swam tears,
A sincere man, whose mournful, thoughtful years,
Have run away in longings for that good,
Which finds he only in some solitude,

Where swing in sunny distances the trees,
And squirrels chirp in frolic to the breeze,
And o'er the grass the green snake winds along,
Curving himself in like the Brook's clear song,
Where pigeons glance about the murmuring boughs,
And beetles hum, and the tall Pine-tree soughs.—
Dear student, in that life, so sad to thee,
Is better Nature, than all this to me.
Thou dost not feel the sweetness of the art,
When strikes the farmer in the earth his heart;
His crops are wise instructions of the power,
Which off his fingers reels the fruitful hour;
With a father's fondness, o'er his rich Fields
He looks content, and what the out-door yields,
Within his bosom meets its answering tone,
Nor is he satisfied to hold alone
This credit of the world, but with his friend
Who owns yon meadow, does his harvest blend
In fair exchanges, as the honest earth
For his just thoughts alone its crop gives birth.
The neighbor in his mind, has his fit place,
And trade is the keen Wizard's shifting mace

By which he deals in untold craftiness
With those about him ; they in turn confess
The profit which this prudent Industry
Has made for them, and kept their wits at sea.
'Tis always the concealed, mysterious thought
Which in his bargains somewhere shall be caught ;
This competition is the mystic thing,
He does not know its strength or power of wing,
And only on his neighbor tries its force,
Who can for him interpret its true source. —
What is the cheer within the village street,
Which makes the Court, the Jail, the Church complete,
Save that each day 't is a new birth of mind,
And these new men experiments can find ?
So like a laboratory smells the town,
These villagers the chemists, — skill the crown
Which decks the royal head, — he is a King,
Who from his cunning competence can bring.
Shall witty scheme or formula compare
With Nature's secret force, which can prepare
Each hour new tactics for this village war,
So gently waged, so little do they jar.

And who do tenant then the Poor-house wall,
And who are fastened in the Prison's hall,
But those that baulk kind Nature in her play,
Who thus has laid them up, and stored away.
Is trade no happier than the game of old,
When iron muscles played the trick for gold,
When Barons led their fierce retainers forth,
Like Kurroglou and battered down the earth,
When no man's life was safe in wood or street,
And the whole neighborhood a martial beat.
Much I prefer to sit on Princeton hill,
And see around me the results of skill,
Where Mind does own the making of the thing,
The age of muscle having had its swing.
Are there no dear emotions in the vale,
Does not the Maiden hear the lover's wail,
Breathe gently forth below the Chesnut shade,
Does not her bosom heave, and blushes fade
Momently on her cheek, like shadows flying
Across the woodlands while soft day is dying
Upon that range of Hampshire hills, — does age
No sweet respect from its young heirs engage,

Sounds not the running Schoolboy's chorus cry,
And village girls do they not smile and sigh;
Are not the wrinkles in that old man's brows,
The fruit of battle with the winter snows,
Or honest strokes beneath the summer's sun,
Of his swift scythe, those curvatures have run;
Are there no merry parties for the lakes,
And nutting frolics in the forest's brakes;
The horse, the cow, and dog play merry part,
The humblest village beats with cheery heart.
Within the plainest School-house lore is writ
As good as Bible-story, part of it;
The city claims a visit every year,
The Cattle-show is held each season near,
A thousand books fly everywhere about,
Of which the secret quickly is torn out,
Sweet bread, rich milk, and apples weigh the board,
The village, by its trade, doth spend not hoard.
He who has craft, he gets respect from all,
He who has none, by his deserts doth fall
To his true level, and Nature dwelling here
Pours out her sacred Instinct strong and clear.

The Student said, — If all this, truly so,
A stagnant element cakes deep below,
The threadbare relic of the elder age,
The heirloom of Judea, that sad page
Recording the fantastic miracles
Done in that day, which read like jugglers' spells,
Or incantations in a tiresome play,
Which later editors might crib away.
How sadly serious is Religion now,
That Seraph with her sparkling, crystal brow,
In whose deep humane eyes the world should read,
Tenderest consolation, and not bleed
At their cold, spectral, grim, forlorn replies,
Like one who stares at us with mere glass eyes.
What awkward repetitions of a Creed,
The pulpit and the minister, indeed,
Where congregations meet for gossipping,
Or boys for show, and girls to learn to sing.
Is *this* Religion, — Nature's other self,
Or the last issue of the thirst for pelf,
How cold to me the worn church-service is,
I wonder that some people do not hiss. —

O Student learn a wiser lore than thine,
Deem me presumptuous, do not call it mine ;
A lore I read upon the steel-blue lakes,
And in the piled white clouds, this soft wind takes
Like sailing navies, o'er the Atlantic heaven,
A lore by Spirits to this mortal given,
That teaches in whate'er our souls revere,
Is the pure oxygen of that atmosphere,
Which God presents our race to freely breathe,
Which he does finely through our beings wreathe,
And that we *reverence* has power sublime,
Whether it be the birth of olden time,
Or the last Spirit-prophecy of him
Who dwelt on earth, a mild-eyed Seraphim.
O Jesus, if thy spirit haunts that vale
Whence softly on the air, the Church-bells wail,
Swells up this silent mount, a prophecy,
That thou didst teach our souls could never die ;
If to some lonely heart, thy memory brings
The healing of thy Beauty on its wings,
And to this gentle heart its truth does say,
That thou wert mild and gentle, pure alway ;

Does promise after that hath left this shore,
And when no longer sounds this hurried roar
Of eager life, a rest in sacred camps,
Where holy Angels tend unfading lamps,
Where all that here this lowly heart did love,
Dwells in the sunshine of that sphere above ;
Where never sorrow, and where never pain
Creep o'er the mind, as on the flowers the rain
Of early winter, crossing out their flame ;
Where music sounds perpetual the name
Of an eternal Beauty, and where day
Dies not in shadow on a mournful way ;
Where shall that lowly heart meet better earth
Than here was present, where shall a new birth,
Quicken her faculties low lying sere,
And thought's rich Compensation shall appear ;
If thus to one pure heart in any vale,
Above which now these vast white clouds do sail,
Thy lesson comes, though taught by miracles,
And in the dark contrivances of spells,
Yet shall each Church to me an altar seem,
Of sculpture lovely as a maiden's dream,

The lowly Hymn-book claim my gratitude,
The least frail office chain my darkest mood,
For I must feel such souls do dwell on earth,
Who look afar for an immortal birth,
And thou, serenest Jesus, art to them,
The lustrous mild-eyed, blissful Seraphim.

It is a busy mountain, — the wind's song
Levels so briskly the oak-tops along,
Which light October frosts color like wine,
That ripens red on warm Madeira's line.
I hear the rustling plumes of these young woods,
Like young cockerels crowing to the solitudes
While o'er the far horizon trails a mist,
A kind of autumn smoke or blaze, — I list,
Again, a lively song the woods do sing,
The smoke-fire drifts about painting a ring
Sublime, the centre of which is the mountain;
It rises like the cloud of some dark fountain
At even-song; the Indian summer's voice,
Bids me in this last tropic day rejoice.
How brown the country is, what want of rain,
But no crops growing, no one will complain.

The Indian summer, wan and waste and tame,
Like the red nation whence it takes its name,
Some relic of the season, a faint heat
Which momently must into Winter fleet,
The dying of the year, — the Indian time,
How well they name it, how it suits the clime.
The race who on this mountain once might stand,
The country's monarchs wide on either hand,
Bold as the July heats, and vigorous
As August tempests, and more glorious
Than splendid summer Moonlights, where are they?
Ah, like this summer, they did fade away
Into the white snows of that winter race,
Who came with iron hands and pallid face,
Nor could the Indian look within his eye;
They turned, their frosts had come, their blight was nigh;
Some praise their stately figure, or their skill,
They straight submitted to the White man's will,
Their only monument, a fading week,
The Indian summer; like the hectic cheek

Of a consumptive girl who ere her time,
In some gay anguish half renews her prime,
Shines in one summer moment, e'er the frost
Crimsons her foliage before all is lost.

Now the veiled sun is drooping to his fall,
Weaving the western landscape a thick pall
From the gigantic Air-smoke, through it slant
His stretching beams, the mighty figures daunt
The eye, far-shading level smoke that side,
While eastward the white towns in sunshine ride.
But all around this wonderful, wild haze,
Like a hot crucible wherein the days
And nights are melted by a giant hand,
A terrible world, neither sea nor land,
As if at last old earth had caught on fire,
And slowly mouldering, sank into the pyre.
To the dull north, a skeleton so dim,
Is gray Monadnoc's head, and half of him,
Looming out vaguely, as Gibraltar's rock
Off Estepona, when the east wind's shock

After a long gale from the sparkling west,
Comes coldly down, but warms the seaman's breast,
Anxious to fly Mediterranean calm,
And clasp the ocean with his daring palm.
Beneath the sun, like Saladin's bright blade,
One glittering lake cuts golden the wide shade,
And on some faint-drawn hill-sides fires are burning,
The far blue smoke their outlines soft in-urning,
And now half-seen the Peterboro' hills,
Peep out like black-fish, nothing but their gills.
Each feature of the scene itself confounded.
Like Turner's pallet with strange colors grounded,
It seems to gain upon me, shut me in,
Creeps up to the brown belfry where I spin
My fancies, like that last Man Campbell painted,
Who finally 't is to be hoped was sainted.

Who can be sad and live upon this earth,
A scene like this would make a Hermit mirth,
And turn mankind to Painters, or forswear
All sympathies save with this landscape-air,
While comes the breeze as gently as caress
Of pensive lovers in first blessedness.

A yellow tone sweeps southward the horizon,
The sun to weaving deeper shadows plies on,
More mountains loom, and hills burst up like isles
Shot in the sea by Earth's galvanic piles ;
One clear black spot hangs o'er the valley there,
A solitary Hawk balanced on air;
Banks of gray squall-clouds swell below the sun,
The lake turns steel, another sketch begun,
Each instant changes everywhere the scene,
Rapid and perfect turns the Indian screen.
There comes a firmer yellow to the North,
The sun just opening showers more glories forth,
A lakelet dazzles like a bursting star,
The landscape widens in that Hampshire far,
The swelling lines of nearer hills arise,
The greater mountains ope their dreamy eyes;
Out bursts the sun, turns villages to gold,
Blazons the cold lake, burns the near cloud's fold,
Drops splendidly a curtain of warm tints,
And at an apple-green divinely hints.
What land is this, not my New England drear?
'T is Spain's south border, or warm Naples' cheer,

Sweet Provènce smiles upon the western side,
And Azores' velvet on the molten tide.
I see in front the great Savannahs lie, —
The endless deserts burnt by Afric's eye,
Shine in that dusky land the Moor's delight;
'T is Tangiers yonder and dark Atlas' height,
Or Mauritania with her sable skins,
And gold-dust rivers, elephants and kings,
And yonder looms the sandy Arab coast,
With yellow tassels of the Palm all crost,
And in that valley bakes a torrid Fez ;
He is not right, who our New England says
Is a dread, cold inhospitable realm, —
Guides not the South this glowing landscape's helm?

I hear the cawing of some drifting crows,
Beneath in villages the watch-dog blows
His bayings to the scene, and King-birds shriek,
And stronger breezes fan the happy cheek,
While purest roseate turns the western sky,
Laughing to think that night has drawn so nigh.
And like a ball of melted iron glows
The sinking sun, leaves his last veil, and throws

Upon the Eastern hills a gentle red,
Upon those skies his rosy pencil spread,
Then dies within that stormy mountain cloud,
That masks him proudly in a leaden shroud.

THE POET.

Each day, new Treasure brings him for his store,
So rich he is he never shall be poor,
His lessons nature reads him o'er and o'er,
As on each sunny day the Lake its shore.

Though others pine for piles of glittering gold,
A cloudless Sunset furnishes him enough,
His garments never can grow thin or old,
His way is always smooth though seeming rough.

Even in the winter's depth the Pine-tree stands,
With a perpetual Summer in its leaves,
So stands the Poet with his open hands,
care nor sorrow him of Life bereaves.

For though his sorrows fall like icy rain,
Straightway the clouds do open where he goes,
And e'en his tears become a precious gain;
'T is thus the heart of Mortals that he knows.

The figures of his Landscape may appear
Sordid or poor, their colors he can paint,
And listening to the hooting he can hear,
Such harmonies as never sung the saint.

And of his gain he maketh no account,
He 's rich enough to scatter on the way;
His springs are fed by an unfailing fount,
As great Apollo trims the lamp of day.

'T is in his heart, where dwells his pure Desire,
Let other outward lot be dark or fair;
In coldest weather there is inward fire,
In fogs he breathes a clear celestial air.

So sacred is his Calling, that no thing
Of disrepute can follow in his path,
His Destiny too high for sorrowing,
The mildness of his lot is kept from wrath.

Some shady wood in Summer is his room,
Behind a rock in Winter he can sit,
The wind shall sweep his chamber, and his loom
The birds and insects, weave content at it.

Above his head the broad Skies' beauties are,
Beneath, the ancient carpet of the earth ;
A glance at that, unveileth every star,
The other, joyfully it feels his birth.

So let him stand, resigned to his Estate,
Kings cannot compass it, or Nobles have,
They are the children of some handsome fate,
He, of Himself, is beautiful and brave.

106

TO THE PAST.

THESE locks so light and thin,
Once waved luxuriant o'er a playful brow ;
The sunlight sends these eyes no pleasure now,
Their harvests gathered in.

Not one is spared to me,
They all have fallen in Life's narrow field,
Green waves the grass, their ashes are concealed,
Remains their history.

They fell not in the fight,
Like steel-girt Warriors in the castle's breach,
Their deeds did nothing high or mighty teach,
A battle for the Right.

But cold Forgetfulness,
And ceremony with a tedious eye,
And worldly Wisdom aping courtesy,
And sickly stinginess;

These were their enemies, —
Farewell! though I am sad, yet in my heart
There burns the splendor of a better part,
That which ye cannot prize.

POEMS OF THE HEART.

I.

There in the old gray house whose end we see,
Half-peeping through the golden Willow's veil,
Whose graceful twigs make foliage through the year,
My Hawthorne dwelt, a scholar of rare worth;
The gentlest man that kindly nature drew,
New England's Chaucer, Hawthorne fitly lives.
His tall compacted figure, ably strung
To urge the Indian chase or guide the way,
Softly reclining 'neath the aged elm,
Like some still rock looked out upon the scene,
As much a part of Nature, as itself.
The passing Fisher, saw this idle man

Thus lying solitary 'neath the elm,
And as he plied with lusty arms his oar,
Shooting upon the tranquil glass below
The old red Bridge, and further on the stream
To those still coves where the great prizes swim,
Asked of himself this question, why that man
Thus idly on the bank o'erhung the stream ?—
Then by the devious light at twilight's close,
He read the Twice-told Tales, nor dreamt the mind
Thus idly musing by the River's side,
Had gathered and stored up from Nature's fields
This golden grain, and sweet nutritious fare,
Nor saw within the blind man's eye that boy,
The Gentle Boy, float o'er the tranquil tide.

Softly from out the well-stored sunny brake,
Or where the great Fields glimmer in the sun,
Such mystic influence came to Hawthorne's soul,
That from the air, and from the liquid day,
He drank the subtle image of deep life.
And when the grand and cumbrous Winter rose,
Sealing the face of Nature as with stone,
He sat within the Manse, and filled the place

With all the wealth of Summer like a sun. —
Yet were these plains more sacred in my eyes,
That furnished treasure for his Kingly purse.

II.

To thy continual Presence in me wrought,
Vainly might I, a fallen creature, say,
That I partake the blessedness of day,
To thee, thou essence of Creation's thought.
That on my verse might fall thy healing dew,
And all its faults obscure, its charms renew.
I praise Thee not, because Thou needest praise,
What were my thanks, thou needest not my lays,
Yet will I praise thee, for thou art the fire
That sparkles on the strings of my dark lyre.
Sole majesty, yet 'round us softly flowing,
Unseen, yet in the common Sunset glowing,
The fate of Universe, the tide of things,
Sacred alike to all beneath thy wings,
If Passion's trance lay on the writing clear,
Then should I see thee evident and near,
Passion, that breath of instinct, and the key
Of thy dominions, untold Mystery.

III.

It was the summer, and in early June,
When all things taste the luxury of health,
With the free growth of foliage on the trees,
And o'er the fields a host of Clover blooms,
And through the life and thought of the fresh world,
Unsorrowing peace, and Love like softest air.
'T was then I took my way along the hills,
Upon the sandy road that devious winds ;
At last, I came to happy Meredith.
This beauteous spot is circled in with heights,
And at a little distance Gunstock stands,
A bare, bold mountain looking o'er the lake,
That shines like glass within the emerald meads.

Much was I pleased, to mark the simple life
That man yet leads among the mountain shades,
Nor failed to see a Farmer, who was born
Upon the side of Gunstock, where his sire
Had tilled the fertile soil, — himself a son
Of Nature, framed to love the heights and fields.
The meaning of the landscapes in his heart,
Shone with a rural splendor, and his eye

Trembled with Humor as it roved abroad,
Gladdened by each familiar scene of youth;
While in his mind the Words of men were stored,
Quaint phrases, and wise sayings manifold.
Not often have I met thus wise a man,
Not often heard such merry words, and learned
That Nature pours her wealth unstinted forth,
Upon the unknown, careless, and remote.

IV.

The day has past, I never may return;
Twelve circling years have run since first I came,
And kindled the pure truth of Friendship's flame,
Alone remain these ashes in the urn;
Vainly for light the taper may I turn,
Thy hand is closed, as for these years, the same,
And in the substance nought is but the name,
No more a hope, no more a ray to burn.
But once more in the pauses of thy joy,
Remember him who sought thee in his youth,
And with the old reliance of the boy,
Asked for thy Treasures in the guise of truth;

The air is thick with sighs, — the shaded sun
Shows on the Hill-side, that the day is done.

V.

Tomorrow comes; dost say my friend Tomorrow?
Far down below those Pines the Sunset flings
Long arching o'er, its lines of ruddy light,
And the wind murmurs little harmonies,
And underneath their wings the tender birds
Droop their averted heads, — silent their songs.
But not a word whispers the moaning wind,
Nor when in faint array the primal stars
Trail with the banners of the unfurled night,
Nor even when the low-hung moon just glints
And faintly with few touches seres the wood,
Not there, nor then, doth Nature idly say
Nor whisper idly of another day;
That other morn itself its morrow is,
That other day shall see no shade of this.

VI.

A green and vaporous cloud of buds, the Larch
Folds in soft drapery above the glade,

Where deeper foliaged Pines high over-arch,
And dignify the heavy, stooping shade,
There yellow violets spring, in rarest show,
And golden rods in secret clusters blow.
There piping Hylas fill the helpless air,
And chattering Black-birds hold their gossip by,
And near I saw the tender maiden-hair,
With the fine, breeze-born, white anemone;
The Glade, though undisturbed by human art,
Has richer treasures than the busy mart.

VII.

As in some stately Grove of singing pines,
One tree more marked than all, decisive rears
Its grand aspiring figure to the sky,
Remote from those beneath, and o'er whose top
The first, faint light of dawn familiar plays,
So in Count Julian's face there was the soul
Of something deeper, than the general heart,
Some memory more near to other worlds,
Time's recollection, and the storied Past.

His pure slight form had a true Grecian charm,
Soft as the willow o'er the River swaying,
Yet sinewy and capable of action ;
Such grace as in Apollo's figure lay,
When he was moving the still world with light,
So perfect balanced, and convinced with art.
About his forehead clustered rich black curls,
Medusa-like, they charmed the student's eye.
Those soft, still hazel orbs Count Julian had,
Looked dream-like forth on the familiar day,
Yet eloquent, and full of luminous force,
Sweetly humane that had no harshness known,
Unbroken eyes where Love forever dwelt.
This art of Nature which surrounded him,
This made Count Julian what he was to me,
Which neither time, nor place, nor Poet's pen,
Nor Sculptor's chisel can e'er mould again.

VIII.

O band of Friends, ye breathe within this space,
And the rough finish of a humble man,

By your kind touches rises into Art.
I cannot lose a line ye bend to trace ;
Your figures bear into the azure deeps,
A little frail contentment of my own,
And in your eyes I read, how sunshine lends
A golden color to the dusty weed,
That droops its tints where the soiled Pilgrims tread.

IX.

Believe, that thus a humble worshipper,
Who in soiled weeds along this pathway 's going,
To one of Nobler kind may minister,
His lowly hope in such faint words bestowing ;
O Lady, that my words for thee were more,
But I have not the right to richer store.
Thou art of finer mould, thy Griefs are proof,
Only those nearest to the sun do burn,
While we sit merry underneath the roof,
And vainly to those larger empires turn ;
Had I been heir of brightness such as thou,
Then might a Sorrow seal my rounded brow.

X.

Ye mournful walls, that with a look of woe,
Idly stand gazing in each other's face ;
Ye eager, soulless crowds that coldly pass
Forever 'neath those walls darkly contrived,
And streets that are the wards of Misery ;
Thou poor, and hunger-stricken, needless Town,
That I delved lonely on some sea-washed moor,
Delved with a hand of Pain the barren sands,
All day beneath the scorching eye of Heaven,
Or vacantly stood cold within the wind,
Where rugged Winter nursed his rugged child,
Yea ! on some bleak, bare, desolate place of rock,
Yea ! anywhere but here, in these dim shades,
Within your shades, you high and gloomy walls.
For I have been a walker in the fields,
Oft in the woodland arches have I played,
Seen many times the golden Day-god roll
His round, expanded eyelids in the West,
And bravely flaming, bid the world good-night,

And to my ear the soft, pearl-handed Moon
Hath played her ivory songs beneath the fringe,
That night hangs over edged about with stars,
But thou, sad City, thou art not for me.

119

THE FADED FLOWERS.

SEE these modest little Flowers,
They were nursed by summer's rain,
Many a day broad, sunlight hours
Kept them free from chilling pain ;
They that shall never feel again.

Their little stems are broke away,
Their bells so proud are withering,
Child of dust, poor Child of clay,
To thee does it no feeling bring,
Does it no shadow on thee fling?

Mind me, in a certain hour,
Hour when coming know not I,
Like a little modest Flower
Thou shalt wither, soon to die,
Friends, near thee musing with wet eye.

Then a bell shall toll I ween,
Of the old Church sad and high,
And they shall put thee 'neath the green
Thick grass on the worn Hill-side nigh,
Where many a year may thy bones lie.

And a good Legend may be graved
Upon the marble white and bold,
Hoping that thou may'st be saved,
Thy pure Virtue there enrolled,
While thou sleepest in Death's large fold.

Then shall modest, cheerful Flowers,
Scatter their sweet colors on thee,
All the livelong summer hours,
Keep thee pleasant company,
Gentle memories be to thee.

Life's mystery is fearful large,
What grows, — decays, is now, — then gone,
Of thee, then let the Flowers keep charge,
Small guardians not quite forlorn,
And we will sit, and sing, and mourn.

121

TO READERS.

Dear reader! if my verse could say,
How in my blood thy Nature runs,
Which manifesteth no decay,
The fire that lights a thousand suns,
How Thou and I art freely lent,
A little of that element.

If I could say what landscape says,
And human pictures say far more,
If I could twine the sunny days
With the rich colors on the floor
Of daily Love, how thou and I
Might be refreshed with charity.

For grateful is the softened smile
Of Winter sunset o'er the snow,
And blessed is the spheral isle,
That through the unknown void must go
The current of the stream is sweet,
Where many waters closely meet.

123

THE WINTER LANDSCAPE.

So pure and cold, the bleachèd Snow
That loads the pine, and crowds the wood,
That even as I lonely go,
I feel no touch of Solitude.

This drapery hangs so loosely o'er
The leafless boughs, a passing breeze
Shakes down a tribute to the floor,
For life the Seasons cannot freeze.

And merry sounds the passing Sleigh,
In this bright Winter's softened air,
For Nature ever will be gay,
Her seeds, soft Blossoms ever bear.

You could not frown or scowl abroad,
  Whate'er your indoor malice plied,
So bountiful this winter Lord,
  So splendidly his thought supplied.

Like marble pillars are the tall
  Straight, oaken boles that close the lane,
And alabaster carves the wall,
  The very path is free from stain.

What if this wondrous purity
  Should pass within the human Will?
But Winter will not always be,
  And Summer smiles above that hill.

TO MY COMPANIONS.

Ye heavy-hearted Mariners
    Who sail this shore,
Ye patient, ye who labor,
    Sitting at the sweeping oar,
And see afar the flashing Sea-gulls play,
On the free waters, and the glad bright day,
Twine with his hand the spray,
    From out your dreariness,
    From your Heart-weariness,
    I speak, for I am yours
        On these gray shores.

In vain, — I know not, Mariners,
    What cliffs these are

That high uplift their smooth dark fronts,
And sadly 'round us bar;
I do imagine, that the free clouds play
Above those eminent heights, that somewhere Day
Rides his triumphant way,
Over our stern Oblivion,
But see no path thereout
To free from doubt.

127

A WOODLAND THOUGHT.

THE crashing Tree, the merry call
Of woodmen in the frosty air,
The voices of the drovers clear,
And ringing axes here and there,
These occupy the lonely ground,
And scatter Human life around.

No more that charming solitude
Where swinging branches roar and sigh,
For level is the Church-like wood,
Its spires no longer pierce the sky,
The partridge and the red deer fled,
Where treads the swain, and creaks the sled.

The oak shall never shed again
That fawn-like Harvest in the fall,
Nor acorns in the Autumn rain,
From its deep clefts the squirrels call,
But far away it rolleth free,
And soon is planted in the sea.

And when the frowning Tempest drives
Those pinioned planks like dry leaves down,
And when the billows wildly rage,
And Men by death are quickly sown,
'T is Autumn in the ocean's tide,
And men to Acorns are allied.

ODE.

If we should rake the bottom of the Sea
For its best treasures,
And heap our measures;
If we should ride upon the Winds, and be
Partakers of their flight
By day, and through the night,
Intent upon this business to find gold,
Yet were the story perfectly untold.

Such waves of wealth are rolled up in thy soul,
Such swelling Argosies,
Laden with Time's supplies;
Such pure, delicious wine shines in the bowl,
We could drink evermore,
Upon the glittering shore,

Drink of the Pearl-dissolvèd brilliant cup,
Be madly drunk, and drown our thirsting up.

This vessel richly chased about the rim,
With golden emblems is
The utmost art of bliss,
With figures of the azure Gods who swim
In the enchanted sea,
Contrived for deity,
Floating in rounded shells of purple hue,
The Sculptor died in carving this so true.

Some dry uprooted sapling we have seen,
Pretend to even
This grove of Heaven;
A sacred forest where the foliage green,
Breathes Music like mild lutes,
Or silver-coated flutes,
Or the concealing winds that can convey,
Never their tone to the rude ear of day.

Some weary-footed mortals we have found
Adventuring after thee;

They, — rooted, as a tree
Pursues the swift breeze o'er a rocky ground;
Thy grand, imperial flight,
Sweeping thee far from sight,
As sweeps the movement of a Southern blast,
Across the heated Gulf, and bends the mast.

The circles of thy Thought, shine vast as stars,
No glass shall round them,
No plummet sound them,
They hem the observer like bright steel wrought bars,
And limpid as the sun,
Or as bright waters run
From the cold fountain of the Alpine springs,
Or diamonds richly set in the King's rings.

The piercing of thy Soul scorches the thought,
As great fires burning,
Or sunlight turning
Into a focus; in its meshes caught
Our palpitating minds.
Show stupid like coarse hinds,
So strong and composite through all thy powers,
The Intellect divine serenely towers.

The smart and pathos of our suffering race
Bears thee no harm,
Thy muscular arm
The daily ills of living doth efface;
The sources of the spring
From whence thy instincts wing,
Unsounded by the lines of sordid day,
Enclosed with inlaid walls thy Virtue's way.

This heavy Castle's gates no man can ope,
Unless the lord doth will
To prove his skill,
And read the Fates hid in his horoscope;
No man may enter there,
But first shall kneel in prayer,
And to superior Gods orisons say,
Powers of old time, unveiled in busy day.

Thou need not search for men in Sidney's times,
And Raleigh fashion,
And Herbert's passion;
For us, they are but dry preservèd limes;

There is ripe fruit to-day
Hangs yellow in display,
Upon the waving garment of the bough;
The graceful Gentleman lives for us now.

Neither must thou turn back to Angelo,
Who Rome commanded,
And single-handed
Was Architect, Poet, and bold Sculptor too;
Behold a better thing,
When the pure mind can sing,
When true Philosophy is linked with verse,
When moral Laws in rhyme themselves rehearse.

In city's street, how often shall we hear,
It is a period,
Deprived of every God;
A time of Indecision, and doom 's near;
When foolish altercation
Threatens to break the nation,
All men turned talkers, and much good forgot,
With score of curious troubles we know not.

By this account their learning you shall read,
Who tell the story,
So sad and gory,
People that you can never seek in need;
The pigmies of the race
Who crowd the airy space,
With counterfeit presentments of the Man,
Who has done all things, all things surely can.

We never heard thee babble in this wise,
The age creator,
And clear debater
Of that which this good Present underlies;
Thy course is better kept,
Than where the dreamers slept,
Thy sure meridian taken by the sun,
Thy compass pointing true as waters run.

In vain, for us to say what thou hast been
To the occasion,
The flickering nation,
This stock of people from an English kin;
And he who led the van,

The frozen Puritan,
We thank thee for thy patience with his faith,
That chill delusive poison mixed for death.

So moderate in thy lessons, and so wise,
To foes so courteous,
To friends so duteous,
And hospitable to the neighbor's eyes;
Thy thoughts have fed the lamp
In learning's polished camp,
And who suspects thee of this well-earned fame,
Or meditates on thy renownèd name.

Within thy Book, the world is plainly set
Before our vision,
Thou keen Physician;
We find there wisely writ, what we have met
Along the dusty path,
And o'er the aftermath,
Where natures once world-daring held the scythe,
Nor paid to Superstition a mean tithe.

Great persons are the epochs of the race,
When royal Nature
Takes form and feature,
And careless handles the surrounding space;
The age is vain and thin,
A pageant of gay sin,
Without heroic response from the soul,
Through which the tides diviner amply roll.

The pins of custom have not pierced through thee,
Thy shining armor
A perfect charmer;
Even the hornets of Divinity,
Allow thee a brief space,
And thy Thought has a place,
Upon the well-bound Library's chaste shelves,
Where man of various wisdom rarely delves.—

When thou dost pass below the forest shade,
The branches drooping
Enfold thee, stooping

Above thy figure, and form thus a glade;
The flowers admire thee pass,
In much content the grass,
Awaits the pressure of thy firmest feet,
The bird for thee sends out his greetings sweet.

And welcomes thee designed, the angry Storm,
When deep-toned thunder
Steals up from under
The heavy-folded clouds, and on thy form
The lightning glances gay
With its perplexing ray,
And sweep across thy brow the speeding showers,
And fills this pageantry thy outward hours.

Upon the rivers thou dost float at peace,
Or on the ocean
Feelest the motion;
Of every Natural form thou hast the lease,
Because thy way lies there,
Where it is good or fair;
Thou hast perception, learning, and much art,
Propped by the columns of a stately heart.

From the deep mysteries thy goblet fills,
The wines do murmur,
That Nature warmed her,
When she was pressing out from must the hills,
The plains that near us lie,
The foldings of the sky,
Whate'er within the horizon there is,
From Hades' cauldron, to the blue God's bliss,

We may no more; so we might sing fore'er,
Thy Thought recalling,
Thus waters falling
Over great cataracts, from their lakes do bear,
The power that is divine,
And bends their stately line;
All but thy Beauty, the cold verses have,
All but thy Music, organ-mellowed nave.

139

HYMN OF THE EARTH.

My highway is unfeatured air,
My consorts are the sleepless Stars,
And men, my giant arms upbear,
My arms unstained and free from scars.

I rest forever on my way,
Rolling around the happy Sun,
My children love the sunny day,
But noon and night to me are one.

My heart has pulses like their own,
I am their Mother, and my veins
Though built of the enduring stone,
Thrill as do theirs with godlike pains.

The forests and the mountains high,
The foaming ocean and the springs,
The plains,—O pleasant Company,
My voice through all your anthem rings.

Ye are so cheerful in your minds,
Content to smile, content to share,
My being in your Chorus finds
The echo of the spheral air.

No leaf may fall, no pebble roll,
No drop of water lose the road,
The issues of the general Soul
Are mirrored in its round abode.

141

AUTUMN.

ONCE more I feel the breezes that I love
  Of Spanish autumn stabbing leaf and flower,
Cold cuts the wind, the gray sky frowns above,
  The world enjoys a gloomy hour.

I love thee, Autumn, ruthless harvester!
  Thou dost permit my stagnant veins to flow,
And in my heart a Poet's feelings stir,
  To thee a Poet's fruits I owe.

My boughs shall hang with ripened tribute due,
  I will repay the life that in me lies,
The cold wind shakes off fruits the which if true,
  Must gathered be by those sweet eyes.

MARIANA.

HE loves me not, — she stands as if entranced,
He loves me not, and I am all alive, —
Around her waist her floating tresses dance,
I gave, — she said, — what woman has to give,
My life, my love, my heart, and I am now,
The crimson leaf upon the frozen Bough.

I gave, such agonies are in that thought,
The jewels of an Empire for his song,
The vestments that by purity were wrought,
Which should of right to Princes high belong,
I stand a beggar now beneath the throne,
I am a wanderer forsaken, and alone.

Would the calm Hope of childish sleep was mine,
Would I went gathering flowers across the fields,
When innocence did the pure sense confine,
And the enjoyment that young nature yields,
I see upon the landscape a dull cloud,
The shadow of a weary Heart, and shroud.

And I have sat upon a Parent's knee,
Listening to stories of the immortal few
Who in this sinful world were good and free,
Longing to follow and that life pursue ;
'T is past, the world contains their form no more,
I am unanchored, distant is the shore.

Repent! how bitterly, I might repent!
It could not give me back my dreams of youth,
It could not bathe me in the element,
The lovely radiance of unspotted Truth ;
My love is false, but I am worse than he,
I have no hope, — he has Dishonesty.

144

THE ISLAND NUKUHEVA.

It is upon the far-off deep South Seas,
The island Nukuheva, its degrees
In vain, — I may not reckon, but the bold
Adventurous Melville there by chance was rolled,
And for four months in its delights did dwell,
And of this Island writ what I may tell.
So far away, it is a Paradise
To my unfolded, stationary eyes,
Around it white the heavy billows beat,
Within its vales profoundest cataracts meet,
Drawn from the breasts of the high purple mountains,
And to those Islanders perpetual fountains.

One vale there is upon this southern Isle,
This seal of velvet on the Ocean's smile,

One vale, all breasted in with precipices,
Whose ample side the clinging root caresses,
And from the Ocean to the mountain's face,
But some few miles their interventions trace:
Within this narrow limit there are men,
Of whom I loved to read, and read again,
Such strange and placid lives there seem to be,
Upon that vale far on the deep South Sea.
There, like our village elm, the Bread-fruit grows,
Its green pavilions in broad circle shows;
The scollopped leaves group splendid in decay,
Their rainbow tints oft parted in display,
Upon the brow of the gay Islanders,
Whose heart more serious business rarely stirs.
And when the fruit shines golden in the sun,
Like citron Melons on the vast vine hung,
The Typee farmers gather in the grain,
That in great forests heaps its verdant wain,
No dusty Ploughman breaks the heavy clod,
But crops in native clusters freely nod.
There the smooth trunks of the tall Cocoa-nut,
Rise in abundance near the graceful hut;

The scarce-seen fruit in Heaven it seems to be,
But Typee men ascend the slippery tree,
Where from the centre shoot the waving leaves,
With rich grain burdened like our Indian sheaves,
From which is drawn that nectar most divine,
Nature's blanched vintage of Marquesan wine;
There, waving Omoos vibrate in the air,
Bananas spread their yellow clusters fair.
Along this Typee vale, houses are strown
At easy distance, separate not alone;
Of bamboo, reed, and cocoa-nut's fine boughs,
The hut is built, whose pliant strength allows
Many reverses, — the interlacing sides
Of open cane-work, where the windy tides
Circulate free, and colored Sinnate binds
With various hues the light ethereal blinds;
Then, almost to the ground, the sloping roof
Thatched with Palmetto's tapering leaves, is proof
Against the rains, while from the modest eave
Its tassels droop, and thus the eye relieve.
Two trunks of Cocoa-nut lay polished high
Within, — upon the ground the mats descry

Which gaily-worked form grateful seats by day,
While there at night, the supple limbs obey
The natural instinct sunk in sleep profound,
Upon the simple couch nearest the ground.
The path that goes by these light cottages,
Was never made for horse to pace with ease,
Broad, dusty, strait, and lined with smooth stone-walls,—
Here, droops the pathway with the vale's deep falls,
Now leaps upon the curving hillock's side,
Then, down the glens in rapid mood doth glide,
Crosses the Brook's flint-channel, then away
Turning stupendous rocks, or where the day
Rarely descended in Time-hallowed groves,
Where rotting trunks give to the earth their loves,
By shade and flashing sunlight parted oft,
Or gently winded o'er the verdure soft.

King of the Typees, reigned Mehevi tall,
His mighty stature rising above all,
Of Paradise plumes his gorgeous head-dress made,
With the cock's gaudy plumage interbraid,
A semi-circle high in beads is laid.

His neck-lace of Boars-tusks like ivory bright,
Depending freely o'er a breast of might,
His ear-rings fabricate of sperm whale teeth,
The fronting ends freshly-plucked leaves enwreath,
And wrought with odd devices at the other,
Of which the Typee worship is the mother ;
His loins girt round with Tappa-cloth in folds,
Dark-colored, clustered tassels, — who beholds
His wrists and ancles, sees the curling hair
Of some dead enemy, in circles there.
His well-carved spear of bright Koar-wood is made,
One end points sharp, one is the flat oar-blade ;
His decorate pipe a sinnate loop doth hold,
Hanging from his girdle, painted like red gold
Its slender reed-stem, and the Idol-bowl
Flutters with thinnest Tappa, so the whole.
Over his skin like finest lace-work drawn,
Endless tattooings the great limbs adorn,
And a broad triangle upon his face,
Across his eyes, across his lips finds place.

'T is different, the sweet shape of Fayaway,
To her, the grand Mehevi, night by day.

The Typee maiden with her olive skin,
Through which a soft vermilion shines within,
Her dazzling teeth, like arta's milk-white seeds,
Her soft smooth form contrived for fairy needs.
Upon her naked shoulders flowed her hair
Of deepest brown, which like a mantle rare
In natural ringlets dressed her in its pride,
Her hands as soft as Countess', — she, the bride
Of Nature, who in captivating mood,
Sculptured this maiden for this solitude.
Her dress at home was a slight belt of bark,
With some leaves, like those Fig leaves (save the mark),
Which our first Parents found, but in this she
Moved like a creature wove of sanctity,
Fell like a sunbeam in that summer world,
Beneath those skies her native grace unfurled.
Her jewels were the small Carnation flowers,
Strung in necklaces, rubies for some hours,
On a slight thread of tappa, — in her ear
One small white bud, its stem behind, a sphere
Of purest pearl, its delicate petals close,
Her bracelets flowers, and anklets, like a rose

Set in a folded circle of sweet things,
Or like a soft Spring hour when one bird sings.

Upon the vale the white snows are not sown,
Winter has never been there, but alone
One endless early Summer reigns content,
Ripens sweet fruits in this fine element.
Temperate live the Islanders, the trees
Themselves prepare their food, their perfect ease
Ever consulted by the passing wind ;
They live, like youthful fancies, in the mind.

Into the sparkling streams the Maidens spring,
Dash in the cool, clear waters, laugh and sing,
Anoint themselves with "aker," or that oil
Of cocoa-nuts, prepared with pleasant toil,
Shut as it is, within the "moo-tree's" nut,
Which when carnation-tinted then is cut,
The odorous globe within fragrant with rind,
Of a light yellow all perfumed they find ;
Then wreathed with flowers their sportive dances try,
Or couched the pipe to their sweet lips apply,

Or to their nostrils put the scarlet reed,
And with soft lullabies their fancies feed.
Some in gay parties with their lovers find,
In the deep groves the bright banana's rind,
And never doomed to labor's slow decay,
Shall these fair Typee maids wear out the day,
But like a band of spirits linked together,
Weave through the landscapes dances in fair weather.

In that sweet vale where Nature serves her lord,
The land is equal, sounds no Tyrant's word;
Upon the doors no padlocks shall you see,
The Warrior's spear stands out against the tree,
The maiden's brooch hangs careless from the roof,
The door is open, but the heart is proof.
There is no prison, neither fence nor road,
The land is but the man's desired abode,
What there is worth is freely shared by all,
No man is sad, and life a festival.
Within the forests ne'er the Lion's hum,
No wild beasts from the mountain-deserts come,
No snakes crawl hissing o'er the fruitful ground,
But sportive lizards golden-hued abound,

And purple-azure birds flit freely by,
Or crimson, white, and black, and gold come nigh,
Fly not at man's approach, and fear no harm,
Sometimes alight upon the extended arm,
But trill no reedy notes in those high woods,
Silent save roar of Falls those solitudes.

And in this happy vale the "Taboo" rites,
Cast a religious awe o'er many sites,
And feasts of Calabash are freely set,
In "Hoolah-Hoolah" grounds the men are met;
The delicate fair maids are all forbid
To enter there, and cannot be Priest-rid.

Ah! lovely vale, why art thou called that name,
The land of Cannibals, — did nature tame
Thy happy groups, and Paradise make thee
In some forgetful moment, savagely
Turning, and for her frolics bid thee eat
Her Happar children, yon the mountain's feet?

153

THE ICE RAVINE.

NEVER was the sight more gay,
Down the rapid water flows,
Deep the ravine's Rondelay,
Stealing up the silent snows.

Like an Organ's carved wood-work,
Richly waxed the Ice-tubes stand,
Hidden in them stops do lurk,
And I see the Master's hand.

Swift his fingers strike the keys,
Glittering all with rings of light,
Bubble's break and born with ease,
Sparkle constant, swift and bright.

Now upon the rocks, the roar
Of the Streamlet beats the bass,
Deeply murmuring through the floor
Of sparse snow and frozen grass.

Red as ruby wine the hue
Of the running Brook that brings,
Through the Ice-ravine this true
Music for the native kings.

Solemn stands the Ash-tree near,
Not one leaf upon his crown,
Still the Barberry, still the clear
Landscape of the meadows down.

Thus they listen every day,
Wind may roar and rain may run,
Clear or dull the Streamlet's play
Sounds that music, All in One.

155

THE BARREN MOORS.

On your bare rocks, O barren moors,
On your bare rocks I love to lie, —
They stand like crags upon the shores,
Or clouds upon a placid sky.

Across those spaces desolate,
The fox pursues his lonely way,
Those solitudes can fairly sate
The passage of my loneliest day.

Like desert Islands far at sea
Where not a ship can ever land,
Those dim uncertainties to me,
For something veritable stand.

A serious place distinct from all
Which busy Life delights to feel,
I stand in this deserted hall,
And thus the wounds of time conceal.

No friend's cold eye, or sad delay,
Shall vex me now where not a sound
Falls on the ear, and every day
Is soft as silence most profound.

No more upon these distant wolds
The agitating world can come,
A single pensive thought upholds
The arches of this dreamy home.

Within the sky above, one thought
Replies to you, O barren Moors,
Between, I stand, a creature taught
To stand between two silent floors.

WALDEN.

It is not far beyond the Village church,
After we pass the wood that skirts the road,
A Lake, — the blue-eyed Walden, that doth smile
Most tenderly upon its neighbor Pines,
And they as if to recompense this love,
In double beauty spread their branches forth.
This Lake had tranquil loveliness and breadth,
And of late years has added to its charms,
For one attracted to its pleasant edge,
Has built himself a little Hermitage,
Where with much piety he passes life.

More fitting place I cannot fancy now,
For such a man to let the line run off
The mortal reel, such patience hath the lake,
Such gratitude and cheer is in the Pines.

But more than either lake or forest's depths,
This man has in himself; a tranquil man,
With sunny sides where well the fruit is ripe,
Good front, and resolute bearing to this life,
And some serener virtues, which control
This rich exterior prudence, virtues high,
That in the principles of Things are set,
Great by their nature and consigned to him,
Who, like a faithful Merchant, does account
To God for what he spends, and in what way.
Thrice happy art thou, Walden! in thyself,
Such purity is in thy limpid springs;
In those green shores which do reflect in thee,
And in this man who dwells upon thy edge,
A holy man within a Hermitage.
May all good showers fall gently into thee,
May thy surrounding forests long be spared,
And may the Dweller on thy tranquil shores,
There lead a life of deep tranquillity
Pure as thy Waters, handsome as thy Shores
And with those virtues which are like the Stars.

159

OF KEATS.

'Tis said, a Keats by critics, once was killed,
Alas! they have lacked power to do this thing
In these late days, or else some blood was spilled,
They softly bite to-day, or kick and fling.

Let them pluck courage from the Bravo's knife,
And stick their victims in small streets by dark,
Or somehow skillfully cut out their life,
Do something that must pain them, but not bark.

And most of all let them kill Keats alway,
Or him that can be killed, as sure as steel,
For many Keats's creep about our day,
Who would not furnish Heroes half a meal.

Who writes by Fate the critics shall not kill,
Nor all the assassins in the great review,
Who writes by luck his blood some Hack shall spill,
Some Ghost whom a Musquito might run through.

Of Keats' poetry I have small taste,
But trust some Critics still are in the field,
Whose well-puffed Pills are not composed of paste,
Whose swords of lath with wisdom they do wield.

For me, I trust they will not spare one line,
Or else in frozen silence may abide,
Pray may they hack like butchers at all mine,
And kill me like that Keats if it betide.

Or if they courteous damn me with faint praise,
Let some old Hunter of the pack be set
To track me out, and fasten on my lays
His toothless gums, or let them all forget.

I ope my arms to them, — the world beside, —
O awful God! who over verse dost sway,
Thine eye does scan me, — in thy flowing tide,
I, like a leaf, am eddying whirled away.

Could but the faintest echo from my lyre,
Within Thy ear awake one choral thought,
I then had gained my earnest Heart's desire,
This battle then securely I had fought.

THE WOODMAN,

AND

OTHER POEMS.

BY

WILLIAM ELLERY CHANNING.

BOSTON:
JAMES MUNROE & COMPANY.

MDCCCXLIX.

BOSTON:
THURSTON, TORRY AND COMPANY,
31 Devonshire Street.

CONTENTS.

CONTENTS.

POEMS.

THE WOODMAN.

Deep in the forest stands he there,
His gleaming axe cuts crashing through,
While winter whistles in the air,
The oak's tough trunk, and flexile bough.

Upon his floor a leafy bed
Conceals the grass, and o'er his head
The leafless branches trimly rise,
The lattice of his painted skies.

Within the tree the circles are,
That years have drawn with patient art,
Against its life he maketh war,
And stills the beating of its heart.

The fibrous chips spin far and near,
A tangled net of twigs around,
The dry leaves whisper to his ear,
He stops to hear the cheering sound.

Nought but the drifting cloud o'erhead,
Nought but the stately pine afar,
A glaze o'er all the picture spread,
A medium that far suns prepare.

Above the wood the ravens call,
Their dusky murmurs fill the space,
And snow-birds toss above the wall,
And flickering shadows span the place.

In distant grove the fox-hound bays,
Where fainter strokes of axes beat,
And thin snow drives across the ways,
Untrampled by the Woodman's feet.

Beneath his axe the green moss grows,
Its cups stand stately on their stems,
Above the rock's divine repose,
With bright red in their diadems.

He must beware the dulling stone
Where drifts the snow, nor swerve his hand,
A hair shall make his axe atone,
For his mad carnage in the land.

Bravely he toils with patient blow,
While warmer grows the melting sun,
And damp the snow his feet below,
And from each twig bright jewels run.

The rough Pitch-pine with scaly stem
Crashes in thunder to the ground,
Its dark red mail is hid from him,
Till in the pile its worth be found.

The tough white Oak commands his eye,
He sees it in the saw-mill's power,
Its rustling leaves fern-colored fly,
Its winding limbs have met their hour.

When handsome noon fills out the day,
Behind the pile he stoops content,
And needs no fire, the sun's kind ray
Tempers the stinging element.

And opes the pail stored with corn-bread,
And frosty cake baked cheap with art,
And apples that last Autumn shed,
Like russet leaves from his good heart.

And then the snow-white bunting came,
To peck the crumbs that near him fell;
He did not give the bird a name,
He knew its pouting breast so well.

And single woodmen tramp the road,
Silent and staring, striding by,
For onward is their own abode,
There with the noon they hungry hie.

And when his robust treat is done,
He marks the hour by a true clock,
Glancing a moment at the sun,
His timepiece that shall never mock.

Then on the whetstone brights the steel
That polished enters easy in,
And cheered with his pinched, frosty meal,
The place reëchoes in his din.

And many a catch he sings with cheer,
And puts his soul into the work,
Such songs they should convince the ear,
That no regrets within him lurk.

Then piles the wood, in cords so high,
Thus the close trees are cut apart,
So grateful to the Woodman's eye,
The forest shade is in the mart.

'T is nearly eve, his taper gleams
Behind the horizontal pines,
That dark upon the setting beams
Draw shapely forms, in perfect lines.

And with a flood of amber light,
His candle sinks below the west,
Around the wood smiles still Good-night,
'T is time for home, 't is time for rest.

Thus shall he fare, nursed in the snow,
Child of the thaw, and son of frost, —
Who sweeps his floor he may not know,
A form his eye has never crost.

6 THE WOODMAN.

One blast each morn blows fresh and clean
Its greeting through the withered leaf;
His coldest day shows fair demean,
It pets him, and its stay is brief.

He cannot grieve for any hour,
His roof is painted so complete,
The gray tints of the sleety shower
Are soft, if savagely they beat.

The perfect trees that rise in air,
Composed, content they seem to him,
There 's nought but pleasure everywhere,
His cup is always at the brim.

Within the marsh, the muskrat gnaws
Sweet flag-root at his piquant meals,
And where the sly fox touched his paws,
The tell-tale snow his track reveals.

And all things press to him as one,
All times salute him as a day,
'T is nought with him save sun to sun,
Life is a short and skilful play.

His house is 'neath a pine at night,
A nest beyond the next stone wall,
The sky his roof so true and tight,
The ground hard timber for his hall.

The stone his chair, the cushions moss,
With lichens varnished neat and fine,
His flagon is a spring, its boss
Some twisting bramble-thorn and vine.

His opera plays a full-keyed wind,
That brushes spray-shower from the leaves,
His waltzes in the shadow find,
That every twig and leaflet weaves.

His picture is continual change,
The lights and shadows shifting fly,
His eye shall simply shift its range,
The landscape changes for his eye.

His glassy temple carved the ice,
Where with the brook the ravine runs,
There obelisks and porches rise,
Pagodas, palaces, by tons.

If a dead branch trail down the stream,
A white pavilion builds the linn,
That juts o'er mirrored walls, that seem
So clear that you could pass therein.

If a spent rail bridges the brook,
Along its length thick columns stand,
Their bases bright as silver look,
So polished by the cold stream's hand.

They rise propped on a silver stone,
Thin as a crystal bubble's robe,
And silver shields spread out alone,
Serrated fine, a lustrous globe.

And lower down white temples rise
Of alabaster free from scar,
The Woodman rubs his puzzled eyes,
And thinks his cities wondrous are.

An ashen swamp his banquet room,
Hung with an alder tap'stry fine,
Where chocolate globes paint red the gloom,
And cupped spiræas' branches twine.

And light-gray mossy rocks peep up,
Specked with the steel-black lichen smooth,
Where tufted plumes wave moroon cup,
Marsh-feather is the name forsooth.

And rugged trees hedge in the space,
Their outline costly oaks confuse,
Behind the beechen forests lace,
Here sits the wight, and spells the news.

Then whirls the powdery snow-storm down,
And pitch-pines go for chandeliers,
And powder-puffs the birches crown,
And stones are alabaster tears.

The bold north wind his cannon fires
Sweeping the pine, the smoke flies fast;
They shake the pointed, twinkling spires,
While o'er the field ploughs the cold blast.

TO JULIA.

I.

I AM not dumb,
When to thee I come;
'T is only that thine eye,
Puts out my reply.

A chosen word,
My tongue could thee afford,
Were not thy ear,
Too beautiful to hear!

In thy warm, hazel eye,
Some deeper colors lie,
Than I have felt elsewhere,
In sky, or sea, or air.

In that persuasive mouth,
Still heaps the south
Its orange-bloom,
And makes the lip perfume.

Thy cheek whose tint is soft
May gently float aloft,
There, for angelic shows
Paint its smooth, peachen rose.

And if a seraph dare,
To steal thy raven hair,
To ornament his plume,
It darkened that high room.

Why wilt thou on me smile,
From a divine profile,
And in thy easy chair,
Show so much beauty there ?

Or wilt thou dream that I,
Can look in that dark eye,
And no kind feeling share,
With that which is so rare ?

TO JULIA.

No love between us goes,
Thou art an unplucked rose,
And yet thy rich perfume,
Hangs sweetly in the room.

If thorny is the hedge,
I stand on its bright edge,
And plums and cherries see,
And peaches not for me.

The grape I cannot steal,
Nor the ripe pear conceal,
But still my eye can see,
The richness of the tree.

Who eats sweet fruit is cloyed,
And 't is bliss unalloyed,
To trace the beauty there,
Through the soft, golden air.

II.

I worshipped at the shrine,
I brought the fruit and wine,

Milk and rich olives spread,
And wreaths for thy dear head.

I might have worshipped there,
Until my youthful hair
Had turned to silver gray,
And come my latest day.

What is a goddess worth,
If she smile not henceforth,
And if the worshipper
Has no return from her?

Thine eye might be as sweet,
As the soft hues that meet
Within the sunny brook,
Yet never on me look.

And honied be thy mouth,
As the unvaried south,
But if thou breath'st not here,
A winter I must fear.

I should have soothed thy heart,
Thou wouldst have felt the smart

Of love, as sweet as pleasure,
That flows from other measure.

We might have ended pain,
And filed away the chain
Of dullness and the world,
Love's silken flag unfurled.

Thy cheek had been as smooth,
After my kisses sooth
Had stirred some blushes there,
Amid the peachen air?

SONG.

Who would go roving
  Far from his love,
Banish his loving,
  Wearily move?
Give me the heart that is mine for to-day,
To-morrow I care not what life takes away!

Give me the smiling
  Eyes of my heart,
The sorrow-exiling
  Sweets of love's art;
Give me the joys that are mine for to-day,
To-morrow I care not what life takes away!

16 SONG.

Turn from me never,
Friend of my soul,
And the hopes sever,
In thy control;
Then may I move o'er the land and the sea,
Still dreaming so fondly of love and of thee!

Speak to me kindly,
While I remain,
Gaze on me mildly,
Ease me of pain;
Then shall be joy, and to part without sorrow,
Remembering thy mercy on the lone morrow!

TO LYRA.

So warm an air I ne'er have felt,
As breathed from thee upon my heart,
When near thy golden shrine I knelt,
Child of the summer! Nature's art!

Thy radiant smile seemed more to me,
Than music from a well-toned lyre,
Thine eye as gentle as the sea,
When soft afar day's beams expire.

Why should I breast the shining foam,
And weary the wild wave pursue,
If Beauty light the path at home,
Near thee, as fresh as morning dew?

18 **TO LYRA.**

What were the Indian gems if thou
Art brilliant as the sapphire's glow,
Or frozen Alps all blanched as now,
With their perpetual crown of snow?

If cold thine eye upon me fall,
And motionless thy brimming heart,
Thou 'rt nothing to me, and art all,
Child of the summer! Nature's art!

Some shadowy years may fold o'er thee,
Far in the dark-veiled future's hand,
And tears bedim the smiling eye,
And fruitless vows the heart command.

And life that is a weary thing,
May twine a wreath of care for thee,
And sin, and time, and sorrowing,
O'er the smooth brow trace their decree.

Thus on my thought the line is traced,
Thus sin, and time, and woe have done,
Yet in thy beauty are effaced,
As night is lifted by the sun.

TO LYRA.

Cold is the heart if Beauty's power
May wake no murmur in its tone,
That feels no more the early hour,
When first the sun of Beauty shone.

We met, — to part, few words to speak,
The hour by fate's chill poison sped,
My pathway leads o'er snow and bleak,
Thine, where the blushing roses shed

A richer glow than day's last smile,
A purer light than morn's first beam,
My heart is but a rock-girt isle,
Thine, like the gently gliding stream.

Then, fare thee well! speed joyous far,
Then, fare thee well! my queenly child,
Like Lyra, or the evening star
That o'er the meadow shines so mild.

OLD SUDBURY INN.

Who set the oaks
Along the road?
Was it not nature's hand,
Old Sudbury Inn! where I have stood
And wondered at the sight,
The oaks my delight?

And the elms,
All boldly branching to the sky,
And the interminable forests,
Old Sudbury Inn! that wash thee nigh
On every side,
With a green and rustling tide:

The oaks and elms,
And the surrounding woods,
And Nobscot rude,
Old Sudbury Inn! creature of moods,
That I could find
Well suited to the custom of my mind.

Most homely seat!
Where nature eats her frugal meals,
And studies to outwit,
Old Sudbury Inn! that thy inside reveals,
Long mayst thou be,
More than a match for her and me.

THE SUNSET LAKES.

The day had been a day of partial storm,
For the gray mist was drifting from the sea,
And o'er the moorland hung a heavy veil,—
A day of storm, yet fell no rain. I stood
Near sunset on the upland sere, and marked
A still, blue lake, far reaching to the east,
Skirted by woodlands deep, and nigh one house,
So placed, that he who dwelt there may have been
A lover of the field, and of the wood.
And while the dark mist drifted from the sea,
There flushed a sudden gleam of sunlight warm
Out of the west, at which the blue lake smiled,
And nature seemed inwardly glad. The scene
O'ertook me with a pleased surprise,—I stood

Wondering at the wild beauty, like that man
Who lost within the forest, from some hill
At evening sees his home afar, and shouts.
Then westward moving, I stood suddenly
Upon the curve of a clear lake, where no eye
Had fancied it, dropped in a hidden dell,
Embosomed in bright copses and dark pines,
And one low cottage on the swelling shore,
Its pleasing lines drawn clear against the sky,
A little rustic dwelling near the lake.

Glad in this new-found wealth, I sought the way,
Yet facing westward on the dusky moor,
Where solitude was native to the air.
And in a moment, further on, I came,
Not dreaming of these waters in that place,
Upon the bank of a round mirror, framed
In the brown hills. There, stretched on the crisp moss,
And more than joyous for the charming scene,
I thanked good Nature for the generous skill
By which she multiplied my happiness,
Made me three lakes, thrice to rejoice my eyes,

The careless eyes that slowly seek the good.
And as I mused, upon the yielding moss,
A flashing beam of day's last glory fell
In unexpected splendor, through the gloom,
Slanting across the silent, lonely hills,
Until the place seemed social in this fire.
Then rising, with a love for the wild spot,
I hastened westward, as the day grew faint,
And climbing a low hill, stretched at my feet
A gray and dimpled lake lay in the shade;
A shapely basin rounded in soft curves,
Whose little lines of beach betray the waves,
That with a lapsing murmur touch the sand,
And loftier shores, with rain-swept grooves of soil,
And pleasant headlands crested by green trees,
And longer reaches pictured with proud woods.

Upon the steepest bank was reared a house,
Where sign of life or occupant was none,
Not e'en a barking dog or lowing cow,—
A tall and narrow structure on the sky.
Now had there been true feeling in my eyes

For nature's pure enchantment, — had I seen
Intelligently what her forms express,
And had my heart been loving as it should,
Touched by the concords of the sunset hour,
I might have made a hymn, and sung it there.

ON LEAVING ROME.

There is an end to all we know,
A swift Good-bye to all we have;
Beyond the present thing we go,
No sovereign hand can hold or save.

Still echoes in my ear thy voice,
Majestic city of the Past!
And bids my doubting heart rejoice,
As now I quit thee speeding fast.

Whirled down the dark blue gulfs I float,
Toy of relentless Ocean's tide,
And brave the surging empire's note,
And bridge the emerald mountain's pride.

And I would seek the rolling war,
Nor fear, and with the wave contest,
To touch again the things that are
So softly folded o'er thy breast.

The airy arches tinted soft,
The moonlit fountain trilling clear,
The beauty of the landscape oft,
Thy pictures, and thy art so dear.

I sought thee not a traveller vain,
My heart was neither glad nor gay,
My life had proved a life of pain,
The flowers I love had bent away.

Few friendly voices cheered me on,
Few dear caresses went with me;
Alone I loved thee, I have won
A present happiness from thee.

The truth that I had felt before,
I now can paint with clearer eye,
And that I did not reach, the more
Comes near me, and the reason why.

28 ON LEAVING ROME.

My native land, the proud and strong,
Stands stronger matched with thy decline,
I learn from thee that hate is wrong,
And loving-kindness most divine.

To Rome, farewell! that faltering word,
Dear name! — so far thou art to me
The sweetest sound I ever heard,
Save the brave cry of liberty.

QUARLES.

Dry as a July drouth,
And a simoon from the south,
Art thou, Sahara Quarles!
I love thee not;
Blaze 'neath the pot,
'T is the best thing that I can do for thee,
To make thee accelerate cookery.

Dusty and dry,
Thou wouldst the eyeball of a saint defy;
Thy emblems seem
A staircase in a choking dream,
Yet Herbert said,
Thy chip had his provoking hunger stayed.

HERRICK.

I READ in Herrick's verses,
I could see
The spirit of each tree,
Each quality that he rehearses,
Bodily.

I saw bright Herrick's flowers,
With which he binds the hours;
His rural fare,
A ripe and russet literature,
And sweet as nuts his songs to Larr,
And of himself rich lines a store.

When a pure wit he lauds,
'T is in such sense,
That no pretence
Of being less the verse affords;
Herrick is good as best,
And has the fact confest.

Then, Herrick, from thy blood
I draw some fire;
Better my desire,
And be my muse as good
As thine,
Who came of race divine.

DONNE.

Scholastic Donne!
Acme of self-conceit,
The Phaeton of Poets! one
To whom distinct concern was counterfeit,
At first thy song made me feel sick at heart,
Plaited with not a line of Goethe's art.

Perplexing Donne!
The enemy of a strait road,
To whom the honest sun
Must have as a traitor showed,
I learned to love thee soon,
Pleased with the subtle tune.

Heady yet wise!
As far as thy blind scrannel goes
Not to be imitated,
Searching, with thy deep eyes,
Thoughts that by no one have been said
Except thyself; the dies
For thy rich coin no later Muse bestows.

TO ROSALIE

Girl, so beautiful,
And sweet, I dare not love;
Girl, so dutiful,
That my heart will move
With a pure delight,
A tranquil worship, at the sight:

As a dewy rose-leaf falling
Loosely in the summer wind,
Or the twilight fancies calling
Far the buried sun behind,

Or on high a vesper bell
Softly tolling day declining,
In the mountains sounding well
Answer to a heart repining,
Or a sigh of the wind-harp's tongue,
By a silken zephyr rung.

As thy liquid eye
Sent a still reply,
As thy rosy mouth
Painted the warm south,
As the beauty flowed o'er me,
Noble maiden, born with thee,
Only could I wonder long,
For it frame this feeble song.

I might love when passion dances
In the dark, entrancing eye,
Answering to my dim glances,
Answering — I know not why,
But the lovely, simple Child,
Figure holy, spirit mild,

That angelic Rosalie
Without the least thought of me,
I could not love,
For her heart I ne'er might move.

Then I knelt before her beauty,
And I woke from idle longing,
Made it my most chosen duty
To this child to love belonging,
Her to lead in wood and dell,
Where the streams conceal their spell
In the breathless solitude,
And the leaning Silence nods
O'er the old, complacent wood,
Seat of unpretending gods,
And where'er the secret bird
With her melody is heard.

Be the weather cool or warm,
May it soothe her like a charm,
With its blossom spring enfold her,
With blushing flowers summer mould her,

With ripe fruit may autumn bless her,
With brave cheer white winter dress her;
And more, may I
Resist the force of every tie,
And on this spotless errand bent,
With a duty abstinent,
Vow to her the steadfast heart,
Silent tongue and sleepless thought,
Vow to her the spoils of art,
And the gold the mind has brought
From her rivers in the Reason,
To regild the faded season;
Vow them all,
And her my mistress call,
Whom to love were hopeless folly,
Maiden mild, and pure, and holy,
Whom to love ne'er was for me,
But to worship sacredly.

THE BOLD BARON

Spring to your horses,
My merry men all, —
So shouted the Baron,
Across the old hall, —
Away with a cheer
O'er the mountain and meer,
For the hart is aroused
From his bed in the heather,
And long has caroused
In the sweet Spring weather. —

Then hearing the Lord,
Twenty men took their bows,
And tossed on their caps,
And their quivers of arrows,

And in dresses of green,
They to horse all have sped,
And away they have rid,
Down the steep thundered,
And waked the wild deer,
From his couch that was near,
And him coursing have gone,
By the light of the moon.

But Alice was left
By the window alone,
Of her slumber bereft,
And gaily bestrown
With sweet thought that bright morn,
Looking out on the vale,
Far away o'er the corn,
And the lake where one sail,
Was tipped by the light of day,
That shot o'er the mountain,
And fleet ran along,
To river and fountain,
And the covert bird's song.

Young Alice was beautiful,
Wondrous and fair,
Hazel rich were her eyes,
And rich brown was her hair,
And her form was a sight
To adorn every dream,
In her lover's brief night,
And her soft, lovely eyebeam
Was a spell of such power,
That it filled every hour,
With a light of its own,
And a fanciful tone.

Where, where is my lover! —
Thus the sweet Alice sung,
And where has he rid
The bold hunters among?
Is he chasing the deer,
O'er mountain and meer,
Or sits he alone,
In his proud father's hall,
And ponders his book,
Or leans o'er the wall?

Come Clarence, come now,
In my ear breathe thy vow!

On my cheek may thy lip
Seal the first kisses there,
As deep in my heart,
Thy dear form I may wear;
They all to the chase,
On the fleet coursers race.

Not one is left here,
Save old nurse who well knows
The love of my Clarence,
And shares my dear woes! —
When into the window,
Beyond where Alice leaned,
There sprang in a youth,
By the broad shadow screened.
His arm round her waist,
Her rich beauty embraced,
And her lips to his own,
Were pressed in a swoon.

Her cheeks dyed with blushes,
Were than roses more red,
And her heart beat like flushes
The thunderstorms shed,
And still to the youth she clung,
Who sweetly thus sung:

Dear Alice! my Alice!
My own lovely child,
I have heard thy low words,
Thou bride undefiled,
And below is my steed
Who is fleet for the war,
But can carry at need,
A lady full far,
And below on the lake,
Is my boat with her sail,
And the wind shall us take
Till the four towers fail,
Of the castle so old,
Kept by the Baron so bold.

O my father! said Alice,
But my father has gone; —
'T is the thing that I love! —
And he pressed her cheek long,
Thy father has sped
To the chase of the deer,
There is nothing to dread,
There is nothing to fear,
Then come, haste away,
And be quick, wastes the day.

O my father! said Alice,
But my father is kind! —
Fear not, said the youth,
He shall be of our mind,
Fear not, I shall come
To the castle again,
And bring my Alice home,
And fill the old keep with men,
And the Baron so bold,
Shall laugh when he sees

My prowess and courage,
And fire flash from his eyes. —

Then dim the mist gathered
Along the low shore,
In a phantom all gray,
And the wind sighing o'er,
Made the castle to echo,
And the shrubs at its base
All mournfully rustled
Along the brown space,
And the Nurse from her room,
Beneath the fond pair,
Cried, — the hunters are coming,
My Alice! take care! —

And the thundering crash,
Of their hoofs on the stone,
Whirled up the steep ascent,
And the court-yard forlorn,
Thou wilt fly! Alice cried,

'T is my father's wild band,
Fly, fly, for thy life!
And whither? — his hand
On her shoulder is placed,
And they two are now bound;
Down the steep castle-side,
They had slid to the ground,
When the Baron so bold
In the arch of the tower,
Looked out from his hold,
At that merciless hour;
The youth with his prize,
Had just lit on the earth, —
Shoot, shoot! said the Baron,
Touch not child of my birth,
But kill me this thief,
Who would rob me so brief!

Four bows bent amain,
And four arrows off sped,
But touch not the twain
With the copse overhead,

Nor touch the proud courser,
Whose silken rein shook,
Not a whit in his hand
As the youth up it took,
Then dashed in his spurs,
O'er the heath, o'er the moors,
And away they have flown,
For a second alone.

Out! saddle your steeds!
Said the Baron so bold, —
Ride, ride, for your lives,
Strike that knave, ne'er be told
That we missed him this time,
If the chase be not prime. —

They sprang to their horses,
With might and with main
They drave like the lightning,
After the twain,
But the fleet-footed courser
Was steady and far,

Their deer had been chased,
And that morning their war,
Yet they lagged not behind,
And swept on like the wind,
The Baron 'fore all,
With plumed figure so tall.

Down fell horse after horse,
Until three only were left,
And two more than the Baron,
Near the shore's sandy cleft,
And they saw as they ran,
The white sail shake and fill,
And across the vexed water,
As they plunged down the hill
To the desolate beach,
Did the little bark reach.

And the Baron was frantic,
And maddened alone,
For the rest drooped behind,
And his arrow has flown ;

It strikes in the breast
Of the sweet Alice then,
And the Baron falls helpless,
A corse for his men.

Alas! for the day! —
Sang the Nurse when they came,
With the bold Baron home,
And they told her the game,
How the arrow had sped,
And the boat had sailed on,
Alas! for the day,
And our Lord who is gone.

And woe for the day!
For our Alice so sweet
And her Clarence so true,
And the courser so fleet;
Ye tell me that Alice died not
In her pride,
And the lover drew out,

The red shaft from his bride;
Alas! in her heart, the arrow is left,
And her father is dead,
Of all pity bereft!

TO ——, THREE YEARS OLD.

A LITTLE boy,
To be his parent's joy,
A tender three year old,
Close in a shapely fold.
Whose trusty eye,
Draws a great circle of new sky!

His eye is blue,
As loved Italia's heaven,
Or the mid-ocean hue,
And Mediterranean even,
Or the bright petal of a star-shaped flower,
Autumnal Aster, or the Gentian's dower,
Or the just god's cerulean hall,—
How shone this eye o'er us at all?

How smiled its birth,
O'er trifling Concord earth;
How is it here,
Shining blue above the bier
Of the dead autumn flower,
And in my November hour?

Thou little boy,
To be thy parent's joy!
Thou angel sent,
Angel eloquent,
To drill the close-grained moment,
How gaze our wondering eyes at thee;
One, whom the god has anchored
In a bare plain, from the clear sea
Of his creative pleasure,
Moored thee to measure
The fathoms of the sense,
In the hard present tense!

Child of the good divinity,
Child of one,

Who shines on me
Like a most friendly sun;
Child of the azure sky,
Who has outdone it in that eye,
That trellised window in unfathomed blue,
Child of the midworld sweet and true,
Child of the combing, crystal spheres,
Throned above this salt pool of tears,
Child of immortality!
Why hast thou come to cheat the Destiny?

By the sweet mouth,
Half parted in a smile,
And the fat cheek,
And upright figure,
And thy creamy voice so meek;
By all thou art,
By the pat beating of thy criss-cross heart,
How couldst thou light on this plain, homespun shore,
And not upon thy own aerial riding,
Fall down on earth where turbid sadly pour,
The old perpetual rivers of backsliding?

Since thou art fast
In our autumnal ball,
Of thistle and specked grass weave thee a nest;
Renounce if possible the mighty air-spanned Hall
Cups of imperial nectar,
Vases of transparent porphyry,
Amethystine rings of splendor,
Bright footstools of chalcedony!
The alabaster bed,
Where in the plume of Seraph sunk thy head,
To the full sounding organ of the sphere,
By the smooth, hyaline finger of thy peer,
So amorously played!

Catch the sack, examine it!
Here are prickly chestnuts
That tinkle when they fall,
And the meat of oily walnuts,
And a pitch-pine tall
In his scaly cone,
And a terrace with alders sown,
Along the fleet brook's grassy side,
Little child! down this, thou mayst glide.

In the sack 's an oaken chip,
Be thy skiff no more,
Sedge-grass for thy whip,
And a fountain for the roar
Of the brazen chariot-wheel,
Buzzing at thy pinkish heel.

Fix a blue jay's scream
For the whistle of thy car,
Hear no costlier music in thy dream,
Than the tap of the hard-billed woodpecker,
And suck ambrosia from tipped columbine,
And out the red fox-grape crush a tart wine.

Be those blue eyes,
Thy only atmosphere,
For in them lies,
What is than earth, than Heaven more dear!

THE FISHER-BOAT.

ALL day the cobble dashed,
All day the water splashed
Along her sides;
The wind rose high,
Said Alfred, I can spy
That we must have high tides.

See, father, how the Crested rock,
Proudly flings off the shock
Of hurrying seas,
And yet its height,
Should ere the night,
Be dry beneath the breeze. —

Old Peter shook his head,
And soberly to Alfred said, —
My boy let's take our chance,
And throw the lines,
And let the signs
Of wind and wave go dance. —

So Alfred threw
His sealine in the blue
And rolling wave;
The cobble spun,
The boiling crests among,
And faced the billows brave.

— My hands are cold, —
At last said Peter old, —
Alfred, my boy,
The day must soon be done,
And soon will set the sun,
Then heave-a-hoy. —

Heave-o, heave-o,
The cobble's anchor rises-o,
She whirls away;
The dashing oar,
Dips more and more,
Among the shadows of the day.

Let 's make some sail! —
Cried Alfred pale
With the moon's first beam; —
The wind 's so high,
Our boat will fly,
Like spirits through a dream. —

Haul up! my lad, —
Said Peter glad,
The sail flew out,
Then dashed against
The mast. — All saints!
Defend us! — said Peter stout.

Then bellying full,
A sudden lull,
Rested them on the foam
Of a high crest;
They saw afar their nest,
And the red light of home.

From chimney top,
The smoke stole up,
As Mary by the fire,
Stood frying neat
Some flounders sweet,
Joe had just speared for her.

— When will they make
The beach, and break
Across the ugly surf?
Said Mary dear,
To Peggy near,
The heaped-up fire of turf.

And Peggy's heart,
From Mary's caught
Half of a mete of woe,—
My Alfred come,—
Cried Peggy,—home,—
Mary, how the wind does blow!—

The little house,
Rocked in the rouse,
And the one window creaked,
A cold, still moon,
Far up looked down,
And into it half-peaked.

'T is cold,—said Mary,—
As January,
A bitter mad October,
My stars! that blast
I hope the last,
And that they both are sober.—

Meantime the boat,
Sped like a shot,
From some deep cannon's mouth ;
The spray flew in,
Amid the din,
There ne'er was such a drouth.

Keep her head strait, —
Said Peter, great
Amid the frantic pother ; —
Run her across,
The Devil's horse,
And nothing can her bother. —

The rudder creaked,
The water leaked,
Fast through the surf she flew,
And high she 's beached,
And Peter dashed
Upon the sand below.

The old man lay,
Drenched in the spray,
And Alfred lifted him
Across his back,
And took the track,
To the low cottage dim.

And reached the door,
As Peter o'er,
His trance had fairly come, —
Cried Mary, — See!
Peter! what's happed to thee? —
Why wife, I have got home!

And Alfred laughed,
And Peter quaffed
Some spirit from the can,
And Peggy saw
What it was for,
And Alfred felt a man.

I guess, — said Alfred,
Father had been dead,
If I had not brought off
His shattered body,
To his glass of toddy,
And *was* buried half. —

And so they ate,
A supper late,
And still the gale blew strong,
But the red fire,
And the mug higher,
Circled with song.

This is a storm, —
Cried Peter warm, —
But we have had our day;
Alfred my boy,
I give you joy,
That we sailed safe away.

SONG.—TO-DAY.

In the old time,
Listening to the chime
Of the melodious world,
Before despair
Darkened the air,
And woe his flag unfurled.

In the old days,
When life was crowned with bays,
And pleasure's glass went round,
Or we thought it did,
Not heeding what was hid,
In the sweets profound.—

In the Future's hand,
In the promised land,
Fair hopes are building
Palaces and towers,
And gay reception-hours,
Bright with beauty's gilding!

In the coming dream,
How glitters every stream,
Singing a low song
Down the clove of the mountain,
And sparkling in the fountain,
The shady valleys among.

But better is To-day!
Than all the fine things say,
To-day! is a dusty hero rough,
And his muscles are firm,
And his heavy arm,
Is both fit to strike and tough.

He has no couch of pleasure,
But war's sternest measure,
Is that he best shall know;
He is a bold man,
And the chief of a bold clan,
No bolder or stronger rules below.

He would not be dashed,
If his sparing armor clashed
With the rapier of a ghost,
And his hearty cheer,
A battle may safely dare,
Even with a mighty host.

Then let us all be bold,
And grow not ever old,
But strike through thick and thin,
And conquer if we can,
And if not support the man,
With at least brave hope to win.

THE XEBEC.

A soft wind rose, the Xebec sailed, —
She left the sunny port with glee,
Her lateen sail how gently failed,
Far o'er the laughing, azure sea.

No more the high brown shore in view,
The white Sierra coldly grand,
But stretched around its sparkling hue,
A wave that never washed the land.

The Xebec was a sharp, swift boat,
Her polished side was black as night,
Well did she trim, and gaily float
Like sea-bird o'er the water light.

Four sailors bold her crew compose,
And one fair youth who tempers these,
The swarthy men who feared no foes,
The rovers of the rolling seas.

And noon came on, the sailors slept,
The youth his watch kept in the stern,
When a levanter softly crept,
Poured from the desert's Arab urn.

Then freshened on so merrily
The Xebec leapt along the foam,
And left a long wake on the sea,
And parted further from her home.

And freshened on the fiery breeze,
Until the blue wave curled in air,
And fast they flew along the seas,
And gay they felt no further care.

Then clearer grew the sky all o'er,
And bolder blew the steady wind,
And now the Xebec plunged the more,
Whirling the eddies far behind.—

Haul fast the sheet ! — the crew obey,
The bending mast hung o'er the waves,
And brighter shone the dazzling day,
And louder, louder the wind raves.

She strains and pulls, the rudder creaks,
They tack the sail, and on she drives,
While in her bottom start the leaks, —
They run a race, — 't is for their lives.

Take in the sail ! — in vain they try,
It splits, and surges off the mast,
Along they plunge 'twixt sea and sky,
And driving onward, — onward fast.

One moment in the deep blue wave,
The next upon the topmast spray,
The winds weave riband as they rave,
Long lines of foam that glide away.

Then sweeping o'er the Xebec's side,
A monster wave pours crashing in,
No bark could brave the sea's blue tide,
Spares not the crew the rolling din.

The Xebec tosses on the sea,
A battered wreck to sail no more,
And still the youth how wearily
Dreams of a warm and sunny shore.

He sleeps how softly on the tide,
The Xebec drives upon the beach,
The youth dreams silent on the wide,
Cold couches of the sandy reach.

He wakes! — and in a fruitful isle,
Dark groves vine-covered steal his eye,
Ripely the waving harvests smile,
And perfumed breezes gently sigh.

He sees the Xebec's broken shape,
And stepping slowly seeks the field,
From loaded vine he plucks the grape,
Beneath, clear springs cool water yield.

If it was Home! — he sadly says, —
Alas! my vessel ne'er shall sail,
With the green isle must end my days,
Could I not perish in the gale?

And fell his tears in showers to earth,
Where proudly ruined temples stand,—
Why was I noble in my birth,
Alas! this is not my own land!

THE MAGIC CASTLE.

Wind the horn, —
Said the Forester bold,
Blast the bugle,
The night falls cold,
Pathway shimmers,
Fire-fly glimmers,
How the gude-wifes will us scold.

Then blew a blast,
Those hundred foresters
Upon a hundred shining horns,
The old wood stirs,
The trees in motion,
Rise and fall like an ocean,
Organs were the ghostly firs.

Blast again,
My hunters strong! —
Cried the hardy Forester,
They blew a blast more loud and long,
The dogs did clamor,
And in a second,
As they ne'er reckoned,
Uprose a castle there.

Lofty sprang the ivied walls,
Blazing shone the handsome halls,
Open stood the doors and wide, —
My hunters bold! — thus cried
The jolly Forester,
Welcome the lordly cheer.

Spur every one his horse,
On rushing dogs and men,
Wind clear your shining bugles,
Spur and dash ye then,
Within the open gate,
And banquet in that state. —

Then like a whirling sea,
The fiery cavalcade,
Poured through the courteous gate,
And the coursers played
A merry march,
By the sculptured tower and arch,
And when the last was gone,
Close together the gates swung.

Of all this host,
But one was left behind,
He was a feeble Minstrel,
With some verses in his mind;
On foot he weary was,
Nor sped with their light horse.

He saw the splendid hall,
Fade like a dream in air,
No more of man, of horse, or hound,
And in a strange despair,
He sung the halting verse,
Which we may now rehearse.—

Where have vanished horse and hound,—
Thus the Minstrel sang,
Hunters flying o'er the ground,
And the gates that clang,
While I linger sighing here,
In the misty evening air.

No lady's eyes,
No sweet girl's flatteries,
Nor learning's pride,
Nor riches, nor the tide
Of fortune carries me,
Whither the hunter's destiny.

I saw the gates together fall,
The building rise in air,
And chill the night creeps slowly down,
And the star is gleaming fair,
And my heart is cold,—
O for the life of a hunter bold!

WALDEN SPRING.

Whisper ye leaves your lyrics in my ear,
Carol thou glittering bird thy summer song,
And flowers, and grass, and mosses on the rocks,
And the full woods, lead me in sober aisles,
And may I seek this happy day the Cliffs,
When fluid summer melts all ores in one,
Both in the air, the water, and the ground.
And so I walked beyond the last, gray house,
And o'er the upland glanced, and down the mead,
Then turning went into the oaken copse,—
Heroic underwoods that take the air
With freedom, nor respect their parent's death.
Yet a few steps, then welled a cryptic spring,
Whose temperate nectar palls not on the taste,

Dancing in yellow circles on the sand,
And carving through the ooze a crystal bowl.
Here sometime have I drank a bumper rare,
Wetting parched lips, from a sleek, emerald leaf,
Nursed at the fountain's breast, and neatly filled
The forest-cup, filled by a woodland hand,
That from familiar things draws sudden use,
Strange to the civic eye, to Walden plain.
And resting there after my thirst was quenched,
Beneath the curtain of a civil oak,
That muses near this water and the sky,
I tried some names with which to grave this fount.
And as I dreamed of these, I marked the roof,
Then newly built above the placid spring,
Resting upon some awkward masonry.
In truth our village has become a butt
For one of these fleet railroad shafts, and o'er
Our peaceful plain, its soothing sound is — Concord,
Four times and more each day a rumbling train
Of painted cars rolls on the iron road,
Prefigured in its advent by sharp screams
That Pandemonium satisfied should hear.

The steaming tug athirst, and lacking drink,
The railroad eye direct with fatal stroke
Smote the spring's covert, and by leaden drain
Thieved its cold crystal for the engine's breast.
Strange! that the playful current from the woods,
Should drag the freighted train, chatting with fire,
And point the tarnished rail with man and trade.

INDIAN BALLAD.

GIVE me my bow,
Said the Leaping Deer,
And my arrows sharp,
With their feathered cheer.

Then, the Graceful Fawn
Who sat in the tent
Of the bison's skin,
Felt half sad and faint.

But she handed him
The long strong bow,
And the poisoned arrows,
She handed too.

And the dark papoose,
From his panther-skin
Rolled o'er on the floor,
And laughed with a din.

They called his name,
The Star of the East,
So mellow he was,
And so gay in the feast.

And give me my moccasin,
Said the Leaping Deer,
For I must to the brake,
With my feathered cheer.

Low was the sun,
When the Graceful Fawn
Looked forth from the tent,
From her soft boiled corn.

Bright was the morn,
But the Leaping Deer
Came not to the tent,
And they 'gan to have fear.

She asked of the Wise,
Why the warrior stayed,
And she asked the old squaw,
And the bright-eyed maid.

And the warriors strong,
Now girded them up,
And each took his bow,
And his arrow so sharp.

Twenty and tall,
Were those warriors red,
Painted and plumed,
Was each haughty head.

And they sung a hoarse song,
As they tramped to the wood,
Beyond the last lodge,
To the green solitude.

O where is our brother,
The swift Leaping Deer,
And where has he fled,
With his arrowy cheer?

Has he sunk in the marsh,
Where the dog-wood is wet,
Has he buried himself
In the panther's net?

Has he fallen in fight,
With the Raven our foe?
Let us seek him till night,
Where'er we may go. —

And he lay in the mouth
Of an old panther's den,
Two cubs dead beside him,
A prize for ten men!

He was torn by the claws,
Of the mother so cross,
And jagged and marked,
Like a heart with remorse.

Then the warriors tall,
From the pine made a bed,
And they bore him along,
Thus torn and thus dead.

Till they reached the low lodge
Where the Graceful Fawn sat,
With the Star of the East,
Upon a hard mat.

The warriors haughty,
Tramped silently on,
And there they paused once,
And with slow step have gone.

She heard their shells rattle,
And saw their furs shake,
As they marched slowly by,
And no word ever spake.

She saw on the litter,
The torn Leaping Deer,
And no tear stained her eye,
She came not more near.

But still to her breast,
The Star of the East,
She held closely and firm.
As she had in the feast.

The old squaws they came,
And surrounded the bier,
Where near sat the Fawn,
By the still Leaping Deer.

They spake to her slowly,
No word did she say,
They touched her cold arm,
Where the dark papoose lay:

Cold as the stone,
Where the spring-water falls,
Her tongue was all silent,
And fixed her eyeballs.

Then this song sung the women,
As the sun painted the east,
Our sister is gone,
And our brother has rest.

To the land of the Spirit,
Flown the sweet Graceful Fawn,
There too is the Leaping Deer,
Both in the red morn.

And the boy shall be ours,
And the tribe shall him make,
A terrible hunter,
For the mountain and brake!

MAID MARIAN AND THE PAGE.

RUN, said Maid Marian,
Run, to the Page,
Hie thee o'er meadow,
And plume thee in rage,
And let thy light heart,
With sorrow split apart!

False fool that thou wert,
To make love so to me,
And claim my soft kisses,
And hope in my eye,
A Page and a boy,
Can ne'er give a maid joy. —

Then the Page spake so cheerly, —
My mistress so fine!
Thou lovest me dearly,
I truly divine,
When thou say'st thou dost need,
A man at thy heed.

And my lovely Marian!
Wilt thou believe,
That I am a man,
And I do not deceive?
How thy cheek is deep red,
And thy lip as it bled!

THE BLACK EAGLE.

SPARE him not! said the chief,
Haughty was the White Bear,
Spare him not! cried they all,
As he smote so now shall he fare,
'T is the foe of the tribe,
The Black Eagle we describe!

They bind the Black Eagle
To a stiff ash-tree,
His hands tied behind,
And thongs at his knee,
And they bare his broad chest
That ne'er tremor confest.

Ten warriors step forth,
Each armed with his bow,
And each took good aim
To kill the proud foe,
When the bright Harvest Moon
Sprang swift, and lovely as June;

And a soft, graceful form
Placed 'tween him and them:
Kill me, if you will,
And spare the brave Sachem;
In my heart is a place,
For that cold, patient face!

BAKER FARM.

THY entry is a pleasant field,
Which some mossy fruit trees yield
Partly to a ruddy brook,
By gliding musquash undertook,
And mercurial trout
Darting about.

Cell of seclusion,
Haunt of old time,
Rid of confusion,
Empty of crime,
Landscape! where the richest element
Is a little sunshine innocent;
In thy insidious marsh,
In thy cold opaque wood,

Thy artless meadow,
And forked orchard's writhing mood,
Still Baker Farm!
There lies in them a fourfold charm.

Alien art thou to God and Devil!
Man too forsakes thee,
No one runs to revel
On thy rail-fenced lea,
Save gleaning Silence gray-headed,
Who drains the frozen apple red,
Thin jar of winter's jam,
Which he will with gipsy sugar cram.

And here a Poet builded,
In the completed years,
For behold a trivial cabin
That to destruction steers.
Should we judge it was built?
Rather by kind nature spilt
To interfere with circumstance,
And put a comma to the verse

And west trends blue Fairhaven bay,
O'er whose stained rocks the white pines sway,
And south slopes Nobscot grand,
And north the still Cliffs stand.

Pan of unwrinkled cream,
May some Poet dash thee in his churn,
And with thy beauty mad,
Verse thee in rhymes that burn;
Thy beauty, — the beauty of Baker Farm!
In the drying field,
And the knotty tree,
In hassock and bield,
And marshes at sea!

Thou art expunged from to-day,
Rigid in parks of thy own,
Where soberly shifts the play,
And the wind sighs in monotone.
Debate with no man hast thou,
With questions art never perplexed,
As tame at the first sight as now,
In thy plain, russet gabardine dressed.

I would hint at thy religion,
Hadst thou any,
Piny fastness of wild pigeon,
Squirrel's litany,
Never thumbed a gilt Prayer Book,
Here the cawing, sable rook!

Art thou orphan of a deed,
Title that a court can read,
Or dost thou stand
For the entertaining land,
That no man owns,
Pure grass and stones?

Idleness is in the preaching.
Simpleness is all the teaching,
Churches in the steepled woods,
Galleries in green solitudes,
Fretted never by a noise,
Eloquence that each enjoys.

Here humanity may trow,
It is feasible to slough

The corollary of the village,
Lies, thefts, clothes, meats, and tillage!
Come, ye who love,
And ye who hate,
Children of the Holy Dove,
And Guy Faux of the State,
And hang conspiracies,
From the tough rafters of the trees!

Still Baker Farm!
So fair a lesson thou dost set,
Commensurately wise,
Lesson no one may forget.
Consistent sanctity,
Value that cannot be spent,
Volume that cannot be lent,
Passable to me and thee,
For Heaven thou art meant!

THE END.

NEAR HOME.

A POEM.

BOSTON:
JAMES MUNROE AND COMPANY.
1858.

CAMBRIDGE: THURSTON AND TORRY, PRINTERS.

TO HENRY.

Henry! though with thy name a nobler verse,
Of theme heroic, or devotion's prayer,
Might fitlier blend, and more inspire
Than these low, halting strains, and lead the way
To more sublime emotions and entrance
The listening city or the landward town,
That spots afar the toppling mountain's base,—
Still let thy name here stand, of one the name,
Who to no meaner service, nobly walked,
Than virtue's service!
Who, by his virtue,
Might compel, from even a reed so low,
Or a weak life consumed in trivial thought,
Spent on the tricks of show, on time's reprieves,
Fate's half-forgiveness for forgotten deeds;
Might still compel from this dull-sounding reed,

In some strange moment truant to its jar,
One note of music that might touch the stars,
O'ercrown oblivious eras of long night,
And so, half live.
Be, then, to me a muse,
And while the day roars downward in the dust
Of crowded cities, and afar on seas
Uplifted rifts the tall hoar billows,
Mid its surge (surge all its own), the blast,—
May I pursue, with thee, thy peaceful walks;
O'er the low valleys seamed by long-past thrift,
And crags that beetle o'er the base of woods,
Which lift their mild umbrageous fronts to Heaven.
By rock and stream, low hill and surly pitch
Of never-opening oaks, let me essay,
To teach their worth, meed of a poet's life.

Yes! be to me a muse, if so, that thought
Which is in thee, the king, that royal truth
Spurning all commonplace details of lie,—
All far-fetched harrowing curb-stones
Of excuse, that fit men's actions to their

Consciences, and so achieve content
At the expense of honor; all low hopes,
Apologies for self where weakness hides,
And those worst virtues that the cozening world
Pimps on her half-fledged brood; old shells and worms
That saw ere deluged Noah at the plough,—
If so, e'en in its faintest radiation
Thy abiding faith in God's great justice
Might arise, and so might I be just,
And trust in him!
For chiefly here, thy worth,—
Chiefly in this, thy unabated trust,—
Ample reliance on the unceasing
Truth that rules the nether sphere about us,
That drives round the unthinking ball,
And buds the ignorant germs on life and time
Of men and beasts and birds, themselves the sport
Of a most healthy fortune, still unspent,
So that all individual sorrows
Butts for jest, leap down the narrow edge
Of thy colossal wit, and shattered hide,

There, at its base.
Modest and mild, and kind,
Who never spurned the needing from thy door,
(Door of thy heart which is a palace gate);
Temperate and faithful, in whose word, the world
Might trust, sure to repay, unvexed by care,
Unawed by Fortune's nod, slave to no lord
Nor coward to thy peers, long shalt thou live,
Not in this feeble verse, this sleeping age,
But in the roll of Heaven; and at the bar
Of that high court, where virtue is in place!
Then, thou shalt fitly rule, and read the laws
Of that supremer state, writ Jove's behest,
And even old Saturn's chronicle,
Works ne'er Hesiod saw, types of all things
And portraitures of all, whose golden leaves
Roll back the ages' doors, and summon up
Unsleeping truths, by which, wheels on Heaven's
prime,

NEAR HOME.

Still burns at Heaven's gate thy golden torch,
All-conquering Sun, and in thy flame at morn
The wearied nations rise; thyself, unwearied,
Urging on the year, and pouring down thy fires
On the delicate flowers, that still trusting ope
Their little half-shut bells.
Above us far
The painter of the dark floods her cold light
Across the dewy meads, with the still stars
Companions of her coil. So the first day,
Had burnt both sun and star, so burnt, so cooled,
As now they lend a virtue to our fields,
Where slow thro' modest valleys creep the streams,
Nor leap to cataracts. So, to the first,
They spoke in kindred voices, and compelled

Just admiration. And, to the last,
If e'er the race die out, they still may speak,
Thus, in an outward dialect. Of this,
We phrase not here; neither how from their seeds
Sprang out the progenies of things, and rose
To haughty empire or commanding state.

On the low hills that skirt the River's side,
Where feebly waves through half-felt joy the grass,
Couched at their frugal cheer a savage host
Held banquet high, nor doubt not in their ire,
Here smoked forbidden dainties, though the fire
Lit by the white men had not scorched their wits.
How silent all! save the lone Sandpiper,
Whose plaintive call a little echo stirs,
When on the brink he idly plagues his mate.
Soft sways around the Spring's consoling air,
And up the sallows, like a distant camp,
The never-ceasing hum of bees; birds soar,
And gay the insect tribe flit in the beams
Of the low-falling orb.

I do not walk alone;

For still I feel thy arm is round me,
And thy law above, Thou, who art all in all,—
Whose goodness guides, whose truth endears the
whole,
Without whose presence what were all to man,
Save a far clouded gleam of deepening night.
I do not walk alone, for still the Spring
Calls up my old companions; and I see
The old familiar faces: once more hear
Notes that I once had heard, touches of joy,
Beyond all words of mine expressions glad,
Thoughts linked to brightness, and joys twined with
joys,
So that the far-off chimneys, as they rear
Their tall unmoving pillars to the sky,
Permit from their broad roofs sweet in the sun,
A solace in their hospitable thoughts,
Intent on home.
That was my thought, my Home!
And those dear memories that with thee build,
Like youth's first love throned in unfading light.
For like this Spring's soft sunshine, like the kiss

Of this first sunlight, like these smiling hours,
That never seem to bid farewell to day,
Safe in my heart is home with all its joys;
The blessed security of love that in one place
There, I am truly loved; and there no thought
Of usury upon the warm affections of the soul
Ever may come, no blinding doubt, no frost,
But in the laughing faces of our kin,
Glad in the children dear and matron blest,
And trust that knew no bane, we so shall live,
So die, — then gathered to our graves.

And see,

How quietly the dimpling river laves,
Safe in its pure seclusion, the green base
Of yonder hill, bleached to its core with shells,
Things of the Indian, who, in this retreat
Bent their small wigwams, when the spring's first thought
Jetted the shad up from the usurping sea,
And taught them near to lay their numerous spawn.
Gone, like those leaping fish, that Indian tribe,
Falling like autumn leaves drift o'er the soil,

Where, for unnumbered centuries they chased
The graceful deer, wild bear, and cumbrous moose.
To thoughtful eye, their arrow-heads appear,
Turned with the furrows of the farmer's plough, —
Or pestle smooth, or chisel sharp of slate,
And soap-stone pot, the heirlooms of a Race
That *owned* these lands.
So fared the fatal Indian,
So decayed, so fell like grasses unrenewed,
Down, where the white man builds. Thus drop the races,
Annihilate and spoiled, not to return.
Yet at their base the dimpling river laves,
Base of these low, lone hills. The blackbird's trill
Calls up his dusky mate, from the stiff twigs
Of copse, the Button-bush that brings no leaf
As yet, and on his wing the stripe of flame,
Darts like a crimson meteor o'er the blue.
On floating logs grave tortoises enjoy
The watery dream, for hope returns, to all,—
The everlasting hope returns with Spring.
Save that the Indian bow no longer twangs

Along the meadow, nor his watch-fires light
The lonely tresses of the ambushed wood,
Even as for countless ages all pursue
The same immeasurable round. Why fear
The pangs of penury, the student's curse,—
Or love abandoned when some victim's heart
Tears up from thine its fibres, and so graves
A wake of living anguish in thy soul?
Why live and droop beneath the weight of woe,
That unsuccessful effort piles o'er pride,
Half measuring its strength, thence prone to earth
Hurled by self-accusation? Could not thou,
Leagued with the universal law pursue
Like it, a sympathetic journey;
Nor fail thy sunshine to the sun, as he
Ne'er to thee fails; bud as the laurel buds
Deep in the hidden swamp, like the pinxter
Hang flowers along the edges of the wood,
Where save the savage hunter none delights,
Or the green bittern brooding from the light?—
Alone, deserted? then art thou alone,
On some near hill-top, ere the orb of day

In early summer, tints the floating heaven,
And far around thy sleeping race endow
With their oblivion the dim village roofs;
Nor yet the wakeful herdsman folds his kine
So to prolong their hours?
Alone, then listen hushed!
A living hymn awakes the studious air!
A myriad sounds that to one song converge,
As the added light shows the far hamlet
And the distant wood. These, are the voices
Of the unnumbered birds that fill the sphere
With their delicious harmony, prolonged
And ceaseless, so that at no time it dies,
Vanquishing the expectation by delay.
Still added notes, from the first Robin's 'larum
On the walnut's bough, to the Veery's flute,
Who from the furthest deep of the wet wood,
In martial trills rallies his liquid lay,
And the blithe whistling Oriole pours his joy.
O! mark the molten flecks along the skies
That move not, floating in those rosy heights
Of clear celestial radiance, so far pure

That not the artist in all color skilled,
The English Turner, faintly them could picture.

Yet not this color, not these lovely forms,
That chiefly should engross and ask thy praise;
Rather the revelation of abiding grace
Continuous, as the morning's voice
Lifts up the chant of universal faith,
Perpetual newness and the health in things.
This, is the startling theme, the lovely birth
Each morn of a new day, so wholly new,
So absolutely penetrated by itself,
The fresh, the fair, the ever-living grace,—
The tender joy, that still forever clothes
This orb of Beauty, this, of bliss the abode!
Therefore, fling off poor slumberer, thy dark robe
Woven of night, ungird the dream-claspt brow,
And freely forth exulting in thy joy,
Launch out and taste the dewy twilight hour,
Come ere the latest stars have fled, ere dawn
Perfectly seen, unveil the outlined charm
Of bosky wood, deep dells, and odorous copse,

Where blazed with more than gold, some slow-
drawn mist
Retreats its distant arm from the cool meads!
Forth, forth, and see what thou hast never seen,
Nor thought, nor in thy wildest fancy touched,
The charms of earliest life, the act of Love,
Still in each day repeated, when from the dark
And sleeping chaos sprang all fair, proud forms.
To even express in faintest hints this birth,
This resurrection of the buried earth,
This weaving of new garments in an hour
For our else naked orb, her fairest moment
In the whole long day, must fail the wariest hand.
Yet what these few faint touches may convey,
Be that conveyed.
Is it pure morning light,
And dewy dawn within thy soul upheld,
Who, from the world retired beholds the day,
Creep with slow fingers from the utmost verge
Of the remote horizon; notes of joy,
Do these prelude within thy thought new life,
When the thick cloud of being veiled in dust,

Drops its obscure concealments and renewed
Shoots like the eagle to new-risen orbs,
Far-spent upon the eternal cope?
Or dost thou never soar, and feebly soiled
With matter's low terrestrial cerements,
Conceal by them that dawn which in thy heart,
Gives prophecy of heaven?
These thoughts not here;
Our simple rustic garb for such befit not,—
More that soaring bard, rapt to a sphere beyond
Time's fallible. Rather, let us pursue
The shaded path, that in the thicket ends;
Where in the blueberry the Cat-bird builds
Shapely of twigs his nest, and mewing near
Proclaims his royal emeralds to all eyes.
Here would the mischief-loving boy, a pest,
Deal prompt confusion, dragging to earth,
Remorseless as the fates, the frail design;
Wreck in a moment the neat finished house,
And with capricious finger smash o'erjoyed
The oval of the egg, short funeral!
Nor trust to lesson him, with brass his nerves

Tight-twisted might appal whole decalogues.

Time is the cenotaph of things, of men.
Nature renews with touch incessant, — Death, —
Rears to decay, creates her round on round
Of still rejected being, scaling heaven,
To lay her vast perfection at its feet.
Numbers and dates, shoals of existences,
Myriads of ages to her hand are nought, —
Absolute artist in her least design
As in her greatest. With her rapid eye
She steals with lightning dash from worm to man,
Wriggles in the atom, walks along the brute,
Still to extend her still-extending plan.
Thou need not ask her, wherefore, why hawks
In mad descent dash at the sparrow's brain,
Or leaping pikes the little pikes engulf, —
Why in the volley of the surging main,
Man's fleets blow off like apples and o'erstrew
The Alps and Andes of the sunken world?
Not if she knew herself, where she was bent,
(That some have doubted) could she e'er reply.

Why should she ancwer, — thee? — or canst thou probe
With thy perfection, the unformed expanse
Of anxious fortune where thy being swims,
Even if its elements league with eternity,
And curvet on the blast sweeping the halls
Of the remotest heaven; or if the cup
Of thy existence vapours with the breath
That filled the clay, whence sprang all living forms?
With spines and veins, with hairs and nervatures,
Joints and articulations, leaves and cells,
She calls her varied creatures into space.
But what behind the ever-changeful thought,
If thus the checkers on her board arranged,
With what intention deals she her shrewd game,
And where shall man, feigning his ignorance
To be in league with her, at last arrive, —
Or is he but a leaf tossed on the wave
Creative, one more joint to pass along
To-morrow, to a meaner thing, a throw
Of her wise finger, then displaced.

Forbear!

Such speculation idling fools admit,
But in thy heart of hearts that truth discern,—
God to no worm denies his saving grace,
And in thy darkest hour of mental anguish,
Before his throne fall humbled, there fall,
With thy brief sorrow and thy infant thought,
Let drop the penury of self, and pray
That his true light that never set nor will
Upon the meanest, may o'erbloom thy dust,—
And heal the torture of thy narrow heart.

How like a girl that into maiden glides
The spring has melted into June! O how
She dashed her May of life away, and tied
Her long uncumbered tresses in these knots,
These neat confinèd braids that gird her brow,
Put off her girlish figure springing free,
Her loose attire half-gathered to a plan,
Soothed her capricious form panting with play,
And 'neath the trees her fair companions round
Told them this charming tale to end the day.
Could she not shout a little longer wild,
And in her dark and roguish eyes proclaim

The graver secret, that the half-staid girl
Carelessly cool reserves, when on her tongue,
As if a breath would from its tip, throw off
The sudden meaning? There's no stay to life, —
We thought to pause on May, to hold the world
One moment to itself, to keep her fast,
One long long joyous day, all Spring, and lo!
The foliaged June sways her soft drapery
O'er the waving mead, smiles in the grass,
And pranks Senecios on the side
Of the consumptive ditch.

Yet the Rice-bird,
From the murky south come speeding fast,
Flings from his yellow crown a pulse of heat,
And if the Blue-bird and his mellow trill,
(A kind of joy half-uttered) brings the year,
The hardy Bobolink profuse of notes
O'erflowing, deluges the liberal air,
Exuberant, as if his compact frame
Could not contain his sounds, but in his pang
Of never-ceasing melody his throat
Too rash distended, might defect and end
By one intense crescendo all his strain!

So, it is fabled, that in contest, rare,
The ambitious nightingale expires, her power
Crushed by some instrument that to man's touch,
Volumed a nobler music.
On every hand
Now wakes an insect world, raised from close sheaths,
Strange transformations and unnoticed silks,
Spun in low marshes by imperial worms.
Their scaly lances on the wood-path dash,
Glittering like men-at-arms, the Dragon-flies,
Nerved to the core, and Whirligigs in maze
Weave their continual circles o'er the pool
With their dusk boat-like bodies, things of joy.
Nor fail to note the thick Empheridæ,
That dance along the stream, food for a tribe
Almost as countless of quick-leaping fish.
The Swifts on cutting wing dash through the swarm,
And the familiar Swallow, poet birds.
There are no poor in Nature; only man,
And mostly he who lumbers in the train
Of the commercial city, pride of power,
Where from low allies and thick reeking lanes

The putrid mass of slow corruption breathes,
Infests the air, and with its sallow host
Spawns ragged children for as ragged sire.
Yet man, with his strange ills, deems himself first, —
Lord of the world, and calls the orbs his own,
Because with artificial eye he sweeps their round,
Poor phantom of an hour, graved in the dust;
While bee and beetle his interment make,
And even the owls from some perpetual oak
More stately and ancestral piles inhabit
Than all his short-span race!

But yesterday,
Our fathers pulled their boats ashore and touched
The rock, and now we are an empire, free, —
So free, so utterly free, that never,
No, not in Rome's barbaric hour, when slaves
Of lust, were garnered in from all her lands,
Did such a base and cruel wrong e'er soil
The purple of her conquerors, as spots
The unstained ermine of these blood-dyed States.
I speak of Afric's wrongs, unnumbered wrongs!
So that the summer o'er their wretched huts

Wakes but a fiercer fire of wild revenge,
And shrivels up the mind that rightly sees,
How yet that desolation must ensue,
Fruit of long-chosen sin that could be shunned,
But would not!
Not on the high road, not in dusty cars
Loud-thundering o'er their iron vertebræ,
Where in close boxes sweltering with the speed
Nod in newspaper dreams the broadcloth world;—
Nor with capricious haste of foaming steeds,
Essay thou, rather along the river's smooth
Untenanted domain gliding in peace,
Steal with soft fancies in a silent bark.
On every side the green contrivings wave,
The friendly Willows nodding all their plumes,
Carved Arrowheads and Calla broadly-leaved,
And burr-reed spined, nor slight the floating orbs,
Anchored companions of thy moving thought,
The life of lilies, where the Nuphar's disk
In richest yellow floats its gold repose,
And smaller yet as brave, the Kalmian buds.
O holy rest, O ripe tranquillity!

For who shall dream in what uncounted years,
These realms of peace e'er bent at ruin's knee,
Or when that primal burst, the ancient chaos
Racked these courteous aisles? Rather the arches,
Where the King-bird rears his grassy throne,
And strikes the nerve-fly, strong in tyrant-pride,
Amply excepted from the general roar,
When in the whirling war all seeds of things
Together mixt, shook to their base old empires,—
These soft scenes, wholly at peace still smiled,
As now they smile, and took the sunsets
In their peaceful arms and rocked them sleeping.

Here, thing eternal, day begins not, ends not!
And the night stealing half-ushered in,
Steeps in the trembling wave her pillowed stars,
Or with pellucid silver tints the wake
Of the retiring moon, when from her couch
She half withdraws, like some faint nymph
Flushed by the hunter's horn, her bath profaned.
Time nowise here, her rapine wakes, nor save
The spray-voiced toad or bull-frog deep, whose
music

Half-finished, e'er it folds the ear,
The weary question of the living bears.
Nor can you here, voluptuous worldling,
Flaunt your silken train, nor in your gay
And Cleopatra-barges bear away
The old simplicity that breathes in things.
Nought but the solitary fisher comes,
More like a weedy tuft than living man,
Lest he should lose his finny prey,
And half-concealed along the green copse side,
Or on the shore unmoving calmly spread,
Mimics the maple-stump and core of soil.
Strange fisherman! whose highest aim may soar
To whirl the pickerel on the grassy bank,—
With watery shoe unconscious of a leak,
Or hot rheumatic thrill or opulent gout
That rides the turtle-lord and shrieks his knell,—
Thou seem'st to own this world, and to despise
The lesser fry who dart about thy lines.
So that the brassy court-bell dinging clear,
Or whirr of engine-wheel, or news from wars,
Where o'er Crimea's fields the Tartar horde

Pours a red freshet on the Saxon steel,
Cannot distract thy cane-pole; — not old Greece
And all its pale, departing history,
Or that in later days they dream Rome was,
Or nearer conscious England, Shakspeare's tomb,
Thee worry; — so bite the fish, thy conquest.
Nor think his strange morality, a jest,
Superior beggar! who in Court or Church,
With braying tongue and curt suspicious eye
Demands romantic homage! think him not,
This ragged fisher, 'neath thy empty state.
What more hast thou, Life, Death, the Infinite,
Above unbounded Heaven, beneath old Earth,
And may be less repose of mind than he,
More aching emptiness, not more content,
And far more self-deception.

If it stood
So that the aspiring crowd, who with their pride,
Declare their thoughts are nice, and coax them down,
Lay o'er these fields long roads, proclaim club law,
And summon lesser virtues to their thrones, —
If these were all, if camp and church were all,

And broadcloth might decapitate green baize,
Then truly we were doomed, and life a dungeon.
With these clerks for bolts, into one slumber
All the social train softly might fall,
And creep supine beneath their awful knees,
Adore their wit, and pray the newspaper
To intermit one afternoon, next year, for sports.
But while the fisher dreams, or greasy gunner
Lank with ebon locks shies o'er the fences,
And cracks down the birds, game-law forgot,
And still upon the outskirts of the town,
A tawny tribe denudes the cranberry-bed, —
Or life remains, we still shall sign, that Time
Is not all sold like grains to the forestaller; —
Still that we, even as the Indian did,
Clasp palm to nature's palm, and pressure close
Deal with the infinite.

Thy estimate?

And wherefore is that thine, my moralist?
Or lays her eggs along the sandy shore
The painted Tortoise by thy section one,
Or on the naked oak long by the blow

Of splintering lightning leafless, does our bird
The white-crowned Osprey read thy paper code,
Sauce to his pouts?
And who shall scale the Heaven,
And with his microscopic eye
Discern, wherefore the Laurel pale adorns
The deep-set swamp fenced by declivities
And sombre woods, where the fierce Hen-hawk screams,
And Screech-owls rear from dusky egg the young?
Why not in trim parterres or shaven lawn,
Or the gay sunshine of the grassy meads?
Flowers of humanity! do ye too ope
Your soft attractions in the lonely shade,
Where the deep sphagnum coats a spongy soil,
And the old spruces hung with lichens gray,
Strive to outlast the annals of our race?
Thou didst not carve the flowers, Philosopher!
Thou, nor thy creed, thy saws, or reasoning forms,
Bred in the lazaar-house of Thought, and shade
Of tedious questions, dull and pale, fungi
Of the Understanding, mere type of Fruit.

O rather learn of the lone laurel, learn
To intermit unprofitable shows,
And harbor God's retirement in thy soul.

Then, let us read in June, Boccaccio's stories,
Told in gardens fair hard by Firenze's walls,
And Shakspeare's mind, here we shall dedicate
To a new purpose, vowed to ampler homage.
Now, let us renew our vows to all delights,
That grow from noble roots, enhance the day,
And turn its passing glories to high purpose.—
She cannot fail us, nature cannot fail,
God's just expression through unrivalled form.
And if the shallow worldling may not join
With our true reverence for God's noble works,
Thoughts of religion, still let us endue
The transitory moment with that bloom,
That on the fruit of Paradise shows purple,—
Color unfading, tint of cloudless skies,
Sapphire and amethyst of burnished spheres,
That ope their crystalline beyond Time's grave.
He shall not mock us, ne'er shall he deceive,—
Nature's progenitor, who from the first,

O'er all presiding still reneweth all!

I see Rudolpho, cross our honest fields,
Collapsed with thought, cool as the Stagyrite
At intellectual problems; mastering
Day after day part of the world's concern.
Still adding to his list, beetle and bee, —
Of what the Vireo builds a pensile nest,
And why the Peetweet drops her giant egg
In wheezing meadows, odorous with sweet brake.
Nor welcome dawns, nor shrinking nights him
menace,
Still girt about for observation, yet
Keen to pursue the devious lanes that lead
To knowledge oft so dearly bought.
For ne'er
Can nature give her secrets without toil,
And long inquiry and an anxious heart;
So that Rudolpho, like the midnight watch,
With eye and ear each strained to their full tension,
Thought and feeling bent keen on one purpose,
Who wonders that the flesh declines to grow
Along his sallow pits, or that his life

To social pleasure careless, pines away
In dry seclusion and unfruitful shade?
Martyr! for eye too sharp and ear too fine,
Hero of facts, who fills his pouch with all
Such life can furnish to a surface-fly,
I must admire thy brave apprenticeship,
To these dry forages, if the worldling
Laugh in his sleeve at thy compelled devotion,
And declare, an accidental stroke
Surpassed whole æons of Rudolpho's file.
Press out the cream of learning, cast away
The nicer sensibilities that fret
The o'er-passioned heart, and eat thy crust
Of brown unleavened dough off platters pine,
Wherewith a grosser cook might light his fire;—
Dust off the film of flattery and ambition,
Drown old conventions in thy acid wit,
Nor leave a peg whereon to hang the times!
So shalt thou learn, Rudolpho, as thou walk'st,
More from the winding lanes where nature leaves
Her unaspiring creatures, and surpass
In some fine saunter her declivity.

Why beats that court-bell on the liquid air
Of June's translucent prime, what caitiffs hold
Base trials in the smug design of wood,
Where sallow prisoners haled from grated walls, —
Dark cells and close confines of misery
Blink at the open daylight unconfined,
Or callous to their doom demand contempt?
Was it for this, he grew, yon thick-browed Murderer
In his mother's arms, nurst in her road-side
Cottage 'neath old elms, umbrageous place, —
And there his boyish days brought to the lore
That liberal nature shares amid the poor, —
Gave to a parent's heart its pulse of joy,
Bade elders smile to mark his urchin trick,
Promise fair for virtue; and for this, he
Walked along the adult's path and took
Another to his side as wife and friend, —
To end in this, felled in the dust ere dead?
Driven by the slave-whip, in dark passion's power,
He struck his bosom friend a murderous blow,
And now where's human sympathy? Will one

Lament, when the dread sentence from the mouth
Of some oblivious Judge, slow-falling, shears
Away ere dead, his once delightful form?
Yes! still in another heart, he lives, a life
Incessant; a simple girl, bride in her soul,
Wears faithfully her crown, and fears his name
Lest on his children's ear its presage fall.
And should not jar the ear that brassy peal,
Summoning these fearful woes to human hearts?

O rather would I hear in murmur slow,
The dying cadence of some funeral bell,
With melancholy echoes far
That lapse to silence, for the good man's soul,
Who, after a long life of righteous deeds,
Now has laid down the burden of his age,
And fitly summoned to his fathers, sleeps
With them, along the green hill-side. Such peal,
Methinks, need not disturb our dim retreats,
The depth of shaded forests robed in night,
Or the true faces of the upland hills,
Where nature wears even in her winter shroud

A look of joy, and calm content, unfading!
Let me hear that solemn-stealing bell,
And pause a moment in the whirling tide,
That bears me headlong on to the still regions
Where our fathers sleep, and reign o'er silence;
Let me reverence their lives, and so prepare
My soul, for higher duties.
                    If thy heart,
Pained by humanity, desire retreat,
This, thou may find and undisturbed secure,
Near the calm bosom of the inland pond,
For storms too sheltered and for forms too free,
Where no vexatious villa greets the eye,
Or blazing chateau proud with whited walls.
Here, save the lone Kingfisher rattling o'er,
Belted with blue, and half an azure wave,
Or the great Northern diver, laughing bird,
Saluting with her lonely peals the shore,
Nought thee shall trouble; here thou canst repose
And dream away the pains of ardent life,
Forego ambition and the world's applause,
Stretching along the bank, fanned by the wind
That even in summer heats, from the cool surface

Quaffs a breath of life, forget thy madness,
Thy contriving wit, that made thee stoop
To things beneath thyself. Around, the woods
Lift up most ample canopies; old Pines,
Yellow with spendthrift lichens, whispering groves
Where youthful Birches frolic in their prime,
And ever-graceful Maples with light leaves
That turn the zephyr's kiss. Nor fail to mark
The distant vision of the Hill-top blue,
Where through the trees a vista opening far,
Lets in a line of landscape on thy thought,
And shows its moral by a fairer scene,
More beautiful with distance.

No palace,
Rich in all Italia's art, e'er showed
Like this calm pond, a store of rivalries.
As if resolved, to outdo the bank,
The tranquil wave reflects in its deep bosom,
Or sleeping rock or soft and shaded hill,
More perfécted than in their real shape.
So Nature plays the artist and defies
Human ambition to surpass her skill.

Here, sometimes gliding in his peaceful skiff
Climéne sails, heir of the World, and notes
In his perception that no thing escapes,
Each varying pulse along Life's arteries,
Both what she half resolves and half effects,
As well as her whole purpose.
To his eye,
The stars of many a midnight heaven
Have beamed tokens of love, types of the Soul,
And lifted him to more primeval natures,
Than adorn the lower sphere. He saw
In those far-moving barks on heaven's sea,
Radiates of force, and while hė moved from man,
Lost on the eternal billow, still his heart
Beat with some natural fondness for his race.
Kind egotist, who still pursuing Art,
Turned with a half-felt joy to lesser things!
In other lands, they might have worshipt him,
Nations had stood and blocked their chariot wheels
At his approach, and cities stooped beneath his foot!
But here, in our vast wilderness he walks
Alone (if 'tis to be alone), when stars

And breath of summer mountain-airs and morn,
And the wild music of the untempered sea,
Consort with human genius, for his soul,—
Climéne's soul leagues with these sources,
These informing depths, and his pure mould
Was laid, in the great sunshine, of the universe.
O could not thou revere, bold Stranger, prone
To inly smile and chide at human power,
Our humble fields and lowly stooping hills,—
Yellow with Johnswort, bright with Blue-eyed grass,
When thou shall learn that here Climéne trod,
Here thought and from these modest surfaces
Plucked fruits of Hesperides.

Who are the great?

They, who compose the current of the state,—
War's conquerors, radiant with rapine,
Bleeding in their seats so that the longest peace
Can never still their memories, or they
Who build leagues of oblivion and their tombs,
Commercial cities! fettering the poor;
Or noisy babblers, in the weary halls
Where legislation crowns her acts with wind,

Or far beyond, Mechanics, who displace
Aged exertion with inventive skill;
Or rather he, whose Thought girds in the whole,
And like a sentinel on the outpost of time
Challenges Eternity and bids it speak?
I know not, let the world decide; but life
I feel, is never spent in vain, that leads
Man to revere himself and so his aim,
Be to rise higher towards the social good,
And so exalt at once with him, mankind.

But if these July fervors sere thy brain,
Parch up thy heart and turn thee to a coal,
Then, rather seek the Sea's capacious verge.
There, stretch at length upon the ocean brink,
On some all-crowning headland, while the wind
Blows cool from off the bay, renew thy strength,
And coping with the element itself
Enjoy the exhilarating bath.
Vigor and pulse shall animate thy frame,
Caught from the wholesome perfume of the main,
New life and new emotions linking thine

To the vast spaces of the untrammelled deep.

Survey the sliding sands, that down the bank
Ever precipitate, next snatched away
By ceaseless waves, so lead a moving life,
Now for a little fixed to mother earth,
Then sweeping far, erect new shoals whereon
The hapless Mariner his chart revoked,
Sleeps his perpetual sleep! The tide-wave,
Whose strange vigor rolls the breaker onward,
Knows no pause, no halt, ever renewed the same,
Curling transparent to long lines of foam
When softer airs dally with summer hours,
Next hurled in surges like a cannonade,
Where worlds in contest join, battles the coast,
Tossing the ship a pebble in its palm.
Strange creature, unsuggestive element!
Forever from the mind that cannot fix
Thy form in horizontal grandeur vast,
Still without likeness, swept; I see the ships,
A never-ending company desert
Their places, onward, out of sight, and feel

That were it not for what there is of life,
Of human life and human hope in them,
But for thy freshening airs, consummate Sea!
And endless beauty and provoking change,
Thou wert a lonely waste.
And yet I link
With thee, fathomless Ocean, that dear child!
A summer child, flower of the world,
Rosalba! for like thee, she has no bound
Or limit to her beauty, framed to spell
Words that the gods might copy; Venus-zoned
She rather, like thy billows, bends with grace.
Nor deem the Grecian fable all a myth,
That Aphrodité from a shell appeared,
Soft spanned upon the wave, for o'er thy heart,
Unheeding stranger! thus Rosalba falls,
And by one entrance on thy privacy
Unrolls the mysteries, and gives them tongue.
Dearest Rosalba! could a clumsy hand
Or paint or shape thy image, thou, who art
Not only fair but good, not only good but true,
Not borrowing from artificial plans thy virtue;

Rather, like the sun that all things warms,
Life in thyself, breath of humanities
That take their rise from milky natures,
Soft and fine and pure, refined so far
Beyond all touch of art, or word of praise,
That an interior sunlight tones thy days
To one profound contentment. O my child!
Child of the poet's thought, if ever God
Made any creature that could thee surpass,—
The lightest sunset cloud that purpling swims
Across the zenith's lake, the foam of seas,
The roses when they paint the green sand-wastes
Of the remotest Cape, or hour ere dawn,
I cannot fathom it; how thou art made,
How these attempered elements that in the mass
Run to confusion and exhale in fault,
Beget all monstrous passions and dark thoughts,
Or slow contriving malice or cold spite,
Or leagues of dulness self persuaded rare,
Or old delusion in the maiden's breast,—
Should rise in thee like the vast ocean's grace,
Ne'er to be bounded by my heart or hope,

Yet ever decorous, modest and complete.
Forgive me, O most beautiful, if I have sinned,
If e'er one feeling in my heart had place,
To link thee to myself! Forgive this song,
That here presumptuous I should name thy name,
Or feebly dare to celebrate thy charm!
Rose on her cheeks, are roses in her heart,
And softer on the earth her footstep falls
Than earliest twilight airs across the wave,
While in her heart the unfathomed sea of love,
Its never-ceasing tide pours onward.—

Yet if those high and echoing shores thee please not,
Seek again the tranquil river's bank.
July evokes new splendor o'er the stream,
In dulcet figures and diviner forms.
Yet more than all the Water-lily's pomp,
That star of creamy perfume, born to be
Consoler of thy solitary hours.
In vast profusion from the store of pads,
They floating rise, with their fine beauty decked,
The habitation of an insect host,

That here pursue and steal the core away.
Nor slight the Pickerel-weed, whose violet shaft
Completes the tall reed's beauty and endows
With a contrasted harmony, the shore.
No work of human art could faintly tell,
Much less repeat in words or colors, all
The unnoticed lustre of these summer plants,
The floating palaces of anchored orbs,
And spikes of untold beauty crowning earth,
Where save the lonely sportsman or some soul
Wandering from heated life and sick of toil,
No creature glides of human shape. Yet here
The Muskrat swims, and pout and perch display
Their arrowy swiftness, as the minnows dart
And break the filmy surface of the pool,
And the high-colored Bream, the fish of gems,
Their circular nests scoop from the yellow sand.
Nay, do not ask why was this beauty lavished
On these spots, do not believe that love in vain
Is poured upon the solitude, nor deem
Absence of Human life, absence of all!
Why is not here an answer to thy thought,

Contriving man, rearing the court-house,
Or rich pulpits lined, or deemest thou the charm
Of endless beauty might not thee avail,
More than a stuccoed wall where pictures hang,
Or rattling street, or state and camp, and town.

Or mark in August as the twilight falls,
Like wreaths of timid smoke, the curling mists
Poured from some smouldering fire across
The meadows cool, whose shadows thrown
So faintly, seem to fall asleep with day!
How softly pours the thin and curling mist!
Now shall the eye half lose in it all faith,
As it were but the mockery of the brain,
Then if it gather denser own its truth.
O twilight world! abode of Peace, how deep
Might we not envy him who in thee lives,
With that same quietness that lives in thee;
And like thy soft and gently-falling beauty
His repose, — dreams in the flood-tide of the world.
Alas! I fear but few who walk these streets,
That wear as deep tranquillity,

Poor slaves of fashion and the prints of form,
Or simply frivolous if first youth gild
An aimless brow with pleasure, or the dupe
Of little weak successes, that deceive
Their shallow owners, martyrs to mere cant,
If cant it be, to not perceive their vice.
And yet those nobler souls, whose hopes were
wrecked
On some remote mischance, remote in time,
But nearest to their hearts.
Forbear such themes;
For now the upland Pastures draped with green,
Invite us to that pleasing task unsung,
The Berry-field, where in a frolic chain
Knit by gay industry, the healthy band
Of bounding children go, and glean the grain
That ripens without cost, to laboring steer,
Or dim domestic horse, the farmer's butt.
Not olden Crœsus in imperial wealth,
Nor the bright jewel-chambers of a crown
Famed for barbaric conquest, pulled from Ind
Wreaths for its queen, like these unnoticed moors,
Pregnant with Blueberries whose colors mock

The overhanging sky, all turquoise gems!
Not that Vitellius wooed or Horace sung
Praise of Falernian, or delightful mead
In Chaucer's time no mythus, could now win
From us a single sentence, while we pluck
The abundant fruit adapted to the hand,
And place and hour, while slowly o'er the hills
The unnerved day piles her prodigious sunshine.
Here, be gardens of Hesperian mould,
Recesses rare, temples of birch and fern,
Preserves of light-green Sumac, Ivy thick,
And old stone-fences tottering to their fall,
And gleaming lakes that cool invite the bath,
And most aerial mountains for the West!
Italy and Greece? and would ye fly to them,
Poor, rash, deluded travellers, art and fame
That they have built afar their gilded seats,—
Capricious children, in our berry-fields,
That bound the horizon's verge from where
Ye sit, near by at ease, here be your shrines!
With but a glistening pail, an honest hand,
And thought that loves the air and heart at home,
Ye safe may laugh at those poor foreign lands,

Where dilettanti apes go clad in weeds,
And ruined temples rear their weary moss.

What leads our people, children of this land,
Born in New England, in New England bred,
To shun their native shores, and with sad eyes
Rehearse on Tiber's banks their homesick woe?
Here, where old races linger in the soil,
(The aspiring Indian elder to them all,
First in great Nature's heart), and where the scene
Is all a long and beautiful delay,
To round a finished life and steep the blood
In temperate pleasures, why should Egypt be
And her colossal mummies such a joy?
Or dusty Babylon where Arabs howl,
Or China's torpid teas, or English tombs.
May God forgive me! I had rather be,
The meanest worm that haunts our berry-fields,
Than wear the purple on those distant thrones,
And love far more the breath of Liberty
Across our poor, uncultured, sandy soils,
Than all the crumbling empires in their shrouds.

The wealth of Penury! — scant phrase indeed! —
Yet to be poor is ever the true wealth!
Poor to the worldly eye, and those who swim
And glitter in their pride cannot aspire
To the deep blessing that the Poor man knows,
Lord of himself, and health, and simple tastes.
And all our youth rush out to feed on whims,
Fashion craves their hours, low hopes their aim.
To win not noble women for their brides,
But titled slaves heirs to some teasing caste,
And beauty without culture seems mere show,—
As if great Nature laid not on her tints
With more contrivance than the brush of art,
Or schools where grammars bide the place of sense,
And shallow stammering drowns the native voice.
Here, in these shades, these deep seclusions hid
Beneath the whisp'ring leaves and o'er our moors
A ragged independence lives at ease,
Wearing those good adornments of the race,
Such as pure air, warm suns, and builds the Hero
Urban pens describe. Such have I seen,
Men to whom palaces might bow in vain,

Inferior to themselves; whose hearts and hands
Conjoined with Nature love the earth they smite,
And while they tease the globe for rye and corn,
Give still an hour to junketing and sport.

So walked our fathers, when the English braves,
Who deemed they owned the land our fathers tilled,
Flush with red jackets, marched along the bank
Of this slow River creeping to the sea.
And said, doubt not, because the tide was slow,
The rustics on its banks had hearts as slow.
Then rang their shot and echoed through the Manse,
Scaring the red-wing, but that noon's brave hour,—
That little hour America endowed
With shores that bound Pacifics, wilds that touch
Base of the Rocky hills and prairies far
Where the fierce bison stalks, the Pawnee's game.
They came up from their ploughs; they fired their guns;
Crushed out the host of England, yet tame slaves,
And while grave queens and lords still on their necks
Weigh an usurping heel, our fathers' sons

May worship God as they list, and choose their best
Or worst to govern, as they will. Brave shot!
That echoes far across the wide St. Lawrence,
And India's depth of jungle, tigers' lair,
And fitfully o'er Westminster and Scotland's hills,
Though many a shot has scared the red-wing since,
Time and the men made of *that* ringing gun
The knell of empire, Freedom's best salute!

O why so soon, most princely Golden-rod,
So soon, — why yesterday all summer,
Now, thy nodding plumes convert our hopes
To Autumn, and endow the verdured lanes
With thy most royal gold? Yet like all wealth,
Thou hast a cold and hidden sorrow in thee,
As to say, Behold in me a flattery!
Think me like an ebbing of the tide,
When purer splendors o'er the curling wave
Seem down its long declivity, to glide.
Ye too, meek Asters, violets' late friends,
Pale tranquil constellations of the fall,
That mark a decadence, why do ye strew

Your fair amenities along the paths
Of these continuous woodlands, come so soon?
Ere half the flush of summer's rosy hours
Had lit the faces of the August hills,
Decked the broad meadows with their base of grass,
Forced Indian corn to flint, or ere the brood
Of the first April birds put on their dress.
Not mournful; no, the world, whate'er its sorrows be,
Will not disclose them. Silent and serene
The plastic soul emancipates her kind,
And leaves the generations to their fate,
Uncompromised by tears. She will not weep, —
She needs no grief for man, our mother Nature!
Is not rude or vexed, or rough or careless,
Out of temper never, still as sweet, though winds
Of Winter brush her leaves away, and life
To human creatures, breathes like frost.
Dear friend!
Learn from the joy of Nature, so to be
Not only quite resigned to thy worst fears,
But like herself superior to them all.
Not only superficial in thy smiles,

For down the inmost fibre of thy heart
Let goodness run, and fix in that
The ever lapsing tides, that lesser thoughts
Deprive of half their patience. Be throughout,
Warm as the inmost life that fills the world,
And in demeanor show thy safe content,
Annihilating change.

So Vernon lived,
Considerate to his kind! His love bestowed
Was not a thing of fractions, half-way done,
But with a mellow goodness like the sun,
He shone o'er mortal hearts, and brought their buds
To blossoms, thence to fruits and seed.
Forbearing too much counsel, yet with blows
In pleasing reason urged, he took their thoughts
As with a mild surprise, and they were good,
Even though they knew not whence it came,
Or once suspected that from Vernon's heart,
That warm o'er-circling heart, their impulse flowed.

THE WANDERER.

A COLLOQUIAL POEM.

BY

WILLIAM ELLERY CHANNING.

BOSTON:
JAMES R. OSGOOD AND COMPANY,
(LATE TICKNOR & FIELDS, AND FIELDS, OSGOOD, & CO.)
1871.

Boston:
Stereotyped and Printed by Rand, Avery, & Co.

The Dedication.

I DREAMED a star from unknown skies
Was shining on the narrow earth:
Or was the beauty from her eyes
The light that gave my spirit birth?

I dreamed the spring caressed the flowers,
And sunshine danced about the tree:
Or was the light, its golden showers,
That soft perfume, thy modesty?

Across the sea thy beauty came
To this far shore so darkly chill;
But now a voice, how sweet! I hear,
And those pure eyes — I see them still, —

A richer hope and nobler traits,
The dowry of a splendid race, —
Oh let us ask the hurrying fates
To leave the spell in Liza's face!

PREFACE.

THE editor of this volume, who has urged the author to permit its publication, and charged himself with its care, has submitted a part of it to my inspection, and requested me to insert in the book my impressions. It is proper to own, that the author has not been consulted, or even informed of this interference, which it is not certain that he will pardon. But the editor affirms his own rectitude.

I would fain conciliate any generous reader by suggesting that there is new matter and new spirit in this writing; that, if the poems are imperfect according to our received canons, they yet point to new art: as the first daguerres were grim things enough, yet showed that a great engine had been invented. These poems are genuinely original, with a simplicity of plan which allows the writer to leave out all the prose of artificial transitions, — a series of sketches of natural objects, such as abound in New England, inwreathed by the thoughts they suggest to the contemplative pilgrim, —

"Unsleeping truths by which moves on heaven's prime."

Here is a naturalist who sees the flower and the bird with a poet's curiosity and awe, — does not count the stamens in the aster, nor the feathers in the wood-thrush, but rests in the surprise and affection they awaken. His interest in nature is not pedantic, much less culinary, but insatiably curious of the hint it gives of its cause, and its relation to man. All his use of it is free and searching, and with too much sympathy to affect more than is compelled.

The author has one essential talent of his art, — surprise. In the "Poets' Corner" of the newspaper we read a line or a stanza, and, perceiving that we can guess the rest, turn to the telegraphic news. But the reader of "The Mountain" must proceed to the end of the canto. We like the poet whose thought we cannot predict, and whose mind is so full of genuine knowledge, that we are sure to be enriched by every verse.

I dare not offer this little volume as a sure prize to the circulating libraries. This book requires a good reader, — a lover and inquirer of nature; and such a one will find himself rewarded. I can easily believe that many a reader and perhaps writer of popular poetry will, after short experiment, turn away with disdain from this rude pamphlet, and thank his stars that his culture has made him incapable of pleasure from such charcoal-sketching. But I confide that the lover of woods and hillsides, and the true philosopher, will search, with increasing curiosity, records of nature and thought so novel and sincere. Here is Hamlet in the fields with never a thought to waste even on Horatio's opinion of his sallies. Plainly the author is a man of large reading in a wide variety of studies ; but his books have not tamed his invincible personality.

I confess to a certain impatience of a needless or even wilful neglect of rhythm in a poet who has sometimes shown a facility and grace in this art which promised to outdo his rivals, and now risks offence by harshness. The reader may reasonably ask, "Is not rhythm worth the study of the poet?" But I remember we once had in Massachusetts a highly-esteemed painter, who was color-blind, and who, after working long on his picture, was forced to call in a friend to tell him whether he had not been using umber instead of cobalt in sketching his sky. One would think the poet before us had fits of deafness to rhythm, and was too impatient, or loved and trusted his fancy too entirely, to risk a critical study of metre. If color-blind painters, why not rhythm-deaf poets, or with that defect at certain hours, when the inspiration is not yet on? Or why should not that befall the bard which has befallen some famed orators, who, when they begin to speak, hesitate and stammer, but, warming with their subject, surmount every barrier, and suddenly command themselves and their audience.

If there is neglect of conventional ornament and of correct finish, which even looks a little studied, as if the poet crippled his pentameters to challenge notice to a subtler melody, yet here are strokes of skill which recall the great masters. Here is the mountain truly pictured, the upland day, the upland night, the perpetual home of the wind, and every hint of the primeval agencies noted ; and the thoughts which these bring to youth and to maturity. There is nothing conventional in the theme or the illustration, — no, but "thoughts that voluntary move harmonious numbers," and pictures seen by an instructed eye.

Perhaps we may even thank the poet, who, in his verse, does not regard the public. It is written to himself, — is his forest or street experience ; the record of his moods, fancies, observations, and studies, and will interest good readers as such. He confides in his own bias for meditation and writing. He will write, as he has ever written, — whether he has readers or not. But his poems have to me and to others an exceptional value for this reason, — we have not been considered in their composition, but either defied or forgotten, and therefore consult them securely as photographs.

R. W. E.

CONTENTS.

WOOD.

MOUNTAIN.

SEA.

WOOD.

The Wanderer.

I.

THE WOOD.

All through the wood I walked : I sought the glade
Where the soft uncut grass makes fittest paths,
And by the pine harp-shaped, of Erin's bards
Or Welsh Cadwallader, or lady graced
To touch the sounding-strings, oft musing, —
Next I reached the eminence whence we look
Down on the village.

That small country-place,
Much domineered by elms (the fathers' care
By each new house to set a votive plant, —

Custom long dead), I sometimes paused to view, —
Not high with palace-walls, or storied keep;
Nor mossy abbeys, green in ivy bright;
Nor towering steeples, mentors of the sky, —
And sometimes heard such bell-notes as it has,
Sound out the common hour, or mortals' years,
Slow tolling from the wrinkled hand of one
Who meekly pulls the rope; and saw the smoke
Rise gradual, as the evening meal progressed,
Product of artists from a foreign strand.
Not wholly strange to me the far-off roofs
That flung, like Virgil's, taller shades at eve,
Nor greatly prized.

I sometimes heard,
Rising in intervals, the speechless wind
Sough through the pines, and touch the whispering oak leaf
In these wintry days, and whiff the snow-cloud
In the chill traveller's face. Not all alone,
Seeing the clouds go over the tall woods,
With patches of blue sky still intermixed,

Or spidery interlacings, as the sun,
Now lowering, drew bright webs out of the twigs,
And sometimes, in the pine, shot out his rays
Prismatic, — fringes of blue, gold, and red, —
Contrived, I think, for fit society,
Such as the titmice or the rabbit, scared
As each new nimble bound echoes his taps
Along the unheeding wood.

How still and spare!
Silent and dedicate the woodland spaces,
As the day's last hour, in dead of winter,
Counts upon the trees its lifeless dirges!
Was there no secret hidden deep in thee,
Thou faltering Silence? Hast thou never asked
Who's coming? standing there, the falling leaf
Alone thy monitor, or wandering breath
Of the unthoughtful air, or partridge-whirr,
Fearing our race as much as we fear thine.
All day the winter sun has spoiled the snow
On all the southern slopes, — melted it off,

And brought the russet forth, coin of the pine.
You almost think there might have lurked a breath
Of mute relenting in the eager frost
That hangs about you like a nettle robe,
Making the pulses ebb ; but Winter's will
Designs more malice, and must chill to the end.

Well, I could pray, — could kneel, and beg the power
That keeps the voiceless solitude for such
As I, to intermit the old decrees,
The fixed resolve, that, in these northern climes,
Killing is the true fact of sharpest frost.
And yet his livelong inattention proves
His skin to hang far looser than my own.
And then fancy the dull man wandering round
As I, vexing the sly world with questions,
Heard his queries solved and plainly answered :
Came, by some-taste of learning, to the sense
Of all the senseless facts, — both heat and cold ;
Four seasons and two poles ; two suns a-top ;
An earth forever spinning to defeat,

Forever spinning to be brave again;
To-day the mute withdrawal; then the bound,
From whence exudes the multifarious kind,—
To walk a pale colossus o'er the dust!
Conceive I held all, clearly explicate,
Here in my hand: might I so front the wood?
Should it not flout and leer? cast grinning outlooks?
Or ask me why I came, the pet of Nature,
With my well-oiled locks to laugh at them,
Poor pensioners, in their rinds straitly enclosed,
And sometimes half allowed to drop a nut,
Cheap accident, if it live? Shall I, the heir
Of this poor wintry ancestor, insist
That I should probe the secret to disclose
The end of Nature's bashfulness, as if
Her breath were sweet as Persian amulet
In her face the shining curls of Helena,
And beauty's eyelash?

Wait! Decided closely,
He who much strives to stay the longest leaves

A little later than the earliest called,
Says a few words, arranges a few facts,
Then drops the veil, and enters Nature's hall.
I hurry forward where the leafless trees
Are wrapped in silence, as the red cold light
Of January's sunset touches each
As with a fire of icicles, — how calm!
Oh! transient gleams yon hurrying noisy train,
Its yellow carriages rumbling with might
Of volleyed thunder on the iron rail
Pieced by the humble toil of Erin's hand,
Wood and lake the whistle shrill awakening.
Transient, — contrast with the unthinking cold,
The ruddy glare of sunset in the west,
And the first flicker of the icy stars,
While the pale freezing moon calmly assists
To point their rays more sharp, — transient and stern!
To-morrow the cold loam spreads over man,
His swelling plans crushed out so utterly,
The deadest of the dead is no more sure;
But bright the snow-drift in the still moonshine;

Bright, as the crystal spicules cleave the air
In shivers ; and the more alone he walks
Whose friends that were sleep in *another* land,
Or those who loved in youth now hate his name.

Brief trace of man goes in these wintry fields, —
A slow, consumptive figure sometime comes
To glean for scattered sticks, or rake his chip,
His poor Bucephalus a wheelbarrow ;
And farther, in the margin of the piece,
A cottage light, precedent of a race
Who rise as far in Nature as her knees,
Wherein they much ignore that Nature lives.
And, in the days made mild by winter thaws,
I sometimes tracked the salient river-shore,
Or wandered on the ridges to the cliff, —
Brown fields devote to pastures, herdless now,
When sear the grasses, — and a wide domain
Whereon a son of earth, who knew this place,
Might cheer his lungs and taste a cheap delight.

Methinks I knew, or heard, of such a one,
Who sometimes came in winter, when the year
Seemed early flowering; he who first explored
The willow in its island, if the heat
Hid in the dark ditch-bottom did not stir
And silver its spruce catkin, and insist
That late or early she should show her flowers.
Oft musing thus, he visited the lodge
Of the sagacious muskrat building domed,
And noted how the fox, going his rounds
Daily and true as milkman's, came each time
To call at the brown cabin, and inquire
Upon the flesh of the inhabitant.
Too much, he thought, may man conceive himself.
Have these consistent creatures no concerns?
Or must we sink them on that poor excuse,
Replete with sound, called "instinct"? Cheap device
Of close self-seeking, which dares not respire
A loving science, nor may grant the fox
E'en the poor drop of brains he ought to have.

He eats the muskrat, and we name him "wild,"—
And what eats man?

Sometimes, perchance, he paused,
Holding mute dialogue with stock and stone;
Nor idly passed the chopper at his tree,
Without demanding what the season wore,
What bird was at its song? if the sap stirred?
And long discussed that puzzling variance
Of maple-bud and willow-bark to know
Whether his eyes, or they, had started first.
From these tough-handed men, with broken nails,
Grimed fingers rich in frost-cracks, and short words,
Clad, like the groves, in bark, he often drew
Useful conclusions. And how much their work
Drives in upon their mind the stores of knowledge
That the small, probing, questionable man,
Who makes the fool of nature, never gets!
And though soft-hearted, and with nervous dread,
Still hearkened to their talk of otters killed,
Stories of snakes, and boat-loads of the muskrat

Slaughtered to-day, and the like crimes of the gun, —
Man being the cruelest murderer.

In March
He traced the warmish wood-depths, glad to explore
The sheltered darlings of the spring, whose leaves,
Earliest unbound in broad veratrum, take
The gazer's eye ; and watched the cowslip's gold
In a forelooking mood ; and heard the bee
Hum in the calla, while the beetle's rings
Drew their white circles on the gleaming sand :
For he could see and trust, — see and delight !
The compensation in his element
Came forth didactic, cousin to the scene,
Still flowering as it should. He, faithful, thus
Unfolded, in propriety, the suits
That his long practising in Nature's court
Had settled with the costs. Sometimes he heard
The partridge in the spring, like a low thunder
Muffled in the wood, swell through the verdures,
And the wood-thrush chant in the green alleys,

Wherein the tough pitch-pine builds her soft bowers.
I think whate'er he found he loved ; kneeling
As some dread worshipper before the shrine,
Wholly desirous to be one with God.
No summer's fire, no winter's blast, nor life
With its unnumbered sorrows for all hearts,
Not that which shuts the door to mortal thought,
Could blot away the fond belief in him,
That even through all Nature he must pass,
So having known her. She would not prove false
To one who loved her, as that poet said,
The eldest of the bards in Keswick's vale,
Who clomb Helvellyn's brow, and loved his rock.
No doubt the knowing critic must have told —
Had there been critics here (a race distract) —
That our delightful wanderer might achieve
More hopeful deeds in cities walled, and marts ;
Yet shall not these crude solitudes permit
At monstrous intervals some special eye
Here interested?

To these quiet woods,
And to the ponds as still, I frequent came;
The waters, late so sparkling, now all rest,
Fast in their icy floors till Spring's warm hand
Pass o'er them, and awake their sleeping forms.
A flat and rustic landscape, loosely done;
Moist bottoms, where the rushes grow; low fields;
Swamps built on sphagnum; most of all,
The shrubby woods, late felled, with brush new-risen;
Small saplings and thin bushes, where the leaves
Hang mournful all the winter, and lament
The hopelessness of life. No stuccoed piles,
Daubed by remoter ages rich in Time,
That write the history of barbaric deeds,
Tall phantoms of the past, towering to shade
The present, mark these hollow vales; if aught,
A recent story, where the actors yet
Walk with the living, and omit the date.
But if thus homely be the novel space,
So chimes it better with the fortune plain
Of them that till the dirt, and make its plum

Their pride. They own no high achievement,
They boast no means but as their labor yields.
No pale, hereditary flame gilds here
A crown; no hives of painted lords exalt
O'er the dull bondsman, whose own name is index
Of what were farmers in the olden day, —
"Bond" meaning "farmer."

And for me, the same,
These dells seemed like my fortunes, as the leaves
That strewed the wayside path, and 'neath my feet
Went crackling in the frost, trod under foot,
And by their living kindred left to die
Unknown, uncared for, e'en their own descent
Hating the thought to mingle with the fallen;
Left for the farmer's wagon to crush down,
Or the wild forest-fire to lick in air,
And snatch for good. In these peculiar scenes
I sometimes caught an echo of the past,
Lessons of sunk religions sounding faint:
The race was born to suffer — so shalt thou;

Was born to perish — so must thou, quickly;
And ever swift the changeful seasons walk;
The icy Boreas comes, and nips thy ears;
The furnace of July consumes the earth;
Round runs the year; and soon the years repass
With an indifferent gait.

Doth the wind
Blowing across the pasture, where the bent,
Long frozen to its core, sighs through the ice,
Survey the landscape? care if green or gray?
Or the swift partridge, o'er the withered leaves
Darting like arrows from an archer's bow,
Demand protection of the season's tooth,
Getting his fill of twigs and frozen buds,
And even the dry leaves, — things to his taste?
Or the unenvied crow, who flaps across
The frequent road, purloining light repast,
Quarrel with the north-west breeze, that mocks
His penury, and beats against his wing
With demon fury? Oft in the season

Dreary to the mind, and at its coldest hour,
A feathery drumming from some wood I hear
Of pine, behind my landscape lying far,—
A softly rolling hum, a feathery sob,—
The music of the owl, softest of sounds,
Half-buried in itself, and far beyond
All pathways that I tread, and yet a part,
Truly a fraction of the winter sum,
When every figure counts. So far from man
This sweetest owl, which human speech calls hooting;
And sometimes in my road I meet a form,
Which all the murderous crew pursue with hounds,—
I mean the slim red fox, his drooping brush
Flitting before me; and his graceful bounds
Bring back Æsop's tradition of his breed,
Giving the fox the mastery o'er the beasts.
Has sovereign Nature spared her faithful court?
The poor fox, gaunt to famine, dreads the sun,
And takes his walk at midnight to devour
Some game less wakeful. Nature is so careless!
She projects her race, then leaves it struggling:

New races hatch, and eat away its heart.
Life is at loose ends. Yet mark the titmice, —
Smallest of the tribe, mere specks of feathers,
Bits of painted quill, so delicate, a flaw
From either pole would extirpate the race :
Such little twittering mites contemn the storm.
That wintry moth I never fail to find,
And the hard snows have spiders of their own.
Let any thaw ensue, how green the plants,
That, mid the russet grass, put forth their leaves,
Spreading resigned their verdure ! clovers bright,
And veiny hawkweeds, and soft, drooping ferns ;
And down the brook, the wild cress moving free
Where'er the ice-chink lets the traveller's glance
Peruse the inward pages of the stream.

II.

THE HERMIT.

Ah, me! what brave content pervades the storm!
How the wind whistles, and outdoes the arts
In raising cornices along the wall!
Or when the gray destroyer from the East
Drives up his frozen troops in cutting sleet,
I feel the thankful chant, that, truly here,
"In these flat pastures and prosaic plains,
Life still has joys, because it still has pains."
Then o'er our upland swells, it cheers to roam,
Where the audacious blast chants loud its hymn,
And the insolent squalls roll by, resolved
To force us downward. Soon, once more below
Into the shelter of the groves I sink,
Delighted with the lee. Of these rich joys,
None can defraud us; and I thank the kind,

That, on our fields dim-moving, — life of fear!
Yet seize their spoil of freedom, — chosen times,
When the tormentor, Man, is barred within;
Then, in the revels of the storm-clad powers,
The howling east or the tempestuous south,
They sally forth contented, and become
Lords of the puny land again, itself
Their own.

Somewhat of this and higher laws
Once brought a hermit to the lowly bank
Of one of these poor ponds that glaze our fields,
Where, for a season, he might quaff the wine
Of nature in full piquancy, and thus
Become well satiate with it. Partly for this, —
Because our man kept other crusade high
Beyond all I pursue; strains of mad faith
And thin tradition rocking in his dream
With their distracting creatures, and afloat
Setting good part of all things sane he knew.
Yet in his stupid moments he half loved

The generous Giver that o'erflowed his cup,
And gave his droning talent chance to shoot;
Filled out his sandy life with our stray pond;
Sought him gay color for his sunset walk,
And morning-lights that were not made in vain,
And icy moonlight, life's true portraiture,
And his own dreadful faith, that praised itself.
Here on the shore, where I more often tread
In the cold season, this conformer dug,
And built a scanty lodge to bar the cold;
For even he, much as he loved tradition,
Never could heat his limbs with ritual Bibles,
But struck up a fire.

I loved to mark him,
So true to Nature. In his scanty cabin,
All along the walls, he hid the crevice
With some rustic thought, — a withered grass,
Choice-colored blackberry-vines, and nodding sedge
Fantastically seeded; or the plumes
The golden-rod dries in the fall; and tops

Of lespedeza, brown as the Spanish name;
And velvet bosses quaintly cut away
Off the compliant birches, of whose trunks
This hermit blest made pillage. Here he sat,
The most contented hermit on the earth,
Full of glad sounds, and full of pleasant thoughts,
Delighted with the village and the pond,
And with himself, the darling of the whole.

Aside from all the jaundice he had caught
From the seducing past, I think he dwelt
As near to nature's heart as most who breathe;
Nor robust woodman, and the sallow tribe
Of dreaming poets or thin writing folk,
Enjoy more comfort in their lonely life.
True, the traditions of the race still ticked
Like spiders in the web, shut in his ears;
And still he heard that drumming in his dreams,
And schemed reforms to agitate the earth
With penny wisdom, and insure the peace.
Yet oft he fed the titmice from his hand;

And the old, cautious muskrat, who, behind
This hermit's hut, had built himself a house,
Felt no alarm at him who daily left
An alms at his back-door, and kept the faith.
When the short winter-days ran rapid out,
If clear the air, he heard the small pond sing
Its well-known strains of pleasure and of praise,
As on the strings of an Æolian lyre;
And saw the sentry pines that fringe the east
Erect their emerald tips along the eve,
While all the singular fibres of the pond
Kept on their whining music.

In those times,
Rarely there passed his door some of those friends
That here survive the downfall of their strength, —
The old inhabitants, the moles and mice;
Perchance upon his roof scenting the stores
Of frugal wheat and corn there left to cool, —
Grains that he ground united, for himself,
In a spent mill, upon his theory,

(For surely he had such a thing, and kept
A theory, on which he lived and moved
And had his being,) slept and sang and piped.
Why should he not? Have we not all some such,
Howe'er we strive to hate it?—a bequest
Of lean tradition from dead yesterdays,
Less wise than this good soul's. Dearly he prized
The hungry winter-nights, when owlets sang,
And pale above the moon careered in heaven,
To such as he a phantom of delight!
And when he heard the frost crack in the tree,
Fancying some ghostly fabled beast come forth
To mock at nature's patience and reserve,
This hermit bawled such ballads to the stars,
The wintry fields, and all the depth of snow,
And that cold, staring moon, that nature's self
Came out to hear his cry, and sat half pleased.

Not always went he lonely; for his thought
Retained the touch of one whose guest he was,—
A large and generous man, who, on our moors

Having built up his thought (though with an Indian
tongue,
And fittest to have sung at Persian feasts,
Or been the prince of Afric, or the lord
Of all the genii in the Arab chant),
Still dwelt among us as the sage he was;
Sage of his days, patient and proudly true,
Whose word was worth the world, whose heart was
pure,
Type of our best ancestrals, English blood
Drawn down in generous measures from the race
Whom Sidney, Milton, and the others knew,
The pious Herbert with the saintly Vaughan,
And splendid Shakspeare, playing Nature's game.
Oh, such a heart was his! no gate or bar:
The poorest wretch that ever passed his door
Welcome as highest king or fairest friend
To all his store, and to the world beside.
And in his tent sometime our hermit sat,
Listening discourse most welcome from the dame
Rarest in shooting darts of wit and love,
Such as most hermits prize.

This English man
(Seldom the hermit's guest) of whom I spake
Could much admire the skill from which he drew
With his small sources those adornments rare,
His curious emblems, — as a blue-jay's wing
Found on my path, a votive from the skies;
Or with the pensile cranberry redly-bright,
Or the less frequent yew's delightful fruit,
Whose coral drops surpass the lustrous blush
Of Southern rubies. Surely this hermit
In his plain-kept hut shaped out a mystery
Deserving of repute, noting his means, —
Mere straws or stems, some o'erspent Johnswort flowers,
And quaint anomaly of pitch-pine cones,

But how could him that hermit quite content,
Creature of custom? Such the spell of love!
A loving heart supplies the occasion ripe.
For if the genius of all learning flamed
Aloft in those pure eyes: if never hour,

Nor e'en the smallest instance of his times,
Could ever flit, nor give that soul reward;
Yet in his sweet relations with his race
Pure mercy lived. He held his noble wealth
For others, as a pearl of rare device,
If set to enterprise in scholar's tasks,
And so less imminent to common life.
But, oh! his goodliness, as that hermit knew:
The merest waif from nothing cast upon
The shores of this rich heart became a gem,
So regal then its setting. I have marked
The silliest apes, the fops of fashion, stand
And think themselves lord arbiters of fate,
Raised by the polished methods of this soul
To rarer problems than their half-done brains
E'er doubted; seen the choughs and cuckoos swell
To bursting, and march off, immoderate.

MOUNTAIN.

III.

THE MOUNTAIN.

At times, the hermit and myself forsook
The narrow boundary of that small place ;
And nothing being left of novel there,
If ever was such element, we roamed
Afar the rocky upland, seeking new
And wilder pastures to contemplate near,
Thinking that thus might come a change of thought, —
Perhaps to me ; for in the hermit's faith,
Thought, like the pumpkin, yielded but a rind.
Wearily he drew his scanty members
O'er the snow-clad ground, in theory as stout
As him fed up on grossness, and more weak,
In my poor estimate, than some slim boy's.
Far we tramped, dragging along the snow,
Through which for very joy I sometime danced

At living still, and knowing one alive;
At which he laughed, to watch me skipping there,
With but a partial looseness in my joints.
Wide pastures, petty woodland, passing soon,
The little cottage where he dwells we reached
Who in great contemplation moulders life,
Or guesses that he does, — one framed to be
Saint of some feverish nation tumbling down
In hot Mahomet's pages, or like Jove,
On that Homeric fable rubbed so bright.

For in the dusty muddle of the time,
When learning goes for nothing, or much less,
He who knows not now triumphs o'er who knows,
And has more glowing honors than a prince.
Who, like the Titans might embroil the skies,
Wears rusty black, and mourns a threadbare seam, —
Him did our hermit love. In him he found
An eremite indeed, a true reformer
Cudgelled from the tomb, — Jerome or Augustine,
Longest breathed of all seraphic writers,

Whose vast tomes, heaps of indifference,
Might furnish forth whole libraries for them,
Who, in these octave days, pop out their books.
There, in his tiny cottage, with no art,
Nor graced with aught but the sublime intent,
Patronus sat upon his learned throne.
He ruled a library, a saint's true prize,
Its covers hanging awkward as the thought,
Done with self-knowledge, cheapest property.
Once as we looked from that divine abode
On those sad mountains shining on the west,
Blue as philosophy, and as far off,
We asked our Mentor if his learned eye,
Drawn outward, had been raised to Nature's height,
Whether he filled the prospect with himself,
Or was himself the creature of the scene.
But you could ask this creature all day long
A hundred questions, and renew the quest.
Reminded thus of those aerial heights,
And nothing doubting, to that point I bent,
I, with the hermit; and once there we sat

On the ascending slope in festive mood,
Across the valleys gazing on dim heights,
And looking in the valleys for a place
To which I fancy I might once pertain.
Strange, a few cubits raised above the plain,
And a few tables of resistless stone
Spread round us, with that rich, delightful air,
Draping high altars in cerulean space,
Could thus enchant the being that we are! —
Those altars, where the airy element
Flows o'er in new perfection, and reveals
Its constant lapsing (never stillness all),
As a mother's kiss touching the bright spruce-foliage;
And in her wise distilment the soft rain,
Trickling below the sphagnum that o'erlays
The plateau's slope, is led to the ravine,
And so electrified by her pure breath,
As if in truth the living water famed,
Recorded in John's mythus, who first dashed
Ideal baptism upon Jordan's shore,

Where doomed Tiberias o'er Gennesareth,
Burns up her smoking columns to the sky,
From Thermæ famed, — dead as her Herod now.

In this sweet solitude, the Mountain's life,
At morn and eve, at rise and hush of day,
I heard the wood-thrush sing in the white spruce,
The living water, the enchanted air
So mingling in the crystal clearness there,
A sweet peculiar grace from both, — this song,
Voice of the lovely mountain's favorite bird !
These steeps inviolate by human art,
Centre of awe, raised over all that man
Would fain enjoy and consecrate to one,
Lord of the desert and of all beside,
Consorting with the cloud, the echoing storm,
When like a myriad bowls the mountain wakes
In all its alleys one responsive roar ;
And sheeted down the precipice, all light,
Tumble the momentary cataracts, —
The sudden laughter of the mountain-child !

Here haunts the sage of whom I sometime spake, —
Ample Fortunio. On the mountain-peak
I marked him once, at sunset, where he mused,
Forth looking on the continent of hills;
While from his feet the five long granite spurs
That bind the centre to the valley's side
(The spokes from this strange middle to the wheel)
Stretched in the fitful torrent of the gale,
Bleached on the terraces of leaden cloud
And passages of light, — Sierras long
In archipelagoes of mountain sky,
Where it went wandering all the livelong year.
He spoke not; yet methought I heard him say,
"All day and night the same; in sun or shade,
In summer flames and the jagged biting knife
That hardy winter splits upon the cliff, —
From earliest time the same. One mother
And one father brought us forth, thus gazing
On the summits of the days, nor wearied
Yet if all your generations fade:
The crystal air, the hurrying light, the night,

Always the day that never seems to end,
Always the night whose day does never set ;
One harvest and one reaper, ne'er too ripe,
Sown by the self-preserver, free from mould,
And builded in these granaries of heaven,
This ever living purity of air,
In these perpetual centres of repose
Still softly rocked."

I looked ; but he was gone.
I saw his robe gleam on the clean-cut stone ;
Nor did I doubt he trod the downward path,
Where we had raised, with competent ado,
That vernal mansion sometimes named in sport
The True Observatory, so to stay
The unversed footstep from these mocking paths.
We found him in the camp (I mean Fortunio) ;
His foot as fleet to scale those pinnacles
As the wild chamois and the Switzer Tell,
Who in the breast of tyrants smote his shaft.
He then resumed his singing, or I dreamed :

Upon the mountain's side no hour is vain,
No fatal thought e'er passes through the mind.
Low in the valley hangs the village church;
I note the tavern with its rusted sign
Creak in the blast, and hear the drover's voice
As on he sweeps his herd, wild as his bulls,
From the pastures high returning: there, below
The cottage lamp gleams forth, ere on the hill
Our daylight flits, or the first tearful stars
Have dallied o'er Wachusett: the hind comes
Home to the evening meal, his children round;
And the coarse village cur, dozing all day,
Essays to hoarsely wheeze largest response
To his adhesive neighbors. On the height,
Diminished thus in distance to mere specks,
I view the fear, the fortune, and the fate
Of that same mortal race chanted in song.
And while the eagles, soaring o'er the peak,
By their shrill echoing whistles fright the hare
Bounding along the naked mountain-side,
And the grave porcupine his shuffling quills

Marches along the ledges black as Ind,
I mark the starry host assert their reign,
Or muse on Nature's income, or my own.
Was there a time when these half-answering hills
Lay at the frown of an ambitious sea,
Grinding along with its cold worlds of ice,
Till, all the furrowed surface deeply carved,
The saline torment took its hand away,
And left a course of splinters in dry air,
To mock the baffled thinker of an orb,
Where somewhat thinks superior to himself.
Oh! what a day, and night of days, swept by,
As, slowly o'er the gray unmoving hills,
In endless march deployed the polar host!
Oh! what an hour when that sea-tossing mass
Began to cut the coast-lines, and map out
The rays of a few continents, and drop
Their bowlders in the path!

Why ask, refused,
Why solitary in the clear expanse

The ceaseless tragedies revolve forlorn?
Nor showman's *bâton*, nor responsive shout
Of all the tribe who make this peak their friend
For a few hurried hours, disturbs the dream.
They speak of questions answered in the deep,
As if these curious carvings were but flung
Aside, like mason's chippings from his blocks,
And left to fill the rut of Nature's road.
They stand forever silent in themselves,
(Whether interior instincts dwell in such,
So speechless, or some deeper cause presides,
Barring out human nature from the ken
Of these presumed concealments,) and disposed
Rather to end, and make no sign, than speak.
Amen! by this neither we lose or gain;
The phantoms of a morn whose blinking sun
Shoots swift combustion, or prefaces death,
And whate'er more, the preface to a tale.

Fair on the hillside as beseemed the state,
Of small spruce-boughs supported by the ash,

Whose crimson berries in September's sun
Lay sparkling jewels o'er the mountain's breast,
There, in a native cot with three stone walls,
I had built out a sort of summer-house,
(As much to nature's trickery owing
As my own) ; and viewed beneath the lowlands ;
The little hamlets with their shining roofs,
When burning noontide fell plumb from the sky ;
The flicker of the tapers from the night ;
And clouding lakes and woods, all still, unless,
Like battle's brunt, I heard the quarries boom
In far Fitzwilliam, where the granite ledge
Hurls forth its masses for the griping town,
Or the far train sighing in lonely fear ;
And never ceased to feel a certain power
That o'er me ruled, uplifted in the height
Of all the crystal sky and perfect air,
Where, but the breath of man were such a thing,
I might have thought vitality a crown.

And here the hermit sat, and told his beads,

And stroked his flowing locks, red as the fire,
Summed up his tale of moon and sun and star:
"How blest are we," he deemed, "who so comprise
The essence of the whole, and of ourselves,
As in a Venice flask of lucent shape,
Ornate of gilt Arabic, and inscribed
With Suras from Time's Koran, live and pray,
More than half grateful for the glittering prize,
Human existence! If I note my powers,
So poor and frail a toy, the insect's prey,
Itched by a berry, festered by a plum,
The very air infecting my thin frame
With its malarial trick, whom every day
Rushes upon and hustles to the grave,
Yet raised, by the great love that broods o'er all
Responsive, to a height beyond all thought!"

He ended, as the nightly prayer and fast
Summoned him inward. But I sat and heard
The night-hawks rip the air above my head,
Till midnight o'er the warm dry, dewless rocks;

And saw the blazing dog-star droop his fire,
And the low comet, trailing to the south,
Bend his reverted gaze, and leave us free.
At times I sat in July's fiercest ray,
Until the solid heat had fairly flayed
Me in her crucible, and the small cisterns,
Where the good mother kept my royal purl,
Had gone to air. Each night renews the waste;
And still each morn the cold pellucid bath
With faith revives the fainting soul, and forth
I step elate upon my chosen path,
Snatching the dewy fragrance of the hour.
Then in the happy sunlight, and the first
Of all those endless hours we name July,
What chosen beauty gleams among the copse
While each lovely tree welcomes its snow-bird;
This his summer-home: his graceful trill,
Perpetually fresh, delights the ear
From spruce to spruce, and the quick glimmering
Of his slaty tail (snow-white its circle)
Sends out most cheerful omens to the eye.

"Here let us live and spend away our lives,"
Said once Fortunio, "while below, absorbed,
The riotous, careering race of man,
Intent on gain or war, pour out their news.
Let us bring in a chosen company,
Like that the noblest of our beauteous maids
Might lead, — unequalled Margaret! herself
The summary of good for all our state;
Composedly thoughtful, genial, yet reserved,
Pure as the wells that dot the ravine's bed,
And lofty as the stars that pierce her skies.
Here shall she reign triumphant, and preside
With gentle prudence o'er the camp's wild mood,
Summoning forth much order from what else
Surely must prove unsound."

Here in the blast,
Drawn from the ranges of our westering hills,
That like far meadows strewn with haycocks lie,
Cool as most well-iced wine, erect the blaze,
Fruit of Herculean labor from the strength

Of one whose hand serves him for others' needs
(No thought of self e'er soils his manly glove),
Blaze of no dry or fitful accident,
The toy of wintry frolic on these slopes,
White as a grandsire's locks ; but of green spruce,
Tough and substantial as her granite roots,
And with strong lights painting the ravine's face,
Or Tintoretto's reds and Rembrandt's shade,
And some fine impulse for our human eyes.
Here let us list the descant bravely raised,
Hymn for the Kaiser, or that seashore lay
Sung on the strand, though inland in its theme ;
O Rolling River! boldly may it swell,
Till the dear creatures on the dark low plain
Catch the sweet strain of music, taught by art
Of distance, to unfold the lenient melody ;
And the loud-blazing torches of birch-bark
Repeat the Indian's war-dance to the cliffs!
Nor let us pass the Spirit of the hills,
One whom no July's blaze has faintly tanned,
No fierce, precipitous slide ever deters

From leaping gladdened down the fearful pass,
His Alpine tira-lira echoing sweet,
And lion curls far sweeping in the blast.
To him such solitudes have been a prayer,
A fount of inspiration, and his hopes,
Whene'er the problem rises, such as youth
From out the store of green expectancy
Brings musing. Then swift he braved the peaks,
Folded his arms, and in the wayward blast,
Tearing the thoughts to ribbons, he would stand,
Composed as silence in the inward heart
Of all the rocking tumult, inly blest.
And now the blaze, uplifting in the breeze,
Shows the mute figures, such as not by art,
To better Gypsy camp, might be improved.
There serious listeners, those undaunted maids,
Vigorous and swift as the lithe Indian girls,
Who in the natural ages sought our rocks,
Lured by tradition to the grotto's gloom,
Or stung by love, here ventured to the taste
Of the cold precipice, and dashed in scorn

Their pulsing hearts on silence and the waste.—
Alertly swift they mount in earliest dawn
The dim Sierra's point, and Persian there,
(Like Oromazdi's tribe or Mexic priest,)
Wait the approaching day on those cold heights,
Clear as the early hour and with the hues
Of blushing morn caught on their Indian cheeks.
Sometimes I see them, standing silent, grace
The rounded rock like statues framed by art,
For worship in these deserts; sometimes hear
Their vigilant step, quick speeding home
To raise the fragrant steam, excite the urn,
Or, drawn from India's shore, the gleaming rice
Responsive boil. Oh! with much patience,
With superior views they frequent strive,
As the cool western breeze, courteously devout,
Salutes the other cheek, and with soft grace
Confers his smoky offering to the orb
Of the delighted worshipper of pan and pot,
Who by her tears proves how sincerely strong
May be a spruce's blessing.

I might deem
That rarely yet had royal hall more seat,
Richer supply of furniture produced,
Rococo or inlaid, and what more light
The Renaissance supplied. The tables, rock;
The chairs carved of the like; and so the floor,
For matutinal or vespernal rite.
And truly nobler ceiling was not framed
Than all that dome of heaven above our heads,
Dappling afar the lazy afternoons
O'er twice a hundred valleys; or, intent
To march upon our banquet, seven wild showers
In misty columns making for the plates.
And much supply of couches spread along.
Behold the mountain's floor! protend your robe
Caoutchouc's glory and the woolly friend,
And lumped therein secure, fast on your rock,
In some sharp crevice where the cornel paints
Immenser scarlet and more smashing reds
Than gorgeous Turner's palette, drop thy bones;
Soothed by the spruces murmuring in thy ear,

The ever-rising, ever-falling sigh
Of the perpetual air, and with the night,
Reserved companion, cool and sparsely clad,
Dream, till the threefold hour, with lowly voice,
Steals whispering in thy frame, "Rise, valiant youth!
The dawn draws on apace, envious of thee,
And polar in his gait: advance thy limbs,
Nor strive to heat the stones."

When August suits,
Some hasten to their haunts, and steal away
The berries blue as heaven that paint the sod
In chosen districts, sweetly edible,
As grape from torrid Spain that commerce wafts,
Or famed Sumatra's fruit, or Cuban pine,
Or where the guava shakes its purple sides,
Glory of camps! Nor let us fail to glean
Proud store of mountain cranberries (more tart
And spicy tasted them the learned deem
Than lowland species), while the faithful maid
Oft stirs the ruddy conserve, nor permits

(Child of inconstancy) the mess to burn.
This task to Madeline was frequent given.
Slight as the daisy bowing in the wind,
She owned a genial grace to charm, persuade,
With copious reasonings on didactic things,
Filled from the springs of genius like a sea,
And touching on the beach of human life
And its smooth pebbles, as a glittering spray,
A fairy music soft as eventide.

Thrice I essayed afar that eastern spur
Where the rude torrents of primeval rock,
Stripped from their canvas, toss in grandeur vast,
A pile tremendous, where four Doric shafts,
Upreared in chaos, front the eager sky,
Graced with an architrave, so that no art
Could more sublime their glory. Wandering here
Once with the hermit, I essayed to speak
Of that conclusive figure on the arch
Of this small temple, carved by nature's rule, —
Things of some prime existence ere our race

Had cast the hammer, and with meted lines
Traced out the right proportions of the form ;
Long ere the Parthenon on the Athenian mound
Constrained the view of him, who from the isles
Cycladean, swift from pirate's prow, flushes
His mainsail till old Sunium's past;
And next we skirted that supinest swamp,
Flowered with the pure white bolls of cotton-grass,
Where the decaying frames of the old trees
(I scarcely know how sprouting from the rocks,
Home of the wildcat, and the panther's house)
Lay prostrate : wrecks of the fiery storm,
That swept away their groves, and, vanquished, cast
To dry and whiten on the careless stones
Beneath the unheeding sky. Then eastward,
As I yet pursued that way, last coming
To the sheer untrammelled precipice that hangs
Forever wall against the small romance, —
The steading small, the little human nook
With its three speaking roofs, some pastoral smoke
Soft issuing from those hearths, a token glad

Sent to the laughing children leaving school,
And the tanned ploughman as he homeward stalks
Ached to the bone, and ragged as the wolf
That preys upon his vitals; soothed he sees.
Poised in my airy pinnacle, I paint
(The darting swallow whirring swiftly by)
At dizzy depths, far in the valley's womb,
The zigzag coil of alders, a black thread,
The serpentine progression of the Stream
That plays its rival flute-notes all the year;
See the herds feeding on the tiresome hills,
Enormous to the herdsman, and to me
As flat and motionless as I to him
Obliterate; and in truth, how sweet,
And never half as sweet the human thought!
Then wished I for some chat with roguish lad,
Or idle gossip fresh from parlors full
Of sewing charities, where ladies meet
And thread the needle, but employ the ear;
E'en the dry call of herd-boy to his cows,
His endless *goaf*, reiterate o'er the fields;

Or the white phantom of an ancient maid
Doing its shopping on a pistareen;
Or the lame parson's sulky, time-worn trap,
Sahara's sermon creaking in the wheel.

In this upraised seclusion from the race
Which holds the mirror to the earnest soul,
And bids it scan itself, and set its rate,
How rapid fly our self-conceits afar!
There in the sole unspeaking life of things,
Only the sky for answer, or the rocks
Stretched out beneath, and seeming clouds asleep;
And the bright spruces that engross the eye
Along the sharp horizon, and content,
So fine and lovely their pathetic grace:
Set in the rocks, apart and sweet and lone,
Like some chaste maid who still attracts us on;
The twittering snow-bird and the red chewink,
All voices for that place, and man so far!
Then search we out the mazy village-roads,
Stealing from town to town, a sweet response

Greeting our hearts where human feet have trod;
And village spire, and gleams of pine-clad lake,
And rippling river playful in the sun,
A glance of human sunshine on the shore
Where labor pulsates; all these signs, and more,
That earth, from this divorce. Oh! far apart,
Then, when the dying orb behind the range,
Gilds the Sierra, and on this, the night
Thrown from his Alpine shoulders, fills our souls.

IV.

HENRY'S CAMP.

AND once we built our fortress where you see
Yon group of spruce-trees sidewise on the line
Where the horizon to the eastward bounds, —
A point selected by sagacious art,
Where all at once we viewed the Vermont hills,
And the long outlines of the mountain-ridge,
Ever renewing, changeful every hour;
And, sunk below us in that lowland world,
The lone Farm-steading where the bleaching cloth,
Small spot of white, lay out upon the lawn;
Behind, smooth walls of rock, and trees each side,
Sifting the blast two ways; and on the south
Our wigwam opened, showing in its length
That flattened hay-stack or repeated hill, —
Wachusett!

Hither, not often wandered
From the vale a sportive lad, whose lessons
Rightly learned, and brought from out-door science,
Still desired the growths of nature, new or old;
Forever in review his choosing thought
Purely might sit; and so as one, the two,
Himself and Nature, truly linked might know.
So strangely was the general current mixed
With his vexed native blood in its crank wit,
That, as a mirror, shone the common world
To this observing youth, whom noting, thence
I called Idolon: ever firm to mark
Swiftly reflected in himself the Whole,
As if in truth he had been rather that
Than what he was, — a mortal as ourselves.
His ever-bubbling wit broke on the sides
Of that small plateau; and the gray rocks smiled,
And all the listening host sent up their crow.
At times, I guessed the giant porcupine,
With his black quill dropping upon my brain,
Or biting on the ledges in the glen;

And sometimes fancied, as the theme became
More cynic, that the bear, lurking below,
Had scaled deep Purgatory and crawled out
To hear the sport, or sharpen up his claw;
So radiant was his talk. Much did he know
The face of all the hills, and stopped to read
Lecidea's black or green parmelia's fruit,
And the round shields that lobe the olive cliffs,
(Tripe of the rock and Muhlenbergian styled),
Or alpine heaths, and where the mosses grew
Most complex in their teeth, and gracious ferns,
Or jungermannia, rich in purple fronds,
Painting the trunks with its delicious tint.
Each hour this laughing boy tenacious caught
A fist full of existence, spread it out
Flat on its back, and dried it in the sun
Of all his breezy thoughts to shape its truth.
Intent to know what meant the outward life
To an unwearied searcher, never slack,
Yet fixed within it all, himself he saw,
Shooting his arrows into all that crowd

Of unaspiring objects, quite engaged
Simply in carrying on their general trade;
Whereat Dame Nature smiled to see her boy.
Oh! let him search in nature, — he who loves
An individual life, prepared to be
The mirror by his notions, if he may;
Yet not too boastful fancy that the kings
Who rule this lower world will stoop their crowns.
Yet the craving soul asks curious questions;
And it asks far more for its usurping pride
Than seats in speechless corners to tell beads.
Thus slumbered not Idolon; ere the day
Had broke the ebon shell, or stretched her pink
Upon the auroral curtains, he set forth,
Making as if the shepherd of the dawn
To drive his scattered flocks, and sum the tale;
In a self-comfortable pride resolved
To equalize things mundane. Much he sought
The limit of the exact. He testified
By painful art how much his world produced,
Precisely how he stood with every fact

Wherein co-adjutor with Nature's truth:
So of the mountains he would draw the map,
And thus, by circumambient tape
Deduce the just extent of those vague rocks,
What spire was that, and how yon lowland's name ;
To some, such searches in the intricate
A cold vacuity sliding and cheap :
Such scorn the petty, harnessed to the vast,
And pray for wings, and sure release from time.

Not far below our tent an Indian camp
All softly spread its shelter in the glen
Where the old mountain-road circuits the gulf:
Three wigwams here they held ; and one old man,
The hunter of the tribe, whose furrowed brow
Had felt the snow of sixty winters' fall,
At eve would mess with us, and smoke the pipe
Of peace before our cabin. He gave voice
To many a story of the past, else dim, —
Things he had done in youth, or heard them told,
And legends of religion, such as they

Who live in forests and in hardships tell.
One day Idolon said, musing of him,
"As there's no plant or bird from foreign shores
That just resembles ours, so, behind us,
Figures transported off an ancient cast, —
The Indian comes, and just as far from us.
I never dream how wildness fled from man
Among those Arab deserts, and how Greece
Fetched from the Lycian seacoast her tame myths,
Or why that fiery shore, Phœnicia's pride,
Should be so civil in her earliest creed.
But on our wild man, like this Sagamore,
Nature bestows her truthful qualities, —
Fleet on the war-path, fatal in his aim,
More versed in each small track that lightly prints
Some wandering creature, than the thing itself,
And wreathed about with festoons of odd faiths,
By which each action holds a votive power.
He hears the threatening wood-god in the wind,
That, hollow-sounding, fills his breast with fear;
His eye, forelooking as the night unrolls

The forked serpents darting on the cloud,
Sees all the great procession of his saints ;
And, while the gloom rolls out the thunder's peal,
Listens the voices of his god command.
Truly the evil spirit much he fears,
Believing, as he drains the calabash,
Or solemn fills the calumet's red bowl
With Kinni-Kinnek, that a god of love
Will not produce for him much fatal loss
To be considered. When the lightning came
And snapt the crested rock whereon he played
With all his Indian boys, he felt the bolt
Crash through his heart, and knelt before the power.
Thus with the careful savage culture fares
As the event looks forth. He does not preach
And pray, or tune of violin the string,
And celebrate the mercies of the Lord,
But flings in his fire the fish-bones, lest the fish,
Whose spirits walk abroad, detect the thief,
And ne'er permit the tribe a nibble more :
So, in the bear-feast, they are firmly bound

To swallow absolutely all that hangs
Appended, cooked or raw, about the game,
Lest he, the figment of the bear, should rise,
And thence no drop of medicable grease
The Indian coat should show, nor poll of squaw
Shine like a panel with protrusive oil.
They thus insure the state, and give the fiend,
The evil one, due homage, — pay the cash ;
And the tribe say, 'What will the good god do?
Alack! the evil one is full of wile,
And black and crafty as our Indian selves ;
Far better for us to keep peace with him.'

"A catalogue of woe the Indian's fate,
Drawn by the holy Puritan, and all
For his divine religion. Thence the names
Fixed to the aborigines, sweet titles, —
Cruel, fiendish, brute, and deeds to match,
At which the earth must rise. The Indian maids,
Oh, lovely are their forms! No cultured grace
Superior breeding, finer taste has shown ;

And tints of color in their modest cheeks
Shaming Parisian beauty with its glow.
And the young hunter, or the agile boys,
As that plain artist claimed who named the first
The Belvidere (of all the statues known to art),
Sunbright Apollo, a young Mohawk chief.
Alas! the race, possessors of these hills,
Would not at once desert their hunting-grounds,
Loved by the Pilgrim, — martyred to the cent!"

Thus could Idolon image his red race,
While o'er our heads the night-hawks darting swarm
(On sharded wing the unwary beetle
Like Indians to the godly, falling in),
Ripped through the empty space, and the young stars, —
The glittering Pleiades and Orion's crest,
Or she who holds the chair, Cassiopeia,
Or swift Boötes driving from the north,
And the red flame of war, the torrid Mars —
Oft added to our strange society
On those religious nights when all the air

That lingered on the rocks was fragrant with a flower
Not of that lowland kind. Then flit abroad
Dim figures on the solitary stones.
Almost I see the figure of my friend
Scaling the height, or running o'er the slabs;
I hear his call for which I listened long;
His fresh response, as swift I shouted back,
Echoes in the space; see his light form
Bound o'er the dark crevasse, or thread the slide
Where never from the year deserts the ice.
Stay! 'twas a shadow fluttering off the past,
A multiplex of dreams that kindled thus;
And, if near eve, the circle of small lakes,
Around the Mountain's foot securely drawn,
Like smoothest mirrors sent me back the world
Caught from their cheerful shores; and, slow revealed,
Came forth new lakes, or even seemed
A river in one path, — I thought I heard
My old companion's voice, who in his heart
Did treasure all their joys!

And great those days,
And splendid on the hills, when the wild winds
Forever sweep the cloud, at once re-formed
From off the plateau's slope; and at a breath
Uplift the sunlit valleys sweet with morn,
The hamlet's homely Grange, the dappling shades
Thrown from the sultry clouds that sail its heaven;
And in a second instant, the wild mist
Instantly obscure, the valley vanishes,
Gone as a flitting vision from the skies,
And by our camp the spruce in brightest green
Laughs at our brigand jackets shining wet.
And night, that eateth up substantial things,
Leads us strange dances o'er the chopping shelves,
Down bosky slide and gravitating cliff,
Where we go plunging madly for our lives,
All safe divisions, paths, and tracks foregone;
And balances we strike, and learn the rule,
That downward motion soon appears reversed.

At times, the hour admitted of debate, —
High topics breaking on the rocky fells
Of Church or State, and how devised their metes,
Whether such bounds are sure, or will not sway
For each superior soul. And once of love,
That subject of burlesque. "I," said Miranda,
Goddess of an isle that sleeps in Grecian seas, —
"I crave a real passion, not a ghost
Dancing about o'er airy vacancies.
May I meet human sympathies not less
Demanding lively truth of me than I
Of them! For who can fence and gesture here
In this swift-moving world, and cast away
Precarious fortune on a thin-spun web
Of blank deception, blowing in the air?
May be that saints and lovers stupefy
Themselves and others with a threadbare dream,
Like famous Dante, that translated great,
To whom poor Beatricé was a myth,
As to his last translator, gaping still.
Ideal love, my friends, do you desire?

Write some congenial sonnets to the moon,
As Sidney did, or spend your soul on one
Whose face you never saw and only guessed."

To her, who sometime spake as full of jest,
Replied a doctor of less lovely sex:
"In that ideal love I see the life
Of a confiding soul destined to soar
Beyond the vain realities he flies,
And, by his deep affection purified,
Become like Dante in a far-off dream,
Worshipping forever a superior soul.
Shall not that star to which I distant tend,
Pure in its crystalline seclusion set
To be an altar of the constant truth, —
Shall not that being, ever to my heart
Utterly sacred, some small grace impart?
Raise my dejected fortunes sunk so low?
And as I see the sunset from the peak,
Before me far the ever-reaching chains
Figured by their blue valleys thrown between,

And raised above to purer skies sublime, —
As the last beams of day o'erpass the scene,
I still forever feel the saint I love,
Never by me to be approached more near;
A distant vision lighting up my soul,
Like Helen to her lover on the heights,
And Beatricé shining through the cloud."

SEA.

V.

THE ISLAND.

DREAMING the sea the elder, I must search
In her for tidings of the olden days, —
Oldest and newest. For how fresh the breeze
That blows along the beaches! and the cry
Of the small glancing bird who runs before,
And still before me, as I find my way
Along the salt sea's ooze, seems like the frail
Admonitor of all the birds: and mark,
Forever turning, that green-crested wave,
Curve of the gleaming billows, and the weed
Purple and green and glistering, the long kelp
Swaying for ages towards the foaming strand;
For here the world is endless. On the marge
I sit of that small Island in the bay,
As an observatory anchored there,

And view the shores receding, where afar
The long sand-beach pursues his lonely way.
Sweet the scene adorned with early sunrise,
Or when a golden hour lifts the faint mist
Of the retreating dawn, and half reveals
The far green hillsides, or the scattered town,
And bits of lovely wood, a moment seen,
Like beauty smiling in her curtained couch.
And then we turn, and meet the curling swell
Roll crashing o'er his sands, — unending Surge,
Voice of another life in worlds how far!

Even like the sea himself, torn down the past,
That wrecker shows, Antonio, an old man,
Patched and repainted like his time-worn craft,
An odd tarpaulin o'er his wild gray locks,
And ever in his hand his wrecking-hook.
Cold as the strand whereon he walks he seems;
His eyes put out with gazing on the deep,
Together with the wear of seventy years,
And scanty food, chill breezes, and the spray

Running their courses in his life. Nor less
The ocean is his friend ; that mystery
Still stranger as he studies it the more.
With tempests often striking o'er his path
Linked to the wrecker's eyes with the far heaven,
Upon whose omens patiently he pores,
And dreams of crashing decks or corpses pale
Washing alone Time's melancholy shore :
Thus are they filled with wisdom who compute
The sea as their companion. Books to them
Are the faint dreams of students, save that one, —
The battered Almanac, — split to the core,
Fly-blown, and tattered, that above the fire
Devoted smokes, and furnishes the fates,
And perigees and apogees of moons.
Despite the rolling temper of the main,
He knows by sternest laws the tide revolves,
And mows his marsh disdainful of the flood :
Held by firm rules, old ocean shall obey,
Indifferently fatal, friend or foe.
Her things so new, her creatures so unlike

All which the dull unmoving shore concerns,
Amid her briny passion pledged to be
Sailors unsocial, darlings of the sea.

How smooth the seal's complexion! finely haired
To shed the searching moisture as if oiled,
Like brave Mahomet's, that unhappy sheik;
Awfully human, the seal's bearded face
Lifts in the cold green current. On the tide
That rakes the channel, there he bolts his horse;
Then stretches off his bulk on the black rocks,
Spread on the seaweed with his heated pile;
Or on the polar cake, politely warm,
Expires his fat. Nor scorn the coots that take
Cold-water treatment, riding on the surf
That combing breaks now spilt upon the sand;
All swimming as one coot from pole to pole.
Nor scare the little beach-birds, dainty thing
Mounted on stilts above the long sea-sands,
Skipping and piping by the whirling tide;
And one, neatest of all, the peep, whose nes

In the remote recesses of the north
That bird constructs, scarcely by Brewer robbed.
A manless thing, a creature with no heart
For human prayers, the cold unfeeling brine.
That tale survives all annals of the past, —
Of an old-fashioned flood, when earliest boat,
An ark, was fairly launched, victualled and stocked,
With patriarch Noah and his constant dove.
Chinese or Persian, old or newly made,
In all the creature's legends I may hear
The same relation, the same flabby tale.
'Tis Ocean's independence. " Launch your ark;
Get out the long-boat; tow a raft astern,"
Cries Ocean to her sons; " for sure am I
I cannot oil your coats, nor stamp your seals."
And man obeys, and in cork-jackets swims.
They dam the restless beach, they stone and pile.
Alack! the sea pours on its flood the same,
Turning us back, and bowing its regret.

Where the Ægean on its cerule wave
Bore forth the Grecian fleets, what green parade

Was that, to populate the sea with gods,
And tossing heroes, who the mortal state
Had raised diviner! There in peace they rolled, -
Tridental Neptune and his spouting team,
Tritonia, and the Nereids cool
Taking perpetual baths, and who the first,
(Above description) from the sea spumed forth, —
Idalian Venus, on her pink conch-shell,
Smoothing the lovely wave, and throwing smiles
Over the laughing billows. But to-day
To the depths descend the gods of ocean,
When mackerel fishers ride the hollow main,
And in the room of Phosphor, worship gold.
Honest Herodotus who marched afar
O'er Egypt's sands and Babylonia's fall,
Telling strange stories of the deaths of kings,
Gives out that Homer made the gods for men,
Some few short centuries before his time.
How vivid the Greek fancy took the sea!
Making the grave of waters yield its dead,
And in its splendid figures live and burn.

Afar upon the sky the unmoving ship
Stands leaning, her place unchanged, still leaning;
And so she stands until below the line
Of that lone horizon she silent falls;
And some fond mother's heart watching her sail,
And children's prayers that guard a father's life.
He hears the billows grating on the keel,
With their gay sheets of foam and splashing lights,
The gulf-stream past, where over Pico's cap
Sail the rich odors of the Western Isles,
And sweeping showers that cut like wings of steel;
And the long steady gale that never lulls,
Drawn through the rigging with its awful moan,
Most like the concert of the monarch-pines
That line Katahdin's walls, when the nor'westers
Scourge that woodland brig: these sounds he hears,
These sights, unmoving, sees; Neptune forgot,
Thinks of his mother knitting by the fire
In his far-sheltered cot, his wife, who lists
As o'er his cottage-roof tears the wild gale,
And hears the children, "Mother, the storm!

Will father feel the gale?" — "My child, my child!"
And folds them to her heart. Oh, mother dear!

Had but those ancients ventured o'er the wave
Like patient Colomb, urging vessels small
Across the ocean's heap, and thus surpassed
Their shining bays and sands of Punic cape,
Where still bold rovers from the Grecian isles
Dart their swift galiots at the opiate Turk;
Then had the Muse of Homer taken flight
In things cosmopolite, leaving the gods
To curl their locks unsung. But so a race
Born on that midland sea achieved new fates,
And first essayed the arts of culture there,
Founding vast cities on the mud of Nile,
Where the great river, treasure of the earth,
Spawned affluence. If old Egypt be
The creature of the river, or reverse,
Becomes me not; if mimic Palestine
Took its first lessons off Egyptian stones,
As that Sidonian with Astarte's name,

On Eshmunezzar's soros found so late;
Or when great Nineveh threw up its halls
Cased with prodigious bulls and bearded saints,
And conquering tyrants trampling on their slaves;
Whatever prescience or rank assigned
To those veiled dynasties sunk in the sleep
Of superstitious gods, and what the priest
That worshipped Moloch sprang from: grant the sea
Gave impulse to those countries, and from that
They flowed with fresh existence. Yes! that sea
And its expanse of isles blest by each other;
In azure waves where rugged Rhodes piles up
Eternal sunshine, and Telmessus sweet,
With Lycian bays, the wood-nymphs' chosen haunt,
(For here the mainland floats upon the sea);
Or Cyprus, where the Paphian goddess built
Her tall melodious shrine, and, as some think,
Called from the tree to Aphrodite vowed,
And earlier to Astarte, whence it passed
From proud Phœnicia's Tyre to Carthage bronzed;
These isles, good halfway-houses to new shores,

Nurtured the mariner on fruit and wines,
Honey and figs, and more, the grace to touch
New customs, and deport novel religions
'Mid a hulk of freight.

The timid sailors
Made small prime essays, and, venturing forth,
Amused themselves with colonies. At first
How limited the risk! The single ship
Bore off from Egypt's shores the chosen troop.
Soon, to the Grecian palm directly steered;
Where o'er Morea's hills the setting sun
Shames our opaque seclusion in its pomp;
There with the Corybants, or Bacchic priests
Lighting on Latmos, or by Delphi's shrine,
Unnamed, unknown, in those anterior days,
They sowed the seed upon the rolling heights
Of new religions, whence Olympus sprang;
And oaks Dodonian, comedy of creeds
Bred on the banks of Nile; and the tall stones
Now standing in her deserts, lone, not mute,

Bear witness that the race, forever one,
As on Mount Serbal, worships in high place,
Or still preserves the forest as its shrine,
And builds its altars on erected hills,
That mark Cholula's platform, to this hour.
Spring and fruit and fall the like traditions.
See the bold ranks of sepulchres that mask the vale
Of Kedron, line Telmessian hills; their doors,
Oblivious still, sealed up for ages.
As o'er the plains of Memphis, and the tomb
Of royal Cheops, where the Grecian stood,
That flaming star of Macedon, whose trail
Burnt from the shores of Greece to India's vale
Of far Cashmere, dreaming 'mid snowy crags, —
And wondered at the mass, what ages gone,
Whose ignorance shall boast? or by whose hands
The placid sphinxes fronting Karnak's mass,
Or Memnon's figure, musical at morn.
Ever the tomb, the dead, the mummied faith,
As if our race, the phantom of a day,
Spurning their nature's flight, had haughtily fixed

Upon our frame, cheap mirror of the dust,
For great enduring; scattered pyramids,
Sculptured the soros, and o'er Euxine's plain
Marched out the line of tumuli that stalks
Across the steppés, league on league afar,
Thoughts for Herodotus and Strabo dead,
And Clarke! that proudest of the Anglic race;
Or Calmuc, with his brandies made of milk;
And equine Cossacks, from whose hairy lip
Norse or Icelandic vocals lingering fall.

Thus did life's youthful mood vouchsafe,
Glimpses unknown to us, when Grecian isles
Were first discoveries, and all westward lay
Regions unkempt, the haunt of wolf or elk;
Seas unmolested, where no keel e'er trod,
Save of the savage proa, flying thing,
With long outriders propping up her sides.
Grand opened on the lids of Carthage fierce,
Sicilian isles, the granaries of Rome;
Vast to the spoiling Romans towered the snows

Of Alpine glaciers, or the rushing shaft
Where the unfathomable crevasse
Nurses her torrents, — feeders of Lucerne,
And wild moraine, slow moving to the foot,
Lifts not its head, nor heeds the avalanche
Crashed o'er its face. From Asia's heated soil
A fiery race wide roving spread around,
Whate'er their famed progenitors enjoyed ;
At Suez, where the Red Sea ends its toil,
Or through the gate of tears pursued their way
Into that Indian Ocean. The great king,
Famed for his tastes barbaric, fetched his pearls,
And peacocks, apes, and Sheba's queen, be sure,
From fertile islands in spice-wafting-roads,
Whate'er distortion later critics paste
Upon the Hebrew story.

So the page
Of human action prints the rolling trait.
So, in the Malay races Vedic creeds,
Cut on rock-temples of the Indian main,

Transport by sea, revive the Brahmin's faith;
So, o'er the yellow desert's weary sand
The fainting legend flies its thirsty way,
Flows down Euphrates' valleys, or encamps
On her flat shores. And wandering tribes of men,
Gypsies that rob all nations of the orb,
And Arabs, whose sharp letters serve the Turk
And Persian, Indian, Hebrew, all as one,
Drifting the seeds of knowledge o'er the lands,
Reflex portray in all the human symbols.
As in the Indian's Veda, so to us.
Even if beneath a cloak of legend
Supernaturally strange, whate'er the Greek
Raised to devotion, yet o'ermastering thrills;
The Pythian shrine, its oracle we hear,
Whether from hempen drug or nitrous air
Frankly diffuse, or trance mesmeric deemed,
Coming in dress of spirits, or such things
As nervous Macbeth played through Shakspeare's
brain,
Or writing morals on the mountain wall,

And raising circles from Druidic stones ;
Yet must the curious instinct of the race
Demand its mystery. Still St. Peter's shrine
Holds its portentous shadow o'er old Rome,
And Abraham's oak at Mamre blossoms on.

Where'er the glass you hold, reflected clear,
Priesthood and king, — names of the fatal powers, —
On most the nations' signets stamped full deep.
Always the nations marvel at themselves ;
Responsive to the past, serve king and priest ;
Such as the hoary Shagpat on the slab
That Layard at Koyunjik dug, and sent
To English halls, one like this mitred saint
From learned seats and colleges to us
Preaches obedience to our cherished creeds,
A secular law, or an unlovely prince ;
Drawing glazed portraits of the Prussian king
Who took Silesia, justice in his strength.
Forever cutting in the claw of might, —
The sword, that hell-born cruelty, our race,

Crudely regarded human, venerate!
Kingdoms are bolted to this butcher-sword;
And poor defenceless knaves, wrenched from their hearths,
Soon at the cannon's mouth blown into rags.
The ruling princes searching swift (those sateless wolves!)
More means of shedding blood, and their poor tools
Hang up in Heaven their dismal reeking corpse,—
Glory and murder burden of their strain.

From Macedonia's chief to the last wolf
That ravaged Roman earth, or what the race
Who people the new world have there essayed
To emulate the elder, whence they sprang;
Age after age the red procession goes,
Sateless, unsated, lapping at the pool
Of useless carnage, as if thus alone
The humane soul, born to the noblest thoughts,
Bred on choice reasons, and devoutly tasked,
Could found their best religion, raised to heaven,
By multiplying human miseries.
To try how clean the whizzing shell impelled

Shall shear in twain the hamlets of the poor;
Or by what law of steam and iron, ships
May smite, and with their fiery rain submerse
Walls of civility and cultured works;
Then, maddened on the wave, in frenzied strife
Sink with their crews to Pluto's tireless arm.
Noble the ghoul who swills most human blood,
Who makes the solitude, and calls it peace!
Would glory, honor, or the crimson chain
Scored on the conqueror's lurid brow, pour forth
Their ruddy flame as signet-rings of Oude,
If the grim field, planted with loathsome trunks
Of what this morning were the living pride
Of happy nations, now in sackcloth clad,
Got its true name, — the shambles of a king?
There see the sad array of captives march,
Sent to the cruel prison, long to bide,
Till the two angry monarchs, murder-tired,
Cease battling, all their recompense a grave!
Then mayst thou hear the anthem of the Church,
The proud *Te Deum* echoing to the skies,

As in Vienna's walls, when Pandours wild
Burnt some lean village on Bavaria's front,
Roasting the peasants in their frenzied rage.

On Nineveh's long wall in sculpture huge,
Where'er the regal pageant of the time—
Nebuco or Semiramis—crawls forth,
Upon the patent of the numerous wars
Done by the bearded peacock and his tail,
Behold, always with special emphasis,
Slaves trailing their chains. So downward far
To Rome's triumphant hours, the slave.
There Cleopatra in her beauty gleams,
And dark Jugurtha facing Rome goes by.
On Afric's sand, as well where Bornou's lake
Through the green sedges bears the fellah's boat;
As in the desert, when the caravan,
Bound for Morocco, marks its deathly trail
By the bleached bones of fainting youth and maid,
(Slaves captured for Numidia); or where Nile,
Wrenched from the Abyssinian mountains

Black and wild, whirls down the cataract
The coffle swart of wretches stolen to sell, —
With war, its source, treads human slavery!
Should a free Roman dig, or press the grape,
Save as Falernian to his weary lips,
With the scourged victim of his cruel wars
Crouched in the atrium, shuddering o'er his scars?
So triumphed down the demon; so espoused
The cause of blood: and from our shores, slavers,
Firing their guns along the Guinea coast,
Signal to send their human freight aboard;
Where the ripe culture of the Portuguese
In Christian morals and the Holy Faith,
Is the slave-factory, and its horrid field,
On which the corpses of the victims, flung
To Hades at the fever's mad command,
Bleach in the pestilent suns; and those who live
(Worse doom), wafted to states of liberty,
Employ the constant lash, and sate the hound
Brought from good Spain with all his native taste
For human gore; then shall they hoe and plant

For the North, till the white fields of cotton,
The government maintain, and on the cross,
Bleeding and nailed for life, die in their tears.
That fatal freedom to this hour ruled all!
But for a son of justice, lent from heaven,
Great Ossawatomie; who dashed his own,
His children's hearts against the demon-power,
And broke the captive's chain, and gave his name
Such glory as shall still less fade from thought,
(As time demanding damns the slavish fiends
Who drank his blood), but all the more blaze forth!

Oft on the marge of that small isle I sat,
Recalling all I knew about the sea,
And how much pleasure I to it had owed, —
A sheltered island tenderly caressed
In the soft billows, parted from the main
By a continuous beach, that miles along
Lists to the wail of ocean, and the cry
Of the light sand-piper: daintily his way
He picks along the cobbles of the marge,

Nor fears the wild commotion. In these frail,
These touching correspondences of love
In nature's vast dominion, man should build,
If anywhere, foundations for his creed,
And find on Alpine summits daisies bright,
And beds in bloom, fragrant of strawberry, —
There, on the concave of the eternal snow!

At times, I traced the fast foam-speeding boats
Whirl like the herring gulls along their track,
As if about to sink in ocean's maze,
Then in the narrowing pass obscurely lost,
I saw them turn, and with forecasting skill
Against the wind, a sinuous course retrace.
Not the mysterious voice that Hugo hears
Comes forth to them from ocean; not to them,
But a poor rag their canvas stilled the gale;
To such the sea is but another field,
Their saving care like the dry husbandman's, —
Fishers of men? That voice they seldom hear.
Save the old cedars eying the four winds,

Pledged to the azure sky and the gray stones,
And russet fields, parched in the July sun,
Upon that isle, Poseidon more is king,
Than lobster-fishers skimming o'er the wave.
Here, in the rudest clime of all our year, —
In stern December, — touched the Pilgrim boat,
Shallop then called; just where I muse, perchance;
And onward marched the crew, and sought the rock
Loftiest of all, to view the neighboring bay,
Albeit the isle should then in thickset wood
Have closed their view, — came off the Mayflower,
While their worn vessel lay outside the beach.
O'erhead December's frown, ice at their feet,
And the old ghostly cedars whispering, "Peace!"
Grandly they raised a hymn of cheerful faith;
The sacred chorus mixing with the gale,
And stormy snow-cloud trailing down the path.
Far lay their homes, — those English homes so dear;
Vacant their hearthstones, and their fields untrod;
Soft with Atlantic mist their vaporous skies
Draping with mossy wreaths the churchyard-stones;

Their hallowed abbeys sweet with eglantine
And old traditions in the English heart,
Built up of love. Oh, unlike this, so drear!
A savage air they never felt before
Amid the ice-clad bowlders on the snows;
The owl far hooting and the panther's scream,
And Indian war-cry echoing down the wood,
And fears, in courage quenched forevermore.

VI.

THE CAPE.

On native soil, pushing yet southernward,
Where the gay sand-dunes color Wellfleet's brow,
And earlier some few years adventuring brave,
Old Gosnold struck the land, searching this way
For treasure; and despatched a company,
Who viewed off Truro's height the Atlantic wave
Far reaching down the east its purple shades,
Chasing the green with red, and the low moon
Trail her soft radiance o'er the glimmering sea.
Then, too, the unceasing music of the surf,
Heard in our waking dream, disturbs the air
Not merely with its sound, but that salt savor
Dear to inland minds. Brave Champlain earlier
Touched these golden sands, castles afar
Skirting the icy bay, then sped his flight

Across to Acadie ; while Gosnold, lingering,
Found Naushawn, and Indian isles he gave
Eliza's name, where in the currents build
The coral insects, as on Omai's shore,
Their curving foliage for the gracile sea,
Warm from the Gulf Stream. Seeking here, he met
Groves built of sassafras, then filled his bark,
And sped an ocean flight. But Champlain bold
Tracked the great river, there where Cartier sailed,
Long ere those days, to Montmorenci's fall,
And where, o'er all the land, her piercing gaze,
Proud of her shining bulwarks, Quebec throws,
And eyes afar the trackless brush that sweeps
Its wilderness far north, where Baffin steered;
And near, the vast St. Lawrence, a deep tide
Coursing from inland seas than it more vast;
Waters like greenest gems of ocean mass
Compact, that proudly roll their emerald sheets
Over Niagara's edge ; and farther down,
Below fair Orleans isle, the traveller seeks
Thy roar, St. Anne, hymn to the voyageur, —

Clad in primeval Thuyas, ghostly trees,
Where thy uncounted fall shakes the dark earth:
So Verrazani and Sebastian stern,
With brave Sir Humphrey, sailed our baffling shores.
Then, even to the lake that loves his name,
And holds the haughty Adirondacks glassed
Within its mirror, where the Iroquois,
A race sepulchral battling for their scalps,
Swept clean the war-path, Champlain fearless went.
Far greater than them all, that trusting soul,
The patient Genoese, whose name this land
Most fitly bore. How are they sped to nought! —
All save the Mayflower's children, or their race;
And, if not done, surviving in lean tribes
Haunting the Cordilleras and the Plain,
And such as 'neath Potosi dig the ore,
Or for their Cuban slave-pen fiercely strike.

If, now, a fable held, the legend old,
That gives the hardy Norse, seafaring men,
The true discovery of our rock-bound world,

And the strange name of Vineyard to the sound,
From Vinland and the Dane, perchance is truth.
So the first human craft seen on this coast,
A Biscay shallop with its crew, one clad
In seaman's costume and their copper pot,
That welcomed Gosnold on the Eastern shore,
Spake of another captain, other ship,
As sea-King Norse from Iceland's fords, whose
words,
Household to us, flow in the English tongue.
What unknown ages, what crude centuries,
Since first New England's cape and that Blanche bay,
Our Massachusetts water, flowed with life!
Since first Cape Cod kept the tautog secure
From the cold ocean north his narrow stripe,
Or bade the crowd of shells south of his sands,
Never to pass that line; what eras past
Had the hot Gulf Stream, torn from Carib seas,
Rounded Nantucket's shore, and warmed the wave
That sweeps Fairhaven ere the trembling sloop,
Product of human labor, touched her strand!

And when shall ride a future deluge forth,
Back to the royal Proteus sweeping all?
Man questions deep in nature; but the plan,
Darkly significant of struggling chance,
Repeats the conflict of a rising world;
Ages where he did not participate,
With one-horned donkies and wing-fingered bats
Shuffled together, and the type obscured;
Lizards that flew; and armadilloes vast
Flopping in orchid-swamps, or dreaming out
Primeval leisures beneath tree-fern bowers.
Then came a page scrawled with hyena lines,
Species of bears and hairy elephants
Lumped at the pole, as if, prolific mind,
The generous mother never could enough.
In vain she crept, she flew at large, she crawled,
And sought to bridge the swamps by making peat,
Age after age, or sketched patterns of trees,
Pine after beech, and beeches after oak;
Beast following beast she tried, and nice
Condensed her shelly refuse into hills;

Then pushed the flashing quartz and granites red
Up the volcano's spout, or earthquake's scar.
Yet she succeeded crudely, striving on,
In this life-struggle for new living forms,
To mould superior creatures, and a globe
Better contrived for permanence to fill.
Vast was the stride from creatures without spine,
To upright columns, and a pivot crown,
The termination of the cord: here she rested;
Here she said, as 'twere, "The work is done.
Thus much my ages bring." Yet beings stride
Ever to brighter regions, struggling through
The ranks of species to complexer form.
May not the winged prototypes be joined
To human structure, now too much embayed,
Collapsed in its own gravity, fixed to support,
Or hang upon the orb, a two-legged thing;
For slowly up, a downcast race, man trod:
Tried the gorilla rough and clumsy built,
Or, on all fours, protrusive crept about
Till times of principle evoked back-bone.

Years ere the Pilgrim Mayflower came and found
Those Plymouth treasures, Gosnold with his men,
As oft we say, landed on Wellfleet's sands;
And Brereton and Arthur crossed the cape
To scan the broad Atlantic, where to-day
The Beacon stands: the Highland light upon
The clay-pit's brink, well should the sailor know,
Lest he confuse this Pharos with the next,
That stars its long Cape Race, or that more east,
With Nauset. Often have I dwelt content,
Pleased with the extending scene, and loved the man
Of genial nature and observant eye,
Who kept the light.

As old tradition lives
Along this coast, like those who came of old
(Danes or bold Norse), and named it Wonder Strand,
The men are fishers. Venturous their craft,
Quick-speeding schooners ploughing the blue main;
And rightly in its bud they named this shore,—
A silent hamlet sown on lonely sands,
Watered with widows' tears and children's sobs,

The fishers' home, — calling it Dangerfield.
And if the gale from George's in its wrath
Rolls o'er these passive fields, as if its power
Would sweep the humble houses off the land,
And make new barks of them to search the seas,
Well may the hamlet shudder in the gale.
That fatal line upon the graveyard sod,
That far amid the lonely wastes is set,
Where fifty souls out from this little flock,
Sunk in one fatal storm, buried alive, —
There in the mountains of the ingulfing wave,
Reads the dread lesson common on these hills!
Ask of your guide, who in the modest house
On that side lives, or this. Each house alike
Widow and children left to mourn the loss
Of him buried at sea. And nothing less,
Each fresh recurring season views the sails,
Bent forth, whiten the azure circumstance,—
The fleet just parting off for George's banks.
From that high cliff I looked o'er Truro's beach,
And saw beneath, the far unending strand

Coping with all the waves, and never wrecked.
There, too, town of the Province, built on sand,
Like Venice, lovely, sheltered in the wave,
With all its spires bright looming in the air,
When the mirage puts forth a playful arm,
And draws the smiling pageant through the haze.
Here first the pilgrim touched; he praised her soil;
He sung about her groves, like mariners
Hungry for inward pleasures, emerald green,
To whom the sward is heaven.
There's no place
I ever wandered in upon this earth,
Sweeter at sunset than the little vale
Crossing above the lighthouse, where is seen
No trace of human dwelling, nor a track
Scooped by the toilsome wagon in those sands;
So still, so fragrant with the fresh sea-air
Caught from the beach. The broad-leaved golden-rod;
And grass ill-named of poverty; and that plant,
The perfumed Mayflower, with the long beach-grass;
And copses blushing all of bright wild rose, —

Enhance the scene; and the soft sparrow's note
Comes from the ground, so well Savanna named,
As if her song in that pure element,
Blest in seclusion, welled up from the herb,
One with the peaceful cricket's twilight strains.
Yet ever haunts the ear a hush of sounds,
Making the silence sweeter; and how soon,
(If your adventurous foot demand,
And standing on the verge) you see beneath,
The sparkling lines of ever-rolling surf,
On the patient sand crashing their cannon! —
The glistening sprays torn off the breaking waves,
Bright lights and changeful greens, and floating wrack,
And that *unwearying* breeze. Oh! yet withdraw,
And in sweet contrast find the silence deep,
As if the pulses of the earth were stilled
Beyond the power of thought, or dream to speak,
Communing with the spirit of the sea,
Most like the mountain's voice when evening greets
You, silent, on his cliffs.

And often came
To this consoling valley one whose bloom
Partly had faded off a cheek of rose,
When not yet twenty summers for her form
Had wound their wreaths of beauty. She had known
The city's culture, nursed by ceaseless love,
And that devoted heart to mothers lent,
And unto them alone. But oft her thoughts,
In the proud mansion on the city street,
Strewed with the loans of luxury that time
Wafts down o'erpowering from the burdened past,
Wandered to this seclusion. And she saw
The rolling wave tossing its sand and shells;
The shining pebbles murmuring at her feet,
And felt the breath of the pure living waters
Thrill her reviving frame. Her song she raised:
"Oh, I would be a daughter of the sea!
On the dull land I feel the death of life,
That bars away my soul from all I love,
Where sleeps the heart I never thought to lose.
The open air, the bright and cheerful day,

Bringing my frame their reasonable toil, —
They make repose, seem joy. But in these streets,
On custom pensioned, and constraint in form,
My thoughts feel feverish as an imprisoned bird
Against life's narrow bars, — narrow and steeled.
Oh, I would be a daughter of the sea!
To list its ceaseless song, and think no more
Of all this weary and incessant shore;
Hiding a breaking heart behind a mask
Made of conspicuous trifles, pointed fine,
And wounding to the last. Afar my boat
Should ride the foaming distance, as the prow
Tossed off the whitening rancor of the wave,
And let the breeze blow free, and my wild speed
Shall emulate its own."

VII.

HILLSIDE.

Eve coming slowly down, at peace we marked
From higher places the low sun decline
Across the bay, pouring o'er Monimet
A flood of ruddy light that made more rich,
Her decorous robe of crimson, — autumn's robe
Of berry-bearing plants and changing trees,
Responsive to that glory. Thence I gazed
With a more fond emotion; for the hills
Contained, or rather might conceal, that house, —
Mansion I fitlier call it. Gothic hall,
With colonnade like Reinsberg's own, contract
To a more private scale; and slated roofs
So purely French, pierced with such frames, that one
Not comely in herself, thence looking, gained
A face. Below were sheltering lattices,

With ample steps beat from the granite ledge,
That borders the fleet brook, most merrily
And in all seasons running down the lawn, —
Stream like Voltaire's, heard in the cheerful rooms.
Far and in lavish taste were ranged around
The labyrinthine walks, their ample shades
Contrived from growths of cultured affluence.
The medlar here pursued his quaint decay,
Near by the chalky hazel's stunted limb,
Or loaded figs sweet as e'er Smyrna grew;
Bohemian olive, orange-scented joy,
And sunny laburnum. Here shrubs divine,
Noble wigelia, roseate-blushed and white,
A summer wreath of glory, clothed the copse;
Or rich forsythia glittering like the fall,
And delicate as lace the pure white fringe, —
Each in its season on the enamoured air,
Breathed its soft beauty. And such flowers unveiled
As might adorn the Psyche in her bower, —
Gay-leaved geraniums, with rich fuchsias lake,
Pendant as graceful drop in loveliest ears;

And Scottish daisies like the peasant's song,
That taught its tender fame, Eolian Burns,
A flower to shine beneath the Scottish birch, —
Tree Wordsworth calls, "the lady of the wood."
The gardens delicate with quality
Of luscious spoil, from Eastern realms conveyed, —
From Japan's fields her lilies' golden gleam,
Or whate'er Fortune in his pleasant trips
O'er China, thought an English charm; all lands,
And farthest skies raining their splendors down.
On the two sides touching the garden, fields
Social in grain, or lapped in orchard-wealth,
The succulent pear, braced apples, or blue plum,
Nor less there bloom, dusk clusters of ripe grapes
Rounding the vines, and walnuts stately gold,
As tallest column of Sierra's stone,
On mellow autumn's hillside.

So within
Genially spread presides refining taste.
The buoyant day, forth wheeling in his car,
Revealed in Guido's dream, here lights the wall

Upon soft Phosphor's blush; and near, the gaze
Instinct with manly genius and young strength,
Of Raphael; his hand so sensitive,
Ne'er touched the pencil but to lift the art
Above the saint he drew, — St. Barbara,
Or holy Catherine bending on the tomb.
And copies of the famous or the fine,
From graver ages ferried to compel
Our admiration, — Dante's shrunken form
Thinking immensely, aquiline and spare;
And polished Milton, creature of the court,
Munificent in diction; and the one
Whose face, traditionally drawn, reveals
To thirsty hearts Judea's loveliest soul.
While from the humble shelves mild rural books,
As liquid Maro dulcet on his flute,
And timorous Cowper with his three pet hares,
Regale the evening circle in their verse;
Unless the sweet piano fill the ear
Blithe in its strings, or with some soft-toned voice;
The courtly grandam, nodding o'er her glass,
And famished girlhood studying out her eyes.

On the same spot, led down the sallow years
From the first impress of the Pilgrim's foot,
Mark this home, succeeding generations;
Cordial descent, more with each added stock
Perfecting the true kind; more mellow fruit,
More culture of the mind, by skilful grafts.
Thus even in the comforts of the house,
The early architecture swept remote,
A costly and convenient mansion stands.
And as in England, skilful heralds rate
The arms and quarterings of good families,
So here the annals of the line descend,
By ladies treasured up, who knit composed
In quiet corners; or by robust sons,
Walking behind their ploughshares; and wise clerks,
Who trace the lineage from town histories.
So that the workmen on such peasant farms,
If never king with garter violet,
And sword of diamond hilt, impressed the blood
With knightly crest, yet by well-ordered work,
Or what the patient mind contrives to raise,

Keep memory and pride about the place:
In these plebeian homesteads is the stamp
Of true nobility. A lettered boy,
Drilled in collegiate walls, perchance, ascends
The pulpit's height, or thunders at the bar;
Another to new shores ordains his wit,
Viewing Calcutta's halls, — a traveller;
The gentler fabric softly weaving in
With other households similar in gift;
Till from the fragile and short-lived estate,
As thought in foreign lands where entail holds,
Rises the solid profit of the farm.
And time above the dear familiar place
Depends in venerable elms;
Like citron bright their lichen-painted trunks,
Fruit of parmelia's skill; meantime the house,
Pride of aspiring builders, slowly brings
The right results. For in our tragic clime
The keen north-west drives through the gaping
boards;
Nor less the east, rich with the sea it loves,

Undoes the shingle, and abstracts the nail;
Slates bloom instead, and rocks of trust,
Replace the wood-foundation; blithe the flowers
Drawn on the wainscots, and the Indian vase
Floating from Canton's river tints the porch.
When evening calls the family within,
Social and warm the ruddy curtains fall
Around the dreamy casements, till the war
Of the continuous surf upon the ledge,
That shores the ocean's ingress, whispering, lulls,
And fancy brings the forms of other days.

O loved and gone, the darling of our hearts!
With thy soft winning ways, caressing smiles,
And step more light than tracks the forest fawn;
Who taught the old how kind the young might be;
How often thy soft figure, wandering o'er
The breezy lawn, or couched within the shade,
Made sweeter music than all sounds beside!
Gone, oh, forever gone! alone she sleeps
Upon the hillside looking o'er the sea;

Alone? when every heart, full of thy worth,
Enchanting Julia, sends its love to thee.

Safe is this peaceful haunt, far from the town,
With all its noise forgot, and steeped in silence.
No shrieking train let forth pants rumbling by;
No factory-bell, the presage of man's toil,
Infects the ear. Soft in its sovereign groves
The dwelling stands of one I knew of yore, —
He truly for seclusion framed, yet graced
With kindly instincts and delightful tastes,
I ever valued, as a hope for them,
Who love the simple scenes of rural bliss.
In cities' throngs might he have haply moved,
And held conspicuous reins in civil crowds,
Had not the charitable God supreme,
With lovelier council given him space to be,
The happiest man of all this earthly state, —
A valued scholar, and, addition blest!
Who made his hillside lovely to his friends,
And, loving, was beloved.

There, in soft dreams
Of hope, I half forgot the old complaint
Against the ambitious crowd who throng the mart,
Supreme each in his own conceit, or first
Might prove, if but allowed due scope, and ripe
For quick promotion. So the centuries flit;
And yet the god admires to people cities,
Arch over arch rebuilds their gates, and fills
The gaps cut by besiegers with their guns,
When the hot fight, on Prague or Warsaw fell,
Or Wolfe outdid Montcalm, and sealed his days.
How fulgent speed the suburbs, once the torch
Of Hecate to the walls applied! Sudden
In empty air the granaries fly aloft,
The year's tanned labor wasted on a spark,
Leaving the land disconsolate, where peace
Just softly cradled raised her Saviour's head.
Not from poor hamlet's sheds go forth the ranks,
But Potsdam rich in palaces, or Ghent
And Paris, camp supreme since Julian's days,
Where yet his thermæ fast by Cluny's halls

Attest the spot, where the vague soldiery
Of latter Rome, swore fealty to their lord.—
Clustered together much like bees in cells,
Close, if unmingled, the associates dwell,
Where meagre penury hitches the skirt
Of silken grandeur, and hungry beggars
Swarm, gathering up cast-out bones, envious
Of the dogs well-fed. Just God! my heart
Bleeds to its depth to feel the children's woe,
Nurtured in rags, uncombed, unwashed, and starved,
Squalid by brutal license, reared in pain,
Old ere their youth has come, to steal and beg
Their joyous privilege. Who grateful sees
The scarlet carriole and the pampered steeds,
With a bedizened load of sickly dames?—
A tatter from their lace enough support
For poor folks half the month, good Christians too;
Fatal such contrast, accident at best.
No farthing wasted on the shivering child;
Then to the prison haled, the wretched thief
Plaything of grizzly sinners, learns his task,

Bible of righteousness, preached in those schools,
And graduates soon fine scholar.
One I knew,
A thinking man, his days in mercy spent,
Who sought to mitigate these carrion forms,
And raise some fresh emotion in the heart,
For them, cast out to ignorance and vice.
But then the o'ercrowded city crowding grows,
And breeds the plague that riots in its squares;
Builds up foul court-yards and unholy lanes,
The fountains of pollution; and endows
The university of thirst and lust
Patron of wickedness, — the lodger's crib; swiftly
The prison's cell receiving its refuse.
What are the costly prints that hide the walls
Where swelling Angelo his prophet seats,
And sibyls, big in muscle; what the stone
Smooth in Canova's taste, or gaslit throng
Clapping the tiresome Hamlet?
Can we sink
The dark and dangerous classes in the mire,

Safely obliterate? and at our ease
Napping behind the curtains, and delight
With spendthrift opulence of ill-got wealth,
And sideboard blazed with plate, omit the claim
Of human misery, fainting at the door?
Or shall we haunt the porches, taste the cool
And philosophic shade where wisdom sits
Upon its nodding throne, and heaps the page
With fruit luxuriant from the spells of Greece,
What Gorgias taught? There, in those seas of froth,
On which the unballast mind pursues
Its vagrant theories, with helm suppressed,
Heaping its dust in weary sophistries
To pamper future pedants; — there forget
In our release, the sufferings of the wretch
In tattered garb, his letters never learned,
Who rakes the city gutter for his meal?

Mother of arts and arms the City stands,
Bred by long centuries to lead the race,
And resting on her hero's head the crown,

Who makes the great occasion civil named,
Term by the learned, fashioned; civil,
Almost polite. Old temples line her streets,
Palace and arch, and Trajan's theatre
Where the Christian fed the starved lioness,
Caught in Numidia, with his lean flesh,
That thus Rome's emperors, applaud by sweaty palms,
Might drink a bloodier triumph. Now, it serves
The pardoning popes. Simply, if handed down,
Race worships most, the custom of the race,
Preserving man, and for long ages pets
The dead prerogative as if man's doom;
In Copan or Palenque, from strange shrines
Plump out new gods; or giant from its mud
Cardiff displays, there near the shallow stream,
Mutely forlorn, half asking to be spared,
Appropriate transcript of the natural man,
Hero of the old days! There he dreams, —
The antique figure, carted from his bed,
Dreams of the time he shot the hippogriff
Trooping about his plains heavy with nightshade;

Or in his torrid swamps bestrode that beast,
The ichthyosaur, and listens to the yells
Of sharp hyena with the savans' talk,
As they debate his bones, and draw the plan
On which young nature laid his wide expanse.
Now drifted to the cities, he may hear
The swarm of pygmies buzzing at the door,
And, for the peal of ages on his case,
Remark the civic clock, politely tuned,
Shoot forth meridian time; the frantic crowd
That worry by his weight breathless to add
A blossom to their days, while his fell off,
Or ever Adam gave the palm to Eve.
Fearing the myth, they ridicule his age;
Less credible, they deem a hero dead
Than insects scarce conceived.

Far eras gone,
Magnificoes like this, old earth put forth,
That pave the brooks in Cardiff to this hour.
Races cropped out, and steady came the dream,—

The giant; the Goliaths fought and fell;
Vain was the search, while every shape of beast
Reckoned incredible the soil produced.
The civil congregation fed and died
In war and peace conceiving; but no work
Of sculpture ere the flood, or man of mould
Twice in his stature topping o'er the kind,
Till that good farmer of the Cardiff vale
Flat in the boggy drain barely concealed,
The fossil creature found. Model the form;
Brow of Caucasian eminence and depth;
His figure average in Camper's scale;
And neck and skull right as a theory.

Behold the entrance of a form in light,
From nations gone ere China or Japan
Baked clay pagodas, and, delightful gleam,
Bushels of Indian hatchets sank to please
Detective Lyell in the Amiens sand,
Or Switzer lake enjoyed the pile-built town.
Form water-worn; the mouth half eaten out,

And half the arm ; the soles all honey-combed ;
The stone of easy grain, and wrought with art.
More as some serious Roman looks it there
Than the brief creatures flitting on the streets
Bandaged in narrow garments fit to hide
Their scanty moulding. For that native drape
(Such as it is) outdoes the Roman baldness
Ere wig or peruke troubled the occiput.
And never in the brilliant forms of stone
That crowd the Vatican more royal shape
Of young Augustus, or Vespasian stern,
Or Sophocles, — the tall, commanding Greek.

Go search the page lucid with polished fiction,
Note the dim fable darkly lengthening down
From Tyre's first castle to the hour that cuts
Our dusty sunshine, — history bereft
Of combination. Selfish crowds still fret
The frosty streets, humanity obscured ;
The grating wheel creaks in the iron rut ;
Never will man his individual brass

Melt in a common pot, nor stretch the roof
For a whole people. Oft the married twain,
Engaged in private broil, deplore the scratch.
Thou crazy Frenchman with a ciphering pen,
Fourier! so scantly fed, yet firmly bent,
Attraction-mad, on sea of lemonade
To float the ripe community, where, knit
In genial temper, the attractive band
Of cohort butterflies, sunning their wings
Along the phalanx walls, and self forgot,
Thus must collapse labor competitive.
Alas! the butterflies loved colored gauze, —
This purple and that brown, for which they struck;
And cider-lemonade became small beer.
This legion envied that; the pivot stood
Slow rooted in the wheel, — a general sleep,
Attractive industry, thy tribes possessed.

Much men enjoy the anxious strife and jar,
And scheme demonstrative for pelf and power:
The toughest rules the trade. In its stone bank

On yonder corner, the Napoleon brain
Controls the dancing stocks, and in a twist
Of its persuasive lid depletes the bond,
And undermines its rate. Such heaven is this, —
The sharp and pungent sniff 'twixt man and man ;
The neighbor's hand pressing the neighbor's throat,
Then fathoming his purse. The bright-rouged clerk
His equipage complete, flown on blood-coursers,
Forges his master's check to sate his duns ;
The decimated globule teased to fame,
And grown profuse on the self-seeking puff,
Carries a simile to beauty's lip.
Books pass by binding ; the tame laurelled bard
Wire-drawing out the pretty, shallow line,
Nurses at Spenser's fount his conscious babe.

Angel of Liberty in simple robe,
The dame, now past her youth, discourses much
Of rights and equities, and asks the urn.
Haste ! let her trail those ribbons in the crush
Of unbribed patriots blushing from the bar,

And drop her vote. Freedom for all decrees
Laws unrestricted; end this imprisoning sex.
As grand Theresa, Austria's fondest boast,
To whose young babe the nation made the vow,
"Yes! for our king as one man shall we die;"
Her woman's breast, too sensitively proud,
And crossed by shadows from an aching nerve,
Drowned in a sea of blood the Austrian land,
Then for peace kneeled; and Cleopatra's heart,
And Helen's, Homer's flame, the woman's right
Held in the throbbing pulse, of blood so frail!
One fruit of civic finesse there emerged,
Conceived in fearful phrase, the pompous laws,
Tradition of the Romans, when there sprang
Diana's temple new from St. Paul's yard;
Narrow old precedents a Cæsar's craft
Bred in his thought to mask his scheming hand,
And into codes fused by Justinian.
Then hurried o'er the Atlantic, by our saints,
The righteous Puritans, their heads as dry
As the remainder biscuit; laws and states

What ages more, riveted to the crowd!
Such bred the deeds of witchcraft, that his muse,
Our gentle-hearted Hawthorne's, touched so well,
Drawing a beauty out of all their cant,
And the self-lauding sect, moral in sin.
Headlong fall arch and fane, Silenus musing
Happy o'er his tun, and gay Bacchus tipped
In Ariadne's garlands; down with heaven,
And blue Olympus and its flashing court
Coming to wine in fashionable vests;
And Persian splendor at Persepolis,
Raised in its burning sunshine on the steps
With bands of dancing girls and horsemen fierce
Darting the jerrid; them we dream no more.

Surest of all the facts of mortal life
Men symbolize the meaning of the thoughts;
The Indian on his skin painting his bears,
And strange Peruvian on his quipo knots
Writing his stanza, down to Europe's pride,
Even to demonic Goethe, feats in words;

Great that Sanscrit's worth, who made the grammar,
Leaving the rest to follow as it might,
And Fin, with sixteen cases to one noun,
And Chinese calm, who wants no alphabet.
Where roams the tribe that never found its tongue?
While the poor beast, squeezed in one fettered strain,
Squeals inaccessible. Oh! should we not
As Indians with each spring consume the town,
Seeking new hunting-grounds and larger game?

Homeless and hopeless in those cruel walls,
Sybilla went, her heart long since bereaved.
She heard the footfalls sear the crowded streets,
Her fatal birthright, where no human pulse
To hers was beating. There she shunned the day!
Tall churches and rich houses draped in flowers,
And lovely maids tricked out with pearls and gold,
Barbaric pomp, and crafty usurers bent, —
All passed her by, the terror in her heart.
So sped she on the train, — a reindeer-course, —
Day's dying light painting the quiet fields,

The pale green sky reflected in the pools.
Oh! why was earth so fair? was love so fond
Ever consumed within the ring of fire?
That soft clear light that marks that heaven afar,
The emerald waters, and the evening star.

No more the tales that once the race of bards
Inspired, — of heaven's high court, or hell,
Of gods or god, Venus, and Mars; no more
The solitude of the high mountain's shrine;
Faded to night, irrevocably passed,
Where they may never be unloosed again:
A simpler and a sweeter lay demands
A new-born age, faintly demanding verse,
(For verse too high, or modulated prose),
The scholar's song, whom thought has made its own.
New times demand new powers; new powers, new men;
The old seems but a pale hypocrisy,
That myth of Serapis or Jupiter,
Vain word for us, and Brahma's holy grass,
Or *Om* (forbidden word), and Odin's skull

Rich with Valhalla's, and metheglin's fume.
But we might launch our gods, as they sang theirs,
Even as our clime and seasons native spring,
So now from us upsprings the myth to-day,
Or shall ere morning gild yon russet field?
Each holds his office, each his native skill,
By self in one part poised, by fate as much:
The rose can never bloom the lily's white,
Nor a still day usurp the whirlwind's roar.
Thus man is but a tool, that yet can draw
His one design on a wide-waving sea;
And though he sails on various voyages,
In different ships, and to as many ports,
The same sagacity, firm will, and faith,
Or luckless chance, yet guides his vessel on.

The glittering bait of power obstructs the mass, —
Mass we may frequent think, so few they stand,
Who, bent on higher ventures, tread Time's shore.
Around us weaves a thought we dimly feel,
As faint some moonlit shadow, flitting fast,

When the mild planet pearls our watery clouds,
And scarce reveals the light herself has made.
A thought is in the trees and seas and skies;
Lurks on the river's breast, or skims the grove;
Glitters at twilight off the folding clouds;
Speaks from young eyes, and throbs within the heart,
Nameless, unfathomed, dark, yet loving light.
This life the scholar loves, this life he breathes;
Without this life he could not tread the path
Of the low-falling world, to heaven the heir.
Who, then, might fitly chant of him whose eye
Is set so firmly in its parent cause?—
Not one of these plain fields and modest lot
The child, but some resplendent bard, whose verse,
Lit with celestial radiance, flashed the skies,
As sunset in her purples bathes the east
With a fore-painted morning.

From the grave he leads
Old glories to new life. His memory throws
Its still soft light across a heavenly path.

With saints, with priests, the wise, the great, he holds
A dread communion, and his thought embalms
Like amber, sweetness of all times. His hope
Hangs in the future; and his aim so high,
That yet through infinite ages vast
He still beholds a stream, where man shall sweep
To excel the glory of his present reign,
And thrones and empires stand where'er a man
Plants his firm tread on the subjected globe.
Make, then, his function saint-like and superb!
Be his the good to teach more than the old,
Revolving new society, new laws,
As in her frolic, nature upward soars
Through bush and glen and cedar-copses dark,
Where the blue berries show like ocean's bloom,
And o'er the chestnut hills whose gray rocks peep,
And far below, beyond, the sandy lake
Bears her retreating skies, and clouds the earth:
Where'er the face of things smiles or grows sad,
The scholar gleans, his faithful eye profound
To read the secret in each thing he sees, —
To love, if not to know.

His soul outbursts
The feebly measured current of his fate.
He rises like the sun in roseate pomp;
Like him, he sinks in splendor down 'mid stars;
As subjects to his throne, the learned haste, —
Focus for all their rays. For him the seas
They furrow with the sparkling keel of ships,
For him they iron o'er the land with flame,
And glass in lightning his projectile thought.
Nor less the star him pleasures in her speech,
Whether in volcan fierce she lifts the heavens,
Or casts in golden sand the river's chain.
His logic suits to each the prize he draws,
In great or less proportions. Let him rise
So long as the race rises, and in him
Its wise perfecting skilled creation claim!

THE END.

ELIOT.

A Poem.

BY

WILLIAM ELLERY CHANNING.

BOSTON:
CUPPLES, UPHAM AND COMPANY.
1885.

610

ALFRED MUDGE & SON, PRINTERS,
BOSTON.

CONTENTS.

ELIOT.

I. IN THE CAVE.

WHERE once the lynx and panther made his house,
Or the fat bear brought up his family,
Poor nurslings of the Wild, I find my place
Of shelter from the world, and man remote.
Nearly two decades of this mortal coil
Run off; my sands of life mostly run out;
And yet the everlasting voice I hear,
And never find the silence.
On these rocks,
Old as the pillars of the earth, I make
My couch, table, and seat; and the iron door
Grates on its hinges to my touch alone, —

6

Alone, alone, alone by night, by day.
No friendly voice e'er sweetness to my ear;
No friendly thought e'er warming to my heart;
Seared by misfortune, with its life-blood scant,
And soon to stop!
Alone! Yes. But I hear!
Was that a human step, or a dry leaf
Dropped from the oak-tree? And that echo soft, —
Was it the splinter of the waterfall
That down the glen flies from the moonlight's clutch?
This awful silence! And I ever hear
Sounds that surprise me, — born, I feel, of fear;
Sounds faint and far, that drench me with affright,
Here as I sit, and see the bloodstained scroll, —
Those letters that I plucked from out his breast,

As slowly from his heart the red drop
oozed, —
Those, and her portrait, and his own!
Lisa!
I see her near me! 'T is her hand I touch!
Her soft brown hair, her gentle hazel eyes.
Cruel, say you, was something in her smile,
And sensual or vindictive? Oh! to me
The very sweetness of God's deepest love
Beamed from those faithful orbs; and
when that mouth
Was pressed to mine I never felt its
scorn.
Thus, thus to live, — should this, indeed,
be life, —
Within this cavern which my hands have
scooped
To the convenient largeness for my wants;
Hight enough, and so secured that none
can come
Without I know them here. And this, my
rifle,
Time once, that was a joy, — far off, in-
deed, —

But now one loathsome thing, since flowed
his blood.
And yet to know that from this dungeon
here
I still must roam the tall wood's broken
gloom;
Far down the glen, where the sharp ripple
glides
Of the cold stream, like arrows in its haste,
Curving and curving fast, — and kill the
deer,
Most graceful of their kind. For I have
vowed,
In this self-punishing, I will not steal my
life;
And naught but these fair creatures make
me live.
'T is late; the night draws on ; no human
love
To cheer me in my grief. Society!
Oh, well I do remember in those days
When I had Lisa, and I owned a home,
How dear the firelight blaze lit up the walls
Of our Kentucky house, — that ample hall,

There where our mother dwelt, and he, the judge,
My father, — all the children round, the dogs
Stretched out along the floor, and often heard
The flying hoof-beats of the full-blood steed;
Some social neighbor, on his round of calls,
Proud of his good gray mare; the kindly hopes,
The tidings from the town, the postman's shout;
And heard afar that soothing Sabbath bell,
Sweet in my childish heart! —
Hush! Was it a step?
Again? Something along the leaves; the night
Crawling in the cool air amid the oaks,
Or the soft panther's foot seeking the meat
That 's hanging at the door. Again! the whisper!
Can it be? Who comes? 'T is Gordon's form.
His hand across his heart, as on that day;

Slowly the red drop oozing from the
spot.
See ! and he shot as well as I; closer!
O God! why was it not his ball through
mine,
Not mine in his ? And Lisa at his side !
I often say it : Eliot, the blow was yours.
And now you live, frozen to the heart, for
life,
Until on yonder heap of leaves you rest,
Mourned for by none unless some wander-
ing wind.
Yes, 't is midnight; I feel it in my soul.
Yon star that strikes beyond the cavern's
roof
Brings me that fated hour, the time to
sleep.
I call it sleep, but all along my mind
Hovers the contribution of the day.
The curse of Cain weighs worlds upon my
soul, —
Whoso sheds human blood, his own shall
flow.
How often have I sought the fatal stroke;

11

How often bared my breast to the lightning's stab,
Or begged the wild man of the woods to dart
His arrow through me; and the venomous snake,
Whose measured warnings in the grass I hear,
As oft I thread the glade, his rattle shrill.
No, no; they harm me not, fated to live.
The sweetest draught that ever touched my lips
Will be the wine of death, a cordial draught.
Would but the sisters brew it speedily,
And let me drain that glass.
And yet I live!
As now, to meet this midnight hour and say, —
One more, one more, another sun must rise;
Another day, the same as all that go;
Tied to myself, and these dread, pitiless thoughts,
As when Prometheus lay and felt the eagle

Lapping his blood, chained on the Caucasus.
'T is silence sears my brain. No pleasant words;
No smile over her lips; no gentlest parting
When she ope'd the door, and lingered long,
Waiting to hear my latest foot-tread fall;
No glance upon her face, as oft she sat
Wondering at my strange fancies and strange acts.
I vainly stretch my hands. I meet the air
Empty and wan and cold and pitiless.
I ask for mercy! On the rocks I kneel,
Long ere this hour is passed, hoping for mercy:
That some voice will say, "Go forth, this penance o'er."
Hoping, I say, Yes; but my hope 's despair.
Decades have fled, and yet my prayers remain,
Like some dull, hollow sphere, untenanted.

13

When I was young, how oft I sang some catch,
Some merry song, when I was left alone,
Gay as the callow bird upon the bough;
My innocent heart responding to the joy
That broods o'er all things. Since that awful hour,
Doomed as the frozen stream, its ripples sunk
To icy stillness.
Hark! That foot again!
'T is Lisa's, at the door. I see her soft brown hair,
Lighter than faintest glass spun at the flame.
How waves it in the moonlight's deadly glow!
And oh! her gentle eyes, they melt the gloom;
And her kind voice, "Eliot! my love, I come.
I never loved but you,— no one as much.
But I was one not framed to love, save one.

Not of the class of women whose shrunk
hearts
Feel but a single friend, and have no more
Than one emotion; and I thought that you
Should still be mine. Oh! Eliot, oh! my
love,
Was jealousy more worth than all my love?
And those poor letters, bathed in his last
blood,
A proof that I less loved you than of
yore?
I know the date 's the same. I know I
wrote
That day to you and him. But my true
love,
Might you not spare his life? I hear the
gun!
I see the fearful flash! the ringing shot
Is pressing through my heart! I cannot
breathe!
I go with Gordon to that other land!
But I will come to you. I will not leave
You, dearest, in that lonely world; but
come

Sometimes, at hollow midnight, when your ear,
Attuned to finer silence, claims new sounds.
'Tis I; 't is Lisa! Eliot, do not fire!"
What did I hear?
Was it the oak-leaf falling in the frost?
Was it the torrent whispering down the glen?
Methought I heard a voice, like Lisa's voice.
There! There! My God! that sound again!
"Eliot, my love,
The nearest to my heart of those I love,
Would that this hand could take and lead you up
In this still land, beyond that temporal day.
I cannot, cannot; no, my child! No hour,
No moment can my loving heart come near
To stanch your wounds; nor this frail form
One touch of consolation to your days

Ever afford. Eliot, why was it I who died
When Gordon fell, doomed by the fatal hand?
Because I loved him thus, you fondly deemed,
Even as I loved yourself. Why look so faint
Across those bloodstained scrolls? My heart is yours,—
Here in the hollow grave, — *all yours*, the same."

II. MORNING.

'TIS almost sunrise; I had long to wait.
I hear the early birds begin their songs;
Would 't were the last. Yet I believe and feel
That life grows weaker, and so it must end,
Nor far away.
How foolish in me still
These shallow, hurried notes to scrawl.
Here will they mold, with those, — the letters!
And the faithful books that true remain,
Silent though speaking, ranged upon the stones,
Facing the long procession of the years,—
Schiller and Shakspere, Spenser, with their kin,
And courtly Addison. Never they dreamed

That things they wrote should float thus far away,
And in such places, here in these rank woods
Nourish an outlaw's breast, haggard with crime,
Save mine, far from all human eyes;
For in your trade-mad town, on Como's street,
Who lives who ever read them? Know I not.
Would I could live and yet destroy no life;
Yet neither roots nor nuts, nor berries scant,
Will save me from destruction. These dim wilds
In their game furnish a thin subsistence,
And I have sworn to breathe till my last sigh
Falls wretchedly to death. Live must I call it?
Once did I live, and knew the morning break
As the sweet herald of auspicious day,

Wherein my thoughts should bloom even
as its blush.
Like radiance o'er the east my hopes shot
forth.
The world was all before me and its
friends,—
Those polite liars, those true, faithful
friends.
On no man yet I ever turned my back.
I was affectionate, or so I thought;
I trusted all, and trustful, tried to please.
They shook me from them like the poi-
soned snake
Whose venom drops when none affects the
cause.
My warm affections, my soft sympathies,
They rated oddity, named them brief
whim,
Caprices, and the wiser called me mad,
The least reprieve they gave, to glance
aside,
Neglect me; cold contempt, indifference,
Silent aversion, indolent remark,
Their sole returns. —

Was that a figure
Moving among the trees, there, where the sun
Begins to gild their moss? Like Gordon's form, —
Just crossing through the glade from where I sit.
Why, 't is a deer, and bends this way to me.
I'll get my gun, shut to my dungeon's door.
And I can feel its soft and liquid eye
Beam on this gloomy cell in friendly fear.
I could not shoot if this viper at my heart
Consumed its blood. Shoot, poor thing!
Never till now,
Driven by hunger was I weeping forced
To slay one living creature, nor to harm.
Nor should I now; 't is part of this dread penance,
And I live by murder.
Could be that Gordon's soul
Impressed itself upon that silly deer,
To tempt a hunter's thought? Its liquid eye,

Perhaps, prefigures happier days in store?
No, no! the same, the gnawing at my heart,
And carking care from anguish unappeased.
Why do I keep those letters yet, so near?
Near, ever in my eyes, and the twin portraits, —
Lisa's and his, — ever, forever there!
Was there no God with pity in his heart
When I lay cradled on my mother's breast?
Or was this fiend who tears my life to shreds
The One who made me, blasted and obscured?
I dreamed in calmer days of pleasing thoughts,
Blest recollections, which like soothing lights
O'ershot my morbid glooms, and made a hope
Of earth, lit up the dark, cold lakes with joy.
And touched the freezing foliage till it laughed;
Honeyed remembrances of good deeds done,

Like angel hymns soft fluting o'er the mind,
Banishing sin and binding up time's wounds.
The unappeasable sky above me shuts
Its iron lids 'gainst every cheerful thought;
No day nor night, nor early morn nor eve,
Nor shapes of things to come nor those all gone,
Are neighbor to my cause.
What moves yon bush?
'T is but the frost-work lightening in the sun,
That gives it verge to move, to right its stems
From the cold grasp of night. These things are loved.
The glade that stoops across the long-drawn wood,
Its unshorn grasses for the deer's supply,
I sought again; a little sylvan temple,
With sober front carved by the wood-god's taste,
For Dryad meetings comfortably adorned.
Around the graceful trees move sensible

To the sweet whisperings of the wind; the
spring
Where nightly come the wild inhabitants,
To touch their lips, adorned with mossy
stones,
Might please some hermit's mind.
Was I happy then?
Was there an hour deep in the past when
life
Half kept some smiling dreams? My
memory fails.
I fancy, as I seek that glade, my mind
Might, if 't were gracious, partly call again
Some thing or day that smiled across my
path,
Ripe with humanity, before that blow
At my own race had shadowed all my soul,
And rooted out all trace of blest emotion.
Why did I love? Had I no joy in that?
I looked in Lisa's face; I saw her shape,
Light and convenient beyond Nature's art,
Made for our race; those hands that did
her thought
Before my clumsy brain presumed her act;

That step so sure and sweet; that modest
eye,
Ever self-humbling, ever soothing me.
I loved her all. Was not there, then, a joy?
Then, but how far off now! I am no more
Of life; all 's fled, all 's lost. —
Again, — her form!
As I was sitting in the glade, herself
Passed at the further end and near the
spring.
Watching for deer I sat, for food is scarce.
My eyes were on the earth, my heart was
faint,
And then I heard a voice. I raised my
eyes.
Was it the oak-leaf falling in the frost?
Was it the torrent whispering down the
glen?
She speaks, soft as the child who prays at
night
His mother's blessing:
"Eliot! thou thread'st alone
The shadowy vale, save that my memory
Its penance bears along thy weary road.

Child to my heart all dear, I loved thee ever!
Nay, thou knew'st not that all my soul was thine.
Frenzied with jealousy, that maddening draught,
The aloes of the heart, and now rusted
With solitude, that by its acid eats
Away the truth ; thought's vitriol, chasing
The fine conceit to ashes, rubbing out
The burnished silver of the social glass,
Reducing every pleasure to a mask ;
A filmy skeleton, through which the breath
Of an unformed despair glides ghostly up,
As midnight's sigh in the cathedral's vault
Where overhead the falling ruins soar."

Methought I knew that voice. Was that his form ?
This hunger at my heart and this fatigue !
I surely saw a figure cross the glen,
As I glanced back, its hands upon its heart.
Gordon, no ! no ! It was not murder, no!

At twenty paces, killed — was he killed by
me?
Oh, mockery! I am frenzied with this life.
Hunger and cold and weariness steal all
sense,
An everlasting faintness in my frame,
And in my mind the fatal consequence,
Brings forth its ghosts and dreams and
fearful thoughts.
Were I not here alone in these wild woods,
Exiled from all which social life holds dear,
Locked in that burial vault, a diseased
mind,
Malady naught can cure, — might not one
heart,
One human heart with a brief tender-
ness,
E'en for me, say one half word of com-
fort, —
Breathe just one sigh, and with a faltering
mind
Touch for an instant to my bleeding soul,
A hope of mercy!
My God! I ask for pardon.

But thou art just! Justice was made for
me,
This miserable doom becomes me well.
A weaker nature might have sought its
life;
But I, whose fibres, like the shattered
oak's,
Wedged to the core with lightning, wreathe
Their pale, white phantoms to the angry
sky,
And roots entwined in earth's unmeasured
halls
Claim property their own; thus I, all
scarred
And blasted, rained on, spat upon by hail,
And winter's silent moons, and still her
voice,
Loud as the earthquake's trump, her still
small voice:
"Eliot, my child, believe me to the end."

I know I saw the sun rise; I believe
That somewhere in that distance was a
world,

And once the woods lay green at summer's breath,
And soft the toying winds that danced in May.
There *must* have been a world, and human life.
I think I might remember childish forms,—
Their soft, wan hair; their little, lovely words;
Questions that break a grown man's heart with joy,
To think that God lets Innocence appear,
And in the weary, worn-out stage of life,
Paint her sweet dreams, the bliss of ignorance.
I had a sister once, cold as yon snow-crowned peak;
A friend, than Judas baser, who did worse,
Than sin, inexpiable crime, who blundered.
Thoughts had I once, anterior to that hour;
Once I had hopes, before all hopes were dead.

I half remember these things!
I must away!
Heavens! how faint I feel. The deer range far;
Slippery the frost shines gleaming down the trail.
That thought was rough, that I need kill these things,
So sacred in these haunts. I dare not keep a hound;
I cannot meet the glances of their eyes,
More than all human. When they lick my hand
They shudder at the touch; there 's blood upon it,
Which naught can wash away. No misery and no wrongs,
Nor day nor night, nor the unutterable voice
That yet forever asks me to repent,
Nor any strength that ever I possessed,
Nor these wild forms that glance across my path,
Can take the stains and clear them from my soul.

30

A deer! Hush! My rifle jarred! If it
should fail
(I did not fail that day), then should I die
A hunter's death, — die, and the deer
should live.
'T were better so; they never kill their
friends.

III. — NIGHT AGAIN.

I WRESTLED with the night,
Then on the rocky, upland ridge found food.
Perhaps another week my breath may spend.
But my limbs falter; methinks they are swollen.
I heard my mother say death lay not far
When that began.
Death! All men fear to die!
To change, to be crushed out into the darkness,
Or sheeted off the scaffolding that swings
Across the deep, unfathomable gulf,
Where all we love and all we hate are dashed, —
No, no, not all! save to themselves, not all,
To such as dream. —

Her blood stains all my soul!
I did not pause; of her I never thought.
'T was all myself, accursed self; her frail
And delicate life I disregarded then.
Soothing, I did not heal her tender fears,
Caress her yielding smile, born of delight;
But rudely swept her faithful heart away.
You tell me Gordon struck me; said I flung
The dice foully, the cards were marked, he struck;
And what was that? One midnight of this life
Would clean wash out centuries of insult,—
Baffled by secret foes, nailed to the Cross,
Far happier than this slowly dropping rust
Curdling about my unprotected thoughts.

Oft, ere I sought these ebon shades, I went
In villages as twilight took their streets,
And saw the laborer halting to his home,
His long day's toil misfigured in the glebe,
And heard his children cry their father's name.

Might I not, too, have had a home, a *life*,
My children's love? Yes! ere these viler fiends
Than all hell's lowest pit supplies, despoiled
My home, murdered my wife, kidnapped my darlings,
Children, — all, flung into one common grave;
And I to weep and *see* them till I die!
That sound again! Was it the breath of moonlit air?
" Eliot! it *might* have been," I list it still;
" But might is *not*, in some men's decalogue.
Mark how the noon of night silvers yon spray,
That tears the crashing cataract in twain,
Then 'mid the dim ravines crushed to wild flakes,
And ever writhing, hurled on heaven again!
See, in the vale beneath, the placid pool
Wherein the tall trees muse and view themselves,

Narcissus like, built in supremer grace
E'en than their own, Nature's prevailing
portraits,
The which she draws to emulate her skill.
Eliot! they never change. The whirlpool
roars;
The tender, silent rivulet pursues
The even tenor of its noiseless way;
Down, down forever smites the tortured
fall,
Its broken agony on life's last beat!
But mark, the stroke of twelve. Dear
love, farewell!"
Her voice? Was it a voice? How my
heart beats!
I thought I heard a voice! My veins are
chill.
Twelve did it say? Who knows the hour
of twelve
Here in this solitude, where never fell
The solemn music of the churchyard
tower;
Here in this fiendish cave, the wild man's
lair,

The *maniac's* cell? Why, I could rend my
heart
From out my breast, and crush it 'neath
my feet!
But I am doomed to live, my own revenge,
And Gordon's death must feast upon my
blood.
That voice again! Eliza's? I did dream!
Yet in these dreams of life I meet with
death.
I live when I am dead, when life is gone;
And when I wake, I die!
My limbs are cold;
I feel the frost, — 't is stealing near my
heart.
More wood upon the fire; but no! Who 's
here, —
Here in my seat? And on the table, —
What?
"All false cards, marked, you say, and
loaded dice?
Well, well, 't is much for you to say to
me, —
Eliot, that never bent to mortal man."

" Yes, loaded all, false, cheating; 't is your
trade.
Take that." A blow, a blow! Why, what
is this?
'T is the cold firelight mocking at the
stones;
They did not hear. My limbs are freezing
now,
I 'll build the fire. " Rifles, to-morrow,
At twenty paces! Eliza will be there."
'T is Gordon's voice, or yet one other
dream.

I cannot *love* such nights; never I may.
Their spirit is a poison to my sense,
And most of them, I fear the moonlight's
spell.
What does *it* comfort? Not my breaking
heart.
No shrub or flower profits its palsied glare.
Silence and gliding phantoms fill the
woods,
And the dim forest glimmers with af-
fright, —

Less like the human life I thought to live
Than all things else, and more like him I
hate.
Myself I mean, most hated of my race!
I must endure it; but when I was young
Then moodish patience was to me a charm.
He who is patient lacks no more; he 's
passed
The precipice; aloft he does not hang
Over the dizzy, threatening gulf, but
glides
In peaceful currents down the greensward
vale.
The night wears on. The fire has sought
my limbs;
Would it could burn this heart, beyond all
warmth
That mortal lips can blow into a flame.
I 'll seek my bed again. —
I loved but once.
He who loves twice has never loved that
once;
Like coldly torpid hearts that slowly drag
(A long paralysis from birth to death),

38

Their small expedient selves. All else to them,
Save their own earnest cant, is rottenness,
Feeling some whim; sorrow a lie, so wise
And temperate their cherished self-esteem;
And they succeed in all, and blazon forth
Most godlike, in the senate halls, in law,
In camps, in literature prevailing.
I was not of them; yet I sought the seats
Where eloquence should rule, and might have played,
Had I not fallen, myself the canting knave.
Was it not better thus to fall and fade
To all things human, than to live and lie?
I know not. What an endless night! Sleep, sleep
Deserts me! Once I loved to muse and think, —
Live o'er the happy hours of past delight;
Think of that creature folded in my heart,
As I in hers; and mark the long night build
Its Spaniard's castle on a dreamer's brain.

Why, 't was a kind of rarer sleep; and when
The glorious morning broke my waking dream,
I did not feel the want, but flung abroad
As light as any bird. 'T is strangely wronged;
Confusion follows swift these sleepless nights,
When nothing goes to cheat me of the loss
That drains my waking hours, nothing to part,
No veil, no dark concealment from those shapes.
Oh, I would die within some happy dream;
I cannot wish to pass and feel the steel
Stirring in my cold heart with its last beat.
But I shall die, as I do live, alone;
This solitude detains no human guests;
No reverend father, with his beads in hand,
Or prayer from trembling lips, or mother's tears,
Or the soft heads of children o'er their sire,—

All 's dark and dumb and chilled.
Daylight ! So dark ?
The notes of early birds ! I must have dreamed.
Have then the sands of night dashed off the hours
In a swift torrent, night that is my prayer?
For then I part forget my outlaw's watch;
Or, if remembered, there hangs o'er the veil, —
That gauzy, thin oblivion men name sleep,—
A breathless falsehood, intermixed among
That which we are, yet are not. Never yet
Since I first faced these woods has the midnight
Found me consoled by this false opiate;
Never the morning light has blotted out,
From off this crime-worn soul, its weight of woe.
Let fate be thanked, 't is not Eliza's soul !
She died, she went to peace; she sleeps the sleep
That should forever soothe her contrite thought.

41

Bless Heaven! it is not hers the frenzy eats,
The solitude devours, its sweetest prey
Some human heart!
Why should I save those letters?
A moment in that blaze, safely consumed;
And the rude scribbling of this traitorous pen,
Were it not handsomer, with them to the dust,
As I shall fall myself? What interest,
What word of good have they for mortal ear?
But these red stains,—*these* will not let me burn them.
Between their life and mine there stands a wall,
Fatality, that says: "Live! These shall live,
Even as you shall live, cursed, ever cursed,
Fate's brand across your deeds."

IV. IN THE PAST.

NOT always this.
My words are frenzy; none can feel them here;
This corse a prey to the green mold, to dust.
Here may the wild-cat crouch and suck my veins,
And the slow snake, the Massasauga, coil
About my throat, or drag his rattles o'er
My harmless bones. I never injured him,
Nor touched his race, no more than if his form
Had been my clannish *totem;* yet methinks,
So wild is Nature, or so self-sustained,
She shows no difference to the cruelest boor

And him who tends her creatures like his own.
At times I seem to swim along the past,
Yet without pleasure; grief 's too near. Could I
But plunge beneath that golden dream, and sleep
Upon the pillow of forgotten days!
I seem to see the city by the shore,
Sullen and tame, where laps the Atlantic wave;
Her gloating palaces, her scornful mites
Hating the poor, but loving much the rich.
Was there a breath of judgment in this world,
That senseless wrack of misers and buffoons
Flung to the simmering billows, served far more
As driftwood to the naked islander,
Crushed in his wrecker's cabin, than 't is now, —
A prison of the soul, where genius dies,
Love withers, and all 's damned.

I do but dream!
Methinks I see the hill-tops round me swell,
And meadow vales that kiss their tawny brooks,
And fawn the glittering sands that hug the grass;
Old valleys shorn by farmers numerous years,
Some mossy orchards murmuring with perfume,
And our red farm-house, — what a wreck that was! —
Its rotten shingles peeling 'neath the winds,
When roaring March fell in the offshore breeze;
Its kitchen with the salt box full of eggs,
And Taylor's " Holy Living " on the lid;
And clammy cellar, redolent of rats,
Had not Grimalkin bought his ticket there,
Braced on lean vermin like a banker's clerk.

Our parlor kept its *buffet*, rarely oped.
Much did I wonder at yon glassy doors,
And stacks of crockery sublimely piled,—
Hills of blue plates, and teapots sere with
age,
And spoons, old silver, tiniest of that
breed.
It was a sacred place, and save I whisked
Sometimes a raisin or a seed-cake thence,
With furtive glance I scanned the curious
spot.
The curtains to the windows kept all
dark, —
Green paper was the compound. And the
floor,
Well scrubbed, showed its vacuities, content
With modest subterfuge of mats, the work
Of some brave aunt, industrious as a fly,
And interwove of rags, yet things to me
I hardly dared intrude on them my shoe.
Such fictions of that past, to-day seem
naught;
And there prefigured lay the ruthless
crimes

That later years have summed up in my
count,
Made me the outlaw of these thick-set
woods,
And bribed the solitude to craze my brain.
Within, within; for things without are
void.
I can remember, on my path to school,
There was upon the road a ledge of rocks,
And on its side red stains. I thought
them blood,
And shuddered when I passed, and some-
times ran,
Ploughed in my conscience by a glittering
pang.
Yet then I was unhappy, my thoughts sad;
My heart was soft, I was not loved enough;
I *felt* all tender impulse; but without,
I found dull answers or averted looks,—
The pale, the selfish, and the worldly
crowd
Who block the paths of life, and drop
their slime
Along the doorways, and bar hope away.

My heart was made to love. I loved the
trees;
The livelong fields, slow slumbering 'neath
the sun;
The barberry thickets, where the cat-bird
builds;
And the green privet's shade, the robin's
house.
I loved the long, low beach that kept the
shore;
The eternal billow, turning in its dream;
The sparkling kelp, slow-moving thro' the
spray,
And the small beach-birds, piping their
faint hymn
Amid the cannon of the o'erhanging brine.
I loved the tall white clouds that the blue
hills
Around my birthplace took to Heaven with
them,
And sailed away upon that azure vault
Till hours made centuries.

And fain I loved
The victories of the mind, that fervent pens

Secured in verse or rhyme; idols to some,
Butts for the jest or jeer; the students' tale,
Read crouching o'er the fire in still midnight,
And poring o'er their books to give the race
Dominion, not themselves. And art became
A passion to my soul; and they who taught
In lands Italian or in Grecian fanes,
Discoverers to cold Nature of herself;
Wheel within wheel, fresh beauty still evolved,
As from the rushing sea sprang Venus forth,
And smiled, till the blue bays grew golden,
And shrines melodious gave soft music forth.
But how chill my race to my emotions!
For such as I encountered most each day,
Low-bent and shrunk, their narrow foreheads carved

Deep by their avarice, scanning each
word,
Ringing their twopence on the grocer's
weight,
Always the leading quest, " What will you
do?"
And " How much can you make?"
I spake of verse,
I praised the master-minds, I praised their
works.
Were not great poets something, artists
naught?
Dante's dark dream, and flowing Shak-
spere's light,
And sweet Correggio swooning in his saint,
And Newton gazing like the stars he told!
" Fool ! " was the word; " fool, go read
the almanac,
Teach you to multiply and foot your sums,
Learning is rank confusion. Science
swims
Upon the floating gulf-weed, and its dream
Flies at the tempest which devours its
strand."

50

There lived a few who laid a claim to me,
Who cried: "This world is vain; here conscience falls
To meanness. Set down your priest, your advocate,
With carp and venison plump his greedy skin,
On couches soft rear his luxurious sleep,
And bring congestion from voluptuous wines, —
That is what science means; to us not that.
Time hath a higher meaning to our hearts.
You can foot a rhyme; chant the right thing, the Good,
Sing friendship, praise the scholar's life, the poet's."
Thus did they brag, and then showed me their gums.
Accursed rot their treacherous, craven breed!
Worshippers of success, idols to themselves,
Bound in conventions, who keep up the church,

And cut each sour malignant who prefers
His unwashed cant to their soaped liturgies.
Such fancy that the law is in the state,
And do not reck of Him who put it there,—
Who made the law and made the state to fit.
If there be one thing in these pathless woods,
One gleam of sunshine o'er their flying streams,
'T is that *they* are not here,—the human vipers,
Warmed in my breast till dawned the hour to sting,
And turn the innocent blood to madness
That had sustained their life, and painted soft
A long and sunny day of true attachment;
Like the Samaritan binding up my veins,
Then stabbing to the heart.
And if I showed aught to the crowd,
They laughed to scorn, or with indifference,

Strangled my offspring. What 's the search of fame?
Why should man care for the applause of man,
Knowing the painted pageant that he is? —
Is that the moonlight gleaming on the lid
That shuts the letters? There it falls across
In a long, narrow line of icy light.
That hand, white and sepulchral, — is 't a hand,
Fringed with its shroud, that lifts the dust-strown lid?
" Eliot! scourge not the past; your heart was locked;
You thought friends loved you not. Not so; 't was you
That did not love them, for your heart was chilled
By its *inherent* coldness. You were vain;
Yourself you loved. You thought your verse was well, —
Now mark this letter; 't is this hand that wrote.

You do not read my letters now; let me: —

'There is an hour when justice seeks her
    own;
  There is a day when love shall find its
    love.
Thou shalt not pace the shores of life alone,
  See the stars shining from that Heaven
    above!

'Eliot! the child of that relentless fate, —
  It must relent. There is a better land,
Smile on thy wounds, and be not desolate;
  And find an anchor on time's lonely
    strand.'"

Her voice! The moonlight sinks!
The hand is gone! A cloud 's across the
    sky!
A flash, — the lightning breaks above the
    cave,
And strikes the vision like the shot that
    kills.
Her voice again, — an echo to the flash:

54

"Thou shalt not wait me long; there is a
place
To which thy steps are bent, and I go
there,—
I wait for thee: not many mornings more
Thy palsied eyes life's blackened sun shall
read."

V. COMO—THE SETTLEMENT.

THEY know me well,—
My long, lank, ebon locks, and still, set face.
(And think me proud, alas!) Once 't was not so.
Como! they call their place. Strange names they take,
As some might deem, for spots along the prairie.
And yet the lake shows fair, and sweet the view,
Broad in its graceful swells and rolling green,
The deep seclusion of the inland world.
On the bare outskirts of this Kansas life
They prize the leaven in the sea-shore news;

As the neat shop-boy deals his costly silks,
Christened at Paris in fantastic French,—
Soiled with the Hoosier's patois. I must come,
Twice in the long twelve months, to purchase lead
And powder for my guns, and trade away,
Poor spoil, the lovely furs I robbed in sooth
From our poor cousins of the ambushed wood.
And oh! how slow did twenty winters fall,
And twenty summers deck the grove with green,
Since constant to the Precinct, shadow dim
Of man's civilities, I needs resort;
See the log-cabins fading off the streets,
See the old settlers sloping toward the west,
Mark the new stations, view the flying train
Glide o'er the dangerous slough, where erst the crane
Stretched his white neck and turned his wary head,

(A hundred rods,) split on my rifle's flash.
Why, all doth change, all goes, all flits but
me.
Their faultless curiosity ne'er cools.
As when the first day I stalked o'er the
plain,
The children stared me, and the drowsy
curs,
A red-eyed swarm, peevish with idleness,
Snarled in my track, scenting the game I
lugged,
To-day the same.
"Who 's he?" "Why, do you know,
He lives within the forest, miles afar,
Alone, — a hunter. He can spoil a deer
At eighty rod." "What! alone there in
the bush?
He looks it. What a face, and eyes so deep
Sunk in his head. I should not care to
meet
Him in the shadows of his forest lair,
And in a cave!" "It takes all sorts of men
To make a world."
"For the last time!"

Strangely that thrilled me. 'T was a showman's puff.
At once the presage to myself I linked;
And some one cried amid the gaping crowd:
"He'll never come this road again" (a clown,
The favorite of the circus, for his wit
And shining heel, potential). I once thought
These callow omens mattered most little.
Such as the blood-red circle at the west
I saw last eve, when tardy sunset slid,
That seemed to carve some gory creature there.
Questions are native here. If so, my mind
Is tasked why they ne'er ask me of myself:
They never question me! Has destiny
Scarred on my form, "This being's beyond life,
And all that draws to life, its interest"?
Ask of the desert sands why lone they bask,
Dreary and bleaching in the lidless sun;
Ask of the surf that 's combing o'er the beach

When the tall breakers lift their awful
forms;
Ask the tornado, as it cuts the trees,
The whirling windrow of the prairie wood,
Like a long swath of hay, to answer questions, —
Or of me, why I live and suffer still,
Who am I, or what?
I would I knew them,
If they need me not. Simply a vagrant
To their laws, I come, at these far intervals,
Tossed like the winter goldfinch on a breeze
In ricochets, against their household gods,
And they are barred from me. I am not
bought,
As they are, day by day, nor sold. I learn
The lessons taught in Nature's school, her
creeds;
My code is but the stream that shuts the
glen;
My market is the herb-field, or the trunk
Where the industrious bee lodges his
sweets;

The lights of my saloon are mournful stars,
That shine and say, " We would, we cannot
come,
To warm your pale complexion by our
fires."
My living suits not them, nor with me
theirs,
Fenced off and barricaded from my race;
And yet would I could please them. I
could take
Not merely of their kindness. If my heart
Would open, it might warm as a new
sun.
Their help I ne'er shall seek again. Rest
there,
Ye implements of hunger, fit for such
As I. Death will come sweet; hunter no
more.
I shall not weep to slay the timorous deer;
Nor clutch her turquoise and her sapphires
forth,
Nature's wet gems, from her cold emerald
streams.
"Eliot," — I read my name upon a sign,

After I heard the warning, — "for the last time."
I am not stooped in form, or shuffling yet;
My hair unbleached, my gaze unerring flies.
Is misery, then, a styptic for Time's wounds?
Does sorrow, like Arabian gums, o'er-spread,
Infix these poisoned images, and mask
A clear transparency that shows all light,
When there 's within a Upas sure to slay?
Perchance there 's wisdom in that outward life,
In the red circle on the sunset sky;
And, as I neared my cell, the owlet's cry
Shook through the pines that weep the torrent's roar, —
That weird, unearthly knell. They say, in sooth,
That men have heard that sob brief ere their deaths, —
Yea, as they died!
My life is foul and poor,
And hunger-bitten, where my sorry bones

Peer through the tightened flesh. And yet
this frame
Seems strong, and I might keep another
century,
If 't were not for the plague-spot at my
breast.
I could embrace the sunshine as it falls,
And list the pleasant song of matin birds,
As if the joys of children tugged my
heart,—
Children! those human birds, with trills
of love.
And when the gems of eve silver the fields
With their soft shower of starlight barely
guessed,
And lay aside the loud and dissonant day,
Which like a noisy school-boy whistled
long
His brawling catch, the old devotion dawns
In figures born of faith. That I might
fly,—
There is no flight for him whose memory
Burns like a meteor through all times and
scenes,

And as a nerve of everlasting pain,
Eats on the rusting shroud he hates —him-
self!
How light I made of omens, called them
cheap,
Foolish dreams; in happier days laughed
them to scorn.
I once could mock at them. Sorrow doth
teach
Such lessons as our gayer hours forget.
I see events prefigured in each mote,—
It floats across my passage, shapes from
dark
And awful regions. I am now become
A sailor on the invisible sea of fate,
That the mist covers.
With man my peace is sealed;
Again I shall not visit Como's shore,—
Not in my living form; but they will find
My bones after some days, and put them
there,
In sad November, when the heart is slow,
Under the prairie, "Eliot, a stranger,"
marked

Upon the place. 'T is right that men outlay
Their compliments on things, to them which are
No more than the thin purple grass that flaunts,
Across the graveyard's swale; for 't is so human!
It floats upon the current of my thought,
When in such places, one of Eliza's rhymes:
"Fear not the end, the quickening hour draws near;
Rise upward, hope, dispel this earthly fear;
The shepherd waits his flock to gather in;
A truce to worldliness, good-bye to sin." —
Little of me could find the villagers,
As mutely on their narrow gaze I dawned,
Denizen of the forest; lean my scrip,
Nothing my business to the eager race.
I trafficked with them, followed up the trail
Across the rolling prairie, struck the ridge,

Took the Oak-barrens, and beneath the
woods
Sank, with the deer I hunted. 'T is near
night;
The journey 's long; the day hangs heavy
on me;
My toil is mostly o'er. Far to the north,
Vibrate the waving lights, that o'er their
ice
Alarm the Eskimo, and furnish forth
Their freezing calendars. To me they look
Repugnant; there 's no warmth, no heart
to them, —
Brilliant and bending as the polished
friends,
Who most me wounded. Hark! the owl's
low sobs
Quiver from out the grove! What world
lies yon,
To whose depths I pass? Do spirits look
therefrom
On such as I, and touch their fading hours
With the brief, borrowed moonlight of the
grave?

VI. LISA.

CHILD of some happier fate, for love's lost hours!
Treasure of household good, of golden days!
The sunshine of all hearts! Torn on the thorns
Wherewith my path was strewn, she sank to death!
Lisa! upon thy grave some violet's breath
Shall softly sigh; and there be set a crown,
As a perpetual token of thy grace,
Rustling upon the banners of our life,
From the gross weight of custom shaken forth.
You see her portrait and her letters there.
I never dare to take them in my hand,
Till now my time 's most spent; and I should look

Through the blank, palsied vacuum of the past,
And then be crushed to silence, by the will
Of ruthless fate.
And 't is the same sweet face?
With half a touch of sadness at the mouth
Gathered, as if the angel smiling there
Might say: "Children of time, hard is our lot;
Yet am I yours. I will not leave you lonely.
But I will come to you, and smile on you.
For I'm a soul, — the cause of pleasure still!
With my devotions, smiles and tears are blent.
Both joys and sorrows keen kindle my lovers.
With me shall sing the unmelodious air,
Sparkle with foam the cold and boundless sea,
And swiftly-fleeting clouds arrest their march,
Till the soft ra liance of my pulses thrill

Their mutely-folded sunshine. I must cull
The odor of the rose, bloom of the peach,
And wave across the forehead in a tress.
I will claim beauty! Take, oh, take, the rest,
You clumsy man! — the war, the weariness.
If you but look at me, in that one look, —
A glance, a touch, one pressure of my
hand, —
Shall all your manhood fall within myself,
Yet not to dissonance. And wonder on!
For to myself I am a mystery still.
That I attract is true, — the secret 's kept.
You come to kneel, — you worship. Love
has lent
Me to the office. I could not refuse;
Though, sometimes, I have thought, 'If
I had scope
For a few selfish hours, with Love's con-
sent!'
Why is a woman's dawn thus toned in
spells
Of music that dissolve, in age, to noise?
*Beauty is youth! For youth forgets her-
self!*"

She looks as if she spoke. I ne'er forget
When her pale portrait left the artist's hand.
And oft I saw that joyous look of life
Upon her face at the faint glow of twilight.
When the dim wood fire lit her pure features,
As in a fairy vision, she would smile.
The past and future were one happy dream;
The present like the laughter of a child.
Eliza! 't is the hour!
And I must ope the casket ere I sleep!
I may unloose the thread. This lock of hair,
Dabbled in gore, Gordon's, — I know the stain, —
I saw you cut it from his head, the morn,
In the cold sunshine of December's scorn.
He did not move, nor lift those loving eyes!
Why do I prate of this? What 's here? A flower!
A withered rose, — a soft, pale rose, your hands

Had placed upon his breast! Be merciful!
That was a sad revenge I took on you!
I loved but thee! Ever within my heart
The murmur ran: Lisa, my darling child!
The idol of my heart! my heart of hearts!
No drop of blood steals ever through my veins
That does not throb with thine! No nerve obeys
A sweet emotion, save of thee it comes.
I saw Time's gorgeous pageant drape the west,
When the low summer sunshine bent the lakes
To fiery gold, and thought, "Were Lisa here!"
Night crystalled on her zenith! Stars blazed high!
Myriads of orbs rolling their myriad rounds!
I said: "Does Lisa see them?" Was it song,
Picture or statue, grove or shrine, one hope

Beat its soft love-march in my faithful
breast.
Did with me Lisa look, that day was bliss.
I dare no more! What words are these?
What sounds?
'T is nigh the midnight hour! This withered scroll,
My hand and spots upon it, Gordon's
name, —
Yes! yes! the challenge! I recall it
now!
And here is hers to him and hers to me,
That morning, both one date. And then,
how sweet
And thoughtful of her kind, considerate
heart:
"Gordon, our life is brief! We are to
prove
A blessing or an evil to our friends.
God, in his mercy, gently lays upon
Our path, the opportunity to good.
O Gordon, take it up! Oh, clasp the right!
Think of my heart, and pardon. Be *my*
friend.

I know the lawless blood, the frontier feud, —
But there 's a better way. 'T is Love's pure law, —
Never can bloodshed right a human wrong."
And but a line —
The least faint line, the smallest hair — divides
A life of anguish from a life of joy.
And there 's no power to keep a human soul
From passing it. — The wolves across the slough!
I fear their thrilling yell. It chills my veins,
And forces out a gasp. Why do they howl?
An echo to my heart, poor hungry knaves!
I humor the least sound. 'T is in myself
The answers must be given. If heard not there,
No gold can taste, no justice purchase them.

There is a star, by which we pledged our faith;
I see it shining through yon glittering sky.
That lamp of promise guides my tearful heart
To calmer regions of unvanquished bliss.
It falls; the cloud is rife. This further page:
"Never despair! for laboring storm-clouds fly,
Softly the west is bathed in Heaven's pure light,
There is a place, beyond Time's sullen sky,
With stars of mercy filled, and ever bright.
Thou gentle heart! Surely thy love was born
To meet return, and find its equal sphere.
The ship glides into port, the streamers torn;
And yet her voyage made good, her record clear,

So thine! The mist is fading off the hills;
Sunshine and verdure light the wintry tree,
Love! in my heart confide thy store of ills;
My faith shall firmly lift thy destiny!"

I read no more!
I must abroad, and soothe me with the air!
The mist is dallying o'er the cataract's tomb;
This hour tastes chill. There is a world within
That outward show the vulgar miscall life.
Why should we then, year after year, submit
To Time's ingratitude? One touch, and all
Was done and ended. We must go one day.
What maddening thoughts! Lisa! I see thy star!
Fondly it climbs that sky's lone zenith far?
The watery clouds tend its pale, soothing light!
Lisa! my heart! Thou idol of my love!

75

If in the planet's soul thine own is set,
If 't is thy figure I see floating there,
Upon a wretched outlaw in these woods,
Look down in mercy from thy spheral throne.
Oh, to be leagued with me, a vagrant's bride!
Cast out, spurned off, detested by his kin;
His children *worse* than dead, his heart a den
Wherein the furies writhe! Where am I strayed?
So near the edge of the black precipice,—
The slippery rock, the dread, uncertain height.
And there, sleeping in peace, the silvery gulf
Whereto the whirlpool reels, maddened at the rush.
Away! away! It tempts me to its plunge! Away!

VII. LIGHT AND SHADOW.

A LOAD of weariness!
And shall I drag it hence? I loathe the thought.
Must I destroy a life in order to save mine?
I'm almost at the cave (not home) at last.
There breathes no home to me o'er life's lone wave.
The door half open; so there 's some within.
And she comes forth, — a female, verily.
Now I can scan her, — wondrously antique,
Stooping and scant of weight, and with a staff
Attuning her frail postures. I 'll touch her quietly,
And then conduct her in the den again.
Her voice :

"I am your debtor. 'T is your home;
I tried your deerskin couch. Surely, I found
Sweet visions there of sleep. Early the morn
I loitered out, plucking strong roots and herbs
Spiced for decoction and for sovereign cures, —
Things that amuse these woods, and white-oak bark, —
That, is a powerful remedy. I tottered on,
Till overhead the vagrant, laughing sun
Had spilled his aureate license o'er the vault,
(In age the sun-god smites my wrinkled brow,)
And far I lingered still. I dearly love
The woods, and sometimes tell them at the Farm
That I could nothing better ask of life,
Than, as a wanderer, down the woods to roam.
The spicy odors would appease my sense,

And by their keen promotion fill my thoughts
With a more sinewy aspect. Light my feet
Then danced along the bed of time-strewn leaves,
The forest loom twines in perennial carpet.
I might seem young those days. The crafty air
Would hazard with my bones, and risk his suit
On the persuasion of my new-laid youth.
Friend, I surmise that here you dwell too blest,
Glad 'mid the soft seclusion of the trees.
And you maintain traditional respect,
Coined for high places and for whirling streams, —
The death-shroud of the rainbow, where he paints
Devices o'er his tombstone manifold.
At early sunrise you must love to kneel
And lift the prayer: 'Oh, God of love! of life!'
But what a fount of loveliness is this,

Each morn surrendered to uncounted bliss;
Record of perfect tones that thrill the air
With their warm, flashing cymbal-dance of
hope.
Chasten this heart. I kneel. Take, take
my life,
And bathe it in thy peace, the silent sun
So softly pours across yon mountain's
breast,
And, like a lawn of pure diaphanous good,
Embalm it with thy mercy!

"A hermit here,
Or fasting penitent, might fitly dwell,
And greet the heavenly carols in the sigh
Of the soft-falling echo from the brook,
That murmurs moisture to the grateful
trees.
Our thoughts are sweet in solitude,
And most at eve. There is a twilight faith
Would steal the foulest wrong, and bear it
cleansed
Into the Invisible Presence; stanch the
curse,

And with the floating glow that stills the west
In its euphonious cradle of the spheres,
Touched in the love of all things, purge the soul
Of every dark emotion. Life brings care.
We love, we are deceived, — most in ourselves.
Our plans deceive us, — they were too ill laid.
The dread omniscient wand that opes the tomb,
Touches her forehead, and the loved one falls.
(Heaven was not heaven before.) I think that pain
Bears, like a vase of beauty carved with skill
In high-born figures of Palladian art,
A homely storax that embalms our stars.
Come weal or woe, come fame or ignominy,
Weaving our colors, dark or bright the thread,
There is a base within us, something given,

More than all things without, may sear or
stain.
If this be not called Heaven, I deem it
called
By its inferior title, as it rates
The low inhabitant of sin and shame,
With true Olympian wealth, banishes care,
Makes desolation friendly, knits the skein
Of our all-ravelled hangings, smooth and
soft, —
I must away! I scent the evening air!"
What, gone?
Such words of life fled off her liquid
tongue, —
I could nor speak nor think. I 'll note her
trace.
'T was there she meant to go. I see her
not.
No one! I heard a voice! What 's here?
this veil,
She left a veil upon the stones, of gauze,
And now it floats, and on the hem letters:
"Fly, youth, fly!" Now the firelight
touches it, —

It brightens fast. A speechless form arises,—
My mother! Then 't was she who raised my dream.
Mother, long lost, forgive thy erring son!
If in that awful realm the spirit hold
Communion with the past, or mortal thought,
Feel for thy son, thy wretched, homeless son,
Doomed to unsated penance for his sins.
Feel with the mercy which thou hadst on earth
For all his failings! Raise him to thyself!
She fades, the spirit 's risen, the veil is air,
"Fly, youth, fly!" The same as Meister's warning.
It is too late for flight; the wind is loud,
I hear the forest creaking in its shroud.
The shadow of the torrent drowns the glen!
And, then, that fisherman?
Could he have been a spy shot from the town

To watch my movements? For he asked
me thrice
As to my privilege in the idle woods,
And how I dragged the leaden hours
along.
He spake of Nature,—said there was to
him,
Bating humanity, a hollow there.
I felt his thought, I marvel at his words,—
The same old things I said this many a
year.
I judge he was the shadow of myself,
Fretted to space on weary monologue.
I kept his words: "Here, in this sylvan
shade,
Alone, always alone, dim as my thoughts,—
Wondering at that which chiefly went
before,
Wondering at that which mostly is to
come,—
I find myself attempting at the bud
The inner life of Nature,—what men call
By that insidious title. Without man,
Or human life to cheer me in the dark,

That thing called Nature (if it be a thing)
Shrinks into paint. All is so shallow there,
These bankrupt days of time, loose as a
fly;
Rather than beg my dole from Nature's
dish,
Procrastinated on her solitudes,
Pray let me die a thousand deaths of pain.
How credulous was my youth, when feel-
ing danced
Elastic in my veins, and I prepared
To hymn the deep oblivion of the groves,
Of Nature, — whate'er its name, — the
somewhat there,
The promise and design I cannot steal.
Struck in confusion from the light of
sense,
I call myself a man, and am the puppet
Of a cheating show."
My brain is turning!
My reason lowers! That spectre of the
stream,
And those poor children's voices that I
hear,

And that pale girl, with her soft, flossy
hair,
A soft, pink blush across her waxen
cheeks,
Who spoke for them: "Father! We love
you still!
Oh! do not curse us, your poor children
still,
Though in the forest, in an outlaw's cave,
You dimly dwell, and nevermore our eyes
Shall see your mournful form, drenched in
your tears,
And nevermore our tender hands shall part
Your griefs away, and bring your joys to
view.
Father! though we are parted for this life,
And only in the grave can ever meet,
We love you still! Our hearts are quite
the same,
Still yours, and all that makes our hearts
is yours.
And she, our mother, resolute and pure,
Ne'er ceased to cherish you, nor ceased to
love.

And we shall come to you once more in life,
Once ere you go from hence. Once more to hear
Our childish voices, as you used before
These days of parting fell upon our love."
Was that a song?
Or the light, infant lisping of the year,
Rocked in the leafy garniture of spring?
There seems a searching inquest at the heart
Of this sad panorama. At the door
He lingers still, that fisherman I mean.
He speaks again: "Come! Come and fly with me!
This mausoleum of the mind is death.
Come! let us fly and touch the dreams of France,
Where gay Garonne pours forth her lively dance,
And dare the meadows that destroy old Rome,
Admire the Stone-pines leaning o'er her hills;

And bright Cycladean suns, all wine and
figs,
Shall steep our noontide fancies for their
hour.
Such closeness in this cave I cannot
breathe, —
All spectres haunting here, and this most
dull,
And gray predicament of thought." Then
ceased.
I voyaged once, — he must have tracked
my road.
I read or dreamed that sometimes ere men
die,
There comes a figure like themselves, and
blabs
Of things they did, or suffered, in their
lives, —
To that intent the shadow speaks. That
sigh, —
The owl again is humming from his
tower,
Ancient and dark upon the tall pine's
dome,

His gossip since some months; and this
last sprite;
And that cold Hecuba who twitched the
herb;
There are strange things in life. I never
guessed
I should become the property of ghosts,
Chime with the scanty brethren of the
tomb,
And take moralities from their weak eyes.
How loud the rapid roars; the wind has
veered,
Raised off the generous sea; the salt-fed
breeze
Loans its luxuriance to our bankrupt
main.
I see the bay softly with islands rimmed,
The dark old fort, the wave with vessels
white;
That wind is but the shadow of my
thoughts!

VIII. THE TESTAMENT.

"O'ER hill, o'er dale; the careless morning's sun
Binds up the wounds of night and makes all sweet.
New flowers flow forth and wander o'er the ground,
Like paradise encumbered by its wealth,
As the ancestral twain delighted roamed."

A boy's fond verses, when my days were rich
In happiness. Careless I threw away
A long life's joy, in one emotion blest,
Not reckoning on the future creeping in,
Stooped and forlorn, a beggar with his scrip.
And later thus: "In youth, we feel so rich,

We draw uncounted sums, we fling about
The revenues of a king, we live and spend
As if unfathomable mines of ore
Gleamed on our bidding. Fame steps smiling in,
Her bonnet on her head, her silken scarfs,
Her laces point device! Sweet fame, good fame!
We do not feel the goblin in the shade,
The pale indifference that leers at hope.
Youth is the glass of fortune, blithe in form.
I follow where you lead, the bridge I cross
That leads to Hela's depths, where Baldred went;
And still hope cheats. Alas! our feet too slow
Go trailing helpless as the future flies.
Success so hovers past the shores of life,
Half seems to light, half touches the cold wave;
We view his bright reflections in the ooze,
Where the slow stream crawls sadly through her weeds,

With newts and sodden tortoises of old,
Or stagnant mosses. The small light that shot
Across our painted youth, and showed her curls,
Was a faint, flickering moonbeam, was the end.
And then comes moldering age, prudent and lame,
A skeptic manifold." And was it I
Who shaped this hollow revery?
Could this be mine?
The page is with her letters, in my hand.
Such days were joy, when I had thoughts like those,
When I had thoughts at all; for now I shrink,
And strive to dam the flow of sentiment,
And leave the turbid pool to clear itself.
There is a grave that opens while we live,
There is a life that ends ere we are dead.
I 'm passing hence; I shall not live the week.
But on this tattered scroll I would express,

Like the brave surgeon who at life's last
beat
Held at his pulse his hand, and dying
said:
" It fails, it ceases," then indeed he died. —

Another verse: " Spirit of the wood,
Who build your bowers amid the forests
tall,
And paint the banks of water-courses
green
With delicate ferns, or feathery grass, that
sways
Like cobwebs at the sighing of the stream,
And the high clouds that gaze below, at
peace,
Far by ethereal culture raised from care!"

In those my early days, amid the trees,
I thought to raise an altar to the Muse,
And with these lines to consecrate its
front,—
The Muse that haunts these bowers and
bends their lives.

Time rubs away the outward, leaves
within,
Merely the cerements that once owned
life.
And, when my numbers failed me, I
essayed
To dwell as might some anchorite austere;
O'er the cold stones to drag the nights
with prayer,
And mortifying arts the convent knew.
Questions I may not answer, may not ask
In this vain world, track my slow flight
to death.
I can but make my will, — what things to
leave,
And to whom, to be left. Who are my
heirs?
Beating upon the sphere no human heart
Claims the least hope in mine; all stone
alike,
Corroded by their unbelief in me.
I see them joyous o'er their cottage fire,
Encased in peace, fretted in comfort's
robes;

Bright shines the ruby blaze upon the group, —
Domestic, cheerful, see the children go,
Playing their evening games, the dance, the jest, —
Who spoke for me, their father, cast away,
A fettered outlaw, to the forest drear.
To them shall aught be left? To them my couch,
Yon pile of deerskins that have warmed my limbs,
In the extremity that winter dares;
And my poor books, sallow with damp and years.
What! could they read the poets, with such hearts,
(Pimping with hollow lies for selfish greed,)
Shakspere and Spenser. And my gun, whose sight,
Baffled by naught, would be a hunter's pride.
Give these, — to hearts like theirs?
I wake once more.
Since those last words a dizziness came up

And took possession of my soul. I went
From out this region of old woods, afar;
I fled this dreary day, this drearier night;
Thought for to-morrow's food, the hunter's watch,
The lurking foe, the chill mistrust of time, —
All these were buried in that swooning fear,
That came upon me as a sudden night
Falls on the face of Nature, when the sun
By interruption dies. I wake so long
I dreamed I ne'er should sleep.
Farewell! thou world!
Unpaid I owe thee naught, — no gratefulness,
No debts of love, no balance of delight.
Thou didst not smile on me, nor crook thy brows
To the contemptuous mockery which poor fools
Adore, and great men name *Success!* not mine
The Halls of Fame, nor sons nor maids, who prize

Their father's life. Only within the grave
One faithful thing, Eliza's sunny heart.
Wealth never fawned on me, and men forbore
To press their knees to flatness before him,
Who could not coin such suppliance. Not a friend,
I ever had upon the fields of time,
Who was not false to me, but him I killed.
And oh! was not that fearful act from God?
Could I, this crouching shadow, in the dust,
With the chill avalanche of fate to bear,
Of my own purpose, shatter Gordon's form?
It might have been. I should have bent
Had I been different; but in this life
Men take upon the wild and boundless pulse
That floats our frontier world, there is a calm,
And it will bear through all things, till it bends,

And then the blow; the shot, fierce as remorse,
Flashed in a second to infinity.
I shall not see this night. The dying eve
Will take me to itself and be my shroud;
And there upon my skins I will compose
My form as if for slumber, to be found
By whom I know not, — hunters in a storm,
Or some foot-weary traveller in the bush,
Who not infrequent tempt the iron door.
All is in order, all that Lisa had,
All that she ever gave me. Be it so;
I could not die should I destroy her gifts.
What is repentance? Can it outwear sin?
Vengeance is Thine, and on the worms of earth
It blighting falls, and blinding all things else.
We are made by Thee, predestined from the womb;
Nor shrine of peaceful monk, nor convent-bell
Tolled up the Alpine passes of the soul,

To lead the blinded traveller through the
snows,
Can keep one sob of anguish from his
heart
Who's doomed to suffering! Days shall
go and come,
And seasons fade and fall, and life renew
More intermittently its palsied beats;
Still woe survives to wring the dying
thought,
And on the Cross of Doom the sufferer
nail!

THE END.

JOHN BROWN,

AND THE

HEROES OF HARPER'S FERRY.

A Poem.

BY

WILLIAM ELLERY CHANNING.

BOSTON:
CUPPLES, UPHAM AND COMPANY.
1886.

708

ALFRED MUDGE & SON, PRINTERS,
BOSTON.

DEDICATED

TO LIDIAN EMERSON.

"A light to them who sit in darkness."

SOUL of a world beyond my lays,
I track in vain thy piercing rays;
Too deep for thought, for life a good
In human nature's daily food.
Earnest in all, most quick to feel
That inward sense, whose laws reveal
States that are founded ne'er on chance,
But built of nature's opulence.
Or high or low, or foul or fair,
Where lies this human fate in air,
Thy instincts touch the natural place,
And teach with thy unerring grace.
Years not on you their signets lay;
Still light across youth's feelings play
In loveliest joy, and those clear eyes
Paint violets in their glad surprise.

CONTENTS.

JOHN BROWN.

I.—CHATHAM, CANADA.

A House on the Outskirts of the Town.—HARRIET, STEVENS; *enter* BROWN, COPPIE, COOK, *and* KAGI.

HARRIET. I do my best; our hearts are right.
STEVENS. We doubt you not;
Heaven knows, I am a soldier;
More than aught else, the child of camp and storm.
Had it been otherwise; would I had breathed
Beneath a parent's eye, and felt the thrill
Of love from some fond heart.
HARRIET. You do not mock me?

8

STEVENS. I know, this is not talk.
Many or one,
Be it myself alone, I take the road
That goes to free thy race. No fresh debate;
For me I should not dare to live, and feel
More like a slave, than now!
HARRIET. My people are unversed in strife and arms;
Peace ever is the music of their hearts;
And, long crushed down, even those who, with us now,
Sit under their own vine, dream but of rest.
What think you of the meeting?
STEVENS. Our men must meet, and each must have his talk.
Thus, in the olden times, the fathers met.
We need this government provisional;
We make it freely and declare its laws;
And in that feast, at which the Saviour sat,
There were but twelve, so few; he felt, —
"Few tho' there be, that number shall prevail."

HARRIET. I have persuaded four to join your band.

STEVENS. Four? One is an army in this cause!

HARRIET. Stevens! I know thee for a man of truth.
I hear the Captain questioned, as too rash;
Risking, upon a throw, the cost of years,
All to one end, — to march a score of men
Against broad States built up on providence,
Leagued by oppression and to crime congealed,
And you, and, like you, some few generous hearts,
Ranked like the Spartans, in a narrow pass, —
Some blue Virginia vale, where throb swift streams —

STEVENS. (Silence! breathe not a whisper!)

HARRIET. Fear not! but think, destruction follows this,
As the forked lightning cleaves its echoing shroud.

STEVENS. Some one must perish. That pure, godly soul,
The Captain, sets not upon his life the price
Would buy an empty shard? Life, — is it life
To breathe this tainted air of slavery's curse?
Republic! — flaunting to the winds its flag,
Free as the stars which spot it, and in truth
More chained than Austrian Hofers, or the vale
Where Tell let go his arrow, laying fast
Heavenly prescripts to each new-born man.

(*Enter* JOHN BROWN.)

BROWN. Harriet! we seldom can make sweet your days.
The woman's heart is aching for its race.
Their fate is hazardous, yet fear it not, —
The sword of Gideon in our hands is set.
Think of the men who till the wide-spread fields,

Lands rolling o'er a continent,
And every brother of the outspread race
Waiting to clasp a brother to his breast.

HARRIET. There is a pulse in that!

COOK. This blow must fall; the sooner 't is the better.
I know that country well; the people hate
The South, and Southern institutions too,
There, where the shot must strike.

STEVENS. How many are there in that town?

COOK. Five thousand.

BROWN. 'T is but their love and gratitude we seek;
It seems as if the planters ask us there.
A price set on my head! (what is it worth?)
From near and far, I hear the ocean-swell,
The voice of Liberty o'er hill and dale,
A sound as blithesome as the wind-shook corn.

STEVENS. I laugh to think how they will stand surprised,—
Our dozen marching like a conqueror's host.

KAGI. Whether to fall or rise, we go content,
And a new government, embracing all,
Goes with us. Small must we seem, our band too few;
But often from dim causes come effects
Of unsuspecting splendor.

COPPIE. The arms, you say, are ready, Captain?
Then, no delay. Some fear this plot is smoked;
Now, for myself, I vow, give me my gun,
And ten sharp-shooters' rifles by my side,
I lit a fire upon those Southern hills,
To burn till that black sky is all one blaze.
Cities shall shrivel in its burning arms,
And the close Nessus-shirt that kills a race,
Fit for a high deliverance, were it free,
Drops like the fetter off the skeleton
At the magician's wand, in midnight's trance.

BROWN. Now, for these thirty years, I kept this plan,

To raise a force, and give the slave *himself*;
Much have I pondered, long have read and
thought;
Was there Sertorius, who thro' his brave
plans
Built up a soul in Spain, artfully strength-
ened;
And Schamyl on the Caucasus, that
nought
Could quell nor break, not all dull Russia's
serfs.
And much I loved that noble hero-man,
Toussaint, so rightly called to be
L'Ouverture to a race who needed that.
But this our cause flies far before them
all,—
Far as unceasing ocean to a tarn,
Securely sleeping on its rock-bound bed.
Now shall Humanity attain due place
To all its neighbor worlds,—a sun of love!
But what to-day has come? The woe, the
pain,
And toiling bondmen, with no wage nor
hope,

"*Knowing no rights a white man can respect,*" —
Drive from the mountain's crest, from sea and shore,
Rivet anew his bonds, send back the doomed!
This must not be! God is a most just God.
'Do unto others, as to you they should."
Forth in the gleaming fields the yellow grain
Waves for the sickle in a freedman's hand.
It falls; the old dead past falls off!

II.—THE PRAIRIE NEAR BAIN'S FORT, KANSAS.

RHODA, ELLEN, KAGI, *then* BROWN.

KAGI. Still dreaming of your home?
RHODA. Be sure, we must remember it for good,—
Our sunny cabin, with its garden-ground,
Its few sweet herbs, its scanty coop of fowl,—
And there my children played the livelong day!
KAGI. And yet you chose to fly?
RHODA. Most surely; had we stayed, to-morrow morn
They dragged us off, the Southern planter's game,
And sold us far from home, to Texan fiends.

KAGI. Men dream there is a Providence, and that
Decrees this life of slavery. Sold? Mother from child,
Torn from each other's lives, banished apart,
To feel the lash, to wear the chain, — tortured
For being born, nor pay for toil, and this, —
This monstrous curse is Providence! is God!

RHODA. Master, in all our woes, yet we believe
There is the Lord above us; He is good.

ELLEN. So, Rhoda, was I taught.

KAGI. Then, were you taught, by whom?

ELLEN. There was an aged slave, bent to the earth
By weight of many winters and much toil,
Who somewhere on this voyage o'er life's cold wave
Had learned to read the Gospel. Oft at night,

When all the field was hushed, save the dogs bayed
The slowly passing moon, or the wind whispered
Thro' the cotton-wood, he read the Word of Life,
And taught us faith in God and human love,
And, most of all, *patience*, — the slave's sole coin!

KAGI. As one of *us* you speak!

ELLEN. Seest thou, my skin is lighter than thine own?

KAGI. I did not note it; for myself, know you,
My birth is Southern. On Virginia's hills
I breathe my native air.

ELLEN. And I, the same; the first in all the county,
Was that one from whom I claim my birth.

KAGI. What deeds! and yet they call us maniacs,
We, who must strive to free a fallen race.
Thus have we fought in Kansas, these hard years,

A battle for the right. How few our
band,
Our arms and means how pinched, our
habit scant.
We lead a savage life; no Indian's trail
Ever by wilder speed was torn along
The pathless prairies, than where we pur-
sue;
The rattle of the sleepless snake, the clear
And ringing whistle from the waving grass
Wherein the gopher stands, and the lone
clouds
Softly and sweetly pacing down the skies;
The creaking cranes that Homer portraits,
far
In heaven o'er our heads, and 'sounding
'neath our feet,—
A land all one profoundest loveliness;
And we, this hunted band, and hunting
others,
Tortured and stung and maddened to fell
deeds;
Versed to the crack of carbines, the wild
fray;

Or, ambushed in the edges of the wood,
With murder in our hearts (men call it such).
Yes, well I know 't is death! My rifle rings;
The quick young life is sped; a mother weeps, —
Her youngest lies in the unburied heaven;
That corpse of human slavery pours forth
A doom, to which the Upas-tree was balm!

(*Enter* John Brown.)

Brown. Is all secure, all safe? Is the watch set?
Nay, do not light the fire, — a long day's march;
It matters not; there may be shorter days,
Of which this march is part.

Kagi. You look beyond these days?

Brown. Yes, Kagi, I have spoken oft to you
Of this; a man must come to break the power
Of slavery, — one fetched upon this errand;

God has set his seal upon that soul;
As in the Hebrew days, the prophets saw;
The ocean rises from an infant spring!
Mark you, now, these things are but the preface
To our work. We crush the fangs of crime,
And spill the adder's venom to that end.
Kagi, I would you loved the truth of God!

KAGI. Not more than I.

BROWN. Have you, then, prayed for help?

KAGI. Oh, utterly!

BROWN. And heard no answer?

KAGI. Never, the least! How could I in this tomb,
That bears cut deep the shapes of slavery?

BROWN. My child, there hangs a mist across your brow,—
You seeing, see not; in God's purposes
There is a wiser meed of goodness fixed
Than human tongues may utter. These are days
When hardness is endured: the well-paid spy,

The bullet at the heart, my children's
blood
Soaking the prairie weeds, and far from
home,
And all that consolation knows on earth
(That mother dear, who weeps on Elba's
height,
Widowed almost),—yet bate I not a jot.
Within my inmost soul I know that peace,
The future's fruit, clear as yon twilight
star!

KAGI. Captain, I never hear your
speech unmoved;
'Tis sweeter to my ear than woman's tones,
When, on her trembling lute, in twilight's
calm,
She sings the vision of her love to rest.
Old man, I never knew a dear one's eye;
And still, I think that true affection
sprung
When first I felt thee, thou so firmly true.
Are men and thoughts null, because oppo-
site?
I caught the histories; I learned the tales

Of sage and saint; the mad Crusader's rage,
And Luther's outspoke hate, and Cromwell's steel
Crushed in the heart-blood of that worthless Charles, —
I could not rest and live, I felt the call, —
A race weeps here in hell; I marked their looks;
Was I not of them, and that shriek of doom,
Thrilling thro' me, to go and breathless take
My life upon my arm and act for them?
But of your gods and priests, and heaven in store, —
I yet must take the thought that's next my mind.

BROWN (*aside*). (I have not known these whims, — what does he mean?
A dreaming youth, — how strange his look, how wild!)
Kagi, there is vouchsafed to each of us
A lesson of his own, and good for each.

To me, the God, who led His people forth
From Egypt's poisonous creeds and withered states,
Is nigh. His guiding touch I feel; He leads
Across life's wilderness my thirsty soul.
My children fell; a price set on my head,
Because I lead these fettered slaves to life;
Affliction, outrage, all that makes life hard,
Must fall upon my fate. And yet I know
A Father's eye is on me, always near,—
I would He filled your thoughts.

KAGI. Oh, look upon me as a man who lives
To bear across this tempest-stricken tide
The olive-branch of peace! Most strange are we;
Culture, dissensions, misformed sentiments
Diversify our aims; yet all must sweep
Into one mighty river of the Free,
As, instruments of forethought, firm we sail
Across the ocean of this strife to calm,
For weal or woe as one bound up to strive.

III. — A RESIDENCE, BOSTON.

ELLEN, MEENIE, FATHER, BROWN.

ELLEN. I trust you rested well, — had pleasant dreams?
BROWN. Yes; always, if I sleep, my thought is sweet,
And better for the many nights I watched,
Chased thro' the wilderness; at least I fancy such.
ELLEN. Are you quite peaceful now?
BROWN. I may be sent for, but my mind is clear,
To sell my life as dearly as 't is priced.
There will be presents for the officers,
Twelve shots, and then the door a barricade;
I shall not hurt your rugs.

ELLEN. We honor you, and all we have is yours,
Nor can we aught return to match your rate,
Poised on that height to free our poor oppressed.
BROWN. The how and why I could point out more plain,
Did I not fear the sport of consequence.
I may seem reticent, and hide my plan;
It is an Indian game. In truth, this cause
Demands the wariest vigilance, closed lips, —
On every turn some hard-eyed deputy,
And our kind friends streams of loquacity.
FATHER. Captain, this is a cause the Lord of Hosts
Must influence, not frail man. There is a guard
Set on your actions, not by constables;
There is a voice that guides you on your path, —
A pillar of flame to light you down the night.

Men like yourself may fall, — they *cannot* fail!
The tide that bears you on comes from a spring
That rises in Judea; that clear fount
Runs never dry until the slave is free.
There 's something here, — here fixed upon my brain, —
Continually hammering; yet before I die,
Mine eyes must see your victory!

ELLEN. Father, be calm! Nay, do not vex yourself.

BROWN. 'T is just; the feeling 's here, within my heart,
And something tells these men, these officers,
Creatures of slavery, crawling in the dust
Of their official meanness, — 't is not manhood's place.

MEENIE. Captain, you are our prophet.

BROWN. Me, my dear?

MEENIE. I 'm sure your beard and head look quite like theirs!

BROWN. Come now, dear Meenie, sit upon my hand;

I 'll raise thee in the air, and then one day
You shall narrate how Captain Brown of
Kansas,
" *Old Brown of Ossawatomie*," took you
And held you on the palm, like this!

MEENIE. Oh, Captain, now be sure I
will remember!

FATHER. Your natural force all una-
bated yet, —
For your deeds you may be censured, and
'tis thro'
That carping world, strict flatterer of the
past,
Starched, uniform, unimprovised;
There may be different lives; there must
be men
Framed of another model, angels sent
To lift their white wings o'er the sunken
race.
I know not where you go, nor wish to know,
Yet mark these shaking limbs, these
bleared blue eyes,
And hear the stroke of hammers on my
brain,

Still beating on these temples for their mirth, —
Eyes, life, and brain fired by some eighty years
Of care, shed on these burning veins, — I say,
That nothing short of purblind helplessness
Can hold me back, this instant, from thy band!
Not seek their lives, not slay these murderers, —
Creatures whose hands are dripping with the blood
Of innocent generations?

ELLEN. Father, dear father! the Captain knows you, —
Knows that your heart is breaking in this cause!
Be calm! God, in his mercy, shows to him
A pathway to more light.

BROWN. Thou noble girl, child of a noble sire!
I go for that I came for, to this life, —
This earthly life, to me no sinecure,

While man makes war on man, and cruelty
Waves his dark sceptre o'er this stricken
race.
Often it makes my heart bleed, as I look,
And find around me all the shows of
wealth, —
The costly synagogue built on the gold
Wrung off the brows of pain, the foul-
mouthed print
Mocking the good man's prayers, the smil-
ing crowd
In jewelled splendor, taught by savage
myths,
But for the millions toiling in their chains?
"Go, go your ways, old man; we know you
not!"
It wears my heart; I think of Plymouth
Rock, —
There, when my ancestor stept from the
boat!
Oh mountains of the North, and you, ye
streams!
Forcing your arrowy coldness down the
rocks;

And ye, uncultured haunts of bear and fowl,—
The eagle soaring o'er your wide domain,
Untrammelled bird; and the wild wind that beats
Forever on your patient, unmoved heights,
Raise, raise my heart, leave it not comfortless;
Bear to me strength, and bid my aims reflect
Those higher natures, those the prophets knew.
I go,—much that I loved is lost; I go,—
I never can return. A voice within
Speaks to my thought,—there is a sacrifice!

FATHER. My son, even for this came we upon our course.
Think of the virtuous saints great England burned,
Chained in the market-place with scorn and hate;
The godless throned above the good; think of our Lord,

Driven, in his youthful blood, and nailed on high,
Scoff for a mocking populace, between the thieves!
Not all may stretch them on the bed of ease.
My broken voice, in its half-stifled force,
Can still pronounce upon thy head
A parent's blessing, — parent, in hope and heart, —
And these my children dear (not recreant)
May yet support thee in the bitter hour,
When the low, wintering sun pales its last rays
Across the fatal door, if that must be, —
My Ellen, is 't not so?

ELLEN. Father, it is! whate'er that coming hour, —
Whate'er the doom, living or dying, — then
My heart, and they who in my heart have home,
Shall always beat as thine. Is it not thus,
Meenie, my child?

MEENIE. Yes, mother; not otherwise, for life and death.

BROWN. Forgive these tears! I was not made to weep;
But such true hearts, thus prest to mine, force out
The drops of tenderness. Do not forget me.
Never forget that still I love you all, —
An old and stricken man, tender for you;
Dear father, bless me! lay thy trembling hands
Across these furrowed brows, and smooth away
My whitened locks. It must be sweet that day,
Upon some scaffold's shrine (it may be that),
And when the closing scene is swiftly set
Of that tremendous drama, to one end!
Now, farewell! There is a heaven above us.
Oh, my friends, — Meenie, dear child, and Ellen blest,

33

And you our father, this poor erring man,
Who came to you a stranger, for his cause
Ye make a brother! God must keep your hearts,
And his firm blessing rest with you forever.

IV.—KENNEDY FARM, MARYLAND, NEAR HARPER'S FERRY.

ANNIE, MARTHA, BROWN, STEVENS, *and Others.*

MARTHA. This is a lovely world.
ANNIE. The hills are charming, and more green and warm
Than the vast mountains which we live beside,—
Home of the free. 'T is quiet here, so still,—
The people well-disposed; I fear that father
Goes, alone, too often to the Ferry.
MARTHA. At least, he does not mind it.
ANNIE. And Watson, too, is often there.
MARTHA. They do not love concealment.

ANNIE. Since we came first, we had a pleasant time;
The boys are kind and gentle, such as grace
A hunter's camp. There must be temper in them,
If they live an unexpected life
(I know dear father cannot bear an oath), —
Noble heart! Oh, why upon these heated days
Of strife and madness, and o'ermastering fate,
Should his wise, gentle character thus fall?
He should have safely spent his life in peace,
Like yonder level sunlight that smiles down
The trees, petting the shadows; and his heart,
Soft as your own, had better heard the bells
Sounding for early church, or faithful prayer
Said o'er the good man's grave; but this, — this blow, —
This agony of fate, of possible death, —
Oh, God, if that must be!

MARTHA. Yes, that indeed. This duty ours, meanwhile,
To cheer the patience of the nervous boys,
Keep their dress whole, answer their modest wants,—
Why, Annie! I believe you're baking bread
The whole long day; and as for me, my needle
Must not rust.

ANNIE. And it is safer so, with them thus leagued,—
Thou and thy husband, and my heart with both.
May not a woman be, more to her love,
More to her vow, than a soft ornament,—
A toy, a thing thrown off, and only worn
Like a quick hurried dream, all smiles or tears?

Enter STEVENS, COPPIE, ANDERSON.

STEVENS. I fear you girls will pine in this dull camp.
It 's true we keep you company, by shares,
But feel you never timorous here alone?

The planters and their gangs are strewn
about.
ANNIE. We carry that upon us might
prove dear
For Southern folks to purchase. Who
are they?
Ignorant all, they not suspect our plans.
As Unseld, many a time upon his horse,
Will sit below the porch and gossip there,
Till the grave mastiff grumbles at his chaff;
They are quite friendly toward us.
STEVENS. Yes! but a single breath
would blast this spark
Of friendliness, to one all blazing fury.
Is Cook a prudent man, so often gone, —
And then his wife, — there at the Ferry?
ANNIE. I do not dream who is, or is
not, safe;
Father controls the movements of the band.
STEVENS. And Coppie, that 's a reckless
lad, hot heart,
Wild as a mountain brook, as quick to rise.
ANDERSON. The tramp was tough.
We 're hungry, girls.
Here comes our father.

(BROWN *enters.*)

BROWN. The arms arrive all safe, the pikes and all.
You girls must be sent off. How nobly, too,
Your hearts and hands have helped us in this cause.
Never can we forget your charities.
Annie, I think your mother's heart has made
Within your own a sphere all like itself;
And Martha, you were fit to mate with one
Who never yet betrayed in deed or thought.
But days may come upon us, far from these;
Forced marches, or a camp 'mid mountain-pines,
Where the slow-moving shades contract the heart
To fibres like their own, bred on the granite;
Biding aloof from men the tides of fate,

Some far-off echo indescribable
In its unspoken faintness, the dim sign
Of human life in sleeping villages.

ANNIE. Father, since first I can recall my thoughts,
You have been always to me a sweet thought,
Oh, so dear! I rest upon thy love,
As if it were a cradle for the sleep
Of a frail infant; — father, must we part?
I know I am a woman, yet I shared
Your ambush, and the fortress on the hills,
For am I not thy daughter, even thy child?
To this thing, the freeing of the slave, is not
My life, even as thine own, forever given?

ANDERSON. Annie, dear child, we soon might call thee back;
But now, in these dread days, our fate is blind.

COPPIE. You are a noble girl; for me, I feel,
I kept you with me if I held the dice; —

Your heart as trusty as the twilight star,
Your step as perfect as the prairie doe's.
BROWN. When we have raised our mountain camp, perchance
You may return, and with your sisters too;
While Martha goes to cheer and bless the cot
We love on Elba's side, — there where the Whiteface,
That bold eminence, uplifts the mind from earth.
ANNIE. Yet, if we part, bethink you is there aught
We leave undone, — something your comfort asks, —
Some brief design, a word or thought of home
For those you love, and leave thus far away?
And we must, too, seem like them, when we go!
But always shall our hearts still comfort you,
True guardian spirits, — firm, immovable,

For that wild want of charity, the unthinking world
Must bear this vast design!

BROWN. Annie, this is a labyrinth that leads,
We know, to danger, if the issue hides.
Be what the persons may, planters or slaves,
We trust that God sees an equal service
We can do; — bringing these out of bondage;
Opening the eyes of those to read the right.
Christ's children to be sold! What then! Is crime,
Because decreed by legal formulas, less crime
Against God's precious words, his firm decrees?

ANNIE. Father, never the hour shall pass, we will
Not think of all thy noble deeds, thy hopes,
Thy fixed reliance on the holy faith
That moves the good man's will.

MARTHA. And may these tears unite us, my dear husband!
Must I, then, leave thee, such a girl as I, —
Scarce sixteen fleeting summers on my head, —
Slight as some bending reed by the brook's side?
To part, it may be ne'er to see thee more.
No more thy well-loved smile, thy cheerful voice;
Perchance, instead, there, in that silent grave;
There, — all to perish with me, at one blow, —
Mother and wife and child, and thee! all there!

BROWN. Poor child! God's blessing on thy tender heart!

MARTHA. And yet for this, even for this cause, I give, —
Yes, give thee and myself. For faith is more
Than my affliction, even if the breath of life

Be spent on death, at my departure hence.
There must be sacrifice and hearts must break!

BROWN. My children! come to your father's arms.
This day is nearly done, — my children dear,
There is another life, — no more we part!

V.—THE LAST COUNCIL, KENNEDY FARM.

JOHN BROWN, KAGI, STEVENS, *and Others.*

KAGI. All are assembled, Captain, as you wish.
I read the roll: to your name each answer. [*Reads.*

BROWN. 'Tis well; I have convoked you thus, at once,
That I may brief unfold my plans of war.
You all are pledged to aid this government,
And keep its laws.

COPPIE. You mean the Constitution of the State,
Formed there at Chatham?

BROWN. I think you are familiar with its words.

MERRIAM. We often hear the words, for good or ill,

But on the venture of our all demand
Its full, explicit meaning.
BROWN. This day will lead us forth to do, or die;
To liberate the slave, or wear his chain.
In a great movement, holding such vast risk,
There needs a plan, — a regulative code, -
To furnish possibilities of rule.
Surrounded by a host of tortured slaves,
When they rush down to join the little troop,
Unless we come provided with a dike
To regulate the flood and stem its wave,
All went to swell a chaos with the wreck.
But in this charter, one to bond or free,
Who comes to join our force, we move secured.
Here stands the pledge to keep the laws writ down;
The penalties are stringent, — death for one.
Unwillingly I speak of this;
But, in a cause so just, our bleeding hearts

Are wrenched with sacrifice, when, to an end
Noble and perfected, the sorry means
Limp on behind shrunken and thin!
This is a day for ages set apart,
Set in the voice of a most living God,
Who singles us as once from Israel's midst,
That stripling David, with his twelve smooth stones, —
He fell, — the great Goliah fell!

COPPIE. Not clearly *all* your plans I learn from this.

STEVENS. And so you think this day the die is cast,
That makes or mars our fortune?

BROWN. Yes, for the time is ripe. Have ye all signed?

STEVENS. All, to a man.

LEARY. All, whether black or white.

BROWN. I thank you for that confidence. List, then:
Our move to-night will aim upon the Ferry, —

The silent armory, its guns and shot;
The bristling arsenal and rifle-works,
Intrenched in nature's fastness of the hills,
That cast their soaring pageant at the sky,
While at the foot the swirling currents roar
Of mighty rivers, raising barriers firm.
Here must we first descend; next, occupy,
Take the weak town, seize the stored arms,
Then fortify ourselves, and sending forth,
Summon as hostages planters of wealth and scope,
Them and their slaves, but no more slaves, — now friends;
And with this army, holding up our course,
Then search yon mountain-wall, and there built out
By circumstance, and its piled granite fronts,
Create our free Republic, in the midst
Of this dread citadel of slavery. Friends!
Tell me, do your hearts echo this?

KAGI. It falls upon me like a clear surprise, —

There in the " hole," plunge down as in a trap,
Like flies within a cage, split on a pin?
BROWN. I know ye, Kagi, for an honest heart;
Now, for these twenty years, this sun hath shone,
Ever from the dark depth of slavery's night,
With healing on its wings.
COOK. You think the slaves might rise?
BROWN. Rise as a whirlwind, when the misty South
Drives her o'ertempered breathing on the cold,
Calamitous ices of the Greenland cliffs.
COOK. Why should they rise for us? They need but step
Over yon frontier, — they are free. This face of slavery
Is drawn by sufferance.
STEVENS. I hold, whate'er the Captain rules is right.

His lead is mine; down in "the hole he pops,"
And I go with him, though I plunge to death,
And strew my corse along yon "rolling river,"
Making the stars much brighter at the sport.

BROWN. This plan so long has been upon my mind, —
It is the will of God! As evening's shades appear,
This Sabbath eve, with earnest, tearful prayers,
We go our way, armed and equipped for fight:
Stevens and Cook scour all the neighborhood;
My sons and I, after the town is held,
Remain there; Kagi and Copeland to the works;
Others to tear away the roads and cut the wires;
While Merriam and his men fall back
And guard the arms.

COPPIE. And all these arms, — hundreds of rifles sharp,
By the score revolvers, a thousand pikes,
All safely dropped behind to arm the foe?
They never had before a stock not made
On contract!

BROWN. Boys, I admire your sport. Men must have temper
Who freely give their blood and take their lives
Upon their arms, unpaid, to suit a cause
Grander than this earth's history records.

KAGI. Captain, we all are firm to follow you,
Even to the last, and shed each drop of blood
That flows within us. What our ends shall be,
Fate and the future keep.

BROWN (*alone*). Father, O look upon me now, in love! —
This day of trial, when my soul is torn
To lift thy feeble children, and repair

Their lifelong sufferings. From my first
faint thought,
This hope beat in my heart, my nightly
prayer, —
Oh Father! grant in mercy to this cause
With me, it may not fail, an erring worm,
(My course is rash; indeed 't is desperate,
Yet thoroughly inspired with love of man;)
And by my expiation, doomed crush out
The slave's blind torture My children's
hearts
Are breaking with me, on this blood-
stained reef, —
Myriads against a little fleeting band.
Father! thy arm
Has held me on since manhood's years
were full,
Upon this single aim; with these gray
hairs,
And this enfeebled frame, always I search
Thy counsels. If it be, that here must
end
All that I sought to do to free the slave. —
If I must die, no happier soul e'er went,

Draining his life-blood for a principle!
My men see in this move more than my
eyes,
But they have other hopes and other
aims, —
Such are not mine. The sun has almost set;
From the high mountains soon the shad-
ows fall;
The cool and colored breath of crystal
autumn
Folds about the stars. How placid is the
scene!
The girls are right, — it *is* a pleasant place.
And I am now to change this peace to
strife,
Arming a race against a race, — their own!
Father! my heart is thine; oh, read its
depth,
And may my thoughts to all be kind and
just,
And sweet and peaceful as this evening air,
And the low sounds of twilight breathing
balm,
And Heaven's unfading mercy to my soul.

VI. — HARPER'S FERRY, NEAR THE ARMORY.

BROWN, HIS SONS, *and Others.*

BROWN. Stevens and Cook, you hear? You are assigned
To take the prisoners, hold them as hostages,
With servants such as ye may find at hand;
First to Washington's and Allstadt's, then Byrne's.
Kagi, you and your men, Copeland, and Leary,
March on the rifle-works, secure the watch, —
The bridge is guarded.

ALL. "For truth and freedom." We have the password.

[*They go out.*

BROWN. My children, this is the crisis of our plan;

Be forward, then, to meet it as becomes
Those who are pledged to die in freedom's
cause.

OLIVER. We shall, dear father; 't is a
desperate deed;
This town, in truth, is taken for the hour,
But our small force is scattered far apart.

BROWN. Yes, dear Oliver; not by our
number
Are we strong; the God of justice aids the
right;
A principle avails more than a host; —
And soon the slaves must rise.

WATSON BROWN. None do rise yet.

BROWN. They have not heard our news;
but fast, at once,
On learning of their brothers flocking in,
From Washington's, and elsewhere, they
will join.
Watchman! watchman! hark ye, open this
gate!

WATCH. I will be hanged if I unlock
that gate, —
My God, don't shoot! four guns across my
chest, —

Well, if you kill me, 't were no better then.
Come on, but on your peril, not on mine;
And now, I say, what is this fuss about?
BROWN. We come to free the slaves, — no more, no less;
We hold the armory and rifle-works,
The town is at our mercy. In God's hand
Our cause is firmly set; he will support
Our forces on this march, furnish supplies,
And cause the guiding light that fell
O'er Israel's pathway, in her darkest hour,
Thus to illume our road.
WATCH. That may be so; my lantern is put out,
And my employers look to me.
Captain, how many men along with ye?
BROWN. You long have been a watchman at this yard, —
How many are the negroes in the town?
WATCH. Just a small sprinkling to the whites.

[*A shot is heard.*

BROWN. Who fired that shot? — quick, Oliver, and learn!
I would not harm a hair of any head,
Save I were forced upon it.

OLIVER. Father, a cruel stroke, — a negro's slain!
A porter of the road, oh, sad mischance!
This man was killed unarmed.

BROWN. That was a sorry deed! but in this strife,
The conflict between races, and within
The narrow boundaries of this close-walled town,
Chance shots might kill. Our men cannot stand fast
As targets for the enemy, nor halt
While they bring in the prisoners; the best place
For them will be the watch-house, — a strong post.

OLIVER. Father, will not these hostages delay
And menace all our motions? 'T is much

If we may save ourselves; nor this, unless
We move, by early morning, for the hills.
BROWN. My son, in war there is a measured course.
The lives of others must become a shield
Between the outside foe and us within.
WATSON. Yes, if we had a force. We are too few.
They have a store of arms outside the armory
Secured against the freshets.
BROWN. Children, we are alone; no other ear
Might list a word of this, except your own.
To you, my sons, dear as my eyes, — the life
By which I live, — I frankly own our bark
May not be shipped upon a sea of oil.
Remember Kansas! think of your brothers' fates.
It may be in our family that blood
Descends, leading us forth to sacrifice.

Perchance our plans may fail for one short hour;
Yet 't is the vast design of God, who leads
A cause to victory by ill precedents.
Failure must prove success!

OLIVER. I hear the wagon!

WATSON. Cook is returned.

BROWN. These men must pass within the watch-house.

[*To the prisoners, who enter.*

'T is cool this early air, and fire is welcome;
Walk in. Your name, I hear, is "Washington," —
I thought as much. As soon as the dawn breaks,
You will oblige by sending off a line,
By which your able-bodied negroes haste
To take your place. We come to free the slaves.

ALLSTADT. Your force, doubtless, is large.

BROWN. We call upon a host that cannot fail.

No harm can come to you; as hostages
We guard you here.

COOK., Captain, I'll make another move for Byrne's.
The morn's so chill, I am completely froze.
Stevens I do not need, while you may get
Hot work before you march.

BROWN. That's well; we shall not linger long.
Our plans are all destructive to delay.

WASHINGTON. And do you think to make us march with you?

BROWN. No doubt for that you are brought here.

WASHINGTON. Without our will, four men full-armed to one.
Had I my sword, — see, that is it you hold.
You do not know the history of that sword.
Frederick, of all the Prussians Great,
This sword to him whose name I bear once gave;
And if I had not been four times outmatched,
Its blade had cut your hirelings to the ground.

BROWN. You are a brave man, sir; we all see that.

STEVENS. Yes, it is true; brave as a slaveholder.

BROWN. Pardon their temper, Colonel.

OLIVER. Father, their scouts are active. One just passed
Mounted, — he flies to raise the neighborhood.

BROWN. Let none go by whom you can stop!

OLIVER. And of the train, the passengers are timid.

BROWN. Has that not gone? You then mistook my order.
It should have gone long since.

[*They go out.*

WASHINGTON. What do these madmen mean?

ALLSTADT. Fanatics, abolitionists. all doomed!

WASHINGTON. And holding us as pledges of their safety.

ALLSTADT. It is their trick of speech.

VII.—THE RIFLE-WORKS.

KAGI, LEARY, COPELAND.

COPELAND. We get no good of lurking.

KAGI. We act precisely to the Captain's order;
He sent us: here we stay.

LEARY. 'T is the last order he will make to us.

KAGI. The hour is after eight. I see more men
Assembling on the street; I note their guns;
The country will be up; another hour
Must seal our doom. Copeland, you know for what
You came,—the general plot or plan.
You came to fight, to conquer if might be.

If not, taking the consequence of war,
Chief of a soldier's portion, to go down!
To you belongs, as to me specially,
An offering for the slave; for I was born,
Even as yourself, upon that poisonous soil,
That curls the shining asp of slavery.
My earliest faith, taught by my earliest thought,
Led me to this resolve: if e'er I grew,
Became a man, and acted for myself,
To live to free my brethren. You the same
In Oberlin, where you have dwelt so long,
Both you and Leary, the same truth were taught.
Thus we have learned life is a sacrifice;
We should expect the ripples on its stream.

LEARY. Yes, Captain, that is true; yet it is false
The slaves would rise, if we came here, — they have *not!*
They did not comprehend our move,
And when they learned it, listened with a cold,
Slow apathy, as if they learned it not.

KAGI. This is the curse of slavery; it
bears weeds.
The freeman knows, and joys to know,
he 's free.
As plants turn grateful to the parent-sun,
And insects warm their wings upon his
beams,
So the free heart delights in each new
growth,
That fettered natures still forever shun.
Now, for myself, the sport of storm and
camp,
Even if a man of letters, 'mid a band
Of strong and robust woodmen, I am
steeled
In my particular province, and my eyes
Look upon death as sure and safe release
From many a mortal pathos. You can live;
For me, I know this day concludes my
dream.
I am not superstitious, yet I see
Now, as I saw at first, the Captain's plan
(That dear, true, sweet enthusiast!) told
our doom.

See yonder band of marksmen crowding in;
Next, by a trifling force added to them,
They seize the armory, the arsenal;
Then, send a score of guns to hunt us down,
Like rats caught in a poisoned trap, — no flight.
Poor boys. I grieve for you, not for myself!

LEARY. I do not fear to die. Better go out
In one fierce struggle, than reserved to live,
So to be caught and hanged.

COPELAND. Whatever doom may happen, bravely meet!
Why, Captain, we might even now move off,
And take the mountain; 'tis an easy thing.

KAGI. His order we obey, the leader; one
Whom willingly we advanced to lead.

COPELAND. Remaining here is of no good to him.
KAGI. That matters not! Copeland, in future days
The Captain's name may ring across the land
From Maine to Georgia; and the pens of France
Engrave his frank, familiar lineaments
Upon immortal dies; his deeds get rhymed
By bards in English verse. As for ourselves,
No more the eye of fame will see in us
Than in a lump flinging our vulgar names,
Confound our histories, and blot their scroll.
Content, I came to work to Freedom's hand!
Friends, for your sake, I hope our leader's plan
May be an overture to pure success!
If not, then let us hail its opposite.
Sustainers of the right, — mistress and friend,

Religion, love, and faith, that make life
sweet:
For me the chief attraction to my heart,—
One with the breath I draw, the sun and
stars,
Lies in my fixed resolve, to free the slave!

VIII.—CURRIE'S SCHOOLHOUSE.

CURRIE, COOK, TIDD, LEEMAN, BYRNE.

TIDD The arms are in the wagon.
COOK. We must unload, and leave them here till dusk.
Our forces now can hold the roads, and soon
We shall be freemen of the hills. Leeman,
You can escort our prisoners to the town.
Byrne, you shall not be harmed; in all our aim,
'Tis but to free the slave,—for that we fight.
LEEMAN. March, if we're going; the time is up;
It is a sleepy world, the day's too cold,

And this sharp drizzling mist pierces me thro', —
Freedom will owe us something on our skins.

COOK. 'Tis nothing, Leeman, my poor boy; 't is heaven
To what we did in Kansas.

BYRNE. If you had stayed there, I should not have cried.

COOK. It is no accident that fetched us here.
You must proceed and go before the judge.
He may exchange you for a negro boy,
Or keep you as a hostage. Nothing fear;
Your rights will be respected.

BYRNE. From the Federal troops I look for that,
And do not ask your leave.

[LEEMAN *and* BYRNE *go out.*

CURRIE. My scholars are much frightened with your doings,
And know not what they mean. Were it not well
To let them forth? They cannot study now.

COOK. Yes, presently; leave them with us awhile.

CURRIE. One of my boys now I should like to take
Home to his house; he seems quite ill.

COOK. Well, go your ways; lug in the boxes!
You must not feel alarmed. All those
Who voluntarily free their slaves
We shall protect; the rest we must employ
For our supplies, and confiscate their means.
Tidd, this is a weighty business; I mean,
The boxes crammed with guns, some hundred-weight;
And, in the cabin, those nine hundred pikes, —
We cannot go and bring them; there they rest.
Hark! the guns again! There's fighting forward.
Down at the Ferry our men are in the brush, —

The slaves will come by hundreds at that sound.

A SLAVE. Master, there be no hundred slaves to come!
Why you have lived there at the Ferry, years;
That is the white man's country.

COOK. Yes, it is so. I mean far off, from Charlestown,
Or Winchester, and Martinsburg, — that way.
As apt as runs the prairie fire alight,
Swift pacer thro' the dry November grass,
Licked by the persuading breeze that bears
Its ceaseless wave o'er the vast rolling fields, —
So this eruption, blazing on the sleep
Of that dead pageantry, the planter's shroud,
Shall burn it to a cinder, and calcine
The vampire beak that feeds on human gore.

A SLAVE. Master, that may be, or may not.

COOK. Certainly, boy; yet you believe in freedom?

A SLAVE. Yes, Captain; ye see the slaves are stupid,
And half the time asleep; if they could wake,
They might get started somewhere.

TIDD. 'T is a bold argument. Sleep is a fact.
Poor Leeman! what a child, scarcely across
His brow twenty brief years have run, and this, —
There 't is again! That 's sure the crack of rifles
From our men; I know their ring too well.

COOK. The mischief 's on us to be stationed here,
Just on the line of action, with hands tied
To all that 's going forward. Matters not, —
Such is the Captain's order, and I 'd hang
Over the gibbet, if he spoke the word,

If on the other side a bed of down
Gaped for my carcass.
TIDD. How long are we to hold this watch, here in
This lonely hollow, made for darksome deeds,
Rather than childish pranks? and what on earth,
What can be d ne with all this store of arms
And heap of pikes and cartridges and food?
They have no wings, and we have simply legs.
COOK. Crack, crack! Sharp work is going, and I hear
Surely the beat of drums, faintly and far!
Yes, I am not deceived, the troops have come,—
The railroad whistle! *My God, the Captain's lost!*

IX.—THE ENGINE-HOUSE, HARPER'S FERRY.

BROWN; WATSON, *his Son;* COPPIE, BREWER, *and the Rest.*

BREWER. Your terms are not accepted.

BROWN. I could have burnt the town. My son is killed;
My men, carrying out flags of truce,
Are shot like dogs. I spared the place;
I could have burnt it; all I ask for, now,
Is the permission to retreat as far
As the Potomac bridge; then a free fight.

BREWER. Mercy is not the password of this day!
It was a horrid deed, the death of Thompson.
Young Hunter, maddened with his uncle's death,

Demands the prisoner be brought forth, —
His arms pinioned, he cannot resist;
Many stand round and Thompson in their
midst.
Hunter with four men, armed with guns,
half-mad,
Insisting on his blood; when there rushed
forth
To him, Foulke's sister; threw herself be-
fore him
And held her arms, her form, to shelter
him.
"Shoot, if you will," she says, "you kill
me first!
For shame to murder him, a helpless pris-
oner,
Tied, and in cold blood, — you dirty cow-
ards!"
They dragged him forth, and ere he went,
he said,
"You may kill me, but there remains be-
hind
A countless race, who must avenge my
death, —

The day will come!" Down-stairs they flung him;
Forced him upon the bridge, ho'ding their guns
Closely to his side, and through him fired six balls.
Then dashed him from the truss, into the stream,
Where, slowly sinking, now he lies a ghastly corse.
This is the answer to your flag of truce!

BROWN. And what of Stevens?

BREWER. I went, as I had leave, and helped him up,
Fearfully wounded, — three balls in his head,
Two in his breast, another in his arm, —
And brought him to the tavern, nearly dead.
When they had finished Thompson, then they cried,
"Another of the cursed fiends! This one
Shot Turner and Barley! Kill the ruffian!"
Another, "No, let him die as he is,

Wounded to death; he suffers more, — more thus.
Let 's go and make a mark of the dead nigger,
And fire at him!" Such is the talk I heard.

WATSON. Father, my pain is awful! Put an end
To my dread agony. Oh, in mercy,
Kill me! These torments rend my soul.

BROWN. My son, strive to endure in patientness.
These wounds may be a crown of glory to you.
The lives we give to free the slave, a hope
To suffering millions!

FITZMILLER. (*A hostage.*) You brought it on yourselves; you shot our men,
Murdered the citizens without a cause,
Even the slightest; sent a panic thro'
A peaceful, sleeping town; and all for what?
When Cross went out, Thompson was sacrificed.

Your men should have been patient.
Stevens fired,
And so was shot himself. Then, on your
terms, —
Simply, they are preposterous!

(*Enter* COLONEL SIMMS.)

SIMMS. "Over the bridge!" Give terms
like that to you!
The thought is madness!
BROWN. My son, who lies here dead,
was just shot down
When bearing out a flag of truce. My men
Are killed like dogs.
SIMMS. If you take arms in such a
cause as this,
Like dogs you must expect to be shot
down.
BROWN. We fight not, unless they fight
against us.
COPPIE. And fight I must, as long as
life be left,
Or but my rifle goes, to sell my blood
As dearly as I may, at the highest price.

SIMMS. Beckham was shot by some of you, unarmed
(The mayor of the town, a peaceful man),
Perchance this bragging youngster, a foolish boy.

BROWN. Our prisoners do not fear us, but outside
That drunken crowd, shooting at friend or foe.
This night in strength we may be re-enforced;
Then must we storm a path; now let us pass
To the Potomac bridge, — you not on us,
We not to fire on you. I might have gone
Ere noon, but wished to spare the town.

SIMMS. Useless is debate; such terms are never given
In regular warfare, and much less in this:
A traitorous insurrection, in cold blood,
Planned by yourselves on countrymen in peace. [*Goes.*

BYRNE. Captain, you see how much you took by that;

That job will never fash, so fling it by.
It had been cheaper for you to have moved
By ten this morning, or surrendered since.
Your youngest boy lies dead across the floor;
His brother dying, Kagi and Leeman killed,
And Thompson butchered. That was a brave girl!
(They say she did it, though, to save her carpet.)

BROWN (*feeling his son's pulse, and firing*). You thought of that yourself (in open fields
A bloody corpse looks bad); but, gentlemen,
You know not of the past; my sufferings
In Kansas, — children slain, their houses burnt,
Their trembling wives doomed to a speechless fate, —
Watson, do not move, nor try to shoot.
Your pulse is failing; he needs some water.

Thank you, sir; this beverage will revive you;
Now drink it up; I trust you may yet live,
And bless this hour of precious sacrifice.

(*At a later hour.*)

ALLSTADT. You have been farther South?
BROWN. Once, to the other border of the State;
I marked the kind of country and the slaves,
How to dispose my men, how move.
ALLSTADT. And all you came for was to free the slave?
BROWN. Not more nor less; absolutely that!
ALLSTADT. 'T is now you see the end; your plans have failed.
Had you surrendered earlier, so far well.
BYRNE. Two of your men have fallen at the door
Since night;—'t is now most five, and soon

The dawn will break, — your son gasps
dying here,
Why not surrender now? When morning
comes,
Then Lee moves his marines at once upon
us,
And just as certain his attack succeeds.
BROWN. When the assault is made, be
sure keep low.
The troops will aim at us, not injure you.
WASHINGTON. Insensate leader of a
senseless band!
Your scheme has failed, and but five men
remain,
And one a negro, — and you still resist!
BROWN. Such are the rules of war.
Our terms were fair;
I offered them, they were refused; our
lives
We now must sell as dearly as we may.
BYRNE. Why, what 's the good? You
calculated wrong.
The slaves have slept most of their time
in peace;

And as for those strange pikes you armed
them with,
A pistol in the hand were worth full
seven.
BROWN. I had no proper field to try
their worth.
The present moment fails, if fail it must,
But not for all. Within the brief and
thin
Arrangements of one mortal day
Sleep the grand fortunes of the coming
time, —
When universal freedom pours its beams,
Its brightening radiance, o'er man's fet-
tered soul.

(*Later.*)

BYRNE. I hear the roll-call, Brown!
They come.
BROWN. So far so good; let them come.
Who is it cries,
"I will surrender"? Do, then, as you
please;
I cannot undertake your safety further.

BYRNE. Hallo, men! here's one surrenders, —
Cry Dangerfield, cry surrender!

COPPIE. Get down upon your knees, unless you need
Your head blown off.

BROWN. Now, men, fire!

(The door is burst open, guns fired, ANDERSON *and one of the marines fall dead.* BROWN *surrenders; is struck thrice over the head with a sabre while on the floor.)*

X.—THE ARMORY OFFICE, HARPER'S FERRY.

JOHN BROWN *and* STEVENS *lying on the Floor, badly wounded, covered with old quilts;* WISE, HUNTER, *and Others.*

BY-STANDER. Are you Captain Brown, of Kansas?

BROWN. I am sometimes called so.

BY-STANDER. Are you *Ossawatomie* Brown?

BROWN. I tried to do my duty there.

BY-STANDER. And for your present purpose?

BROWN. To free the slave from bondage.

BY-STANDER. Were others with you in this business?

BROWN. No.

BY-STANDER. And was more aid expected of the North?

BROWN. Those only who came with me were expected

BY-STANDER. Was taking life a portion of your plan?

BROWN. I did not wish to do so, but you forced
Us to it. The town lay at our mercy, —
That I spared; my prisoners I respected.
My son was shot (Oliver, who 's lying dead)
While carrying out a flag of truce; my cause
Was just, — the right to free the slave,
As perfect and as good as God's commands;
And in that cause my right of warfare lay.

(BY-STANDER *goes;* HUNTER *enters.*)

HUNTER. Captain Brown?

BROWN. Yes, that 's my name.

HUNTER. And for your wounds, how fare they?

BROWN. They are the least part in what 's left of me.

HUNTER. The governor, Wise, is at the door, and wishes
To come in, and hold some conversation.

BROWN. Bring him in; you all are welcome.

(*Enter* WISE, LEE, *a reporter*, MASON, *and Others.*)

GOV. WISE. We ask no word of you, save such as comes
All willingly; and what you say will not
Affect your case a hair's breadth.

BROWN. Thus much I know myself, — I never asked
For quarter, do not now. As to my plans,
There 's nothing to withhold; they are made good, —
Free are all to hear just what I say.

HUNTER (*aside*). How purely garrulous this old man is.

BROWN. Among my things there is a document,

Giving the general sense of why I came;
That paper I have sent for — this is it, —
The same, the name of Owen Brown indorsed; —
It is a Constitution I had writ
For a new government. I should have sent
In the next fortnight hence this far and near, —
Yes, you have read the articles I wish.
LEE. Did all your men swear by this oath laid down?
BROWN. It is a pledge; I never take an oath!
WISE. And where set up this novel government?
BROWN. Here in Virginia; I have known this State.
WISE. And then what force and arms did you expect?
BROWN. Three or five thousand men, as might be need.
STEVENS. Do not misunderstand him, — he was not
Sure of this help, though he expected it.

BROWN. Yes, that is right; and then the slaves
And non-slaveholders, they would join our troops;
I could arm at once more than a thousand men.

WISE. And then with these you would stampede the slaves?

BROWN. Never; they had remained here, on this soil,
Here in Virginia and through the South.

MASON. Where did you find the money for this move?

BROWN. Most of it from myself; by my folly
I am here, and all against my judgment;
I was too merciful; I moved too slow;
As to myself, I freely answer you,
But not of others.

MASON. How can you justify these acts?

BROWN. My friend, against humanity and God
You do a grievous wrong. It would be just

For any one, at any and all times,
To interfere with you. I hold the Golden Rule,
"Do as you would be done by"; I am here
Upon that mission, his servant in God's hand.
The slaves to me are equal with yourselves;
And I am yet too young to learn the difference.
We thought of no reward; we heard the cry
Of the oppressed, — that ordered us to come.
The sooner you prepare for settlement
Of this same question (the *negro* question,
That I mean), the better. You may dispose
Of me most easily, have nearly now;
That other may come sooner than you expect, —
The end 's not yet!

XI. — CHARLESTOWN, VA., JAIL.

BROWN, *alone*.

BROWN. A fearful hour is this; it rends my thought.
All that I hoped has gone, and all has come.
My Oliver! my youngest, bravest, best;
No, no. I do not mean it. Watson the same, —
They all were one, and he was but the last,
And so more like his mother. Both are dead, —
Gone, ere they scarcely had grown up to men,
Both dying for me, at my side. Why this
Must be a cause most righteous in His sight,
Who rules impartially the ends of life,

Touching their just proportions. And the rest
Of all my little company, so young, —
Leeman not twenty, the eldest thirty years, —
Eleven shot upon the field, and five
Who came with me reserved for death
By a relentless foe, slave-holding law,
Swift executioner to every hope
Nursed in a freeman's heart. And all so brief;
Now this is Wednesday noon. 'T is but a dream, —
That nightly march, the brisk attack, those deaths,
And Watson by me still with fading eyes,
Aiming his piece; and Stevens who lies there,
My poor brave boys, and I, an old — old man,
Led here to death, led up in mockery.
'T is well; within my soul is peace;
Such clouds must be the prelude to more light.

It may seem I failed;
Granted, 'tis hard to comprehend my aims
Why live thus long, camped on a prison soil,
Yet never organize sufficient force
To save myself upon that narrow pass?
These things may be explained sufficiently
By that which will come after. I shall be
Denounced as a strange madman, and my plans
Misrepresented by the world.

(Avis, *the jailer, enters.*)

Avis. Have you all you wish, Captain?
Brown. So far as I can feel; my sight is poor,
My hearing is the same; I 'm spared the pangs
Of listening to what else might wound the ear.
These senses are defrauded by the blows
Dealt on my naked head after surrender.
A stab from some fiend's bayonet, just then,

Had laid me on the floor; I passed for dead,
Else never here had lain this living corpse.

Avis. Captain, they did not understand your game.
'T was strange that Unseld never smelt your plans, —
Those girls of yours were close.

Brown. That was too great a trust to prate away.

Avis. And Hofmaster, who tried to make you out,
And knew your boys, he said, by way of jest, —
"Yes, but his boys are just old Smith himself."

Brown. These things were so. Avis, when a man's life,
And all that 's dear to him in life, is set
Upon a cause that one short breath may shake
To sundered atoms flying o'er the world, —
A single insobriety, a smart

Or spendthrift word, — their leader should
    accept,
With careful eye and the most searching
    thought,
Men sure to act in faith, conspirators
For a good cause, for love of doing
    right.
No word has ever passed the lips of one
Of my poor boys, that touched upon our
    plans.
(I offered up my all to thee, O Lord!
Impart thy mercy to the consequence.)
  AVIS. I knew you meant it, Captain;
    rest in peace.
So far as I may do, all shall be done
To you and yours. Be, then, not hard on
    me, —
I do not ask your promise; but, in truth,
You will not seek escape, and ruin me.
  BROWN. Avis, doubt not I treat you
    as a man.
I know the chains of bondage are not
    yours;
I know, as far as in you lies, you mean

Me well, and my poor boys. Fear not! never
I wronged a friend, nor struck, but in fair fight.

In the Court-Room. JOHN BROWN, *the lawyers, officers of the Court.*

BROWN. Where are my witnesses? I gave their names,
But none are summoned. This is mockery!
I cannot have a trial just or pertinent.
Robbed of my means, stripped of my purse, and all
Stolen from my pockets, in the engine-house,
When in that swoon I lay, given up for dead,—
I cannot summon counsel in my cause,
Nor bring forth evidence.

CHILTON. Your trial has been fair; the jury must,
As far as in the law is found, decide
In mercy to the prisoner.

HUNTER. To vindicate the law and keep it pure
Concerns the jurymen. Virginia
Rests upon her moral dignity, her rights,
Sure of herself; and Justice is the seat
Of Deity, — Mercy upon another
Column leans, from that we worship here!

After the verdict of Guilty is rendered.

BROWN. May it please the Court, I have few words to say.
I still repeat, to free the slave was all
I came for, — free, and keep him thus for good.
Had I acted for the reputed great,
Suffered and sacrificed as I have now,
By you all the deed had been applauded.
The book that I see here, the Testament,
Teaches me what I might wish from men,
To do for them, with those in bonds be bound!
If justice then demands my blood must flow
And mingle with my children's and the host,

The blood of millions, all whose rights are crushed, —
Then I submit. I hear that some of those
Who came with me (forgetfulness, no doubt)
Have said I *sought* their aid: that was not so.
Freely, and of their own accord, they came.
Now, I have done.
(*The Court then sentences him to execution.*)

In his cell the next day, BROWN, *then* ELLEN.

BROWN. That mockery 's o'er; my time will soon be sped.
"Sentenced to die!" It needed this last word;
The parting hour has come, — a single month
Remains of all the sands of life, granting
No shadowy accident step in to end
Me swifter; for as long as life is left,

The vulture's beak is watching for my
blood.
This trial was of truth a mockery.
For then must justice change, and take
the side
Of the sorry criminal, when laws
Devised by human sins, make head
Against the eternal force of God.
My heart is dreaming. Soft I hear the birds
Piping their matin hymn to greensward
fields,
There in my native town; or faintly list
My cattle on the hills, — the sheep-bell's
tinkle,
And vigorous rush of the imprisoned
streams,
Tearing against the barriers at their flank;
And, dearly loved, the soft-voiced herd at
night,
Sheltering themselves from the lone prairie
winds,
Against the low log-hut, or from the howl
That thrills the sudden blood drawn from
the heart

Of the slim prairie wolf, far in the slough, —
I dream, — wake, wake, oh dream not now!
'T was strange, —
Some words, by me spoke in the court,
Confused the last year's work with this late plan,
But I can write and make that error clear.
I never thought the least to *move* one slave, —
Well, well, these wounds and wars, and my boys' deaths,
They may have crazed me somewhat, but not all.

(AVIS *enters.*)

AVIS. Captain, there is a lady come for you.

BROWN. A lady? How, and what can be her name?

AVIS. She says you call her Ellen, that 's enough.

BROWN. Ellen, Ellen! child of my dream. She here, —
O yes! oh, let her in, — too late, too late.

(ELLEN *enters.*)

ELLEN. Once more, my friend, once more on earth we meet!
Our father sends his love, and Meenie too.
I should have come ere this. It is a thing
Requiring some debate to see you now.

BROWN. And no great sight, methinks. How glad I am
To hear your father's voice; his blessing rests
Still on my head. And Meenie too; they do not feel
As parted from me by these sad events.

ELLEN. Parted, dear friend! close in our hearts you live, —
There 's no more parting when the loved one falls
Into suspicion, incurs obloquy, contempt, —
Then, as the sun poured thro' the threatening rifts
That drape the setting of an angry day,

True loves shine forth, warm and uplifting all.
All moments, in our hearts, your image rests, —
That dear, true thought is sanctified by heaven.

BROWN. You see me here, the same as when they first
Dragged me, half-dead with wounds and sleeplessness,
From that cold engine-house, in felon's rags

ELLEN. Well, I must say it was a prudent cut;
Give me your coat. I 'll stitch it in a trice;
At least your visitors shall find it whole.
But who 's this popinjay that 's staring in?

(*To a* VIRGINIAN, *in the passage.*)

Young man, you just run off and get a brush
For me; I want to clean this coat; look sharp!

BROWN. That was a fatal shot; he'll come no more:
Now tell me, those who may not send are well,
I cannot name, or write to some again.
How do they treat my movements? Does it seem
As if I had thrust back the wheel of time?
ELLEN. We saw, as we came on, the good you do;
Hence all the soldiers round this cruel jail,
And limit to my visit sharply set.
Tell me your needs, of all you wish, at once, —
What messages to give to those you love,
And I can carry with me all you say
Upon my memory; and this same pin,
Rusted with a true patriot's blood, shed
For the coming years, always to keep.
BROWN. I think on some provision made for them,
I soon must leave so poor, my family.
ELLEN. My friend, your wife and children shall not want,

So long as in New England beats a heart,
Sharing in that humanity which all
Who wear our form, should own.

BROWN. 'T is well; you cannot know the joy I feel,
To think their lot will not be destitute.
And, Ellen, sometimes think of these poor men,
Who ventured all they had, to free the slave,
And lost their little all.

ELLEN. Fear not! they shall not be deserted now,
When the dark storm has burst upon their head.
It is a miracle your life was spared
Amid that shower of bullets. Father thinks
It was the hand of Providence reserved
Your bright example for the martyr's crown, —
For nothing earthly, nothing common, mean.

BROWN. Rarely God permits examples like to this, —

So sweet my peace, like a young infant's
sleep
Cradled upon its mother's heart. Must not,
Dear Ellen, something come from this,
beside
The customary sequel of our lives?

(AVIS *enters.*)

AVIS. The crowd begins to clamor;
faith, they think
You plotting treason, when you stitch his
coat.

BROWN. Then, must we part! Tell
them at home
How much I feel their love; tell them my
heart,—
I cannot speak my thoughts; weep not, my
child, —
'T is but a transient parting, soon to pass!

ELLEN. Farewell, oh noble soul! if we
must part, —
And in his mercy may God grant support
To thee, and to the hearts of those you
love!

XII. — THE CONDEMNED CELL.

BROWN, STEVENS.

STEVENS. The leader gets the credit of the act.
Why, look ye, Captain! My wounds are fivefold
What there fell to you, of course, my luck;
And think of Thompson butchered by the fiends;
And Leeman's head blown off, after he cried,
Throwing his hands in air, "Don't shoot!"
And Newby's body eaten by the hogs.
And yet the sympathy is all for you,
The love, — people who live a thousand miles

Away, mending your coat, or writing notes.
Captain, it makes me laugh, or would do that,
If those untutored balls that shelled my head
Had not made laughing out of place.

BROWN. Stevens, you always were a cheerful boy!
There is some truth in what you say, and force;
And yet, right well you know, each friend of mine
Feels just the same for you, as they for me.
And then our men passed off in that sad way:
Kagi died in fair fight, and Leary too;
Stevens, a resolute soldier like yourself
Abides the brunt of war, accepts his wounds,
And never thinks the consequence will end
Of these our deeds with what is sped to-day.
On least events the pregnant issues hang!

Out of the shattered acorn, from that weak
And shredded circumstance, the tiny sprout,
The vast majestic forest fronts the storm,
In peace receives the lurid blaze of heaven,
And doth outlive the gash of centuries;
Then, from its mossy ruin, build new groves.
Not all of us will fall below that floor
With our poor, quivering atoms, downward dropped,
Swinging in empty space.

STEVENS. Old Harper's Ferry well deserved its name,
"The hole," — a trap; just that and nothing more!

BROWN. It seems a moral clear to Southern minds.

STEVENS. A simple story. Down came we in force,
Some twenty strong, into that pit dug deep
Among the mountains, by the flashing streams

That sweep their billows thro' Virginia's vales, —
Came down, swooped up the armory, the bridge,
The railroads stopped, with prisoners filled the jail,
And morning dawned to show a thousand men,
A score of marksmen, shooting at a mark.
As I have often thought, yes! I could laugh
The whole of a long summer's day at that

BROWN. Stevens! I grant you, were our plans revealed?

STEVENS. Avis thinks Cook confesses something.

BROWN. Much as he knows. I never told the names
Of those who helped me. In the end,
The poor particulars of these events
Will be washed off, and only generals
Remain to mirror out their prescience

STEVENS. In our young day, we do not feel the same

As in your age. I never know this more
Then when I hear you reason of these
things.
Kagi, methinks, held somewhat of your
views.
There is in youthful hearts an element
That will not be defined,—Coppie and
Cook
Acted from this spontaneous force,
And the old Kansas life ran in their
veins,—
The wild romance, the charms of the free
air;
To sleep within the moon, and feel the
night wind
Curl around your form, the bending grass
Whisper its lo ing secrets to your ear,
And sing you into utter dreams of peace;
Your friends the wailing winds; the halls
of light,—
Your dazzling halls,—the stars!
BROWN. Yes, youth is hopeful; it the
future hath.
The picture of your sisters yet you keep.

It will be safe, and shall go back to them.
Believe it, not for me more than yourself,
Shall drop the sympathetic tear.

STEVENS. Captain, I did but play! I know it thus,
But this to me seems a slow work in jail,
With all these sores teasing my brain at once!

(AVIS *enters.*)

AVIS. Boys, speak low when you are talking!
I ought not leave you; but I 'll not be starved
For all the Jews or judges on this street.
That growling crowd, outside, thinks both of ye
A team of rattlesnakes. Poor shucks!
If they own slaves, *I* am not one of them.

XIII.—HUSBAND AND WIFE.

BROWN, *the day before his execution;* MARY, *his wife, enters.*

BROWN. Wife, I rejoice to see you.
MARY. Dear husband, this is a cruel fate!
BROWN. Cheer up as best we may! It will be borne,
Let us confess it, for the best.
MARY. God help them, those poor children!
BROWN. Those who have gone from us are angels now;
Their father lives yet, nor repents his course
In just men's eyes, nor in the view of heaven.

MARY. Our daughters yet are well, but bent with woe.
Martha, so young, so widowed, feels her loss
An agony! And Annie, that brave soul!
She weeps in silence for the loved and lost,
And for their dear remains. Dost think the law
Of a slave country will give them up to us?
BROWN. I doubt it not; yet happen as it may,
Where the good man rests, the spot is hallowed,
Consecrated ground; and there the flowers
Of trust and hope and soft-voiced memory bloom,
And fragrant everlasting all its dower.
Nay, do not weep, my Mary! 'T is God's voice —
That still, small voice, — ever I hear, content,
In the cold watches of the prisoner's night,
Bidding me trust in him.

MARY. My husband! glad am I to hear
these words;
And many years it is since you went forth,
With lint for wounds, and ointment for
your hurts.
Always I feared for some sharp, speech-
less death, —
The rifle's knell, the sudden bolt that shears
The heart-blood of the loved one swift
away, —
But this, this ending, and to-morrow's
doom, —
I never thought of this!

BROWN. Oh, no, poor child! poor
stricken heart,
How couldst thou think of this!

MARY. Still, I had felt it better in my
love,
To come, even with these pangs that tear
like death,
Somewhat for the good of the dear chil-
dren.
For them I thought one short, swift hour
might seem

A consolation if I came, spending
It with you, even in one last embrace.

BROWN. Mary, it was a noble thought, worthy
Your generous, kindly mother's truth.

MARY. They told you they would gather up the dead?

BROWN. Yes, fear not for them. Hear your husband's will;
I have just written it.

(*Reads the Will.*)

I know these things are hard;
I strive to make all plain, nor let the end,
The sorry end of all, step in to blot
Our parting. Thus, our dear mother taught me, —
"Most plainly speak the truth, all strictly do."
Remember the last words I wrote you all,
And may the children find the Bible full
Of saving wisdom for their daily lives.

AVIS. The time is nearly up; are all things done?

MARY. Must we then part so soon,
and all those hours
Lost at the Ferry? My husband, from that
world
You go to, oh look down and think of me,
And there uphold my heart. Recall our
love
That nothing can destroy, and all our
hearts
Shall ever point to thee, though gone from
hence.

BROWN. Mary, this parting is for a
brief space;
There is a coming hour when we no more
Must separate; and these dark scenes of
earth,
Born in the hope of lifting up the bound,
Float off like clouds the dewy morning
wears,
Quenched in the splendor of the eternal
day.
Farewell! Oh, dry your tears! you may
not grieve,
True wife, best friend, I suffer all with you;

Nor feel myself, and when you meet them
there
At home, embrace them all for me; and
each,
Tell them each one their father thought of
them
In his last dying moments, each and all!

MARY. Yes, husband; God's mercy on
your soul,
And our poor weeping hearts. Farewell.

(*She kisses him, and goes with* AVIS.)

BROWN. Oh, this is harder, now, than
all that comes
Or went before! O God! this sacrifice
Of this poor weeping heart, that breaks for
mine!

COOK, COPPIE, *in their cell, in irons.*

COPPIE. To-morrow, then, the Captain
dies.

COOK. It is decreed so.

COPPIE. I felt that such must be the
end, that morning
He divulged his plan; the attempt was
fatal;

Suppose we held the Ferry for the hour,
Or for the day, — a town ten miles from this
The county seat; a railroad to the place,
Troops at disposal, — poor ones I admit;
Yet from their number, better than our score.

COOK. And do you yet believe it was his plan
To run off slaves as in Missouri times?

COPPIE. Such is my notion.

COOK. I do not comprehend; I neither heard
Nor thought of running off the slaves, — a stand
Here on Virginia's soil was all I knew.

COPPIE. Yet Copeland holds with me; and did not Brown
Make a like statement in the court? In truth,
He may have been confused, — his mind perturbed.

COOK. Yes, in faith he did; 't was but a blunder.
The loss of those he loved usurped his sense,

And all that sad experience clouded o'er
His eagle soul, and drew a film across it.

COPPIE. I never have regretted that I came.
'T is hard to die just as one's life begins.
But, then, we threw for chances, and we lost!

COOK. Your youth has purchased sympathy; but Wise
Never could pardon you, and live himself.

COPPIE. I know they hate us, look on us as fiends!

COOK. The Captain blames me for what I have said.

COPPIE. He ever is severe and just; at times
I thought him bigoted; but now at last,
When all we hoped is lost, and on that Cross
To-morrow's dawn reveals, all scores are blanked.

COOK. Another week will swing us there, ourselves.

COPPIE. Then let us die as he does; let us show

His firm, unaltering courage, his true faith
In that, — this cause is worth the price we fixed, —
Worthy of living for, of dying for,
Though our brief years have taught a lesson brief
Of human ills and all that life denies.
Still, there was this, this festering cloud of crime,
This much-enduring race fated to Hell!
Could not a few, a score, of living souls,
Mated with one who never was surpassed,
Go forth into that howling wilderness
To do or die? and win a hero's grave,
Leaving the consequence to breed its truth
In other kindred hearts, whate'er our fates?

COOK. If we gain nothing by it; in the book
Of fame, no single line?

COPPIE. The *leader* of an enterprise shines most,
As mountain summits catch the early sun!

XIV. THE LAST MORNING.

BROWN, *alone.*

NEVER I planned
To kill or ravage, torture or destroy,
Not in rebellion, not to slay their foes,
Incite the slave, — solely to loose his cords.
"Do unto me as ye would have me do,
And in my bonds be bound, even as myself":
By that, as far as in me, I have done.
God hath not parted persons in his law.
Father! if by thy will I came to be
What now I am; if ever in my heart,
From my first recollection, still I felt
Thy guiding hand,—be still to me the same,

121

This lovely hour, all gentleness and peace,
Ere the faint dawn has painted the dim sky,
And all her beauty sleeps upon the world.
I am at peace with all men; in my heart
I feel the quiet of thy morn. Oh, give
Me strength of hope and power of faith to meet
This sacrifice I make for man; myself,
A poor and sinful creature, worn and weak.
Unfailing God, our friend, Oh, give me strength!
Truly uplift in love, renew my prayer.
Father, pardon what I have done amiss!
These deeds were sad; they wore a troubled look;
Yet for that principle alone, of right,
I forward moved,—then sanctify these acts.
May they upon the future throw their light,
As yonder rising orb, who paints the morn
With beauteous tints of life; let them awake

The hearts of a great people, who have
moved
Too sluggishly in freedom's cause; and let
My name, if vain, unnoticed, be the word
To lift a struggling race, and free the
slave!
O God! my saviour, my redeemer too,
Receive me to thyself! now that the day
Has dawned when I must die; and those
I leave,
That poor and scattered remnant on the
hills,
Of my contentment something breathe in
them, —
And let their weeping souls be filled with
light,
And from their breaking hearts be heaven
in view,
Seeing that they, who try for duty, so to
live,
However weak, and so to die for it,
May with thee be received.

THE MARTYR'S SACRIFICE.

TO

F. B. SANBORN,

THE MARTYR'S FRIEND, — "FAITHFUL UNTO DEATH."

THE MARTYR'S SACRIFICE.

THAT day, I mind it well, we buried him,
There, in our heart of hearts! From city's wall,
From depth of deepest woods, came up the moan,
The weariness, the wail, all that was grief,
Or could be, in a world all pain and woe.
Gone and forever gone! the good, the just,
The patriot fervid, he who lived — to die,
As he had lived to act, — for the oppressed, the weak.
A shining stone shall be engraved for him.
Thereon a martyr's name, the last and best;
Not Rose, not Lancaster, but "For the Slave,"

Hapless and helpless, for his breaking heart,
He stood, truest and best, that hero-soul,
Old Ossawatomie!
Slow tolled those bells!
Slow and how far away, and yet too near!
Where gray Monadnock lifts a forest front
Over low Jeffrey's pass, sunk in the vale,
(Or what seems such, to them who climb that mount,)
And wide Quonaticut, the Indian's stream,
And those White hills that bend their brows in heaven;
By seas and farthest lands, and sky and shore,
Slow tolled the weary peal, John Brown is dead!
Gone — in his prime of good, and thought, and hope,
Stabbed to his heart so foully by the men
Who wore the Southern Madness in their souls.
Yes! like a falling star, thro' twilight's depth,

He sank in Heaven; his words were like
the hues
Some gentlest eve imprints with zephyr's
touch,
And overlays the ripples of the stream,
In her last glory soothing earth to tears.
And yet that knell, his form, this fatal
hour,
Is swinging on the scaffold!

Mild was that morn, and peaceful was the
day,
When forth from his *last* prison, stepped
this man
Who made the Union sacred, and re-
newed
By heavenly deeds the early patriot's
faith, —
Forth from his cell, a wounded dying
saint,
Far from his home, far from his loved
one's aid,
But closest in their hearts, — with step
unshaken,

And firmly went he forth! And as he went,
A poor devoted slave, a mother stood,
One of the race that Christ came down to
 love,
Bearing upon her breast an infant slave, —
There, by the prison-gate, his blessing
 craved.
Softly, with angel voice, he blessed her
 there, —
One of his children, for whose good he
 lived,
His mind on heaven, his heart still loving
 earth!

Then, forth, that tread of soldiers with
 bright arms,
Rifles in long derision at his side,
Flashed on December sunshine, like a
 pall
O'er all that speechless world, cutting the
 cold
And hard rapacity of civil lines
Across God's sky of light, — on with his
 cheerful thoughts,

That patriot fared, and sitting on the bier,
That soon should hold his silent form, he
said:
"This is a country beautiful, and first
With pleasure have I seen it now."
Serene
And clear, modest and sensible,
He passed along, eying in peace the hills,
That urge the steep Potomac on its flight,
By old romantic wood and cliff-tower tall;
Blue as the skies above them, far away
O'er drear Virginia's vales. Soft russet
shades
The earth, and some few trees, leafless
this day,
Recalling in their grace more vernal bliss.
Oh, had the might been present in that
hour!
To lift his sinking form and bear him on
With the dark race he fondly rushed to
save!
Oh, had the soul, the power acquitted then,
Its future to the world? (his name is
graved,

First on the Capitol, his figure shines
Above the highest, who holds the nation's
heart;)
And now he asked: "Why are not all
within the field,
Not only soldiers, but the citizens?"
Faithful to freedom in this cruel hour.
Why were ye faithless, heavens? Shall
yon chill sky,
Wherein December's sun gleams sadly
forth,
Fail to prefer one pitying look on him,
Who dies to liberate the down-trod race
From stripes, and crime, and legal butch-
eries,
Inexpiable, untold woes, the stake, the
lash,—
Not tears, not pity, mercy, no remorse,
In those who stand around, to slay this
man,
(They called him brave; "That was my
mother's lesson,")
So mild and pure. an infant without
guile!—

'T was o'er, 't was done, the noble, generous soul,
Now more than martyr, met a felon's doom.
He went
To death! — death for a multitude, whose hearts
Were wrung with time-worn suffering, all one pang,
And torn, like desolation's corses chill
Across some mountain-chain, where hungry wolves
Gnaw the still quivering flesh, and reek their thirst
On hearts quick with life's pulses, — went to death,
After those words spoke on Judea's mount,
The text of love, no wild revenge or hate!
"I could have moved,
But there were prisoners within my charge;
I did not fire; this came we for alone,
But this, no more, to free the slave; 't is right;

The poorest and the weakest, these we aid."
He stood; he could not fly;
His children fell; that loss was on his soul;
He spared the lives of them who sought his own,
Weak as a dying infant, spake great words,
Soft as an angel's voice, they clearly fall:
"I think, my friends, you wrong both God and man;
And such as interfere, in this respect
Must act for right, to break man's galling chains!"
They answered, "Yes."
They felt it in their hearts, knew in their minds.
A voice sprang forth from the dark centuries' folds:
"Father, forgive them; they know not what they do."
They could have wept, bound up the brave man's wounds,
And set him on a throne, a hero's throne,
And triumphed him to Alabama's shores,

Or where the hot Caribbean melts her wave
Of fire and silver on the Texan's coast,
O'er Carolina's sands and rice-bound marsh,
And proud Virginia, once of Washington.
That could not be!
God's hand was on the hour, — it must not be!
Never since human breath had moulded sound,
Or given words to sense, more awful truths
Were stretched across the strands of Fate, than those
From that poor, simple, dying. tender soul.
It could not be! by camp, and tower, and ford,
By crashing cannon tearing down the glen,
In the lone forest, up dark mountains hoar,
On sea and land, and graves on earth and wave, —

Sons, fathers falling, doomed without a
shrift,
Unburied, not unknelled, came forth that
voice
From the cold armory of Harper's vale, —
A prophecy of woe: " Prepare, prepare!
The soonest — best; the settlement will
come;
The end 's not yet," a voice of woe and
war, —
Where thro' their valleys dash the liberal
streams,
And at day's dying hour the purple hills
Smile in their forests at the bounteous
heaven.

. . . .

His seat is vacant now.
The son is gone. His mother folds her
hands;
Her hair is gray. " Yes, he was mine: 't is
just!
I gave him for the slave, — that hour was
God's,
The negro's blood was ours, he died for
him,

(Most that I loved sat in his empty chair,)
Died for the mother weeping o'er her child,
Torn from her bleeding arms; the scourging lash
Striping her naked flesh, because she wept
For her young infant's life, sold on the block, —
Sold? God in heaven, yes, for her, he died!"
(Their barren fields dry shrinking in the sun,
The city's pomp is o'er, the grass grows green
Along the silent mart, the drooping flag
Fades in the hot glare of that Southern tomb.)

. . . .

Here, in these quiet fields, John Brown came forth,
Cradled in peace and modest competence;
In pleasant Torrington drew first his breath,
Where swift, a gleaming wave, darts Naugatuck,

And the calm hills stretch off to Wolcott's
side,
Soft in their laurel clumps 'neath towers
of pine,
Birthplace of kindred thought, all purely
reared,
Where mellow Alcott spake and fetched
that strain
Of sweet, melodious converse. Oh, ye
hills,
And groves, and charming greensward
meads
Of rural Torrington, never had yet,
A more devoted soul emerged to life
Among the baffling shades that sepulchre
This large, afflictive, unwound web of
time,
Than him I vainly speak of.
From your force,
A child, he drew perpetual courage,
Full rich in the love of a good mother,
To life's adventure saintly and resigned;
Taught to serve truth, seek God, and do
the right!

Yes! must there move all blessings in this air
Of dear Connecticut, o'er her green fields,
Her lone romantic hills, her torrents bold,
And yonder wave-fringed town, whence busy Yale
Pours forth such learned rivers o'er the States.
And still it stands, the home where he was born, —
The homely house, domestic in its style,
As he who there first felt the wrench of time,
With sloping roof behind, with windows quaint,
And lavish chimney from its centre flung,
Shaming the villa's brick. And here he played,
A merry boy beneath the low stone wall,
Or saw the sunset fade across the lines
That suit yon happy fields. Here, as a child,
Along the meadows, where the streamlet glides,

No future condescension could reveal
The boding years, and yet remain these things:
But he, who saw them so unconsciously
Of days in store, he may not come again,
When even the weeds and tall, neglected grass
Whisper their fitful surmise to the breeze,
That overtops their dreams! Widely the day,
On this uncumbered horizon falls in
From those blue skies, — a house standing so free,
In its society of light and air.
What tho' its casements rattle in the blast:
Immortal deeds within them sprang to life!
Not long his hours among his household gods,
For far away, where bold Ohio's stream
Pours down her volume past Kentucky's vales,
And further yet, and in maturer years,
He spent his strength upon that prairie fight

For bleeding Kansas, when Missouri's crimes
Burnt thro' a freeman's heart and lit its flames.
There came the sorrow o'er him, there his race
Fell at the Southern rifle, there he fought,
And with superior calmness, or swift guile
Such as a woodman's creed sweetly allows,
Thus preached a hero's truth, saintly if strong,
Wise Ossawatomie!
He knew not that,—
The day in Harper's vale. Never he heard
Those pealing strains ascend from camp and town,
"We're marching on," unknown, unheard-of lived,
Where the dark Adirondacks fling the pine
Up the unsounded ramparts of their chains,
And lakes, whence the wild waterfall alone

Whirls thro' the steep-cut flume a curdling hymn.
There, as a settler on the silent lands,
Within his heart musing of many things,
His children near, their mother by his side,
(She, who walked truly with him to the end,
Soothed his affliction, stanched his wounds with love,)
There, in that tranquil Elba, might have lived, —
And all that is, not been?
Most vain that thought!
Before him lay the laws, the swift reward,
The spy, the bribe, the scoff, hunted from town
To town, bearing a charmed life, for death
Grimly prepared. And still that voice, a cry
From breaking hearts more wretched than his own,
That simple, childlike, helpless, loving race, —
Enough, he heard it still!

No, no, not rest;
He knew no rest, sleeping or waking none!
Holding his plow across the fresh-broke swards,
When fell his children in the prairie-fight,
Or at the good man's burial from the church,
In storm or calm, in danger or repose,—
"Do ye for us, as we should do for you,
We are the poor oppressed, and you—the strong."
Nor aid he sought, nor force of arms nor men,
But in his daring heart and soldier's brain,
Matched to heroic Will with earnest prayers,
And those few watchful souls who knew this man,—
As one, a bride, upon a summer morn,
To some sweet sacrifice of all her dower,
Devoted to the death for him she loves,
He went,—not all alone!
That race kept with him,

The oppressed, the weak, those who him needed;
The souls went too, of all the martyred good
Who died for men, stars that adorn the Past,
And light the sky of ages, lamps of fame!
And one whom he had worshipped from his birth,
The Saviour! Those too, him half-way welcomed,
Fluent and loud, fixed pioneers of speech,
Who poured forth Abolition, and preferred
Scant reconcilement in all human souls,
To close companionship. And women
Of tried passion, who surprised man's fortitude,
And off their silvery lips loosed the shrill breath
Of liberty into war's clarion keen,
Shaping man's rancor.
With this host he passed, —
All that was acting on life's stage, he passed;

Or crowding street, or miscellaneous wain
Towering with luxuries, the Mill whose bleach
Was spun from bloody thread; the Court, the Church,
Where never yet that name of Slave was breathed;
He knew them *well*, 't was the loud treacherous world
He oft had dreamed of, masking Human Right,
(Pouring envenomed death, thro' life and love,)
Till one man touch the cords and launch the bark,
With loud acclaim, United Liberty!

He came; he touched the cords; 't is done!
The chain is snapt; the vessel leaves the shore.

THE END.

UNCOLLECTED POEMS

WHY askest thou, friend, for new thoughts never said?
On the same olden lore are all fair spirits fed.

WILLINGNESS.

An unendeavoring flower, — how still
Its growth from morn to eventime;
Nor signs of hasty anger fill
Its tender form from birth to prime
Of happy will.

And some, who think these simple things
Can bear no goodness to their minds,
May learn to feel how nature brings,
Around a quiet being winds,
And through us sings.

A stream to some is no delight,
Its element diffused around;
Yet in its unobtrusive flight
There trembles from its heart a sound
Like that of night.

So give thy true allotment, — fair;
To children turn a social heart;
And if thy days pass clear as air,
Or friends from thy beseeching part,
O humbly bear.

TORMENTS.

Yes! they torment me
Most exceedingly: —
I would I could flee.
A breeze on a river —
I listen forever;
The yellowish heather
Under cool weather, —
These are pleasures to me.

What do torment me?
Those living vacantly,
Who live but to see;
Indefinite action,
Nothing but motion,
Round stones a rolling,
No inward controlling; —
Yes! they torment me.

Some cry all the time,
Even in their prime
Of youth's flushing clime.
O! out on this sorrow!
Fear'st thou to-morrow?
Set thy legs going,
Be stamping be rowing, —
This of life is the lime.

Hail, thou mother Earth!
Who gave me thy worth
For my portion at birth:
I walk in thy azure,
Unfond of erasure,
But they who torment me
So most exceedingly
Sit with feet on the hearth.

THEME FOR A WORLD-DRAMA.

THE MAIDEN — THE ADOPTED FATHER — THE ADOPTED MOTHER — THE LOVER.

I WOULD that we had spoke two words together,
For then it had gone right, but now all still, —
This perfect stillness fastens on my heart
Like night, — nothing can come of it.

Why art thou so sad?

O, I do not know.

But thou must know. Whoever knew not living
Some of his inner self; who had no consciousness
Of all his purposes, his doings, — will?
Why this we call the mind, what is it, save
A knowledge of ourselves?

I would it were so.

What were so?

Come — let us be alone awhile; I'm weary.

If you would be left, I'll leave you.

Do so, — I'm glad he's gone;
I think of him even when my guardian here,
So gentle and affectionate a man,
Would converse with me of myself. Alas!
And yet why do I say alas! — am I
Not happy in the depth of this my sorrowing,
The only treasure which is simply mine,
That watchful eye is now upon me, ever.
If I look abroad and recognise the forms
Of those familiar mountains, my brothers,
And see the trees soft-waving in the wind
This summer's day; — what then? I cannot, cannot!

One thing it is to have an outward life,
Another — such as mine.

Why is she then so sad?

Partly it is her nature to be so.
  These delicate beings look not o'er
The earth and the rough surface of society,
  As commoners. They breathe a finer air,
And their enraptured senses, sudden brought
  Into harsh contact with the scaly folds
Of the enormous serpent, Sin, shatter;
  As if a glass in which an image dwelt
Of an all-perfect seeming were rudely
  On a bitter stone employed, smiting it
Into a million fragments.—She is of this breed,
  This narrow suffrage in a world of dross
Of gold thrice molten, and it seems to me
  That, with a strange peculiar care of love,
We should encompass her with lovely thoughts,
  Forms breathing Italy in every bend,
Scarce enough products of our northern vale.

I feel that, although she is not our child,
  We do regard her with a parent's love

But O, our love is a poor mockery
  Of what that love had been. We do not live,
As marrow in the bone, within her life,
  As parents had. Nature has ministered to these,
In such full kind; they are the double worlds,
  As man, if truly wise, a twice-told tale,
First for himself, and then for Nature.
  I am all aware that with what stress of mind
I strive to paint a parent's love for her
  In my imagination, will drop short
O' the mark; I cannot sling the stone, as one
  Who from his hand the whirling pebble sent
To dive into another's life.

  Let us not despair!

This world is much too wide for that;
  I pity him, the poor despairing man,
Who walks the teeming earth,—a solitude;

Who groans his soul away, as if it were
The conduit pipe of a dull city, or
The dreadful hum of oiled machinery,
Which from the doors, where starveling weavers ply
Their horrid toil, down to the sunset hour
Floats out upon the tune of all this visible love,
A clanging echo of the miser's shrieks.
Our very freedom is to be awake,
Alive to inspiration from the whole
Of a fair universe.

I feel myself, — I do not see myself;
But my particular nature masters me,
Even here, among these waving spirits
Who haunt the reedy banks of this calm river,
Lofty genial presences who fill their place,
Nor will displace a thought their long year lives.
I defy all but this, and this I must
Obey, — I cannot this defy. This is
The oracular parent of the child,
Whose simple look can wind him into tasks
Hateful and hated. — I did not wish
To love; I said, — here stands a man whose soul
The imprisoning forms of things shall master,
Not without a strife convulsed as death;
I stand upon an adamantine basis
Never to rock; I triumphed over much;
The whimperings of the youth I changed to words;
Nor scoffs, nor jeers, nor place, nor poverty
Gained footing in the scale of my design.
This girl came to me on a summer's day,
The day of my o'ermastery, which passes
From my mind but with my life. Up she rose
As the first revelation to the Poet's soul
Of his dear art, thenceforth to him his spring;
A radiance circled her with grace, as I
Have seen about the fronts of Raphael's
Time-defying saints, — a ring of glory,
Waxing immeasurably potent
In its symbolical form; her motion
Flung me to the ground in prayer, I hardly
Daring to translate my eyes again to hers,
Lest another glance would represent a thin
And shadowy lustre fading fast away.

At length, with breath suspended, looked again,
  And there in very form she was. I felt
I know not what. I will not venture on a chance
  That I may hit the sense of my expression,
Yet I was expressed; a copious sense
  Of knowledge that my former mind of beauty
Was inconceivably blind, rushed through me;
  A decided view of perfect loveliness,
Bore information of celestial heights,
  At whose first inch I had thus far stood idle
Into the Ideal in my mind; there fixed
  The simple surface of her body; the hair
Of tender brown, not negligent disposed,
  The unrivalled tracing through her dress
Of a prodigious nature; her life
  Glowed out in the embalming whiteness of her neck;
All that she is in fact came to me then,
  And in me now finds ready utterance.

SONG.

Like seas flashing in caves
  Where stalactites gleam,
Like the sparkling of waves
  Where Northern lights beam;
Like the swift drops that fall
  Where the sun brightly shines,
Like a clear crystal hall
  Amid clustering vines;

Like emerald leaves
All transparent with light,
Where the summer breeze weaves
Its song of delight,
Like wild flickering dreams,
Is the light which lies,
Which flashes and beams
In Angela's eyes.

Like ripples slow circling
Where a stone has been thrown,
Like a sunny spring gushing
In a meadow alone;
Like a fair sea-girt isle
All blooming with flowers,
Is the joy of her smile
In our wild-wood bowers.

Deep as the sea,
As the voice of the night,
Lofty and free
As the vast dome of light,
Are the thoughts which live
In the soul of this being,
To her God did give
The true power of seeing.
Comprehending by love
What love did create,
She seeks not above
Like one weary of fate,
And longing to see
A bright world to come,
Where'er she may be
Is her beautiful home.

PRAYER.

Mother dear! wilt pardon one
Who loved not the generous Sun,
Nor thy seasons loved to hear
Singing to the busy year:—
Thee neglected, shut his heart,
In thy being, had no part.
Mother dear! I list thy song
In the autumn eve along:
Now thy chill airs round the day,
And leave me my time to pray.
Mother dear! the day must come
When thy child shall make his home,
His long last home, amid the grass,
Over which thy warm hands pass.
I know my prayers will reach thine ear,
Thou art with me while I ask,
Nor a child refuse to hear,
Who would learn his little task.
Let me take my part with thee,
In the gray clouds or thy light,
Laugh with thee upon the sea,
And idle on the land by night;
In the trees I live with thee,
In the flowers, like any bee.

AFTER-LIFE.

THEY tell me the grave is cold,
The bed underneath all the living day;
They speak of the worms that crawl in the mould,
And the rats that in the coffin play;
 Up above the daisies spring,
 Eyeing the wrens that over them sing:
I shall hear them not in my house of clay.

It is not *so;* I shall live in the veins
Of the life which painted the daisies' dim eye,
I shall kiss their lips when I fall in rains,
With the wrens and bees shall over them fly,—
In the trill of the sweet birds float
The music of every note,
A-lifting times veil,—is that called to die?

TO SHAKSPEARE.

As the strong wind that round the wide Earth blows,
Seizing all scents that shimmer o'er the flowers,
The sparkling spray from every wave that flows
Through the proud glory of the summer hours,
Sweet questioning smiles, and gentle courteous glances,
The stately ship that stems the ocean tide,
The butterfly that with the wild air dances,
And radiant clouds on which the Genii ride,
Bearing all these on its triumphant way,
Sounding through forests, soaring o'er the sea,
Greeting all things which love the joyous day,
In life exulting, freest of the free ;
Thus do thy Sonnets, Shakspeare, onward sweep,
Cleaving the winged clouds, stirring the mighty deep.

THE POET.

No narrow field the poet has,
The world before him spreading,
But he must write his honest thought,
No critic's cold eye dreading.

His range is over everything,
The air, the sea, the earth, the mind,
And with his verses murmurs sing,
And joyous notes float down the wind.

LIFE.

It is a gay and glittering cloud,
Born in the early light of day,
It lies upon the gentle hills,
Rosy, and sweet, and far away.

It burns again when noon is high;
Like molten gold 't is clothed in light,
'T is beautiful and glad as love, —
A joyous, soul-entrancing sight.

But now 't is fading in the west,
On the flowering heaven a withered leaf,
As faint as shadow on the grass
Thrown by a gleam of moonshine brief.

So life is born, grows up, and dies,
As cloud upon the world of light;
It comes in joy, and moves in love,
Then, — gently fades away in night.

Sweet Love, I cannot show thee in this guise
Of earthly words, how dear to me thou art,
Nor once compare thy image in my eyes
With thy dear self reposed within my heart.
The love I bear to thee I truly prize
Above all joys that offer in the mart
Of the wide world, our wishes to suffice, —
And yet I seek *thy* love; for no desert
That I can boast, but that my new love cries
For love that to its own excess is meet,
And searching widely through this dark world's space,
Hath found a love which hath its holy seat
Within thy bosom's blissfulest embrace,
And to awake this love is at thy feet,
Whence will it not arise till thou accord this grace.

Let not my love implore of thee in vain,
For in its loneliness it dooms to wo,
From whose deep depths I cannot rise again;
Let not thy love conspire to kill me so
With my love, which will only share its reign
With thine its sister; rather may both go
To that high altar, where no longer twain,
In sweetest concord both together grow,
Thence to ascend to the Eternal Love,
And be absorbed and spread through all the life
That breathes in purest holiest bliss above,
Or that incites all mortals to the strife
Of kindness, in this scene of mixed delight
And griefs — of brightest day and darkest night.

W.

SPRING.

With what a still, untroubled air,
The spring comes stealing up the way,
Like some young maiden coyly fair,
Too modest for the light of day.

THE SONG OF BIRDS IN SPRING.

They breathe the feeling of thy happy soul,
Intricate Spring! too active for a word;
They come from regions distant as the pole;
Thou art their magnet, — seedsman of the bird.

AN OLD MAN.

HEAVY and drooping,
By himself stooping,
Half of his body left,
Of all his mind bereft,
Antiquate positive,
Forgotten causative,—
Yet he still picks the ground,
Though his spade makes no sound,
Thin fingers are weak,
And elbows a-peak.

He talks to himself,
Of what he remembers.
Rakes over spent embers,
Recoineth past pelf,
Dreams backwards alone,
Of time gnawing the bone.
Too simple for folly,
Too wise for content,
Not brave melancholy,
Or knave eminent,
Slouched hat, and loose breeches,
And gaping with twitches,—
Old coin found a-ploughing,
Curious but cloying,
How he gropes in the sun,
And spoils what he's done.

C.

AUTUMN.

A VARIED wreath the autumn weaves
Of cold grey days, and sunny weather,
And strews gay flowers and withered leaves
Along my lonely path together.

I see the golden-rod shine bright,
As sun-showers at the birth of day,
A golden plume of yellow light,
That robs the Day-god's splendid ray.

The aster's violet rays divide
The bank with many stars for me,
And yarrow in blanch tints is dyed,
As moonlight floats across the sea.

I see the emerald woods prepare
To shed their vestiture once more,
And distant elm-trees spot the air
With yellow pictures softly o'er.

I saw an ash burn scarlet red
Beneath a pine's perpetual green,
And sighing birches hung their head,
Protected by a hemlock screen.

Yet light the verdant willow floats
Above the river's shining face,
And sheds its rain of hurried notes
With a swift shower's harmonious grace.

The petals of the cardinal
  Fleck with their crimson drops the stream,
As spots of blood the banquet hall,
  In some young knight's romantic dream.

No more the water lily's pride
  In milk-white circles swims content,
No more the blue weed's clusters ride
  And mock the heaven's element.

How speeds from in the river's thought
  The spirit of the leaf that falls,
It's heaven in this calm bosom wrought,
  As mine among those crimson walls.

From the dry bough it spins to greet
  Its shadow in the placid river,
So might I my companion meet,
  Nor roam the countless worlds forever.

Autumn, thy wreath and mine are blent
  With the same colors, for to me
A richer sky than all is lent,
  While fades my dream-like company.

Our skies glow purple, but the wind
  Sobs chill through green trees and bright grass,
To-day shines fair, and lurk behind
  The times that into winter pass.

So fair we seem, so cold we are,
  So fast we hasten to decay,
Yet through our night glows many a star,
  That still shall claim its sunny day.

THE MOTHER'S GRIEF.

I STAND within my garden fair
  Where flowers in joyous beauty spring,
Their fragrance mingles in the air,
  The birds most sweetly sing.

And in that spot a lonely mound,
  Spread o'er with grasses heavily,
My infant sleeps within the ground,
  Nor may the garden see.

The wind sighs sadly, and the sun
  Shines down to dazzle weary eyes;
That buried form the truest one,
  The rest its mockeries.

ALLSTON'S FUNERAL.

THE summer moonlight lingered there,
Thy gently moulded brow to see,
For art in thee had softened care,
As night's mild beams the dying tree.

That storied smile was on thy face,
The fair forgetfulness of fame,
The deep concealment of that grace,
Thy tender being's only aim.

TO THE MUSE.

WHITHER? hast thou then faded?
No more by dell, or spring, or tree?
Whither? have I thy love upbraided?
Come back and speak to me;
Shine, thou star of destiny!

O simple plains and quiet woods,
Your silence asks no poet's strains,
For ye are verse-like solitudes,
Your leaf-like paths the sweet refrains
The muse awakens but in pains.

Yet shines above undauntedly
The star-wreathed crownlet, heaven's great fame,
And azure builds the dome-like sky,
Nor should I make my nature tame,
Lest distant days shall hide my name.

"Thou bearest in these shades the light,
That piled the rugged height of leaves,
Thou rob'st with artificial night
These dells so deep; — he who believes,
The muse enchants not, or deceives.

And let the deep sea toss the shore,
Thy infinite heart no motion hath;
Let lightning dance and thunder roar,
And dark remembrance crowd thy path,
  Thy spirit needs some wider wrath.

That verse, — the living fate within,
Shall truly find its tone to save,
Its adamantine goal to win
Demands no voice, descends no grave,
  They sing enough who life-blood have."

O placid springs which murmur through
The silken grass so glistening;
Are fed your veins with silent dew
So softly that ye onward sing,
  For in the middle earth ye cling.

O gentlest woods, — your birds' kind song,
How had you that so virtuous lay?
Among you let me linger long,
And seek the arborous dim-lit way,
  And listen to your light wind's play.

And thou, the essence of the flowers,
My bride, my joy, my own dear wife,
Who melted in thine eyes those hours,
Those hours with sunlight richly rife?
  Art thou a song of earnest life?

WILLIAM TELL'S SONG.

WHERE the mountain cataracts leap,
  And the stern wild pine builds fast,
And the piercing crystals keep
  Their chains for the glaciers vast,
I have built up my heart with a stony wall,
I have frozen my will for a tyrant's fall.

As the crag from the high cliff leaps,
  And is ground to fine dust below,
As the dreaded avalanche creeps,
  And buries the valleys in woe,
So tyranny sinks 'neath my mountain heart,
So slavery falls by my quivering dart.

THE FATAL PASSION,—A DRAMATIC SKETCH.

BY WILLIAM ELLERY CHANNING.

HENRY GRAY. CHESTER. WILLIAM GRAY, *the father.* MURRAY, *friend to Gray.* VINCENT. MARY. ADELINE.

ACT I.—SCENE I.

A Wood.—HENRY. (*Alone.*)

How like a part too deeply fixed in me,
A shadow where the substance lies behind,
Is this sweet wood. I cannot grasp my thought,
But see it swell around me in these trees,
These layers of glistening leaves, and swimming full
In the blue, modulated heaven o'er all.
I would embrace you kindred tenements,
Where dwells the soul by which I deeply live.
But ye are silent; they call you emblems,
The symbols of creation, whose memory
Has failed in its behest, and so ye stand
Merely dumb shadows of what might have been,
Or hints of what may be beyond these days.
(*Enter Chester and observes Henry.*)

CHES. (*to himself.*) I love these moods of youth, I love the might
Of untamed nature battling with despair.
How firmly grasps the iron-handed earth
The youthful heart, and lugs it forth to war
With calm, unmoving woods, or silent lakes,
Making it dastard in the sun's light dance.
Brave on, ye unbarked saplings, soon your boughs
Shall wing the arrows of red manhood's life,
And then, as your low depths of ignorance
Unfold, how shall you wonder at your youth.
How flaunt the banners in the light of morn,
How torn and trailing when the day-god sets.
'T is a brave sight with all sails up, to see
The shining bark of youth dash through the foam,
And sickening to the most, to look upon
Her planks all started, and her rigging split,
When she hugs closeiy to the beach in age.
But I console myself for my gray hairs,
By spinning such warm fancies in my brain,
That I become a little thing again,
And totter o'er the ground, as when I whipped my top.
(*Approaches Henry.*)
Your servant, sir, the day goes bravely down.

HEN. Through the red leaves, I see the mornings' glow.

CHES. 'T is but the picture of some morning scene;
A fair conceit the sun has in his head,
And when he sets makes fatal flourishes.

HEN. I hear you jest with nature, that you mock,
And fling queer faces at her holy calm,
Write witty volumes that demoralize;
Pray Mr. Chester, do you fear the devil?

CHES. As I do nightfall. I have some night-fears,
Some horrid speculations in my brain;
And when the mice play hangmen in the wall,
Or out the house the pretty frost-toes creep,
I think, pest o'nt, what dark and doleful sounds,
If it were safe I'd raise the curtain's hem.

And when I puff away the cheerful light,
The moonbeam makes a thief's dark-lantern flit;
My head is filled with horribund designs,
And on myself I pack damned Macbeth's part.
I love to nourish such complexed conceits;
I have a vein of dreadful longing in me,
Was born to murder, and excel in arson,
And so I love the devil, though broad day
Has all the devilish aspects that I know.
See, comes the gentle Mary, know you her?

HEN. Not I, my solitude hath its own figures.

(*Enter Mary.*)

CHES. (*to Mary.*) God speed thee, lady, it was opportune
Your footsteps led you up this sheltered walk,
For here is Henry Gray, my friend at least,
And now is yours.

MARY. I willingly would know what Chester does,
And Mr. Gray, I trust, will but forgive me.
I rarely venture in these forest walks,
Where leads that prithee? (*To Henry.*)

HEN. 'T is by the lake, which gleaming like a sword,
One edge of this green path, a peacock lance,
Crosses in sport, and then descends away,
And vanishes among the outspread moors.

CHES. And Mr. Gray, sweet Mary, knows the path,
All paths that frolic in these devious woods,
For he's sworn friends with squirrels, steals their nuts,
Divides with other beasts their favorite meat,
Can show you hungry caves, whose blackening jaws
Breathe out a little night into the air,
Will stand you on the dizzy precipice,
Where all whirls round you like a whizzing wheel,
In truth his skill is perfect, so farewell.

(*Exit Chester.*)

SCENE II.

HENRY AND MARY.—(*By the Lake.*)

MARY. Those hills you say are lofty.
HEN. Most lofty.
I have clomb them, and there stood gazing
On villages outspread, and larger towns
Gleaming like sand-birds on the distant beach.
I love the mountains, for a weight of care
Falls off his soul, who can o'erlook this earth.
MARY. And there you passed the night?
HEN. I have passed weeks
Upon their very tops, and thought no more
To fall upon the low, dark days of earth.
Above, the clouds seemed welcome faces to me,
And near the raging storms, came giant-like,
And played about my feet. Yet even there,
I feared for my own heart, lest I should grow
Too careless of myself. Yonder the town,—
You must excuse my absence, for the clock
Rounds the small air-balls into leaden weights.
(*Exit Henry.*)
MARY, (*alone.*) I breathe, and yet how hardly,—a moment,
What a thing am I,—a passing moment,
Lifting from the earth my weary heart so sick,
O'er-burdened with the grating jar of life,—
This youth,—how sleeps the lake, how blue it gleams.
(*Chester again enters.*)
CHES. Ah! Mary alone,—indeed, has Henry Gray
Shot like a rocket in the rayful air?
A brilliant youth, at least his eyes are bright.

SCENE III.

CHESTER AND MARY.—(*Outskirts of Town.*)

MARY. He is a student at the college.
CHES. Mark you, he *is* a student, and knows the trick.
He has a brother too, Vincent, a gay
Free, dashing animal, or so I hear,
But I hate characters at second-hand.
You know they are towns-people; 't is an old,
And comfortable family, I hear
Pest on't, my brains won't hold much matter now,
I am too old for gossip.
MARY. Has he a sister?
CHES. Who wants that good device? it is a part
Of every comfortable family.
MARY. My father's mansion, will you enter?
CHES. No, Mary, not to-night. (*Mary goes in.*)
(*Chester alone.*) What comes of this,
When two youths come together, but woman
Rarely loves,—a play upon the word, So, So!
As I grow old, I lose all reasoning.
I hunt most nimble shadows, and have grown
A perfect knave for picking out old seams.
(*Enter William Gray.*)
GRAY. Good evening Mr. Chester. I call it evening,
For I see you walk, and they say here your gait
Is nightly.
CHES. I have seen Henry now, and Mary came,
He had not known her,—strange!
GRAY. Mary, the banker's daughter; a girl of promise.
CHES. They are old friends of mine, banker and all.
I've held him on my arm, and made him quake
At jingling coppers. He's richer now-a-days.
GRAY. 'T would please me to make more of them.
CHES. I will contrive it. There are times in life,
When one must hold the cherry to his lips,
Who faints to pluck a fair maid by the ear.

ACT II. — Scene I.

Adeline and Vincent. — (*Mr. Gray's House.*)

Vin. She is a lovely girl.
Ade. And rich as lovely.
Vin. I wish I knew her better.
Ade. One day is not enough, friend Vin., to know
The mind of woman ; many days must go,
And many thoughts.
Vin You will assist me, Adeline.
Ade. So far as in me lies, — I know not Mary.
Vin. But the sex is in your favor.
Ade. I know not that.

(*Enter Henry.*)

Vin. You made a good report on botany.
Hen. I'm glad you think so. 'T is a fair study,
To spy into the pretty hearts of flowers,
To read their delicacies, so near to.
But Vincent, science at the best
Demands but little justice at my hands,
It has its masters, has its oracles,
I am content to gather by the wall,
Some little flowers that sport a casual life,
To hover on the wing ; who comes ? — 'T is Chester.

(*Exit Chester.*)

Ches. Three frends in charming concert act their part.
But Henry, I have news for you.

SCENE II.

CHESTER AND HENRY. — (*Seated in Chester's House.*)

HEN. What is the news, I pray?
CHES. Last night, as I went walking in the wood,
I practise often in these woodland walks,
And on some nights I almost pluck the stars
Like crystal plums from off the tops of trees,—
But, as I said, I walked far down the wood,
In that rheumatic kind of greasy gait
I have accumulated, and I went
Dreaming and dreaming on, almost asleep,
If not quite half awake, until I reached
The lake's dim corner, where one ragged tree
Let in a gush of fuming light. The moon
Now being high, and at its full, I saw
Upon that little point of land a shape,
A fair round shape, like early womanhood
Kneeling upon the ground wept by the dews;
And then I heard such dreadful roar of sobs,
Such pouring fountains of imagined tears
I saw, following those piteous prayers,
All under the great placid eye of night.
'T was for an old man's eye, for a young heart
Had spun it into sighs, and answered back.
And now the figure came and passed by me,
I had withdrawn among the ghostly shrubs,
'T was Mary, — poor Mary! I have seen her smile
So many years, and heard her merry lips
Say so much malice, that I am amazed
She should kneel weeping by the silent lake,
After old midnight night-caps all but me.
But you are young, what can you make of it?

Where Henry's life hangs balanced in its might,
Breathe gently o'er this old, fond, doting man,
Who seems to cherish me among his thoughts,
As if I was the son of his old age,
The son of that fine thought so prodigal.
O God, put in his heart his thought, and make
Him heir to that repose thou metest me.
Ye sovereign powers that do control the world,
And inner life of man's most intricate heart,
Be with the noble Chester; may his age

HEN. What can one make of figures? I can see
The fair girl weeping by the moonlit lake.

CHES. Canst thou not see the woman's agony,
Canst thou not feel the thick sobs in thy throat,
That swell and gasp, till out your eyes roll tears
In miserable circles down your cheeks?

HEN. I see a woman weeping by the lake;
I see the fair round moon look gently down,
And in the shady woods friend Chester's form,
Leaning upon his old, bent maple stick.

CHES. What jest ye? Dare you, Henry Gray, to mock
A woman's anguish, and her scalding tears,
Does Henry Gray say this to his friend Chester,
Dares he speak thus, and think that Chester's scorn
Will not scoff out such paltry mockeries?

HEN. Why how you rage; why Chester, what a flame
A few calm words have lighted in thy breast.
I mock thee not, I mock no woman's tears,
Within my breast there is no mockery.

CHES. True, true, it is an old man's whim, a note
Of music played upon a broken harp.
I fancied you could read this woman's tears,
Pest on't, I am insane; I will go lock me up.

[*Exit Chester.*

HEN. (*alone.*) Ye fates, that do possess this upper sphere,

Yield brighter blossoms than his early years,
For he was torn by passion, was so worn,
So wearied in the strife of fickle hearts,
He shed his precious pearls before the swine.
And, God of love, to me render thyself,
So that I may more fairly, fully give,
To all who move within this ring of sky,
Whatever life I draw from thy great power.
Still let me see among the woods and streams,
The gentle measures of unfaltering trust,
And through the autumn rains, the peeping eyes
Of the spring's loveliest flowers, and may no guile
Embosom one faint thought in its cold arms.
So would I live, so die, content in all.

SCENE III.

Mary's Room. Midnight.

MARY, (*alone.*) I cannot sleep, my brain is all on fire,
I cannot weep, my tears have formed in ice,
They lie within these hollow orbs congealed,
And flame and ice are quiet, side by side.
[*Goes to the window.*
Yes! there the stars stand gently shining down,
The trees wave softly in the midnight air;
How still it is, how sweetly smells the air.
O stars, would I could blot you out, and fix
Where ye are fixed, my aching eyes;
Ye burn for ever, and are calm as night.
I would I were a tree, a stone, a worm;
I would I were some thing that might be crushed;
A pebble by the sea under the waves,
A mote of dust within the streaming sun,

Or that some dull remorse would fasten firm
Within this rim of bone, this mind's warder.
Come, come to me ye hags of secret woe,
That hide in the hearts of the adulterous false,
Has hell not one pang left for me to feel?
I rave; 't is useless, 't is pretended rage;
I am as calm as this vast hollow sphere,
In which I sit, as in a woman's form.
I am no woman, they are merry things,
That smile, and laugh, and dream away despair.
What am I? 'T is a month, a month has gone,
Since I stood by the lake with Henry Gray,
A month! a little month, thrice ten short days,
And I have lived and looked. Who goes? 't is Chester,
I must,—he shall come in.

[*She speaks from the window. Chester enters.*

CHES. You keep late hours, my gentle Mary.

MARY. Do not speak so. There is no Mary here.
Hush! (*Holds up her finger.*) I cannot bear your voice; 't is agony
To me to hear a voice, my own is dumb.
Say,—thou art an old man, thou hast lived long,
I mark it in the tottering gait, thy hair,
Thy red, bleared eyes, thy miserable form,
Say, in thy youthful days,—thou art a man,
I know it, but still men are God's creatures,—
Say, tell me, old man Chester, did thine eyes
Ever forget to weep, all closed and dry?
Say, quick, here, here, where the heart beats, didst feel
A weight, as if thy cords of life would snap,
As if the volume of the blood had met,
As if all life in fell conspiracy
Had met to press thy fainting spirit out?—
Say, say, speak quickly; hush! hush! no, not yet,
Thou canst not, thou art Chester's ghost, he's dead,

I saw him, 't was a month ago, in his grave,
Farewell, sweet ghost, farewell, let's bid adieu.
[*Chester goes out, weeping.*
'T is well I am visited by spirits.
If 't were not so, I should believe me mad,
But all the mad are poor deluded things,
While I am sound in mind. 'T is one o'clock,
I must undress, for I keep early hours.

SCENE IV.

The Wood. — Henry and Murray.

Hen. I cannot think you mean it; 't is some dream
Of your excited fancy. You are easily
Excited. You saw a nodding aspen,
For what should Mary's figure here?
Mur. It was her figure, I am persuaded.
They tell strange tales, they say she has gone mad,
That something's crazed her brain.
Hen. Is that the story? I have been mad myself.
Sometimes I feel that madness were a good,
To be elated in a wondrous trance,
And pass existence in a buoyant dream;
It were a serious learning. I do see
The figure that you speak of, 't is Mary.
Mur. I'll leave you then together. (*Enter Mary.*)
Hen. (*To Mary.*) You have the way alone; I was your guide
Some weeks ago, to the blue, glimmering lake.
I trust these scenes greet happily your eyes.
Mary. They are most sweet to me; let us go back
And trace that path again. I think 't was here
We turned, where this green sylvan church
Of pine hems in a meadow and some hills.

HEN. Among these pines they find the crow's rough nest,
A lofty cradle for the dusky brood.
MARY. This is the point I think we stood upon.
I would I knew what mountains rise beyond,
Hast ever gone there ?
HEN. Ah ! ye still, pointing spires of native rock,
That, in the amphitheatre of God,
Most proudly mark your duty to the sky,
Lift, as of old, ye did my heart above.
Excuse me, maiden, for my hurried thought.
'T is an old learning of the hills ; the bell !
Ah ! might the porter sometimes sleep the hour.
[*Exit Henry.*

The Sun is setting.

MARY. 'T is all revealed, I am no more deceived,
That voice, that form, the memory of that scene !
I love thee, love thee, Henry ; I am mad,
My brain is all on fire, my heart a flame,
You mountains rest upon my weary mind ;
The lake lies beating in my broken heart.

That bell that summoned him to the dark cell,
Where now in innocence he tells his beads,
Shall summon me beyond this weary world.
I long to be released ; I will not stay,
There is no hope, no vow, no prayer, no God,
All, all have fled me, for I love, love one,
Who cannot love me, and my heart has broke.
Ye mountains, where my Henry breathed at peace,
Thou lake, on whose calm depths he calmly looked,
And setting sun, and winds, and skies, and woods,
Protect my weary body from the tomb ;
As I have lived to look on you with him,
O let my thoughts still haunt you as of old,
Nor let me taste of heaven, while on the earth,
My Henry's form holds its accustomed place.
[*Stabs herself.*

TO READERS.

A voice, a heart, a free, unfettered pen,
My life in its own shape not rudely tasked,
If I could journey o'er my path again,
No entertainment could be better asked,
  Not wealth, not fame, nor gentlemen to see,
  Rather would I consort with liberty.

That which I must not buy, I do demand,
My way to worship God, my company,
The service of my own decisive hand,
The love that by its life is deeply free,
  Flattered by those I live with, — O not so,
  If I have dropped the seed, then may it grow.

Yet I would perish rather, and be dead
Within this mortal mind than lose my right
Upon a nobler fruitage to be fed,
And spring where blooms more excellent delight,
  To man, shall time remain the sacred thing,
  Shall poets for reward demand to sing?

Bring to my lays thy heart, if it be thine,
Read what is written and no meaning see,
Think that I am a barren, useless vine,
There is no bond agreed 'twixt thee and me,
  That thou shouldest read the meaning clearly writ,
  Yet thou and I may both be part of it.

O Reader, if my heart could say,
How in my blood thy nature runs,
Which manifesteth no decay,
The torch that lights a thousand suns,
  How thou and I, are freely lent,
  A little of such element.

If I could say, what landscape says,
And human pictures say far more,
If I could twine our sunny days,
With the rich colors, on the floor
  Of daily love, how thou and I,
  Might be refreshed with charity.

For pleasant is the softening smile
Of winter sunset o'er the snow,
And blessed is this spheral isle
That through the cold, vast void must go,
  The current of the stream is sweet,
  Where many waters closely meet.

C.

THE DEATH OF SHELLEY.

Fair was the morn, — a little bark bent
Like a gull o'er the waters blue,
And the mariners sang in their merriment,
For Shelley the faithful and true,
 Shelley was bound on his voyage o'er the sea,
 And wherever he sailed the heart beat free.

And a dark cloud flew, and the white waves hurled
The crests in their wrath, at the angry wind,
The little bark with its sails unfurled,
While the dreadful tempest gathered behind, —
 With the book of Plato pressed to his heart,
 Came to the beach Shelley's mortal part,

Then a pyre they kindled by ocean side,
Poets were they who Shelley did burn,
The beautiful flame to Heaven applied,
The ashes were pressed in the marble urn,
 In Rome shall those ashes long remain,
 And from Shelley's verse spring golden grain.

C.

A SONG OF THE SEA.

Where the breeze is an emerald green,
The breath of the fathomless deep,
Fresh, pure, living it falls on the scene,
While the little waves tremblingly creep,
  So the air of the soul hath this firmness of cheer,
  And over it thoughts like wild vessels veer.

'Tis a breeze from the shore that uplifts
The surface, and tosses it far,
But the depths are unmoved, and the drifts
Of white foam like the cloud o'er the star,
  Hurry on, madly roam, but the light is unmoved,
  Like the heart of the bride for the mate she has loved.

I would sail on the sea in my boat,
I would drift with the rolling tide,
In the calm of green harbors I float,
On the black mountainous chasms I ride,
  I am never at anchor, I never shall be,
  I am sailing the glass of infinity's sea.

Rage on, strongest winds, for the sail
Has ropes to the fast trimly set,
My heart which is oak cannot fail,
And the billows I cheered that I met,
  Cold, — no, good breeze thou art comfort to me,
  There are vessels I hail on the generous sea.

C.

SONNET.

BY WILLIAM ELLERY CHANNING.

An endless round of formless circumstance
The unthinking men go treading day by day,
As in the sparkling sunbeams the motes play,
And, like the busy crowd, keep timeless dance.

Struggles their food, anxiety their mind,
A pile of straws all disarranged and broke;
And tossing in the eddy of a wind,
Or played upon by some quick flail's sharp stroke.

Drink, drink, O men, yon azure's beverage,
Admit the sun's eye to your bandaged brain;
Let the free airs, as free, your thoughts engage,
And exercise to cast the tightening chain
Which now grips round this sinking, fainting age,
In cold paralysis of leperous pain.

CHRISTIAN SONG OF THE MIDDLE AGES.

BY WILLIAM ELLERY CHANNING.

Like waving vine the hard stone bends
Into cathedrals soft and free,
An angel every coping tends,
The fretwork blesses sacredly.

The virgin with the Holy Child,
Shines o'er the altar's golden cross,
A lovely mother pure and mild,
Whose heaven mourns no virtue's loss.

The swelling anthem dies away
In mournful music sweet and slow,
To celebrate that sacred day
On which Christ's blood drank up our woe.

THE FUTURE.

BY WILLIAM ELLERY CHANNING.

A sound of music floats upon the wind,
Tempering the discord of the general mind,
And lovely spirits minister to men
As in old times, their ravishment again.
The time has dawned when no more virtue lies,
Sport for the mocking tongues, whose flatteries
Have whispered consolation, but to make
Our destiny a darker semblance take.
Such was the counsel of the wise and meek,
In future times true nobleness to seek,
With reverence and holy hope alive
Which never from his mind his age might drive.
So onward, onward, men of every clime,
Look for the great wise age in coming time,
And as ye feel how it is now your own,
Let all around you breathe its happy tone.

SOLDIERS' GRAVES.

BY W. E. CHANNING.

For fretted roof, God's brave bright sky,
  Flaming with light, bends over them.
In place of verse—a people's liberty,
  Graved in deep hearts, their requiem;
The fringes, little flowers,—the shining grass;—
Will any for such burial say—Alas!

TO MY WIFE

Back from the false and unbelieving earth;
    Out from the sorrows circling like a sea;
From woe to joy — from grief to chastened mirth—
    True midst the false, true Wife! I come to thee.

Not as I would. The hands of love have wrought
    Strange furrows early on this bended brow;
This heart, that beats with thine, it has not sought
    Always the Good, as it is seeking now;—

But come I as I am, — come seeking Peace,
    And those sweet eyes beam on my soul a sign:
'Still in this world, O Doubting! get increase,
    Since this True Heart is married unto thine!'

"True Heart!" What words to come from tongues like ours!
    True Love! yet yields it here below to dwell!
Hush, it is here, as on the mount-top flowers,
    Larks in the *clouds*, sun-beams in prison cell.

We die not all amidst this so much dying,
    Look up, dear face! look up — I see the sign;
While speaks that tongue all speaking is not lying;
    Two stars there are that shine serene divine.

We die not all amidst this so much dying:
    My Own! we *know* there is no death in this:—
White-winged Seraphs' round the Holy flying
    Are next shadowed by the Death of Bliss:

We die not all amidst this so much dying,
    Look up, dear face! look up — I see the sign;
While speaks that tongue all speaking is not lying;
    Two stars there are that shine serene divine.

We die not all amidst this so much dying:
    My Own! we *know* there is no death in this:—
White-winged Seraphs' round the Holy flying
    Are next shadowed by the Death of Bliss:

And love we not some little in such fashion?
    Less, as the earth the great sky is below—
Know we not something of that wondrous Passion
    The awful Guardians of the Godhead *know*?—

Know we not something of that thick-hushed Thrilling
    Pervadeth, like a sword, the Universe,
Sharp, yet O gentle, — Planets, Spirits filling,
    Thine eyes, True Wife! and this my humble verse?

Won'drous sharp, and yet how kindly gentle!
    Lo! you star-blue it painteth golden warm!
Lo! these white limbs it clothes as with a mantle!
    Lo! this war-wasted Heart it fills with calm!

For this we met: To give worth to our living,
Worth in our short Time — worth (as we pray) for ever:
Great Prophet Souls, in fiery Out-giving,
Have they not said the Love decayeth *never*?

For this we met; sick, found a matchless healing, —
And so go on, two Pilgrim souls together —
Two Pilgrim-souls, each to its mate appealing,
For summer-light in wintry world weather.

Alone, unhelped True Wife, we might have traveled,
(Mayhap such Journey had not been amiss,)
But He — the God, Life's tangled web that cancelled,
Pitied us sore; for such Life gave us this.

Praise be to Him! With knees all lowly bended,
See, with one common Thought, we look above:
'Father of Hearts! *alone* we Pilgrims wended
But now, what change! what Miracles of Love!'

New Bedford, Mass WERNER

TO HESTER.

By William Ellery Channing.

A LIGHT lies on the Western hill,
  A purple on the sleeping sea,
And on the trickling forest rill,
  Though bringeth that no joy to me.

The children of the budding Spring
  Are mantling in the solemn woods,
And clear the forest minstrels sing
  To Nature, in most joyous moods.

But there is that I deeper prize,
  Beyond the form of everything—
The smile within thy vivid eyes,
  The graces that around thee cling.

THE RETREATING ARMY.

By William Ellery Channing.

THE pipes no longer sound in gladness,
Nor glisten arms beneath the sun;
They fold their hands in utter sadness,
The eager day is sadly done.

Over the tottering bridge are going—
That wavers in the misty wind—
Some fugitives, few looks bestowing
Upon the stainéd field behind.

The bridge is high upon the mountain,
It was a long ascent to climb;
Beneath, leaps through a mirthful fountain,
Below, the landscape lies sublime:

Green fields that yield to toil's devotion
The heaped-up granary's golden load,
Encircled by the azure ocean–
The lovely land of man's abode.

Above them, where their steps retreating
Seek shelter with the mountain chain,
The misty wind their entrance greeting,
Enfolds them in a dizzy rain.

'Yond the gray rocks the sun is streaming,
On boldly through the threatening storm:
The peaceful clouds float softly dreaming,
The vale is beautiful and warm.

TO THE READER.

FAR back, when I was young, I had a dream
Of buried Nations ; to my eyes did seem
An ancient City, wide with ruins strown,
A soil that in late times was richly sown
With Beauty's increase ; it was happy there,
The landscape smiled, and love breathed in the air.
Then in the middle of this City old
A brave Church stood, whose dome was high and bold ;
Far fell the light across the echoing floor,
And on the ear the wavy organs pour
Their rolling billows, as the thunders sigh,
When o'er the hills the sudden tempests die ;
So, in cathedrals green of tufted pine,
The weeping wind plays harmonies divine.

And entered there to me the spirits great,
Who rendered Art their joy and best estate;
I heard wise voices speak in later days,
The repetition of those Artists' praise.

Dreams! I revere them; may we not dispel
The shadowy visions that within us dwell!
Bright shapes and fiery forms, be those our care,
And a gay landscape float around them fair,
Have solid gold for ceiling of their earth,
And in the dust a planetary worth!
Let the Soul journey in the land of dream,
And never may the day, with flattering beam,
Look in and light that land; let us see Rome,
As she stands firm within the Fancy's home.

For never on such shapes the sun shall set
As rise within thee; all things else forget,—
Thy friend, thy work, whatever thou dost know,—
Let all decease, and keep thy faith below,
In the austerer cities of thy soul,
Founded where winds and rains have no control;
Their architecture ribbed with subtlest thought,
Their streets that only phantom feet have sought;
There let the ruins crumble, the decay,
Like distant landscapes, smoothed by parting day.
There build thy churches, as St. Peter's high,
There Raphael paint beneath the inward sky,

And the brave Romans, — they were giant men,
Cæsar and Scipio ; may they live again,
Stalk through thy inward Forum ! — seek no more ;
The sands of Europe gleam on Salem's shore.

For if thou art an angel, from the land
Of crystal Heaven, and in thy right hand
Hast the old power to form all things that are,
Can weigh the mote, or whirl the new-born star,
Until it poise itself, and roll in duty,
And thou art fed, like roses, with that Beauty
Which nicer fabrics from the air may steal, —
If thou like Lovers in their trance might feel, —
Still never should thou touch the flowing stream
On which there sailed at morning thy sweet Dream,
Saw nations rise like meadows from the snow,
Saw ceremonies that no courts can show.
Revere thy Dream, seek not the outer part ;
The true description reads within the heart.

Dry pages ! who may turn you gaily o'er,
Hoping for wine ? — forbear, it cannot pour ;
Cobwebs are in the measure, and the spring
Is choked with leaves ; no birds about it sing,
For Winter's frost has fallen o'er the pool,
And flowers, and trees, and sands obey his rule,
And weary people speak with husky cold,
Dispute like crickets, in the frozen mould.

But we must search, and toil, and grope our way ;
Shines not the sun for Students every day.
Think ! if there is plain need of Virtue here,
Thy native Wit shall sweet the atmosphere.

THE CAMPAGNA.

A GRAVEYARD, where some lonely tombs remain,
A desert city, where the long grass waves,
The living figures a slow-moving herd
Of large gray oxen, with their flaunting horns,
Or, keeping watch, a shepherd in his hut ;

But for the most part still, and wild, and waste,
Its wide green levels rounded by bold hills,
Clothed in the verdure of this Southern soil,
And hinting in its pathways where old Rome
And her proud sons marshalled their fearless men.
Here was the Appian Way; with tombs once lined,
And seats of pleasure, in the elder time,
Where now the sallow, ragged herdsman stalks,
Himself, the ruins, and the scene confused.
These plains were furnished proudly as those hills,
Where the Eternal City rears her towers,
And by her shadows from the fading past
Attracts devoted pilgrims to her shrines.
How bathes the desolation Nature's love
In flowing sunlight, and the tall grass waves,
Proud as the tresses on a Roman brow,
O'er all the crumbling fragments, buried deep.
And from the shadow of the graceful hills
A veil of silentness the twilight weaves,
And drapes the elder nations in the gray,
Departing presence of the Modern day.

Here were their houses; near, a Temple stood;
This was a Circus; there, the cheerful home
Of some good family. I see the sons
Come running there at eve, to please the eyes
Of the fond mother, who by yonder gate
Stands in columnar beauty, like the shape
Of some old Goddess exquisite in Heaven.
There bends a hoary Grandsire o'er his staff,

Who seeks his home upon yon rising ground,
Whence we comprise the snow-capped Apennines,
And for his children's children, who did then
Worship the white-haired elder of their line.
Now sweep the way a troop of Chariots,
The solid stones grating their brazen wheels,
And with red nostrils fly the headlong steeds,
In the light harness panting to escape.
In his white, floating robe the charioteer
Bends forward eager, for behind the train
Rush whirling on him, as if their fierce speed
Would swallow the swift conqueror in front.
To that sweet Temple, in slow march, proceeds
A group of lovely Maidens, to the shrine
Of sea-born Venus bear some offerings fine, —
Branches, and wreaths of myrtle, and far more,
Pulsing most tenderly their virgin hearts.
Near this fair band, I see a youth advance,
Like an Apollo in his noble form.
As the soft train of maidens fill the door,
And with slow motion, graceful as a stream,
Then quietly flow through and o'er the porch,
He silently approaches, with light steps
Retreats behind the pillars, nor in vain;
As if the Goddess favors, in the train
He sees that modest form he long has loved,
A maiden, with a snowy fillet bound
Upon her low, white brow, beneath whose shade
The large dark eyes slowly excite his soul
Who gazes on them to celestial hope.

As if in sport, her playful head she bends
Upon the column of her marble neck,
Until he sees her face, and the round form
Hid in her robe of early Womanhood.
It is not long before she idles there,
Behind the column; now have gone the twain,
Pass in the open space, and so away.
I see them turning, where the surface falls,
And look back, laughing at their sweet escape.

Figures of Beauty! who in the old days,
Ruled by some laws that influenced your lives,
Worshipped the delicacies of your dreams,
And kept the rites that later times disown,
How are you only flitting o'er these plains,
Where man once dwelt, now this wide solitude?
Was something blighting in the fevered eye
Of Christian martyrs that befooled old Rome,
And brought the second dear delusion in,
Than worship of old Gods more difficult,
The reverence for something past belief?
I love the Ruins more, be as it may,
Than all thy pomp, and worship, and gay shows.
'T is like the prostrate forest, where we touch
The trunks of giants who for ages past
Had stretched their tall tops to the arms of Heaven,
And in some hissing whirlwind toppled down,
Tearing a path among the lesser growths,
With earnest rush and roar of branches breaking,
To serve content the riches of that soil.

No melancholy voice whispers from thee,
Once the home of men, mighty Campagna!
Along thy graceful swells no sorrow steals,
Though there Malaria fastens his wolf-tusks
Upon the Shepherd's throat, and sends him home
To scale his mountains, yellow as the leaf
That on the ash flutters in autumn frosts.
Shall not the forests of Humanity,
Like the thick pines that load the ravine's side,
After their blossoms, fruits, and leaves have done
Whatever duty fitted them to do,
Gracefully droop, and to the earth rush down,
Tearing away a place for them to grow
Who live in after ages, while their boughs,
And all of them that was, fattens the soil,
In which those Nations who come after thrive?
Of old times these ruins are mementos,
Proverbs, and saws, and Bibles of their art,
Which like the necessary seeds have slept,
Safe covered in the dew, and frost, and snow
Of twenty centuries, for the Planter's hand.

We rapidly rush downward to our graves,
Time, and the storms, and winters are upon us,
Yet let us meet them with an equal heart,
Secure in the old laws which bind the race,
Secure in Heaven, that never was yet false.
In Nature's hand, why should not we delight,
E'en if she paints the plain and silent fields,
Or like a mother softly parts the locks

Of whispering verdure on the column's crown?
Is not her hand still perfect as of old?
Has she yet lost one string from all her lyre?
The nations crumble, down sinks tower and town,
The Greeks are fancies in a dreamer's eye,
The Romans live in song that few may read,—
'T is all man leaves behind him, his decay.
And Nature, with a song of even sweetness,
And Love's caresses, twines the landscape round,
And ere the Greek is buried in his grave,
Or ere the Roman's cuirass rusts away,
With a light, soft, and graceful depth of shade,
She veils the downfall of these human walls,
So soothingly she touches them with rain,
So tenderly her frost strikes through their joints.

Come to these fields, ye rash, deluded tribe,
Who in thick cities, or in crowded towns,
Inflate your lungs, or with well-sharpened pen
Drive out a swarm of serious sentences,
That well declare the moral of our day,
How it alone is Age majestical,
And it alone for evermore shall last!—
Come to these fields, and sit upon these stones.
The stern old Romans are beneath thy feet,
Above thy head the soft Italian skies,
Pulsates the sweet wind like the fire of morn,—
Come to these fields, and listen to their voice.
O shallow host! O vain and idle band!
Here, on the relics of a master tribe,

Confess your vanities, and sit rebuked!
For ye are like the critic, whose wise head
Weighs most exactly in its shining scales
That work of Art, whose faintest line his hand
Never might sculpture; in whose soul no voice
Of linked sweetness from some subtler life
Draws out for him the meaning of the lines;
Who makes the mischief of the thing he scolds.
So would ye weigh golden Antiquity,
Balance the deeds of men by centuries,
Erase the bad, and shape a perfect Good,
That for the perfect state should firmly stand,
Decent, and true, and lovely as a hope.
'T is like the sculptor, who, with cunning hand,
Embalmed in marble a dear mistress' form,
Until he thought she lived, and clasped her charms;
Alas! how cold, how still, and too resigned!
So mould you at your statue, and then say, —
"Live thou for ever by this perfect rule
We have decided for thee; it is just."
And Nature comes, and with a breath of wind
Scatters them o'er thy levels, green Campagna!

Farewell! farewell for ever to thee, Rome!
Fade the last circles of thy mountain dome,
Through rosy twilight's intermingling ray.
Farewell to thee! farewell the southern day!

From a cold region sorrowful I came;
Thou kindled in my heart a searching flame;
The golden orange shone, the vineyards gay, —
My life was all festooned with lovely May.

Farewell to Rome! farewell, ye ruins high,
Whose shattered arches float upon the sky!
Farewell, ye giant Baths, where grandeur dwells!
Farewell, beneath the ground, the Martyr-cells!

Thou, Rome! art centred in my inmost heart,—
Palace of Kings, great storehouse of fine art,
Where Virgil sang his mellow summer hymn,
Where Cæsar made all lesser fortunes dim,
Where Raphael with his pencil moulded men,
Where Michel with his chisel lived again.

Farewell to Rome! a long, a last Farewell!
I shall not hear again the Vesper bell,
Nor stand among the courteous multitudes;
Farewell!—now for the sea's green solitudes!

They rocked me in my dreams, those hissing storms;
I saw a circle of divinest forms
Around the cottage where my Ellen dwelt,
My children's kisses on my lips I felt,
And yet the ambitious surge walled out the sky,
And merry sprays hissed at our fore-top high.

Yet on we sped, and, in the calmer time,
Went o'er the blue sea in a mood sublime,
Watching the lazy drift-weed on its course,
Its thousand leagues sailing by inward force.
So blue those summer days, that Heaven seemed
As if it only slept, or idly dreamed.

Then boiled across our decks the Gulf's hot blast,
And weighed the sails, till bent the lofty mast,
And dizzy waves menaced our headlong flight;
But on we sped, like Sea-bird small and light,
Still in the foaming current shot the bow,
We fed the ocean with unceasing prow; —
Away, nor slacks the motion of the steed,
Through rushing waters, and the whirlwind's speed.

Farewell to Rome! farewell the painted mask
Called life or friendship! — Lethe 's all I ask,
To steep my soul in draughts of murmuring wine
And sing to Gods and men a mystic line.
Farewell to Rome! good-by to cant and show!
He who may love me gives me blow for blow;
Farewell to rule and order! for the Muse
She does all things but bravery refuse.
New England, homestead, friend or hope shall fly,
This plaything for a moment, earth and sky,
Like swift rack driven by the western breeze,
Swift o'er the land, and swifter o'er the seas.
Go, lonely, sad, to men a Hermit seem,
Outrun your life, outdream your subtlest dream,
Live on dry pulse, and quench thy thirst in brooks,
Thy only friendship how the bottom looks,
The world, the day, their Aims, their Thoughts refuse, —
Farewell to Rome! — there 's greater for thy use.

THE AMERICAN SLAVE TO KOSSUTH.

BY W. E. CHANNING.

Where the dark Danube proudly runs,
Mayhap your heart, your hope may be;
There live your brothers,—noble ones,—
For whom you crossed the rolling sea.

And many a vine-clad cottage stands,
And peasant hearts throb aching there;
You pray, you weep, you lift your hands
To God,—for life, for light, your prayer.

You think of your dear sister's form,
Crushed by the impious Haynau's blow;
Your feelings true, your heart so warm,
Feel, then, for us, feel for our wo!

Slaves in the land of Freedom bright,
Slaves on the wild Missouri's side,
And Texan vales in sunny light,
Slaves on the old Potomac's tide!

The lash we feel, the chains we wear,—
God of the Free! shall Kossuth come,
Nor strike for us, and empty air
Pour from his mouth for his lost home?

Awake! thou burning Magyar soul!
  Strike for thy brother slaves in view!
Then calmly shall the ocean roll,
  Nor vex thy heart so warm and true.

Where are our wives?—to torture sold!
  Kidnapped our children,—love disgraced!
Hope, home, affection, all for gold
  At once torn out, and life effaced.

O Kossuth! Magyar! Man, at last!
  Betray us not, nor let there be
Our curses lingering on thy past,
  Our hate a household thing for thee.

Are we not men?—are we not slaves?
  By the dark Danube there's no more:
Thy brothers found right glorious graves
  Along his wild, romantic shore:

And we would die—but galls the chain;
  Die—but in prison foul our lot:
By inches killed, the wretch's pain,
  Who, dying, lives by all forgot.

Strike, then, for us, with thought and prayer,
  God give thee power, most noble heart!
Nor waste thy words on empty air,
  But, flying slave, take the slave's part!

TO KOSSUTH.

BY W. E. CHANNING.

Spurn! spurn the bribe! ford not the Southron river!
Death courses in its crimson tide for ever;
A flood of sin too strong for man's recalling,
Where slavery reigns, and breeds its crimes appalling.

What freezing mockery to make slavery's speeches,
And waft thy blessing o'er its bloody reaches!
That soil wide streaming with the negro's anguish;
Their fetters clank, in prisons still they languish.

Spurned, scorned and branded, they survive, half dying—
Wives sold, child sold—the scourge, the scourge replying—
Our brother-men—true rulers of this nation,
Victims of what? but thee and thy ovation!

On thee their deathless scorn as traitor hanging,
Around thy neck their chains of horror clanging,
Thou dar'st not meddle with domestic duties,
And will accept fell slavery and its beauties.

Our bragging land will wreck, and Freedom perish;
God has some heart, nor doth Hell's statutes cherish;
Soon shall the States be lashed by dread commotion—
One fate to all, one flood, one vengeful ocean.

Those tortured hearts to Heaven for life are crying;
God's angel to their thirsty hopes replying,
" The day shall dawn, this terror dark abated,
I am not spoused with Sin, with Satan mated."

From dismal swamps of Carolina's planting,
From Georgia's hills, the volleyed hymn is chanting,
"Give back our freedom! slaves all past describing;
Hungarian martyr, spurn their loathsome bribing!

"Demand our prompt deliverance! cry in thunder,
And stir the torpid soul to joy and wonder!
Burst off these chains, our freedom just demanding,—
Then ford yon stream, each heart thine own commanding!"

THE BLUEBERRY SWAMP.

BY W. E. CHANNING.

Orange groves mid-tropic lie,
Festal for the Spaniard's eye,
And the red pomegranate grows
Where the luscious Southwest blows.
Myrrh and spikenard in the East
Multiply the Persian's feast,
And our Northern wilderness
Boasts its fruits our lips to bless.
Wouldst enjoy a magic sight,
And so heal vexation's spite?
Hasten to my Blueberry swamp,—
Green o'erhead the wild bird's camp;
Here in thickets bending low,
Thickly piled the blueberries grow,
Freely spent on youth and maid,
In the deep swamp's cooling shade.

Pluck the clusters plump and full,
Handful after handful pull!
Choose which path, the fruitage hangs,—
Fear no more the griping fangs
Of the garden's spaded stuff,—
This is healthy, done enough.
Pull away! the afternoon
Dies beyond the meadow soon.
Art thou a good citizen?
Move into a Blueberry fen.
Here are leisure, wealth and ease,
Sure thy taste and thought to please,
Drugged with Nature's spicy tunes,
Hummed upon the summer noons.

Rich is he that asks no more
Than of Blueberries a store,
Who can snatch the clusters off,
Pleased with himself and than enough
Fame?—the chickadee is calling,—
Love?—the fat pine cones are falling,
Heaven?—the berries in the air,—
Eternity?—their juice so rare.
And if thy sorrows will *not* fly,
Then get thee down and softly die.
In the eddy of the breeze,
Leave the world 'neath those high trees.
Only some admiring fly
Will buzz about thee left to dry,
And the purple runnel's tune
Melodize thy mossy swoon.

O golden green

O golden green on autumn's breast
Thou wilt not bring my sorrows rest;
Console the distant azure hill,
The maze of cloud and tree and rill.

My heart was sad, I walked alone
Around the lake with shadows sown;
For me no sunny vista smiled,
No friends no love my doom beguiled.

And all I had was memory's shrine
Of withered hopes, no longer mine.
O golden green on autumn's breast,
Thou wilt not bring my sorrows rest.

W. E. Channing
Concord, Mass (1850)

LASHED TO THE MAST.

BY W. E. CHANNING.

It was the brave old Farragut,
And he these words did say,—
"Now lash me to the foremast fast,
And then boys fire away;
They robbed our forts, our arms, our ships,
Our sailors' hearts remain,
Take back your own and break their whips,
And free the doomed from pain."

Then boldly up for Mobile Bay,
Lashed to the mast he steered,
"Sail for the forts," cheerful he cried,
As they the passage neared;
Push near and pour your shots within,
And see if Gaines will stand,
The traitors robbed our forts and arms,
We pay them over hand."

Then sank a faithful heart in death,—
Our Craven, in Tecumseh's hold,
A noble soul, a hero, brave,
Like Farragut both sweet and bold.
While flew the shot and shell amain,
No shelter on the open mast,—
They poured their rebel fire like rain,
But Farragut ne'er cried avast.

"Make for the ram and run her down,
All, all my fleet, speed on speed fast,
Tear out her sides and spoil her bows,
Our wooden fleet else her repast.
And deadly was the foe that day,
The iron monster Tennessee,
An insult to the patriots bold,
Who keep their volleys for the free,

And Farragut now cried again,—
"She yields, I see the white flag wave,
The forts are ours, the traitors fall,
And Mobile Bay again is brave;
One hope, one heart, one home for all
Shall yet our guilty sons recall,
And from the pain and peril past,
Thank God they lashed me to the mast."

HOMEWARD.

A FAR-OFF shore
And a beating tide,
With a rustling breeze
Away we ride,—
Sing for the sea,
Sing, sing cheerily.

Swift our painted bow
Cuts the hissing foam,
Swift fly the eddies behind,
Swift we rush towards home,
Sing for the sea,
Sing, sing cheerily.

On the white beach stands
My love with her flowing hair,
She waves her small hands
For love, not despair;
Sing for the sea,
Sing, sing cheerily.

O! blow heavy breeze,
Bend our mast, load our sail,
Rush and dash onward fast,
And roll to the gale;—
Sing for the sea,
Sing, sing merrily.

DEDICATION.

Silent and serene,
The plastic soul emancipates her kind.
She leaves the generations to their fate,
Uncompromised by grief. She cannot weep:
She sheds no tears for us, — our mother, Nature!
She is ne'er rude nor vexed, not rough or careless;
Out of temper ne'er, patient as sweet, though winds
In winter brush her leaves away, and time
To human senses breathes through frost.
My friend!
Learn, from the joy of Nature, thus to be:
Not only all resigned to thy worst fears,
But, like herself, superior to them all!
Nor merely superficial in thy smiles;
And through the inmost fibres of thy heart
May goodness flow, and fix in that
The ever-lapsing tides, that lesser depths
Deprive of half their salience. Be, throughout,
True as the inmost life that moves the world,
And in demeanor show a firm content,
Annihilating change.
Thus Henry lived,
Considerate to his kind. His love bestowed
Was not a gift in fractions, half-way done;
But with some mellow goodness, like a sun,
He shone o'er mortal hearts, and taught their buds
To blossom early, thence ripe fruit and seed.
Forbearing too oft counsel, yet with blows
By pleasing reason urged he touched their thought
As with a mild surprise, and they were good,
Even if they knew not whence that motive came;
Nor yet suspected that from Henry's heart —
His warm, confiding heart — the impulse flowed.

MEMORIAL VERSES

I

TO HENRY

HEAR'ST thou the sobbing breeze complain
How faint the sunbeams light the shore?—
Thy heart, more fixed than earth or main,
Henry! thy faithful heart is o'er.

Oh, weep not thou thus vast a soul,
Oh, do not mourn this lordly man,
As long as Walden's waters roll,
And Concord river fills a span.

For thoughtful minds in Henry's page
Large welcome find, and bless his verse,
Drawn from the poet's heritage,
From wells of right and nature's source.

Fountains of hope and faith! inspire
Most stricken hearts to lift this cross;
His perfect trust shall keep the fire,
His glorious peace disarm the loss!

II

WHITE POND

GEM of the wood and playmate of the sky,
How glad on thee we rest a weary eye,
When the late ploughman from the field goes home,
And leaves us free thy solitudes to roam!

Thy sand the naiad gracefully had pressed,
Thy proud majestic grove the nymph caressed,
Who with cold Dian roamed thy virgin shade,
And, clothed in chastity, the chase delayed,
To the close ambush hastening at high noon,
When the hot locust spins his Zendic rune.

Here might Apollo touch the soothing lyre,
As through the darkening pines the day's low fire
Sadly burns out; or Venus nigh delay
With young Adonis, while the moon's still ray
Mellows the fading foliage, as the sky
Throws her blue veil of twilight mystery.

No Greece to-day; no dryad haunts the road
Where sun-burned farmers their poor cattle goad;
The black crow caws above yon steadfast pine,
And soft Mitchella's odorous blooms entwine
These mossy rocks, where piteous catbirds scream,
And Redskins flicker through the white man's dream.
Who haunts thy wood-path?—ne'er in summer pressed
Save by the rabbit's foot; its winding best
Kept a sure secret, till the tracks, in snow
Dressed for their sleds, the lumbering woodmen plough.

How soft yon sunbeam paints the hoary trunk,
How fine the glimmering leaves to shadow sunk!
Then streams across our grassy road the line
Drawn firmly on the sward by the straight pine;
And curving swells in front our feet allure,
While far behind the curving swells endure;
Silent, if half pervaded by the hum
Of the contented cricket. Nature's sum
Is infinite devotion. Days nor time
She emulates,—nurse of a perfect prime.

Herself the spell, free to all hearts; the spring
Of multiplied contentment, if the ring
With which we 're darkly bound.
The pleasant road
Winds as if Beauty here familiar trode;
Her touch the devious curve persuasive laid,
Her tranquil forethought each bright primrose stayed
In its right nook. And where the glorious sky
Shines in, and bathes the verdant canopy,
The prospect smiles delighted, while the day
Contemns the village street and white highway.

Creature all beauteous! In thy future state
Let beauteous Thought a just contrivance date;
Let altars glance along thy lonely shore,
Relumed; and on thy leafy forest floor
Tributes be strewn to some divinity
Of cheerful mien and rural sanctity.
Pilgrims might dancing troop their souls to heal;
Cordials, that now the shady coves conceal,
Reft from thy crystal shelves, we should behold,
And by their uses be thy charms controlled.

Naught save the sallow herdsboy tempts the shore,
His charge neglecting, while his feet explore
Thy shallow margins, when the August flame
Burns on thy edge and makes existence tame;
Naught save the blue king-fisher rattling past,
Or leaping fry that breaks his lengthened fast;
Naught save the falling hues when Autumn's sigh
Beguiles the maple to a sad reply;
Or some peculiar air a sapless leaf
Guides o'er thy ocean by its compass brief.

Save one, whom often here glad Nature found
Seated beneath yon thorn, or on the ground

Poring content, when frosty Autumn bore
Of wilding fruit to earth that bitter store;
And when the building winter spanned in ice
Thy trembling limbs, soft lake! then each device
Traced in white figures on thy seamed expanse
This child of problems caught in gleeful trance.
Oh, welcome he to thrush and various jay,
And echoing veery, period of the day!
To each clear hyla trilling the new spring,
And late gray goose buoyed on his icy wing;
Bold walnut-buds admire the gentle hand,
While the shy sassafras their rings expand
On his approach, and thy green forest wave,
White Pond! to him fraternal greetings gave.
The far white clouds that fringe the topmost pine
For his delight their fleecy folds decline;
The sunset worlds melted their ores for him,
And lightning touched his thought to seraphim.

Clear wave, thou wert not vainly made, I know,
Since this sweet man of Nature thee could owe
A genial hour, some hope that flies afar,
And revelations from thy guiding star.
Oh, may that muse, of purer ray, recount,
White Pond! thy glory; and, while anthems mount
In strains of splendor, rich as sky and air,
Thy praise, my Henry, might those verses share.
For He who made the lake made it for thee,
So good and great, so humble, yet so free;
And waves and woods we cannot fairly prove,
Like souls, descended from celestial Jove.

With thee he is associate. Hence I love
Thy gleams, White Pond! thy dark, familiar grove;

Thy deep green shadows, clefts of pasture ground;
Mayhap a distant bleat the single sound,
One distant cloud, the sailor of the sky,
One voice, to which my inmost thoughts reply.

III

A LAMENT

A WAIL for the dead and the dying!
They fall in the wind through the Gilead tree,
Off the sunset's gold, off hill and sea;
They fall on the grave where thou art lying,
Like a voice of woe, like a woman sighing,
Moaning her buried, her broken love,
Never more joy,—never on earth, never in heaven above!

Ah, me! was it for this I came here?
Christ! didst thou die that for this I might live?
An anguish, a grief like the heart o'er the bier,—
Grief that I cannot bury, nor against it can strive,—
Life-long to haunt me, while breath brings to-morrow,
Falling in spring and in winter, rain and sleet sorrow,
Prest from my fate that its future ne'er telleth,
Spring from the unknown that ever more welleth.

Fair, O my fields! soft, too, your hours!
Mother of Earth, thou art pleasant to see!
I walk o'er thy sands, and I bend o'er thy flowers.
There is nothing, O nothing, thou givest me,
Nothing, O nothing, I take from thee.
What are thy heavens, so blue and so fleeting?
Storm, if I reck not, no echo meeting
In this cold heart, that is dead to its beating,
Caring for nothing, parting or greeting!

IV

MORRICE LAKE

(Written for E. S. Hotham.)

On Morrice Lake I saw the heron flit
And the wild wood-duck from her summer perch
Scale painted by, trim in her plumes, all joy;
And the old mottled frog repeat his bass,
Song of our mother Earth, the child so dear.
There, in the stillness of the forest's night,
Naught but the interrupted sigh of the breeze,
Or the far panther's cry, that, o'er the lake,
Touched with its sudden irony and woke
The sleeping shore; and then I hear its crash,
Its deep alarm-gun on the speechless night, —
A falling tree, hymn of the centuries.

No sadness haunts the happy lover's mind,
On thy lone shores, thou anthem of the woods,
Singing her calm reflections; the tall pines,
The sleeping hill-side and the distant sky,
And thou! the sweetest figure in the scene,
Truest and best, the darling of my heart.

O Thou, the ruler of these forest shades,
And by thy inspiration who controll'st
The wild tornado in its narrow path,
And deck'st with fairy wavelets the small breeze,
That like some lover's sigh entreats the lake;
O Thou, who in the shelter of these groves
Build'st up the life of nature, as a truth
Taught to dim shepherds on their star-lit plains,
Outwatching midnight; who in these deep shades

Secur'st the bear and catamount a place,
Safe from the glare of the infernal gun,
And leav'st the finny race their pebbled home,
Domed with thy watery sunshine, as a mosque;
God of the solitudes! kind to each thing
That creeps or flies, or launches forth its webs,—
Lord! in thy mercies, Father! in thy heart,
Cherish thy wanderer in these sacred groves;
Thy spirit send as erst o'er Jordan's stream,
Spirit and love and mercy for his needs.
Console him with thy seasons as they pass,
And with an unspent joy attune his soul
To endless rapture. Be to him,—thyself
Beyond all sensual things that please the eye,
Locked in his inmost being; let no dread,
Nor storm with its wild splendors, nor the tomb,
Nor all that human hearts can sear or scar,
Or cold forgetfulness that withers hope,
Or base undoing of all human love,
Or those faint sneers that pride and riches cast
On unrewarded merit,—be, to him,
Save as the echo from uncounted depths
Of an unfathomable past, burying
All present griefs.
Be merciful, be kind!
Has he not striven, true and pure of heart,
Trusting in thee? Oh, falter not, my child!
Great store of recompense thy future holds,
Thy love's sweet councils and those faithful hearts
Never to be estranged, that know thy worth.

V

TEARS IN SPRING

THE swallow is flying over,
But he will *not* come to me;
He flits, my daring rover,
From land to land, from sea to sea;
Where hot Bermuda's reef
Its barrier lifts to fortify the shore,
Above the surf's wild roar
He darts as swiftly o'er,—
But he who heard that cry of spring
Hears that no more, heeds not his wing.

How bright the skies that dally
Along day's cheerful arch,
And paint the sunset valley!
How redly buds the larch!
Blackbirds are singing,
Clear hylas ringing,
Over the meadow the frogs proclaim
The coming of Spring to boy and dame,
But not to me,—
Nor thee!

And golden crowfoot 's shining near,
Spring everywhere that shoots 't is clear,
A wail in the wind is all I hear;
A voice of woe for a lover's loss,
A motto for a travelling cross,—
And yet it is mean to mourn for thee,
In the form of bird or blossom or bee.

Cold are the sods of the valley to-day
Where thou art sleeping,
That took thee back to thy native clay;
Cold,—if above thee the grass is peeping
And the patient sunlight creeping,
While the bluebird sits on the locust-bough
Whose shadow is painted across thy brow,
And carols his welcome so sad and sweet
To the Spring that comes and kisses his feet.

VI

THE MILL BROOK[1]

THE cobwebs close are pencils of meal,
  Painting the beams unsound,
And the bubbles varnish the glittering wheel
  As it rumbles round and round.
Then the Brook began to talk
  And the water found a tongue,
"We have danced a long dance," said the gossip,
  "A long way have we danced and sung."

"Rocked in a cradle of sanded stone
Our waters wavered ages alone,
Then glittered at the spring
On whose banks the feather-ferns cling;
Down jagged ravines
We fled tortured,
And our wild eddies nurtured
Their black hemlock screens;
And o'er the soft meadows we rippled along,
And soothed their lone hours with a pensive song,—

1 *One of the most labored pieces I ever wrote. But it was not helped by work. W. E. C.*

Now at this mill we 're plagued to stop,
To let our miller grind the crop.

"See the clumsy farmers come
With jolting wagons far from home;
We grind their grist,
It wearied a season to raise,
Weeks of sunlight and weeks of mist,
Days for the drudge and Holydays.
To me it fatal seems,
Thus to kill a splendid summer,
And cover a landscape of dreams
In the acre of work and not murmur.
I could lead them where berries grew,
Sweet flag-root and gentian blue,
And they will not come and laugh with me,
Where my water sings in its joyful glee;
Yet small the profit, and short-lived for them,
Blown from Fate's whistle like flecks of steam.

"The old mill counts a few short years, —
Ever my rushing water steers!
It glazed the starving Indian's red,
On despair or pumpkin fed,
And oceans of turtle notched ere he came,
Species consumptive to Latin and fame,
(Molluscous dear or orphan fry,
Sweet to Nature, I know not why).

"Thoughtful critics say that I
From yon mill-dam draw supply. —
I cap the scornful Alpine heads,
Amazons and seas have beds,
But I am their trust and lord.
Me ye quaff by bank and board,

Me ye pledge the iron-horse,
I float Lowells in my source.

"The farmers lug their bags and say, —
'Neighbor, wilt thou grind the grist to-day?'
Grind it with his nervous thumbs!
Clap his aching shells behind it,
Crush it into crumbs!

"No! his dashboards from the wood
Hum the dark pine's solitude;
Fractious teeth are of the quarry
That I crumble in a hurry, —
Far-fetched duty is to me
To turn this old wheel carved of a tree.

"I like the maples on my side,
Dead leaves, the darting trout;
Laconic rocks (they sometime put me out)
And moon or stars that ramble with my tide;
The polished air, I think I could abide.

"This selfish race who prove me,
Who use, but do not love me!
Their undigested meal
Pays not my labor on the wheel.
I better like the sparrow
Who sips a drop at morn,
Than the men who vex my marrow,
To grind their cobs and corn."

Then said I to my brook, "Thy manners mend!
Thou art a tax on earth for me to spend."

VII

STILLRIVER, THE WINTER WALK[1]

The busy city or the heated car,
The unthinking crowd, the depot's deafening jar,
These me befit not, but the snow-clad hill
From whose white steeps the rushing torrents fill
Their pebbly beds, and as I look content
At the red Farmhouse to the summit lent,
There,—underneath that hospitable elm,
The broad ancestral tree, that is the helm
To sheltered hearts,—not idly ask in vain,
Why was I born,—the heritage of pain?

The gliding trains desert the slippery road,
The weary drovers wade to their abode;
I hear the factory bell, the cheerful peal
That drags cheap toil from many a hurried meal.
How dazzling on the hill-side shines the crust,
A sheen of glory unprofaned by dust!
And where thy wave, Stillriver, glides along,
A stream of Helicon unknown in song,
The pensive rocks are wreathed in snow-drifts high
That glance through thy soft tones like witchery.

To Fancy we are sometimes company,
And Solitude 's the friendliest face we see.
Some serious village slowly through I pace,
No form of all its life mine own to trace;
Where the cross mastiff growls with blood-shot eye,
And barks and growls and waits courageously;
Its peaceful mansions my desire allure

1 *From Groton Junction (now Ayer) to Lancaster along the railroad.*

Not each to enter and its fate endure,—
But Fancy fills the window with its guest;
The laughing maid,—her swain who breaks the jest;
The solemn spinster staring at the fire,
Slow fumbling for his pipe, her solemn sire;
The loud-voiced parson, fat with holy cheer,
The butcher ruddy as the atmosphere;
The shop-boy loitering with his parcels dull,
The rosy school-girls of enchantment full.

Away from these the solitary farm
Has for the mind a strange domestic charm,
On some keen winter morning when the snow
Heaps roof and casement, lane and meadow through.
Yet in those walls how many a heart is beating,
What spells of joy, of sorrow, there are meeting!
One dreads the post, as much the next, delay,
Lest precious tidings perish on their way.
The graceful Julia sorrows to refuse
Her teacher's mandate, while the boy let loose
Drags out his sled to coast the tumbling hill,
Whence from the topmost height to the low rill,
Shot like an arrow from the Indian's bow,
Downward he bursts, life, limb, and all below
The maddening joy his dangerous impulse gives;
In age, how slow the crazy fact revives!

Afar I track the railroad's gradual bend,
I feel the distance, feel the silence lend
A far romantic charm to farmhouse still,
And spurn the road that plods the weary hill,—
When like an avalanche the thundering car
Whirls past, while bank and rail deplore the jar.
The wildly piercing whistle through my ear
Tells me I fright the anxious engineer;

I turn,—the distant train and hurrying bell
Of the far crossing and its dangers tell.
And yet upon the hill-side sleeps the farm,
Nor maid or man or boy to break the charm.

Delightful Girl! youth in that farmhouse old,
The tender darling in the tender fold,—
Thy promised hopes fulfilled as Nature sought,
With days and years, the income of thy thought;
Sweet and ne'er cloying, beautiful yet free,
Of truth the best, of utter constancy;
Thy cheek whose blush the mountain wind laid on,
Thy mouth whose lips were rosebuds in the sun;
Thy bending neck, the graces of thy form,
Where art could heighten, but ne'er spoil the charm;
Pride of the village school for thy pure word,
Thy pearls alone those glistening sounds afford;
Sure in devotion, guileless and content,
The old farmhouse is thy right element.
Constance! such maids as thou delight the eye,
In all the Nashua's vales that round me lie!

And thus thy brother was the man no less,—
Bred of the fields and with the wind's impress.
With hand as open as his heart was free,
Of strength half-fabled mixed with dignity.
Kind as a boy, he petted dog and hen,
Coaxed his slow steers, nor scared the crested wren.
And not far off the spicy farming sage,
Twisted with heat and cold, and cramped with age,
Who grunts at all the sunlight through the year
And springs from bed each morning with a cheer.
Of all his neighbors he can *something* tell,—
'T is bad, whate'er, we know, and like it well!—

The bluebird's song he hears the first in spring,
Shoots the last goose bound South on freezing wing.

Ploughed and unploughed the fields look all the same,
White as the youth's first love or ancient's fame;
Alone the chopper's axe awakes the hills,
And echoing snap the ice-encumbered rills;
Deep in the snow he wields the shining tool,
Nor dreads the icy blast, himself as cool.
Seek not the parlor, nor the den of state
For heroes brave; make up thy estimate
From these tough bumpkins clad in country mail,
Free as their air and full without detail.

No gothic arch *our* shingle Pæstum boasts,—
Its pine cathedral is the style of posts,—
No crumbling abbey draws the tourist there
To trace through ivied windows pictures rare,
Nor the first village squire allows his name
From aught illustrious or debauched by fame.

That sponge profane who drains away the bar
Of yon poor inn extracts the mob's huzza;
Conscious of morals lofty as their own,
The glorious Democrat,—his life a loan.
And mark the preacher nodding o'er the creed,
With wooden text, his heart too soft to bleed.
The Æsculapius of this little State,
A typhus-sage, sugars his pills in fate,
Buries three patients to adorn his gig,
Buys foundered dobbins or consumptive pig;
His wealthy pets he kindly thins away,
Gets in their wills,—and ends them in a day.
Nor shall the strong schoolmaster be forgot,
With fatal eye, who boils the grammar-pot:

Blessed with large arms he deals contusions round,
While even himself his awful hits confound.

Pregnant the hour when at the tailor's store,
Some dusty Bob a mail bangs through the door.
Sleek with good living, virtuous as the Jews,
The village squires look wise, desire the news.
The paper come, one reads the falsehood there,
A trial lawyer, lank-jawed as despair.
Here, too, the small oblivious deacon sits,
Once gross with proverbs, now devoid of wits,
And still by courtesy he feebly moans,
Threadbare injunctions in more threadbare tones.
Sly yet demure, the eager babes crowd in,
Pretty as angels, ripe in pretty sin.
And the postmaster, suction-hose from birth,
The hardest and the tightest screw on earth;
His price as pungent as his hyson green,
His measure heavy on the scale of lean.

A truce to these aspersions, as I see
The winter's orb burn through yon leafless tree,
Where far beneath the track Stillriver runs,
And the vast hill-side makes a thousand suns.
This crystal air, this soothing orange sky,
Possess our lives with their rich sorcery.
We thankful muse on that superior Power
That with his splendor loads the sunset hour,
And by the glimmering streams and solemn woods
In glory walks and charms our solitudes.

O'er the far intervale that dimly lies
In snowy regions placid as the skies,
Some northern breeze awakes the sleeping field,
And like enchanted smoke the great drifts yield

Their snowy curtains to the restless air;
Then build again for architect's despair
The alabaster cornice or smooth scroll
That the next moment in new forms unroll.

VIII

TRURO

I

Ten steps it lies from off the sea,
  Whose angry breakers score the sand,
  A valley of the sleeping land,
Where chirps the cricket quietly.

The aster's bloom, the copses' green,
  Grow darker in the softened sun,
  And silent here day's course is run,
A sheltered spot that smiles serene.

It reaches far from shore to shore,
  Nor house in sight, nor ship or wave,
  A silent valley sweet and grave,
A refuge from the sea's wild roar.

Nor gaze from yonder gravelly height, —
  Beneath, the crashing billows beat,
  The rolling surge of tempests meet
The breakers in their awful might. —

And inland birds soft warble here,
  Where golden-rods and yarrow shine,
  And cattle pasture — sparest kine!
A rural place for homestead dear.

Go not then, traveller, nigh the shore!
  In this soft valley muse content,
  Nor brave the cruel element,
That thunders at the valley's door.

And bless the little human dell,
  The sheltered copsewood snug and warm, —
  Retreat from yon funereal form,
Nor tempt the booming surges' knell.

II

THE OLD WRECKER

He muses slow along the shore,
  A stooping form, his wrinkled face
  Bronzed dark with storm, no softer grace
Of hope; old, even to the core.

He heeds not ocean's wild lament,
  No breaking seas that sight appall, —
  The storms he likes, and as they fall
His gaze grows eager, seaward bent.

He grasps at all, e'en scraps of twine,
  None is too small, and if some ship
  Her bones beneath the breakers dip,
He loiters on his sandy line.

Lonely as ocean is his mien,
  He sorrows not, nor questions fate,
  Unsought, is never desolate,
Nor feels his lot, nor shifts the scene.

Weary he drags the sinking beach,
  Undaunted by the cruel strife,

Alive, yet not the thing of life,
A shipwrecked ghost that haunts the reach.

He breathes the spoil of wreck and sea,
No longer to himself belongs,
Always within his ear thy songs,
Unresting Ocean! bound yet free.

In hut and garden all the same,
Cheerless and slow, beneath content,
The miser of an element
Without a heart, — that none can claim.

Born for thy friend, O sullen wave,
Clasping the earth where none may stand!
He clutches with a trembling hand
The headstones from the sailor's grave.

III

OPEN OCEAN

Unceasing roll the deep green waves,
And crash their cannon down the sand,
The tyrants of the patient land,
Where mariners hope not for graves.

The purple kelp waves to and fro,
The white gulls, curving, scream along;
They fear not thy funereal song,
Nor the long surf that combs to snow.

The hurrying foam deserts the sand,
Afar the low clouds sadly hang,
But the high sea with sullen clang,
Still rages for the silent land.

No human hope or love hast thou,
Unfeeling Ocean! in thy might,
Away—I fly the awful sight,
The working of that moody brow.

The placid sun of autumn shines,—
The hurrying knell marks no decline,
The rush of waves, the war of brine,
Force all, and grandeur, in thy lines.

Could the lone sand-bird once enjoy
Some mossy dell, some rippling brooks,
The fruitful scent of orchard nooks,
The loved retreat of maid or boy!

No, no; the curling billows green,
The cruel surf, the drifting sand,
No flowers or grassy meadow-land,
No kiss of seasons linked between.

The mighty roar, the burdened soul,
The war of waters more and more,
The waves, with crested foam-wreaths hoar,
Rolling to-day, and on to roll.

IV

WINDMILL ON THE COAST

With wreck of ships, and drifting plank,
Uncouth and cumbrous, wert thou built,
Spoil of the sea's unfathomed guilt,
Whose dark revenges thou hast drank.

And loads thy sail the lonely wind,
That wafts the sailor o'er the deep,

Compels thy rushing arms to sweep,
And earth's dull harvesting to grind.

Here strides the fisher lass and brings
Her heavy sack, while creatures small,
Loaded with bag and pail, recall
The youthful joy that works in things.

The winds grind out the bread of life,
The ceaseless breeze torments the stone,
The mill yet hears the ocean's moan,
Her beams the refuse of that strife.

V

ETERNAL SEA

I hear the distant tolling bell,
The echo of the breathless sea;
Bound in a human sympathy
Those sullen strokes no tidings tell.

The spotted sea-bird skims along,
And fisher-boats dash proudly by;
I hear alone that savage cry,
That endless and unfeeling song.

Within thee beats no answering heart,
Cold and deceitful to my race,
The skies alone adorn with grace
Thy freezing waves, or touch with art.

And man must fade, but thou shalt roll
Deserted, vast, and yet more grand;
While thy cold surges beat the strand,
Thy funeral bells ne'er cease to toll.

VI

MICHEL ANGELO—AN INCIDENT

Hard by the shore the cottage stands,
A desert spot, a fisher's house,
There could a hermit keep carouse
On turnip-sprouts from barren sands.

No church or statue greets the view,
Not Pisa's tower or Rome's high wall;
And connoisseurs may vainly call
For Berghem's goat, or Breughel's blue.

Yet meets the eye along a shed,
Blazing with golden splendors rare,
A name to many souls like prayer,
Robbed from a hero of the dead.

It glittered far, the splendid name,
Thy letters, Michel Angelo,—
In this lone spot none e'er can know
The thrills of joy that o'er me came.

Some bark that slid along the main
Dropped off her headboard, and the sea
Plunging it landwards, in the lee
Of these high cliffs it took the lane.

But ne'er that famous Florentine
Had dreamed of such a fate as this,
Where tolling seas his name may kiss,
And curls the lonely sand-strewn brine.

These fearless waves, this mighty sea,
Old Michel, bravely bear thy name!
Like thee, no rules can render tame,
Fatal and grand and sure like thee.

VII

OLD OCEAN

Of what thou dost, I think, not art,
  Thy sparkling air and matchless force,
  Untouched in thy own wild resource,
The tide of a superior heart.

No human love beats warm below,
  Great monarch of the weltering waste!
  The fisher-boats make sail and haste,
Thou art their savior and their foe.

Alone the breeze thy rival proves,
  Smoothing o'er thee his graceful hand,
  Lord of that empire over land,
He moves thy hatred and thy loves.

Yet thy unwearied plunging swell,
  Still breaking, charms the sandy reach,
  No dweller on the shifting beach,
No auditor of thy deep knell;—

The sunny wave, a soft caress;
  The gleaming ebb, the parting day;
  The waves like tender buds in May,
A fit retreat for blessedness.

And breathed a sigh like children's prayers,
  Across thy light aerial blue,
  That might have softened wretches too,
Until they dallied with these airs.

Was there no flitting to thy mood?
  Was all this bliss and love to last?
  No lighthouse by thy stormy past,
No graveyard in thy solitude!

THE HILLSIDE COT.

AND here the hermit sat, and told
his beads,
And stroked his flowing locks, red
as the fire,
Summed up his tale of moon and
sun and star:
"How blest are we," he deemed,
"who so comprise
The essence of the whole, and of
ourselves,
As in a Venice flask of lucent shape,
Ornate of gilt Arabic, and inscribed
With Suras from Time's Koran, live
and pray,
More than half grateful for the glit-
tering prize,
Human existence! If I note my
powers,
So poor and frail a toy, the insect's
prey,
Itched by a berry, festered by a
plum,
The very air infecting my thin
frame
With its malarial trick, whom every
day
Rushes upon and hustles to the
grave,
Yet raised by the great love that
broods o'er all
Responsive, to a height beyond all
thought."
He ended as the nightly prayer and
fast
Summoned him inward. But I sat
and heard

The night-hawks rip the air above
my head,
Till midnight, o'er the warm, dry,
dewless rocks;
And saw the blazing dog-star droop
his fire,
And the low comet, trailing to the
south,
Bend his reverted gaze, and leave
us free.

FLIGHT OF THE WILD GEESE.

RAMBLING along the marshes,
On the bank of the Assabet,
Sounding myself as to how it went,
Praying that I might not forget,
And all uncertain
Whether I was in the right,
Toiling to lift Time's curtain,
And if I burnt the strongest light;
Suddenly,
High in the air,
I heard the travelled geese
Their overture prepare.

Stirred above the patent ball,
The wild geese flew,
Nor near so wild as that doth me be-
fall,
Or, swollen Wisdom, you.

In the front there fetched a leader,
Him behind the line spread out,
And waved about,
As it was near night,
When these air-pilots stop their
flight.

Cruising off the shoal dominion
Where we sit,
Depending not on their opinion,
Nor hiving sops of wit;
Geographical in tact,
Naming not a pond or river,
Pulled with twilight down in fact,
In the reeds to quack and quiver,
There they go,
Spectators at the play below,
Southward in a row.

Cannot land and map the stars
The indifferent geese,
Nor taste the sweetmeats in odd jars,
Nor speculate and freeze;
Raucid weasands need be well,
Feathers glossy, quills in order,
Starts this train, yet rings no bell;
Steam is raised without recorder.

"Up, my feathered fowl, all," —
Saith the goose commander,
"Brighten your bills, and flirt your
pinions,
My toes are nipped, — let us render
Ourselves in soft Guatemala,
Or suck puddles in Campeachy,
Spitzbergen-cake cuts very frosty,
And the tipple is not leechy.

"Let's brush loose for any creek,
There lurk fish and fly,
Condiments to fat the weak,
Inundate the pie.
Flutter not about a place,
Ye concomitants of space!"

Mute the listening nations stand
On that dark receding land;
How faint their villages and towns,
Scattered on the misty downs!
A meeting-house
Appears no bigger than a mouse.

How long?
Never is a question asked,
While a throat can lift the song,
Or a flapping wing be tasked.

All the grandmothers about
Hear the orators of Heaven,
Then put on their woollens stout,
And cower o'er the hearth at even;
And the children stare at the sky,
And laugh to see the long black line
so high!

Then once more I heard them say, —
"'Tis a smooth, delightful road,
Difficult to lose the way,
And a trifle for a load.

"'Twas our forte to pass for this,
Proper sack of sense to borrow,
Wings and legs, and bills that clat-
ter,
And the horizon of To-morrow."

THE SHOWS OF NATURE.

By WILLIAM ELLERY CHANNING.

SHE woos me on, never may I retreat;
Cold woods, bare fields, and you, ye winter skies,
In you my thoughts, responsive feelings meet,
Within your forms I look, and with your eyes.

And man! that curious copy of *myself*,
I still pursue, as tired dogs hunt the deer,—
That silent mouthpiece, that sly, subtle elf.
I oft shall seek, and rarely find, with fear!

Where roves the Nymph who smoothed the fountain's crest,
And the cold Dryad of the hazel's dell,—
Egeria's couch, where sparely she could rest,
Of its dry ferns, the gleaming icicle?

Some sprouting youth, some knowing miss instead,
The painted moral of a grandam's eye,
Or cold-complexioned adults with small head,
The sticks which our Dodonas now supply.

Nature! I come, fed with thy homely cheer,
  Nature! I kneel, part hopeful at thy shrine,
Form of the Solitude, decline the ear,
  And if considerate, then, confess me, thine!

Court the sleek herd! and hopelessly be drawn,
  Into that false and slimy serpent's lair;
I long must love in mossy groves, the fawn,
  And in the blue lake, bathe, my late despair.

And when the emerald pine-woods' murmuring shell
  Reflects the cadence of the much-voiced sea,
As there some mournful air rings his small knell,
  Or the cold sunset fades, there let me be;

Then as the dying day his saffron plume
  Wafts o'er the purple of these Indian hills,
Dreaming, I mark red warriors leave their tombs,
  I see their tawny columns bridge the rills,

Weird bends their tragic dance across yon mead,
  Dashed on day's fleeting light gleams lance and bow,
And the young lover lifts his mystic reed
  To a dark eye of sloe-like glimmering hue.

Then, as the day-god dies beneath the lake,
  The ruby glasses of the copsewood oak
Their last Madeira promise ripely shake,
  That evermore in midnight's frost is broke.

Soft thro' the east, her silver pomp I see,
  The mistress of the lone romantic night,
O'er sleeping hill, bare stone and leafless tree,
  She pours her careless world of dewy light.

Then, in that roof, a million lamps of spar,
  Set in the brow of heaven's high azure screen,
Gleam slowly down, while some revolving star
  My bark guides radiant o'er the mystic green, —

Of a serener land, than space or time,
  Carve for the cold and worldly breasted man;
Compel me not to fly the foolish rhyme,
  Nor to desert poor nature's secret plan.

I know that charming glows both camp and hall,
  Where beauty's eye outshines its daily fire,
Too true, the poet cannot hope for all, —
  Be his to creep in dust, and yet aspire;

For in the heart of these neglected things,
The thin, deserted field, and wood-road wild,
A virtue breathes, a cheerful patience sings,
Mother! thou never couldst forget thy child.

Original Hymn. By W. E. Channing.

(Sung by the Choir, under the direction of Mr. Thomas Reeves, Musical Director of the Institution for the Blind.)

O'er the pall of a Hero the laurel should fall,
'Tis the love of a Father our voices recall;
With hope, like the sunshine, it paints the dark air;
O God, with thy mercy, interpret our prayer!

From isles of the Muse, over Hellas' blue wave,
From homes of the North, for the hearts of the slave,
Let swift-flashing memory his requiem be,—
Unfaltering, unfettered, unselfish as he.

Our fond hearts reëcho his cry for the race,
For himself not a wish,—speed, speed to the place
Where anguish lies wailing, there always his home,—
O God, with thy mercy, illumine his tomb.

Unseal the veiled orb, for his eye, that ne'er slept,
Unfetter the mind from the darkness he wept;
The light of the soul is the star of life's sea,—
As loving, as hoping, as constant was He.

CHILDREN'S SONG.

NOW the trees are on the air,
Now the flowers are in the vale,
Now the earth shows sweet and fair
As our mother's tale.

Bright is every violet's eye,
Yellow-deep the cowslip hues,
Where the wide-winged butterfly
Feeds herself with dews.

But the rising wind away
Turns the flower-bells bending low,
And the thunder-clouds do say
Their sublimest now.

Leaps the flashing sword of light,
Rushes breeze and hisses rain;
Yet the trees are laughing bright
At the watery gain.

EDITH

Edith, the silent stars are coldly gleaming,
The night wind moans, the leafless trees are still.
Edith, there is a life beyond this seeming,
So sleeps the ice-clad lake beneath thy hill.

So silent beats the pulse of thy pure heart,
So shines the thought of thy unquestioned eyes.
O life! why wert thou helpless in thy art?
O loveliness! why seem'st thou but surprise?

Edith, the streamlets laugh to leap again;
There is a spring to which life's pulses fly;
And hopes that are not all the sport of pain,
Like lustres in the veil of that gray eye.

They say the thankless stars have answering vision,
That courage sings from out the frost-bound ways;
Edith, I grant that olden time's decision —
Thy beauty paints with gold the icy rays.

As in the summer's heat her promise lies,
As in the autumn's seed his vintage hides,
Thus might I shape my moral from those eyes,
Glass of thy soul, where innocence abides.

Edith, thy nature breathes of answered praying;
If thou dost live, then not my grief is vain;
Beyond the nerves of woe, beyond delaying,
Thy sweetness stills to rest the winter's pain.

TO MARJORIE—DREAMING

WE must not weep, we will not moan;
Let all such things be deemed unknown.
Now for the words of livelong hope
In Marjorie's white horoscope!

Good-by to all that dims our eyes—
Welcome her, kind futurities!
Anthems of joy and hymns of gold—
All these let Marjorie infold!

Yes, for that sweet and peaceful child,
That gift of beauty undefiled,
A smile of love, a song of joy,
Shall Marjorie's dream of life employ.

I see the sunset o'er the hill,
The level meads with glory fill—
A gentle light, a heavenly balm,
Like Marjorie's soul, so clear and calm.

THE BYFIELD HILLS

(1836)

THERE is a range of little barren hills,
  Skirting a dark and purely idle stream,
  Which winds among the fields, as in a dream
Of weary man a heavy sorrow rills
The down-prest spirit; whoso buildeth mills
  To break the grain on it? Yet never deem
  These barren little hills low as they seem—
They draw away from us a host of ills.

A lone flat rock is sleeping at its ease
  Upon their topmost line, beneath a wind
That oozes from the sea, nor touches trees
  In that bare spot, but murmurs to the mind
A misty tune of gray felicities—
  Salt Ocean's heart, thy pulse is strangely kind!

SUNDAY POEM

This is the strange title given in the author's manuscript to a long autobiographical poem dwelling on the sadness of the poet's childish life, the loss of an early love (a subject to which he often recurred, as will be seen), and the consolation that he drew from the beauties and protections of Nature—here typified under the Goethean name of *The Earth-Spirit.* This latter part was printed in 1843 as *The Earth-Spirit*, but without this weird, pathetic introduction. A portion of the unprinted lines are omitted.

I

ONWARD we float along the way
Like straws upon a rapid river.
Changeth the weather every day;
So change our human feelings ever—
Yes, most of them thus change,
And have a wider range,
But there are those no time can sever.

Withers not the sun, my love!
What of thee is mortal now
That was framed in worlds above;
Thy full-thoughted archèd brow,
And the light of those clear eyes,
Death and change and Time defies.

The immortal there hath place,
Gladly sits upon thy frame,
Lurketh in thy sunny face,
In a wildness none can tame.

II

Away! the night is dark and drear;
  Loud howls the storm, the clouds uproar,
And chill as broken love the atmosphere.
  Away! thee, Nature, I can woo no more:
    Thou art at war, and naught at rest;
    With thee I never can be blest.

Thy whirling seas my feelings jar,
  Thy weeping winds and twilight cold;
Thy ways my seekings idly mar,
  And I was in my youth-time old.
    Thou didst set a glowing stone
    In a golden belt alone,—
To me thou sayest: "This treasure thine—
It is the richest thing of mine."

III

  I stood amazed; my blood o'erran
    Its usual channels, till my veins
  Would burst; I was again a man;
    Ending was here of all those pains—
Those cold, chill pains that crept about my way,
Those hidden shadows in the light of Day.
  What! no more of them to see?
  Chains were off and roaming free?

Then cried I to the corners of the Earth:
"It cannot be—ye mock at my despair!
For I was destined from my earliest birth
To be beloved by nothing sweet or fair:
And I have made my bed, and now am heir
To all that blackens and has naught of mirth.

"I tell you, sudden fates which come to me,
Ye are not faithful! Hear: my mother died
Before I clasped her, and that parent's knee
Me never knew—my tears she never dried;
But with the unknown upward then I grew,
Far from all that which was to me most true."

That early life was bitter oft;
And like a flower whose roots are dry
I withered; for my feelings soft
Were by my brothers passèd by.
Storm-wind fell on me,
Dark clouds lowered on me;
Many ghosts swept trembling past;
Cold looks in my eyes they cast.

IV

Older I grew then, but I was not more
Joy's child than in those earlier, other hours;
It was the same unyielding penance o'er.
My crown was not of thorns, but withered flowers,

Dry buds, and half-blown roses dry with dust;
Thorns had been glorious, glorious by their side,
For in their frantic pain there rises trust,
While these are phantoms of what may have died.
I see ye still around me;
Why is it said? To sadden?
That there is some joy for me?
Ah! think you me to gladden?

Sang the voice sweetly: "We say what we say;
There is joy in thy cup, there is sun in thy day."
I groaned aloud: "Alas, they mock!
Stood other form in other years,—
Her song,—then came the lightning's shock,
And the sharp fire of those wild tears;
I carry them within, on many biers.
I stand like one who came to sing with those
That sang so sweetly, all of love and joy;
Their voices yet!—while I am hung with woes;
Life comes to me, yet comes but to destroy."

V

Then spoke the Spirit of the Earth,
Her gentle voice like gliding water's song:
"None from my loins have ever birth
But they to joy and love belong;
I faithful am, and give to thee
Blessings great—and give them free.

"I have woven shrouds of air
In a loom of hurrying light,
For the trees which blossoms bear,
And gilded them with sheets of bright:
I fall upon the grass like love's first kiss,
I make the golden flies and their fine bliss.

"I paint the hedgerows in the lane,
And clover white and red the pathways bear;
I laugh aloud in sudden gusts of rain
To see the Ocean lash himself in air;
I throw smooth shells and weeds along the beach,
And pour the curling waves far o'er the glassy
reach;
Swing birds' nests in the elms, and shake cool moss
Along the aged beams, and hide their loss.

"The very broad rough stones I gladden, too—
Some willing seeds I drop along their sides,
Nourish the generous plant with freshening dew,
Till there where all was waste true joy abides.
The peaks of aged mountains, with my care,
Smile in the red of glowing morn, elate;
I bind the caverns of the sea with hair
Glossy and long, and rich as king's estate;
I polish the green ice, and gleam the wall
With whitening frost, and leaf the brown trees
tall.

VI

"Thee not alone I leave—far more
Weave I for thee than for the air;
Thou art of greater worth than the sea-shore,
And yet for it how much do I prepare!
I love thee better than the trees—
Yet I give them sun and breeze;
More than rivers thou to me,
More I shall be giving thee;
Tears of thine I 'll dry fore'er,
To thee joys and blisses bear.

"Believe thy Mother for her worth
(And thou art a son of Earth).
Thou hadst many years of woe;
Life was many times thy foe;
But the stars have looked from where
Hang their sparklets in the air,
And their faith is pledged to me
That they shall give joy to thee."

VII

It came upon me in a sudden thrill,
It stood before me—'t was a thing of life.
The thoughts rushed out; I had not form nor will;
I was in hurrying trance, yet felt no strife.

I laughed aloud—Death had crept back awhile;
I looked abroad—the sunlight seemed to smile.
Joy, joy! was now the song,
Like a torrent crowding strong
To the endless Sea along.
She stood before me in that veil of form
(The stars' first light, dropt from an urn of air);
Within her eyes there melted sunlight warm,
Which its soft heat did with the moonbeam share;
The gushing of her smile was like a stream
Which, when all round was crisped with feathery
snow,
Went surging through the drear its liquid dream,
In sweet dissolvèd style, as angels know.
The spell that dwelt within each faintest word
Was Love—the first my eager ear had heard.
She stood before me, and her life sank through
My withering heart as doth the piercing dew,
That sinks with quivering tenderness within
The moss-rose breast—till it to ope doth win.

VIII

'T was so—'t was thine! Earth, thou wert true!
I kneel—thy grateful child, I kneel;
Thy full forgiveness for my sins I sue.
O Mother! learn thy son can think and feel.
Mother dear! wilt pardon one
Who loved not the generous sun,

Nor thy seasons loved to hear
Chanting to the busy year;
Thee neglected, shut his heart—
In thy being had no part?
Mother! now I list thy song
In this autumn eve along,
As thy chill airs round the day,
Leaving me my time to pray.

Mother dear! the day must come
When thy child shall make his home—
My long, last home—'mid the grass
Over which thy warm hands pass.
Ah me! then do let me lie
Gently on thy breast to die!

I know my prayers will reach thine ear—
  Thou art with me while I ask;
Nor thy child refuse to hear,
  Who would learn his little task.
Let me take my part with thee
  In the gray clouds, or the light—
Laugh with thee upon the sea,
  Or idle on the land by night;
    In the trees will I with thee—
    In the flowers, like any bee.

IX

I feel it shall be so; we were not born
  To sink our finer feelings in the dust;
Far better to the grave with feelings torn—
  So in our step strides Truth and honest trust
In the great love of things—than to be slaves
  To forms—whose ringing side each stroke we give
Stamps with a hollower void;—yes, to our graves
  Hurrying or e' er we in the heavens' look live
Strangers to our best hopes, and fearing men,
Yea, fearing death—and to be born again.

A SONNET TO JOYCE HETH, CENTENARIAN

(1835)

INTOLERABLE Time grasps eagerly,
With hideous Destiny, who sits him near;
Some name him Fate—it matters not to me,
So that thy awful durance shall appear.
Old ebon Heth, eternal Black! strange sight!
Strange, that thou dost not bend to Father Time,
But, rather, holdest confident thy prime,
In this quick-speeding world, where hovers Night.

Yes, bleached Anatomy! dry skin and bone!
Thou Grasshopper! thou bloodless, fleshless thing,
That still, with thin long tongue dost gayly sing!
I would not meet thee at broad noon alone;
For much I fear thee, and thy yellow fingers,
Thy cold, sepulchral eye, where moonlight
lingers.[1]

[1] This woman was shown in Boston and elsewhere as the nurse of George Washington, and about one hundred and sixty years old; she was, in fact, over one hundred. This sonnet is one of the three earliest poems, the *November Day* and *The Spider* preceding it; all were written before Channing was seventeen.

CHARACTERS

A GENTLE eye with a spell of its own,
  A meaning glance and a sudden thrill;
A voice—sweet music in every tone;
  A steadfast heart and a resolute will;

A graceful form and a cheering smile,
  Ever the same, and always true.
I have heard of this for a long, long while—
  I have seen it, known it, loved it too.

THE CONTRAST

THE gray clouds fly,—
There is war on high,—
Their pennons flying, their soldiers dying;
They fall in rain,
But they leave no stain.

But the heart's flight
In the gloomy night,
Its trusting over, its changing lover?
There falls no rain,
But tears that pain.

NATURE

BLUE is the sky as ever, and the stars
Kindle their crystal flames at soft-fallen Eve
With the same purest lustre that the East
Worshipt; the river gently flows through fields
Wherein the broad-leaved corn spreads out and loads
Its ear, as when its Indian tilled the soil;
The dark green pine, green in the winter's cold,
Still whispers meaning emblems as of old;
The cricket chirps, and the sweet, eager birds
In the sad woods crowd their thick melodies;
But yet, to common eyes, life's poesy
Something has faded.

The Summer's breath, that laughed among the
flowers,
Caressed the tender blades of the soft grass,
And o'er thy dear form with its joy did pass,
Has left us now. These are but Autumn-hours,

And in their melancholy vestures glass
A feeling that belongs to deeper powers
Than haunt the warm-eyed June or spring-time
showers—
The destiny of them like us, alas!

Think not of Time; there is a better sphere
Rising above these cold and shadowy days—
A softer music than the gray clouds hear,
That spread their flying sails above our ways,
Where rustle in the breeze the thin leaves sere,
Or on the leaden air dance in swift maze.

THE SLEEPING CHILD

(WALDO EMERSON, DEAD)

(1843)

DARKNESS now hath overpaced
  Life's swift dance; and curtained Awe
Feebly lifts a sunken eye,
  Wonted to this gloomy law.
Lips are still that sweetly spoke;
Heedless Death the spell hath broke.

Weep not for him, friends so dear!
  Largest measure he hath taken.
Now he roams the sun's dominion,
  Our chill fortunes quite forsaken;
There his eyes have purer sight
In that calm, reflected light.

Let your tears dissolve in peace!
  For he holds high company;
And he seeks, with famous men,
  Statelier lines of ancestry;
He shall shame the wisest ones
In that palace of the suns.

ENGLAND, IN AFFLICTION

(1843)

THOU Sea of circumstance, whose waves are ages,
  On whose high surf the fates of men are
    thrown!
Thou writing from the calm, eternal pages,
  Whose letters secret unto Him alone
  Who writ that scroll forever shall be known!
I deem not of thy inmost to discover,
Yet oh, forget not I am thy true lover.

Home of the Brave! deep-centred in the Ocean—
  Cradle where rocked the famous bards of old,
Consummate masters of the heart's emotion,
  Free, genial intellects by Heaven made bold!
  My blood I should disown, and deem me cold,
If I did not revere thy matchless sons—
Of all Time's progeny the noblest ones.

What though the calm Elysium of the air
  Hangs violet draperies o'er the Grecian fanes?
What though the fields of Italy are fair?
  Above them England towers, with mightier
    gains;
  Yet, tell me, are her sons bound fast in chains?
The fearful note of misery sounds so high
From her wide plains up to her clouded sky.

In woodland churches rising forest-free,
  Network of threaded granite, textured fine,
And stamped with countenance of sanctity,—
  With arches waving like the pointed pine,
  Where spires and cones and rugged barks
    entwine,—
Their cloisters shadowy in the light of noon,
Their tall, dim steeples misty in the moon;

Thy surplice—shall it hide a purse of gold?
  The smooth and roted sermon doff to Fame?
Extinguished every aspiration bold,
  While only sounds some formal, empty name?
  Shall her old churches make proud England
    tame?
Throw ashes in those hearts where once coursed
    blood,
And blind those streaming eyes from sight of
    good?

England!—the name hath bulwarks in the sound,
  And bids her people own the State again;
Bids them to dispossess their native ground
  From out the hands of titled noblemen;
  Then shall the scholar freely wield his pen,
And shepherds dwell where lords keep castle
    now,
And peasants cut the overhanging bough.

Fold not thy brawny arms as though thy toil
  Was done, nor take thy drowsy path toward
    sleep!
There never will be leisure on thy soil,
  There never will be idless on thy steep;
  So long as thou sailst the unsounded deep,
New conquests shall be thine, new heritage,
Such as the world's whole wonder must engage.

THE BEGGAR'S WISH

(1843)

O SPARE from all thy luxury
  A tear for one who may not weep!
Whose heart is like a wintry sea,
  So still and cold and deep.

Nor shed that tear till I am laid
  Beneath the fresh-dug turf at rest,
And o'er my grave the elm-tree's shade
  That hides the robin's nest.

THE POET

EVEN in the winter's depth the Pine-tree stands
With a perpetual summer in its leaves;
So stands the Poet, with his open hands—
Nor care nor sorrow him of life bereaves.

Though others pine for piles of glittering gold,
A cloudless sunset furnishes him enough;
His garments never can grow thin or old;
His way is always smooth, though seeming rough.

For though his sorrows fall like icy rain,
Straightway the clouds do open where he goes,
And e'en his tears become a precious gain—
'T is thus the hearts of mortals that he knows.

The figures of his landscape may appear
Sordid or poor; their colors he can paint;
And, listening to the hooting, he can hear
Such harmonies as never sung the Saint.

'T is in his heart where dwells his pure desire,
Let other outward lot be dark or fair;
In coldest weather there is inward fire—
In fogs he breathes a clear, celestial air.

Some shady wood in summer is his room;
  Behind a rock in winter he can sit;
The wind shall sweep his chamber, and his loom—
  The birds and insects weave content at it.

Above his head the broad sky's beauties are;
  Beneath, the ancient carpet of the earth:
A glance at that unveileth every star;
  The other, joyfully it feels his birth.

So sacred is his calling that no thing
  Of disrepute can follow in his path;
His destiny 's too high for sorrowing;
  The mildness of his lot is kept from wrath.

So let him stand, resigned to his estate;
  Kings cannot compass it, nor nobles have:
They are the children of some handsome fate,
  He of himself is beautiful and brave.

ALCOTT

LIGHT from a better land!
Fire from a burning brand!
Though in this cold, sepulchral clime,
Chained to an unambitious time,
    Thou slowly moulderest;
Yet cheer that great and lowly heart,
Prophetic eye and sovereign part!
And be thy fortune greatly blest,
And by some greater gods confest,
    With a sublimer rest!

Strike on, nor still thy golden lyre,
That sparkles with Olympian fire!
And be thy word the soul's desire
    Of this unthinking land!
Nor shall thy voyage of glory fail;
Its sea thou sweepest—set thy sail!
Though fiercely rave the heaviest gale,
    It shall not swerve thy hand.

Born for a fate whose secret none
Hath looked upon beneath Earth's sun—
Child of the High, the Only One!
    Thy glories sleep secure!
On Heaven's coast thy mounting wave
Shall dash beyond the unknown grave,
And cast its spray to warn and save
    Some other barks that moor.

UNFAITHFUL FRIENDSHIP

You recollect our younger years, my Friend,
And rambles in the country; life could lend
No choicer volumes for the Student's eye.
You must remember that it was not I
Who brought conclusion to these rambling
moods—
Our joint connection with the streams and woods:
'T was ever thou—thou who art steeped in
thought,
Subtle and dexterous, wise—but good for naught.
I mean no harm; thou art not good for me—
Thou reasonest, demandest; I ask *thee.*

Thou didst not know that Friendship is a kiss—
Not thought, philosophy,—some Sage's bliss,—
But a strange fire that falleth from above;
The gods have named this star-shower Human Love.
No—thou wert blinded; thou saidst, "Friend,
forbear!
Do not come nigh—my heart thou canst not share."
(My heart, alas! I gave that all away.)
"I do not love thee near me; bide thy day!
Fashion I seek, and whirling gayety,
Not thou, sad Poet! what art thou to me?

More—I have married an angelic wife,
Who wreathes with roses my enchanted life;
Thou art superfluous—come not thou too near!
Let us be distant friends, and no more dear.

"What were thy eager fancies, running o'er
Half of the world? I anchor near the shore:
Thy silly jests for idlers' ears are fit,
And only silence complements thy wit.
I love thee at arm's-length; my quarantine
Declares pacific measures, and divine.
I would it were not so—poor, helpless thing,
That like a blue jay can but shriek or sing
Those lamentable ditties that refuse
To call themselves productions of the Muse!
Nay! walk not with me in the curling wood!
I stride abroad in quest of solitude.
I love my friends far off; when they come near,
Too warm! too warm the crowded atmosphere."

THE POET'S DEJECTION

THERE are no tears to shed; the heart is dry,
And the thin leaves of hope fall from the bough,
Rustling and sere—all winter in the tree.
Some smarting pain, some swiftly shooting ill,
Needless alarm or interrupted fear,
Chances and changes, and the soul's despair,
All we can suffer—all that we deplore
Were happier far than these unmoving hours,
When I sit silent on the sandy shore,
Silent, uncomforted, hapless, and lone.
Why are ye bright, why are ye sunny, days,
With the blue sky that arches over all,
And the sweet wind that with a breath of love
Touches the golden hilltops till they smile?
I murmur from my soul its cherished thoughts,
All I have known or suffered; and I ask
The friends I love to come and sit with me,
And call to memory for their cheerful smiles.
They cannot answer me; no visions rise;
And in such ebbing hours life passes as
A faint and burdened man, whose aching feet
Support him tottering o'er the sandy wastes
In the unlidded blaze of Afric's eye.

Yet let me suffer with a patient thought;
'T is but another turning of the tide
That from the far-off ocean of our fate
So slowly murmurs through its rock-bound cave.
Oh, little feel the gay, remorseless crowd,
Intent on pleasures, of the poet's care;
The path he treads must be by them untrod;
His destiny a veil, his heart—unsealed;
While all around him swims dancing in joy,
And smiling faces and soft azure skies,
Tantalus-like that he shall never touch,
Look in across the dead sea of his life,
Like goblin masks, fleshless and cold and pale.

Would that the heart might break, the mind
    decease,
Or ever these dark hours that do not move,
Sullen and stagnant as the marshy pool
Whose side the rank sedge crowds, while the green
    ooze
Spreads o'er the shallows its soft, slimy veil!
Will the prevented waters ne'er o'erflow,
Burst down their muddy dams, and, leaping clear,
Dance through the valleys like a song of joy?
Is there imprisoned winter through my heart,
Frozen to its centre like an icy shroud?
Am I embraced in stone or filled with dust?
Tell me, kind destinies, who rule our days!
In vain; ye ne'er reveal it. There 's no soul
Within us that applauds these sullen hours.

Ever the tide returns; but now at ebb,
When the white sands gleam bare and nothing
stirs
Save the salt seaweed fringe of little streams
That trickle from lone pools o'er the dented sand.
Cannot I, as the mariner, recline,
Waiting the longed-for hour when with a stir
Of soft, delicious fragrance from the deep,
And heavenly alternations in the kiss
Of the sea-breeze, elastic as young hopes,
The swelling waters hasten, and his bark
At last floats off, rising so steadily,
Her sails all filling with that sweet surprise,
Till her bright keel cuts sharply the green floor,
And tosses off the billows till they laugh.

Yet must we wait, whose voyage knows no content,
Whose compass turns within the eternal stars—
A voyage beyond illimitable worlds;
Yet must I pause upon this earthly ebb,
And play and smile at care and soothe the pain,
Until the raven hair of misery shines.

Brave be thy heart, O sailor of the world!
Erect thy vision, strong and resolute.
Let disappointments strike, and leaden days
Visit thee like a snowdrift across flowers;
Be calm and truthful, and outcheer thy pangs.

And, when thou sufferest, learn from all thy woes,
Those faithful teachers who shall spell thee all
Hope's alphabet and Bible lore. Be calm—
Even in a little this rude voyage is done.
Then heave the time-stained anchor, trim thy sails,
And o'er the bosom of the untrammelled deep
Ride in the heavenly boat and touch new stars.

MURILLO'S MAGDALEN

HER eyes are fixed; they seek the skies.
  Was earth so low? Was life so vain?
Was Time such weary sacrifice?
  This hopeless task, this eating pain?

Smooth, smooth the tresses of thy hair;
  Release that cold, contracted brow!
I have not lived without despair;
  Look down on me—some mercy show!

977

I cannot bear those silent skies;
The weight is pressing in my heart;
Life is eternal sacrifice,
The livelong hour, the selfish smart.

I wake to tears, in tears I close
The weary eyes so fixed above;
I cannot see the skies of rose,
My heavy tresses will not move.

Hope cannot heal my breaking heart,
Heaven will not lift my dread despair;
I need another soul to part
These brows of steel and join in prayer.

Sails there no bark on life's wild sea
That bears a soul whose faith has set,
Who may renew my light in me,
And both shall thus the past forget?

SLEEPY HOLLOW

(1855)

This poem was written at Mr. Emerson's request, for singing at the consecration of the Concord cemetery where his ashes now repose. But finding it could not easily be sung by the village choir, Mr. Emerson desired me to write an ode that could be sung — which was done.— F. B. S.

NO abbeys gloom, no dark cathedral stoops,
  No winding torches paint the midnight air;
Here the green pine delights, the aspen droops
  Along the modest pathways—and those fair,
Pale asters of the season spread their plumes
Around this field, fit garden for our tombs.

Here shalt thou pause to hear the funeral bell
  Slow stealing o'er thy heart in this calm place;
Not with a throb of pain, a feverish knell,
  But in its kind and supplicating grace
It says: "Go, Pilgrim, on thy march! be more
Friend to the friendless than thou wast before."

Learn from the loved one's rest, serenity;
  To-morrow that soft bell for thee shall sound,
And thou repose beneath the whispering tree,
  One tribute more to this submissive ground.
Prison thy soul from malice—bar out pride—
Nor these pale flowers nor this still field deride!

Rather to those ascents of Being turn
  Where a ne'er-setting sun illumes the year
Eternal; and the incessant watch-fires burn
  Of unspent holiness and goodness clear;
Forget man's littleness—deserve the best—
God's mercy in thy thought and life confest.

THE NEW ENGLAND FARM-HOUSE

IN CANTON, MASSACHUSETTS

METHINKS I see the hilltops round me swell,
  And meadow vales that kiss their tawny brooks,
And fawn the glittering sands that hug the grass,
Old valleys shorn by farmers numerous years,
Some mossy orchards murmuring with perfume,
And our red farm-house. What a wreck that was!—
Its rotten shingles peeling 'fore the winds
When roaring March fell in the offshore breeze;
The kitchen, with its salt-box full of eggs,
And Taylor's *Holy Living* on the lid.
Our parlor kept its buffet rarely oped—
Much did I wonder at yon glassy doors,
And stacks of crockery sublimely piled—
Hills of blue plates, and teapots sere with age;
And spoons, old silver, tiniest of that breed.

It was a sacred place, and, save I whisked
Sometimes a raisin or a seed-cake thence,
With furtive glance I scanned the curious spot.
The curtains at the windows kept all dark;
Green paper was the compound; and the floor,
Well scrubbed, showed its vacuities, content
With modest subterfuge of mats (the work
Of some brave aunt, industrious as a fly),
And interwove of rags, yet such to me
I hardly dared intrude on them my shoe.

TRURO, ON CAPE COD

OFT would I tread that far-off, quiet shore,
And sit allayed with its unnoticed store.
What though nor fame nor hope my fancy fired,
Nor aught of that to which my youth aspired,
Nor woman's beauty, nor her friendly cheer,
That nourish life like some soft atmosphere?
For here I found I was a welcome guest
At generous Nature's hospitable feast.
The barren moors no fences girdled high,—
These endless beaches planting might defy,—
And the blue sea admitted all the air—
A cordial draught, so sparkling and so rare.

While there I wandered,—far and wide between,—
Proud of my salt expanse and country clean.
A few old fishers seemed my only men,
Some aged wives their queens, not seen till then;
Those had outsailed the wild, o'er-heaving seas,
These closely nestled in their old roof-trees.
Too dull to mark, they eyed me without harm;
Careless of alms, I was not their alarm.
The aged widow in her cottage lone,
Of solitude and musing patient grown,
Could let me wander o'er her scanty fields,
And pick the flower that contemplation yields.
Oft had she sat the winter storms away,
And feared the sea, and trembled at its play;
Noticed the clouds, and guessed when storms were
nigh;
Like me, alone, far from humanity.

Her straw all plaited and her day's work done,
There as she sat she saw the reddening sun
Drop o'er the distant cape, and felt that May
Had outbid April for a sweeter day,
And dreamed of flowers and garden-work to do,
And half resolved, and half it kept in view.

This census o'er, and all the rest was mine.
The gliding vessel on the horizon's line,
That left the world wherein my fancy strayed,
Yet long enough her soft good-by delayed

To let my eye engross her beauty rare,
Kissed by the seas and mistress of the air.
That, too, was mine—the green and curling wave,
Child of the sand—a playful child and brave;
Urged by the breeze, the crashing surges fall—
Let zephyrs dance—and silken bubbles all;
But let the gale lift from yon Eastern realm—
No more the ship perceives the patient helm;
Tranced in the tumbling roar she whirls away,
A shattered ghost, a chip for thy dread play.
Wild ocean wave! some eyes look out o'er thee
And fill with tears, and ask, Could such things be?
Why slept the All-seeing Eye when death was
near?
Be hushed each doubt, assuage each troubled fear!
Think One who made the sea and made the wind
May also feel for our poor humankind;
And they who sleep amid the surges tall
Summoned great Nature to their funeral,
And she obeyed. We fall not far from shore;
The seabird's wail, the skies our fates deplore;
The melancholy main goes sounding on
His world-old anthem o'er our horizon.

TRURO

A REGRET

THE vain regret, the foolish, wasted tear,
Old memories, and most my thought of thee—
Why will they rise and darkly haunt me here,
Whilst the gay blackbird whistles o'er the lea,
And water-lilies shine, and the blue sea
I little dream of, yonder o'er the hill?
Alas for Hope! since not again to me
Thy form shall rise, thy life my being thrill—
Gone as thou art—gone and forever still.

Forgive this weak lament! and still forgive
In our past days a foolish, erring man!
And yet that I was true thou must believe—
An empty heart that with thy life o'erran,
Creature of beauty—Nature's rarest plan!
So beautiful, who would not love thee near?
We are not carved in stone. The day that ran
Our passion into form why should we fear?
Nor more that silent Past, closed save to some
cold tear.

Then bloomed the flowers along Life's sandy waste,
The waters sparkled in the glancing sun,

And Fate for thee prepared with eager haste
  The festive measure—sorrowful to one
  Who on thy beauty gazed, but could not run
To slake his thirst at that unfathomed spring;
  But feverish looked, and only looked upon,
While Nature hastened with her queenly ring
And crowned thee fairest—her most charming
    thing.

Why must we live? why pause upon this shore?
  Its cold despair our flying souls must chill;
And, sitting lone, I hear the ocean's roar,
  While most subdued my heart and wish and will—
  Like its unsounded depths my hopes are still;
A moment I may pause, and ask the Past,
  Since in the Present frozen is Life's rill,
Had she no joys that might their sunshine cast
On these Siberian wastes and slippery glaciers
    vast?

Though beauty smile not on a wasted heart,
  And with the years I must my lot deplore,
Though Love be distant,—Life an actor's part,
  One moment moored, then sailing off the
    shore,—
  Still, while thy thought remains, I weep no more;
For in thy sweet yet artless dignity,
  Thy polished mind, in Youth's unlearned lore,

There yet remains a happiness for me,
And thee I still remember, Rosalie!
Where went thou straying, when the heart was young,
And green the leaf swayed on Life's bending tree?
When the eye saw, and nimbly sped the tongue
To tell of stream and bird and heaving sea—
And human fate glowed for eternity?
Then Hope on high poised her romantic scroll
Where poets' years are writ—not the cold plea
For having lived: as the long surges roll
Across my years, now but my knell they toll.

JULIA

JULIA—at her name my mind
Throws its griefs and cares behind:
She, the love of early years,
Smiling through her childish tears—
Julia! child of love and pain,
One I ne'er shall see again.

And forgive me, Julia dear,
For the sins of that long year!
Think of me with kindly thought,
And condemn me not for naught.

By thine eyes, so softly brown,
By the light and glistening crown
That so gently o'er thy head
Did its shining lustre shed;
By that sad yet loving mouth,
Rose of fragrance from the South;
By thy form, oh, lovelier far
Than a seraph's from a star;
By that ankle small and neat,
And thy little twinkling feet;—

I must still thy loss deplore,
Since the fatal hour sped o'er
When we parted, ne'er to meet,
On the silent noontide street.

Should I live a thousand years,
  I cannot forget thee,—never,—
Nor the hot and weary tears
  That I shed, from thee to sever;
Never will thy truthful eyes
Leave me, in this world of lies.

Girl of love and graceful youth,
Girl all beauty, girl all truth!
Spirit clad in purer air
Than Time's hateful fashions wear!
Angel, shining through my dreams
When Youth, Hope, and Joy were themes!
Dead seems all Youth's memory,
Save one thought—the thought of thee.

From the blossoms of the Spring
Beauty wreathed thee in her ring;
From the airs of dewy skies
Melted sadness in those eyes—
Speechless, soft and fearful glances,
Maidenhood's enamoured trances—
Faintly trembling, dimly felt,
With a name not aptly spelt.

Now, the moods of passion over,
I am loved by none, nor lover;
'T was not thus when Julia's eye
To my own made sweet reply.
Orphan from her earliest years,
Cradled on a couch of tears,
Dark as Winter's dreariest night
Was her lot—yet she was light;
Never closed her feeling's spring,
Faithful life's best offering.

"Time shall never wile me more
On its dark, its frowning shore."
So felt I for Julia's fate,
Like my own, most desolate;
Years of pain, those years all sorrow,
To-day wretched as to-morrow;
Never finished, never fast,
Falling slowly to the Past—
What a youth was this to me,
Born for love and sympathy!

There was sorrow in her air,
Sweetness married to despair,
In her mouth, that would have laughed
And Love's ruby vintage quaffed;
In her softly shaded cheek,
Where Love could his vengeance wreak;
In her sweet, entrancing eye,
Whence Love's arrows sought to fly:

Could, then, Fortune frame a creature
Perfect so in every feature?
Beauteous as the dove's soft wing,
Or a fountain of the Spring,
Or the sunset as it sinks,
While the Night its radiance drinks
For a glowing beverage,
Nectar of Day's purple age:
Could Fortune, mocking her, declare
Lovely Julia to despair?
Such dark mystery is life,
This debate 'twixt sleep and strife.

But thy heart grew never old!
Naught was there save sunset's gold,
Crimson evenings, blushing mornings,
And all Nature's wise adornings.

Where art fled ne'er have I heard;
In this earthly state? No word.
Art still near the wide blue river
That beyond the meads doth quiver?
Or beneath yon mountain's shade,
By the murmuring chestnut glade?
Shadow of departed years,
Draped in Beauty, draped in Tears,
Where, across life's shadowy main,
Child of sweetness, child of pain!
Art thou drifting, then, to-day?
Dearest Julia, to me say!

GRACE

GRACE was perfect, fresh, and fair,
Cheerful as a mountain air;
Blithely fearless, glad and free,
Pouting lips, with hazel ee.
O'er her firm-set figure played
Charms to make a saint afraid;
To this magnet strong and sweet
Swift my willing steps must fleet.
Grace was all a paragon—
Oh, she drew me like a sun!

Round about her valley lie
Purple mountains on the sky,
And within her valley's fold
Lakes that set no price in gold,
Tracks that climb the crag and glen,
And a race of frugal men.

Buoyant, wilful, frank, and gay,
Grace ne'er lived a wretched day—
Joy of parents, loved by all,
Warmed and cheered her father's hall.

Years of sadness now thrown over,
Once again was I a lover;
Laughed again the lake's low shore,
Laughed the hilltops ten times more,
And the birches in the wood

Fluttered midst the solitude.
"Grace was lovely, Grace was fine—
Could not Grace, dear Grace, be mine?"

Many times around my light,
Darting at the centre bright,
Have I viewed a wretched moth
Singe his feather, by my troth.
I had wept and I had loved—
Frail and fatal all it proved;
Might have known it ne'er could be—
Might have guessed she hated me!

Girl of Life's determined hours,
Clad in glory as the flowers,
Virginal as Venus came
From the sea at Morning's flame,
All a sunny, fond surprise,
With her wealth of hazel eyes—
She was not, if I was, poor,—
Parents prudent,—life in store,—
Could I sing her virtues more?

Grace had beauty, Grace had truth—
Well I loved her in my youth!
And she taught me a fine word—
This (I might have elsewhere heard):
That not all I wish is mine—
What I have should seem divine.

MADELINE

Many days have never made
Me forget that oak's green shade
Under which, in Autumn fair,
While October gilt the air,
Madeline was musing lone
On a cold and mossy stone.
Below her feet the river ran
Like the fleeting hopes of Man;
Around, the unshorn grasses high,
O'er her head the deep blue sky;
Best of all was Madeline,
Gypsy figure, tall and fine.
Yes, and she was Nature's child:
Airs and skies to her were mild;
Never breeze her thoughts perturbed,
Never storm her cheek disturbed.

In her skiff she glided o'er
Foaming crests that swiftly bore
Her to the many-wooded shore;
In her bark, far o'er the tide,
Madeline would smoothly glide
On the wild and whirling wave,

In blasts that 'gainst the islands rave,
Madeline swept 'neath the sky—
Born of Nature, but more high.

Child of grace, to Nature dear,
Be the sky her broad compeer!
Lists her song the sighing wood,
Where she like a statue stood,
But with low and heartfelt voice
That could bid my soul rejoice;
Be her light yon star so keen,
Pure and distant, Heaven's Queen;
Let the sea, the boundless sea,
Her perpetual anthem be,
While the gray gull wets his wing
To the green waves' murmuring,
And the white beach lines the shore
In its sandy curvature.

Sinful cities not in her
Could a feeble passion stir;
Filled with love, her lyric eye
Gave its figure to the sky;
Like a lyre, her heart obeyed
Whispers of the forest shade,
Buds she sang, and fresh spring flowers,
Birds that carolled in her bowers,
And the lonely, sorrowing sea,
Still she sang its lullaby.

Slave to each impulsive hour,
How could I resist her power?
Or not kneel and worship there,
When she tinged the Autumn air
With her joy or with her pain—
Lit the chill October rain
O'er the low and sullen hill
(Outlined, if the hour were still,
By some leaden cloud behind)
With its scanty grasses lined,
Serely russet, as the day,
Hermit-like, went out in gray.[1]

Muse of the Island, pure and free!
Spirit of the sapphire sea!
How can I forget the time
We went wandering in our prime,
And beneath the tall pine-trees
Felt the tearful Autumn breeze?

Hope had I of lofty fame
To embalm a poet's name,
In some grandly festive measure
Fitliest for a nation's pleasure:

[1] This passage shows a clear reminiscence of the happy days at Curzon's Mill, and that region where young Channing spent so much time, and where the best of his early poems were written. These portraits are much idealized, but traces of several of his youthful friends may be found in them. The Julia afterward mentioned as buried in Plymouth was a different person; but possibly an earlier Julia was the Sibylla of *The Wanderer*.

Thus it was I dreamed at first—
Madeline! thy beauty nursed
In me finer thought and feeling,
To myself my heart revealing.

Ghost of wishes dead and gone,
Haunting hopes still limping on,—
Echoes from a sunken land
Falling on a desert strand,—
Cold content and broken plan—
Still the boy lives in the man!

CONSTANTIA

Best of all Constantia proved—
Best of all her truth I loved;
Free as air and fixed as Fate,
Fitted for a hero's mate.
Beauty dear Constantia had,
Fit to make a lover mad;
Every grace she 'd gently turn
Strong to do and swift to learn;
Truthful as the twilight sky
Was her melting, lustrous eye—

Full of sweetness as the South
Was her firm and handsome mouth.

Child of conscience, child of truth,—
Treasures far outlasting youth,—
Would my verse had but the power
Again to shape that brightest hour
When beneath the shadowy tree
First I pressed the hand of thee!
While the sighing summer wind
Toned its murmur through the mind,
And the moon shined clear above,
Smiling chaste, like those we love.

I can ne'er be loved again
As I was on that sweet plain,
Though I sigh for fourscore years,
Watering all Earth's sands with tears.
I am old—my life is sere;
Beauty never can appear
As it was when I was young,
Love and joy upon my tongue.
Give me Passion, give me Youth!
More than all, oh, give me Truth!
Let the beauties steal my heart
In their deep, entrancing art—
Yet the safer shalt thou prove,
Dear Constantia! in my love.

How the feverish glances fly
Off the dark, the laughing eye!
Mark the brown and braided hair,
To weak hearts a fearful snare.
I have seen the Southern skies
Shut their soft, love-laden eyes,
Seen the floor of those calm seas
Rippled by the orange-breeze;
But I fled such azure dreams
For thy frozen Northern streams.

If my heart is growing old,
Thine is neither worn nor cold;
If my life has lost its flower,
Thine still wears its crimson dower,
And the early morning beam
Pulsates on its golden stream.

May a cold, sepulchral breeze
Every feeling in me freeze,
Stab me through and through with pain,
If I ever love again!
More—let all the Graces go,
And the Muses thickly sow
Harsh and crabbèd seed all o'er
Helicon's harmonious shore,—
Subtle Venus snap her zone,
Phœbus carve me into stone,—
If I leave Constantia's side!
My joy and hope, my peace, my pride.

EMERSON

(1857)

HERE sometimes gliding in his peaceful skiff
Climéné sails, heir of the world, and notes
In his perception, that no thing escapes,
Each varying pulse along Life's arteries—
Both what she half resolves and half effects,
As well as her whole purpose. To his eye
The silent stars of many a midnight heaven
Have beamed tokens of love, types of the Soul,
And lifted him to more primeval natures.
In those far-moving barks on heaven's sea
Radiates of force he saw; and while he moved
From man, on the eternal billow, still his heart
Beat with some natural fondness for his race.

In other lands they might have worshipped him;
Nations had stood and blocked their chariot wheels
At his approach—towns stooped beneath his foot!
But here, in our vast wilderness, he walks
Alone—if 't is to be alone when stars
And breath of summer mountain airs and morn
And the wild music of the untempered sea
Consort with human genius.

Oh, couldst not thou revere, bold stranger (prone
Inly to smile and chide at human power),
Our humble fields and lowly stooping hills,
When thou shalt learn that here Climéné trod?

ROSALBA

WITH thee, fathomless Ocean, that dear child
I link—a summer child, flower of the world,
Rosalba! for, like thee, she has no bound
Or limit to her beauty; Venus-zoned,
She rather, like thy billows, bends with grace.
Nor deem the Grecian fable all a myth,
That Aphrodite from a shell appeared,
Soft spanned upon the wave; for o'er thy heart,
Unheeding stranger! thus Rosalba falls,
And by one entrance on thy privacy
Unrolls the mysteries and gives them tongue.

Child of the poet's thought! if ever God
Made any creature that could thee surpass,—
The lightest sunset cloud that purpling swims
Across the zenith's lake,—the foam of seas,—
The roses when they paint the green sand-wastes

Of our remotest Cape,—or the hour near dawn,—
I cannot fathom it; nor how thou art made:
How these attempered elements in the mass
Run to confusion and exhale in fault,—
Begetting monstrous passions and dark thoughts,
Or slow contriving malice, or cold spite,
Or leagues of dulness, self-persuaded rare,—
But rise in thee like the vast Ocean's grace,
Ne'er to be bounded by my heart or hope,
Yet ever decorous, modest, and complete.

Rose on her cheeks, are roses in her heart,
And softer on the earth her footstep falls
Than earliest twilight airs across the wave;
While in her heart the unfathomed sea of love
Its never-ceasing tide pours onward.

1001

A HOUSEHOLD FRIEND

(December 15, 1866)

If the winter skies be o'er us,
And the winter months before us,
When the tempest, Boreal falling,
Hurls his icy bolts appalling,
Let us yet thy soul inherit,
Equable and nice in spirit!
Whom in turbulent December
With still peace we can remember.

Muses should thy birthday reckon
As to one their foretastes beckon;
Who in thought and action never
Could the right from self dissever;
Taken with no serpent charming,
By no tyranny's alarming;
In thy sure conviction better
Than in blurred Tradition's fetter;
Would the State such souls might cherish,
And her liberties ne'er perish!

Age must dart no frost to harm thee,
Fell reverses ne'er alarm thee,
Having that within thy being
Still the good in evil seeing;
Faithful heart and faithful doing
Bring Life's forces humbly suing.

Now we bid the dear Penates
(Inward guardians with whom Fate is)
And the Lar, whose altar flaming
From thy household merits naming,
And Vertumnus we solicit,
Whose return brings no deficit,
Bacchus with his ivy thyrses,
And Pomona's friendly verses,
Or what other joys may be
Pouring from Antiquity:

Let them o'er thy roof, displaying
Happiest stars, stand brightly raying!

In thy thought poetic splendor
This late age spontaneous render,
Shed o'er acts of love divine,
Fit for thee and fit for thine!

1003

SYBILLA

In the proud mansion on the city street,
Strewed with the loans of luxury, that Time
Wafts down o'erpowering from the burdened
 Past—
Homeless and hopeless in those cruel walls
Sybilla went—her heart long since bereaved.
She heard the footfalls sear the crowded streets,—
Her fatal birthright,—where no human pulse
To hers was beating; there she shunned the day!

Tall churches and rich houses draped in flowers,
And lovely maids tricked out with pearls and gold,
Barbaric pomp! and crafty usurers bent—
All passed she by, the terror in her soul;
Then sped she on her flight—a reindeer-course.
Day's dying light painted the quiet fields,
The pale green sky reflected in their pools,—
A soft, clear light,—and in that heaven afar
O'er emerald waters glowed the evening star.
Oh, why was Earth so fair? was love so fond
Ever consumed within its ring of fire?

EPITHALAMIUM

(1862)

FRIEND! in thy new relation
There is no provocation
For Thought's demise;
Be all more nobly brave!
Assist each slave,
And yet more share
Thy hours and thoughts and care
With others,
Thy kinsmen and thy brothers!
And more a patriot be
Through Love's wise chemistry!

Long have I watched thee rule
Thyself; and if a still
And lustrous guardian school
Thee to a stiller patience now,
In this dear vow,
And nearer to the stars
(Save that all-reddening Mars),
More consonant with the train
Of evening and sweet Hesperus,
And her who walks the night,
In blushing radiance strayed,

A well-proportioned light,
A sea-born maid,
Who from old Ocean's foam
Laughed, and made men at home;

In truth, if this prove so,—
If her soft beams
Silver the rushing streams,
And gild the moss
Where the ancestral brothers toss—
Dark oaks and murmuring pines,
Stags of a thousand tines;
These rocks so grave, if they
Smile with humected day,
And silken zephyrs thrill
The maple's foliage, where the bird
Rose-breasted rings
With Music's clearest springs,—
What then?
Though softer, we 're still men!

MEMORIES OF FANNY McGREGOR

This poem recalls a voyage down Boston Harbor in company with Miss McGregor during the Civil War. She was, not long after, accidentally shot near Franconia, in the New Hampshire mountain-land. A person of great beauty and wit, perhaps exalted poetically in this tribute.

WE felt the shadows build the Fort,
And touch Cohassett's withering hills;
The breeze that cooled our Boston port
Ran fresh, as leap the mountain rills
Down gray Franconia's hoary woods,
Saved from the axe, dear solitudes.

The sky's deep blue adorned the Flag,
That pathos of our nation's cause,
Battled in blood from sea to crag,
For home and hearth, for life and laws:
Lovelier than all, a woman's heart,
Reflecting all, and taking part.

How void the play still Nature makes
Where thrills no breast with human fear!
Dull sets that sun—no wavelet breaks
Till woman's loveliness appear;
Heat of the light we coldly bear,
The radiant of Time's atmosphere.

O lovely day that died so soon,
Live long in Her, more fairly planned!
And like the sea when shines the moon,
Reflecting in its ebb the hand
Inscrutable that flings the star,
Thy beauty leads my thoughts afar.

To thee respond the dancing waves,
To thee the grace-encircled shore,
Whose lonely sands old Ocean laves
And pebbles bright flows lisping o'er;
Thy tranquil heart was ever bent
In beauty to be eloquent.

From envious skies thy star shines down,
Not unacquainted with its place;
They wreathe for thee an angel's crown,
And gem the virtues of thy face.
Ah, fated shot! devoid of power
O'er her whose beauty was her dower!

. . . .

Called from the voice of life, the tasks of pain,
Thine eye no more the rounding day shalt see
In sunlit hours or chill and sobbing rain;
Nor we hear trace of old-time melody
That told in music of another shore,
Where rests Time's mournful wave, ne'er breaking more.

THE LATE-FOUND FRIEND

(1901)

ALL, all had long-time gone;
On Earth's wide bound I wandered lone,
By sweeping waves, whose glittering tides
Once safely o'er, no sailor rides—
When out of that soft greensward shore
I saw a vessel steer once more,
And at her prow a tall, straight form;
'T was Margaret, poised so high above Earth's
storm!

Simple and sweet she surely is
As opening dawn or day's last look;
Within her heart, within her eyes,
Meet all the charms of mead and brook,
When rings amid the open fields
That dear, delightful strain along—
Great Nature's heart in little birds,
Piping their unmaterial song.

Late in the deep and dying night,
When sounds are still, and frozen the moor,
There echoes, far from human plight,
The cottage curs' unceasing roar;

Then, in that strange funereal pall
  That veils the Earth and hides the skies,
I seem to hear a note that falls
  Sweeter than tidings of surprise.

I need not ask—I do not stay;
  'T is Margaret's voice—no other sound
Could ever wake a rondelai
  Within this heart by Sorrow bound.

"Wanderer of pain! I am a truth to be
  For those I stoop to, mercy to implore;
  A certain lighthouse on Earth's murky shore;
O God! I kneel and ask that those in me
May trust their heart's best love implicitly—
  Trust and believe—see in my soul their own,
  As one sweet viol clears another's tone."

So from the drooping skies
The quicker lightning flies,
And makes our shadowed hearts bright 'neath those lovely eyes.
For whom now would you raise the tower of Scorn?
Now when yon azure distances, upborne
In their far-shadowed folds of ruby light,
Pale and grow gloomy as the wondrous Night
Pours forth her stream of stars o'er Heaven's deep sea,
And mocks our wandering, far Futurity.

THE SAGE

(EMERSON)

(1897)

WHEN I was young I knew a sage—
A man *he* was of middle age;
Clear was his mind as forest brooks,
And reams of wisdom in his looks.

But if I asked this sage-like man
Questions of wisdom in *my* plan,
Faintly the smile shed o'er his face,
A beam of joy, a smile of grace.

The answer that I needed bad
Ne'er reached my ear, nor gay nor sad;
"That might be so," the sage would say,
Exactly flat as mere "Good day."

Within his mind there seemed to be
A fixed reserve, a pleasant lea:
"Not I—I cannot mend your state,"
To Yes, to No, inveterate.

To all alike he charming was;
His words were wise in Virtue's cause;
Distinct, clear-minded—old and young
Upon his words in rapture hung.

"Come to my woods, come to my fields!
There Nature her revision yields;
These things were made to be enjoyed—
Great is the pleasure, great the reward.

"Unnumbered shine the nightly flowers,
To man the wonder of his hours;
The heavens themselves invite his gaze,
Those actors in their native plays."

Forth went he, armed, to see the world;
Love was his weapon—joy it hurled;
Yet ne'er a word he spoke of them—
Silent, yet shining like a gem.

WELCOME TO THEE NOT GONE

(A TRIBUTE TO MARSTON WATSON,
WRITTEN IN 1899)

FRIEND of my early years! friend of my hours
Fast fading from these shores, from Time's dim bowers!
The same to-day,—e'er living in my mind,—
Sweet, thoughtful, tender, patient to thy kind—
Marston, I would not weep that thou art gone,
Leaving me hapless on these shores alone;
Dear Heart, I will not grieve, since God allowed
So vast a tribute and a soul so proud;
Since thou wert sent to teach me to forget,
By these low shores where my poor voyage was set,
These steep obliquities that shade my path,
While thy far-reaching view o'ergoes their wrath.

Marston! I see thee still—that far-off look
Away, across the skies, the ever-rolling brook,
Or that dark, troubled Sea among the isles;
The breeze blows up; the flowers, the heavens, all smiles.
Smiling we take our way across the tombs,
Stand on the hilltop, hear the rushing looms

In the long valley nestling at our feet;
Scan the vast basin where the heavens meet
Their own blue pageant, sent from skies to greet;
Marston delights in all—or sandy reach,
Or sparkling billows on the Gurnet beach;
The poorest weed, the smallest fly that waves,
To him the same as the great Heroes' graves.

"I am not gone; I live—I 'm with thee still!
I stand off-looking from the windy hill
With thee; 't is just the same; weep not for me!
I murmur in the breeze, I sail upon the sea;
I see with far-off look the westering sun
Play o'er the oak-groves when the day is done.
No, not a tear! let us be cheerful now!
I am not dead—why, what a thought! my vow
Was always sped to life; in Death's lone camp
I do not walk alone; I have my lamp,
My steadfast light, burning from ancient shades,
Eternal remnants from prophetic glades.

"The breezes fan my cheek; I am not dead;
My soul has only waved its wings and fled
From these low-hanging equinoctial storms;
Hail, Heaven and life! hail, gods and sempiternal
forms!"

PRIMAVERA, THE BREATH OF SPRING

With the rush and whirl of the fleet wild brook,
And the leap of the deer thro' the deep wild wood,
And the eyes of the flowers with that gentle look
That shines in the hearts of the truly good,
Dost thou refresh my weary mood.

And chantest thy hymn in the forest old,
Where the buds of the trees and their hearts of fire
Start to the song of thy harps of gold
As the maiden with a timid desire
At the thrill of her love's soft lyre.

Thou passest thy hand o'er the yellow fields
With a light caress like a mother's smile,
And the bright, soft grass to thy impulse yields
The green of its life that has slept the while;
Sweet Spring! Thou knowest many a wile.

And joyfully, Spring, I welcome thee down
To the heavy hearts of my fellow-men;
To the windows dark of the thick-built town,
And the scholar who sits with his tiresome pen,
In the shadow of his den.

Frolic, sweet flowers, along the wall-side,
Along the roadway where the foot-path goes,
And, ferns, in the pines where the rivers glide,
Be as cheerful as where the musk-rose blows,
And gay as a child each thing that grows.

INDEX OF TITLES

INDEX OF FIRST LINES